Shaker
Communities,
Shaker Lives

Shaker Communities, Shaker Lives

Priscilla J. Brewer

University Press of New England

Hanover and London

UNIVERSITY PRESS OF NEW ENGLAND

Brandeis University University of Connecticut   University of Rhode Island
Brown University Dartmouth College   Tufts University
Clark University   University of New Hampshire University of Vermont

Printed in the United States of America

LIBRARY OF CONGRESS CATALOGING-IN-PUBLICATION DATA

Brewer, Priscilla J.
Shaker communities, Shaker lives.
Bibliography: p.
Includes index.
1. Shakers—United States. I. Title.
BX9766.B74 1986   289'.8   85-40930
ISBN 0−87451−362−6
ISBN 0−87451−400−2 (pbk.)

Text Credits

Courtesy of Hancock Shaker Village, Inc., Pittsfield, Massachusetts: Isaac N. Youngs, *Names and Ages of those who have been gathered into the church*; Alonzo G. Hollister, *Book of the Busy Hours*; New Lebanon Church Family *Account Book* (1817−29); Hancock Church Family *Daybook* (1837−1913); New Lebanon Second Order *Farm Journal*; New Lebanon *Journal of Domestic Events and Transactions*; Giles B. Avery, *Book of Records*; Franklin Barber and Philemon Stewart, *A Journal of Garden Accounts*; Grove Blanchard, *Diary*; William Calver et al., *School Journal*; and Asenath Clark, *Ministerial Journal*.

Courtesy of Western Reserve Historical Society, Cleveland, Ohio: WRHS I A 6, 7, 8, 10; I B 37, 46, 82; II A 17; II B 98; III A 2, 8, 14; III B 13; IV A 1−36, 42, 44; IV B 35, 36, 37; V A 14; V B 19, 58, 59, 60−61, 63−71, 80, 84, 85, 90, 92, 93, 97, 98, 104−126, 128, 130, 131, 132, 135, 136, 137, 139, 140, 149, 228, 250; VI A 2, 4, 11; VI B 7, 10−13, 24, 27, 29, 36−37, 51; VII A 6; VII B 22, 59, 61, 107, 109, 113, 133, 258, 266, 267, 270, 270a, 271, 274, 289; and X B 1.

Courtesy, Henry Francis du Pont Winterthur Museum, The Edward Deming Andrews Memorial Shaker Collection, Winterthur, Delaware: SA 748, 750, 756, 760, 763, 766, 770, 772, 774, 776, 779, 780, 783, 789, 792, 795, 797, 799.1, 800, 802, 803, 805, 810, 817, 818, 823, 827, 829, 834, 894, 977, 979, 980, 981, 1030, 1031, 1066, 1077, 1220, 1257, 1261, 1262, 1340, and 1548.

Courtesy of New York State Library, Albany, New York: A2903.

Courtesy of American Antiquarian Society, Worcester, Massachusetts: Thomas Hammond, *Harvard Church Family Record* (1791−1853) in Harvard, Massachusetts, Shaker Church Records, 1790−1875.

Courtesy of The Shaker Museum, Old Chatham, New York: #8831; 10,509; 10,803; 10,804; and 13,357.

Reprinted from *The Journal of Interdisciplinary History*, XV (1984), Tables 1, 2, 3, 4, and 5, with permission of the editors of *The Journal of Interdisciplinary History* and the MIT Press, Cambridge, Massachusetts. Copyright © 1984 by the Massachusetts Institute of Technology and the editors of the *Journal of Interdisciplinary History*.

For my parents
William Dodd Brewer and Alice Van Ess Brewer

Let Zion's children praise the Lord,
Yea, sound His holy name.
Let Wisdom ever be adored,
Her goodness now proclaim.

Let freedom wave her golden wing,
Her scepter gently bow.
Jerusalem, arise and sing,
The victory is now.

Shaker spiritual,
Hancock, Massachusetts,
circa 1850

Contents

Preface

The appearance of another Shaker book requires some explanation. Although the field of Shaker studies has expanded considerably during the last decade both in volume and professionalism, fundamental questions about the sect remain unanswered. Much of the existing scholarship focuses narrowly on Shaker artifacts; the rest broadens in scope to examine theoretical issues about the sect's role as either exemplar or antithesis of mainstream American social and religious values in the nineteenth century. The middle ground bounded by the ideological and social constructs that defined the United Society and the lives of its members is largely unoccupied. It is this territory that I wish to explore.

The Shakers have too often been described as a monolithic mass of sectarian clones. Few of the individual stories about the relationships formed and broken within, and as a result of the sect, the personal struggles, successes and failures have been chronicled. Yet the story of the sect's rise and decline cannot adequately be told or interpreted without this focus on individual members. My goal is twofold: to present the Believers as they were rather than as they wished to be, and to analyze the reasons for, and internal impact of, the Society's decline beginning in the middle of the nineteenth century.

This book is not an examination of the sect in the broader context of American religious and social history. Instead, I have investigated the Society within its own boundaries, as it was experienced by its members. "Worldly" developments appear only when they impinge upon those boundaries. The emphasis here is not on the inner spirit life of the Believers, which an outside observer could not hope to understand fully, but rather on its social and ideological manifestations. This is the circumscribed stage on which individual Shakers acted out their spiritual and temporal lives. It is also, I believe, the perspective from which they and the sect they comprised can best be understood.

This study, of course, owes a great debt to those scholars whose efforts have brought the Shakers before a larger audience. Since 1941, when Marguerite Melcher's pioneering work on the sect appeared, more than twenty major studies of the Society have been published, most of these since 1975. These works fall into four categories.

The earliest group, including Rourke's 1942 essay and books by Andrews and Desroche, is general in focus.[1] Melcher and Andrews produced straightforward chronological histories of the Society: the former romantic in tone and the latter dispassionate. Neither tells much more than what the Believers did, but they nevertheless represented an important beginning. Rourke and Desroche, on the other hand, had larger goals in view. Rourke sought native, non-European "roots of American culture," and discovered in the Shakers a flowering "folk" subculture that she believed to be internally generated. Desroche, too, felt that the Believers represented an important ideological strand within Western civilization. In his case, he traced the development of socialism in the nineteenth century and its various religious roots. Both Rourke and Desroche addressed the issue of the "impulse toward social unity" that has survived even in a capitalist, individualistic society.[2]

The second group of studies is comparative in nature and owes much to the issues central to the sociology of religion.[3] Included here are the works of Whitworth, Kern, Foster, and Marini. All of these scholars focused on American sectarianism and communitarianism by comparing the Shakers with other groups. Whitworth concerned himself with sociological questions about the goals and organizational structures of sects, using the Shakers, the Oneida Perfectionists, and the Society of Brothers (Brüderhof) as examples. Kern and Foster, by contrast, each examined the tension between sexuality and evangelical Christianity in nineteenth-century America and how this was variously resolved by three separatist groups: the Shakers, the Mormons, and the Oneida Perfectionists. Marini, examining the hill country of New England during the Revolutionary era, found important clues to the development of American religious pluralism and anti-Calvinism in the appearance of the Shakers, the Universalists, and the Free Will Baptists. All four of these investigations probe what the authors believed to be the central elements of American utopianism and its relationship to the larger national culture. Though valuable and insightful, their broad focus necessarily obviated an internal analysis of the Shaker Society at the level of individual experience.

The third group of studies investigates various aspects of Shaker material culture.[4] The most significant of these include the Andrews' *Work and Worship*, as well as works by Sprigg and Hayden. In *Work and Worship*, Edward Deming Andrews, together with his wife, Faith, examined the Shaker effort to live *in*, but not *for*, the world—a struggle exemplified by their agricultural and industrial activities. Similarly, both Sprigg and Hayden sought tangible evidence of Shaker ideology in Shaker artifacts, everything from boxes to buildings.

Through their efforts, Shaker architecture, furniture, and craft products have assumed more than mere antiquarian appeal. They are better understood as physical embodiments of religious principles.

The fourth group of studies is characterized by a narrow, specialized focus.[5] Two helpful histories of individual Shaker communities are Piercy's study of North Union, Ohio, and Horgan's study of Harvard and Shirley, Massachusetts. The most sophisticated and useful of these specialized works include Patterson's exhaustive studies of gift songs and drawings, Sasson's work on Shaker spiritual narratives, Morse's edited collection of Worldly responses to the sect from the 1770s to the 1970s, Campbell's analysis of women's lives within the Society, and Bainbridge's study of Shaker population using the national census. All of these works have added considerably to the store of data and interpretation available to current students of the sect.

None of these varied works is wholly satisfying. Before the wider significance of the United Society can be accurately assessed, a fuller, more correct picture of its development must be drawn. This book focuses on Shaker life as it was experienced by a variety of Believers in different periods. Who were they? What were their social, economic, and religious backgrounds? Why did they join? What did they think of life in the communities? Why did some leave and others stay? How did the Shakers respond to social, economic, religious, and ideological developments in the "World?" When did the sect's decline begin and why? Was the decline quantitative, qualitative, or both? How did Believers adjust to these changing circumstances? These are the questions that I will address.

In the search for answers, I have gone to the manuscript record. Work journals, daybooks, business accounts, Ministry correspondence, membership lists, and census schedules have yielded fresh and sometimes startling information about Shaker life and how it was lived by individual Believers in different communities at different times. All quotations from these records appear with their original spelling and punctuation.

I have restricted this investigation to the eleven communities in eastern New York and New England because their story differs fundamentally from that of the western societies. Chapter 1 establishes the background of religious and social ferment in the eighteenth century that fostered the growth of Shakerism after Mother Ann Lee's arrival in New York in 1774. Chapters 2 and 3 trace the organization of the eastern communities under the leadership of her successors, Father James Whittaker, Father Joseph Meacham, and Mother Lucy Wright. Chapters 4 and 5 depart from the chronological order to examine the sect's leadership structure and daily life within the villages during the sect's peak years in the first half of the nineteenth century. The onset of serious internal and external difficulties is traced in Chapters 6 through 8. Chapters 9 and 10 detail Shaker adjustments to these problems and their efforts to sustain their beliefs and way of life into the twentieth century.

I have chosen to restrict this study chronologically for several reasons. By 1900, the Shakers had entered a new phase in their history, one from which they have yet to emerge. They had lost many of their last influential Elders, including Frederick Evans and Daniel Boler of New Lebanon, Henry Blinn of Canterbury, Otis Sawyer of Sabbathday Lake, and Ira Lawson of Hancock, a trend that substantially altered the Society's leadership structure. Then, in 1904, Eldresses Anna White and Leila S. Taylor of New Lebanon published the sect's last major public statement—*Shakerism: Its Meaning and Message*. After that time, the Believers increasingly retired from public view. Their nineteenth-century rise and fall was nearly complete. The story of twentieth-century Shakerism remains to be told.

Acknowledgments

First of all, I want to thank the following current and former members of the staff at Hancock Shaker Village for their support and encouragement: Mrs. Lawrence K. Miller, for her continued commitment; Professor Frederick Rudolph, for his valuable suggestions; John Harlow Ott, who first suggested the book and always believed it would someday see the light; June Sprigg, who introduced me to the Shakers, read the manuscript with both professional and personal care, and wielded a skillful red pencil; Beverly Hamilton, another thoughtful reader of the manuscript whose understanding increased my own; Jerry Grant, whose probing questions led me to rethink many of my interpretations; Cheryl Anderson, who inspired me with a teaching gift; Roma Hansis, who also read the manuscript painstakingly and offered many helpful suggestions; Bob Meader, whose knowledge of the Believers always proved both time saving and thought provoking; and all the interpreters and visitors who asked the right questions.

Second, I want to thank my friends and colleagues in the American Civilization Program at Brown University and at Slater Mill Historic Site who gave me much needed moral support while I tried to finish a book and do graduate and museum work at the same time, particularly: Rheta Martin, Patrick Malone, Sandy Norman, and Carter

Jones. My appreciation also goes to my cartographer, Lyn Malone. A special thank you goes to Nick.

Third, I wish to thank each of the following library staffs for their help during my research and for permission to quote from materials in their collections: American Antiquarian Society, Worcester, Massachusetts; Andrews Shaker Collection, Winterthur Museum, Winterthur, Delaware; Berkshire Athenaeum, Pittsfield, Massachusetts; Federal Archives and Records Center, Waltham, Massachusetts; Hancock Shaker Village, Pittsfield, Massachusetts; New York State Library, Albany, New York; The Shaker Museum, Old Chatham, New York; Western Reserve Historical Society, Cleveland, Ohio; Williams College Library, Williamstown, Massachusetts. My special thanks go to Sarah McFarland and Ann Kelly. I would also like to thank Alice Kimball Smith of Cambridge, Massachusetts, for her thoughtful reading of an early draft of the manuscript and for her many suggestions. Thanks are also due to Rob Emlen of Providence, Rhode Island, for bringing to my attention the letters of Brother John Cumings of Enfield, New Hampshire. I am indebted as well to the staff at University Press of New England, especially Charles Backus, Mary Crittendon, and Sarah Clarkson, for their advice and editorial skill.

Fourth, I want to extend grateful thanks to the Shakers of Canterbury, New Hampshire, and Sabbathday Lake, Maine, especially Eldresses Bertha Lindsay and Gertrude Soule and Sister R. Mildred Barker. They prove by example why Shakerism has worked for so many Americans for so many years.

Last, I want to thank my family, especially my parents. They know why.

Providence, Rhode Island   P.J.B.
December 1985

Glossary of Shaker Terms

Believers: Used commonly instead of "Shakers."

Bishopric: A group of communities, usually two or three, gathered together for administrative purposes under a "Bishopric Ministry" comprised of two Elders and two Eldresses. For example, the Hancock Bishopric included the Hancock community as well as the communities at Enfield, Connecticut, and Tyringham, Massachusetts.

Brother/Sister: Mode of address used for a rank and file member.

covenant: Legal document establishing a member's commitment of goods and services to the Church. The first written covenant was signed at New Lebanon in 1795.

cross: Shakers took up a "cross against the flesh" when they confessed their sins and tried to live a Christlike life. The use of the term "cross" generally referred to the effort to overcome one's carnal nature.

Deacon/Deaconess: Appointed to supervise temporal affairs at the Family level. For example, a typical Family had a Farm Deacon, a Kitchen Deaconess, etc., at least two of each sex altogether. Not to be confused with "Office Deacon" (see "Trustee").

Dwelling: Common name for the building that housed a Shaker Family.

Elder/Eldress: Appointed to supervise spiritual affairs. A general term applied alike to Family Elders, Bishopric Ministry Elders, and Lead Ministry Elders. When used without qualification, the term is synonymous with "leaders."

Elder Brother/ Elder Sister: Specific term used to describe leaders at the Family level. Most often senior Family leaders (one of each sex) were called "Elder Brother" and "Elder Sister," but their assistants were called merely "Brother" and "Sister."

Family:	The smallest Shaker social, economic, and administrative unit, governed by a "lot" of two Elders and two Eldresses, and usually comprised of between thirty and one hundred members.
gathering:	Or "ingathering." An inflow of converts. Also used to describe Novitiate Order Families. Often used as in "first gathering," to describe the first phase of Shaker history, from 1780 to about 1805.
gift:	Any kind of manifestation, frequently physical, of the power of God, as in "whirling gift" or "gift of love." Used colloquially when a member "felt a gift" to sing a new song, institute a new rule, etc.
gospel order:	The establishment of a local Ministry under the authority of the Lead Ministry. Refers to hierarchical governmental structure designed and imposed by Father Joseph Meacham between 1787 and 1796.
Heavenly Father:	Term used to identify the male attribute of the Deity.
Holy Mother Wisdom:	Term used to identify the female attribute of the Deity.
indenture:	Legal document signed by a parent or guardian surrendering a child to Shaker custody.
inspired instrument:	Or simply "instrument." A medium; one who receives messages from the Spirit World. During the 1840s, instruments were officially appointed by the leadership in an effort to control the vast outpouring of gifts that occurred at that time.
joint interest:	Description of Shaker communal economic system. Every convert made whatever contribution he could, either of goods or services, or both, to the "joint interest."
labor:	A concentrated effort to overcome a spiritual stumbling block. Often used as in "labor for a gift" or "laboring meeting."
lead:	A member's immediate superiors.
Lead Ministry:	Quartet of two Elders and two Eldresses, resident at New Lebanon, New York, who shared the spiritual responsibility for the entire sect.
lot:	A group of leaders at one level of the Shaker hierarchy, as in "Elders' lot" or "Deacons' lot." Also used

to describe an individual member's position within the Society.

ministration: Administration, as in "Mother Lucy's ministration."

Ministry: Quartet of two Elders and two Eldresses in charge of a Bishopric. Usually identified geographically, as in "Hancock Ministry" or "Maine Ministry." N.B. "New Lebanon Ministry" and "Lead Ministry" are synonymous.

order: 1) Together with "union," an important goal of Shaker life. "Contrary to order" implied behavior unacceptable to the leadership. Believers who kept their "order" followed the rules and placed the ideals of the Society above any personal desires.
2) Synonymous with "rule." Frequently used as in "gospel orders." Rules governing uniformity of personal belongings, dress, and language were among the common "orders."

Order: Level of membership, as in "Gathering Order" for recent converts or "Senior Order" for deeply committed, covenanted members.

privilege: Usually as in "privilege in the gospel." One of the important "privileges" was the periodic opportunity to confess one's sins to the community's leaders and receive their counsel. Shakers were often reminded that salvation was an on-going process. As Believers, they had an opportunity, a "privilege," to serve God granted only to a few. Occasionally, repentant backsliders were readmitted and given "another privilege."

retiring time: A period of approximately half an hour after supper when Family members "retired" to their bedrooms to think quietly and to prepare themselves for evening meeting.

testimony: Written account of a member's faith and experience, often solicited by the leaders.

travel: Sometimes "travail." Usually used as in "gospel travel." A soul's progress in the Shaker way.

Trustee: Same as "Office Deacon." Two or three appointed in every Family to superintend business affairs. Females assisting in dealings with the outside world were most often called "Office Sisters" and did not legally hold any property. Trustees and Office Sisters typically

	lived in a separate building in the Family, the "Office," where all business with the "World" was transacted.
union:	Together with "order," an important goal of Shaker life. Descriptive of the spiritual bond that joined all Brethren and Sisters throughout the Society.
United Society:	Short for "United Society of Believers in Christ's Second Appearing." Formal title of the sect, first used in the early nineteenth century.
visionist:	Synonymous with "instrument."
World:	Outside world. Non-Believers were called "World's People."
Young Believer:	New convert, young spiritually rather than chronologically.
Zion:	God's Kingdom on earth, the home of Believers in this life.

Shaker
Communities,
Shaker Lives

LOCATION

OF

SHAKER COMMUNITIES

1	Watervliet, New York	(1787–1938)	13	Savoy, Massachusetts	(1817–1825)
2	New Lebanon, New York	(1787–1947)	14	Sodus Bay, New York	(1826–1836)
3	Hancock, Massachusetts	(1790–1960)	15	Groveland, New York	(1836–1895)
4	Enfield, Connecticut	(1790–1917)	16	North Union, Ohio	(1822–1889)
5	Tyringham, Massachusetts	(1792–1875)	17	Union Village, Ohio	(1806–1912)
6	Harvard, Massachusetts	(1791–1918)	18	Whitewater, Ohio	(1824–1907)
7	Shirley, Massachusetts	(1793–1908)	19	Watervliet, Ohio	(1806–1910)
8	Canterbury, New Hampshire	(1792–present)	20	West Union (Busro), Indiana	(1810–1827)
9	Enfield, New Hampshire	(1793–1923)	21	Pleasant Hill, Kentucky	(1806–1910)
10	Alfred, Maine	(1793–1931)	22	South Union, Kentucky	(1807–1922)
11	Sabbathday Lake, Maine	(1794–present)	23	White Oak, Georgia	(1898–1902)
12	Gorham, Maine	(1808–1819)	24	Narcoossee, Florida	(1896–1911)

I

Scarcely Any Sensible Preaching
(1774-1784)

Shakerism was born in a time of upheaval. In the 1770s, Americans were no longer Englishmen, nor were they yet fully Americans. The colonies were still unaccustomed to cooperating with one another, yet they could ill afford to separate. Stirrings of a technological revolution and the impact of an expanding frontier were starting to be felt. The old religion of the Puritan founders had lost much of the vitality it had regained during the first Great Awakening in the 1740s, yet many were reluctant to abandon it completely. Families, communities, and churches were all showing signs of stress. Norms were uncertain and new ideas flourished. Shakerism was one of these. To a generation of evangelical Americans looking for a truly millennial reformation, a life without sin, Shaker theology and social structure provided a welcome combination of spiritual salvation and temporal security. The meeting between Ann Lee, a middle-aged mystic raised in the industrial blight of Manchester, England, and hundreds of Baptists from the hill country of New England and New York, was to result in the establishment of America's most successful communal sect. Its popularity can only be understood against the background of religious and social developments in eighteenth-century America.

The first decade of American independence was a time of exuberance and excitement. New ideological, social, and political forces emerged on every side; to many change seemed the only constant. The philosophy of the Enlightenment had made reason king, and the politics of the revolution had successfully upended the familiar dependence on, and exasperation with, England. Pietism and evangelicalism spilled over from the Great Awakening, engendering new sects and strengthening old denominations.

When Ann Lee and her seven followers stepped off the ship *Mariah* at New York City in August 1774, they landed in the middle of a ferment that was to prove extremely advantageous for the spread of their peculiar religious notions. The product of England's industrial slums,

Mother Ann (as she was called) brought a message of hope to a generation of American farmers who wanted to take part in the reshaping of the world. Many radical Baptists in rural New England and upstate New York had already become disillusioned by the increasing respectability and declining piety of their denomination, and were searching for a pure religion. Large numbers of them were to find spiritual satisfaction among the Shakers, bringing into the new sect attitudes that dated back more than forty years, to the aftermath of the first Great Awakening.

That period of religious fervor in the 1740s had been more than a revival. It had redefined man's relationship to God in ways that were to have a profound impact on politics and society, as well as religion. People had tired of hearing arid, intellectual sermons, interspersed with Biblical citations. They had come to feel that human experience and emotion should be reunited with religion. Arguing that they had received further enlightenment from God, revivalists like Jonathan Edwards and George Whitefield had put the lowly individual in charge of his or her religious life. It was no longer possible to be a good church member without experiencing a provable conversion. Such a conversion personalized God to a certain extent. Ministers and their learning could not help; every person had to have his or her own confrontation with God in order to be saved. The influence of such experiences was, of course, far-reaching.

Thousands of New Englanders were converted to this more active, alive Christianity in the 1740s and 1750s. The accession of confidence and power converts received was probably similar to that of Isaac Backus, a Connecticut youth who was later to become one of the most influential Separate-Baptists in the region. Writing of his 1741 conversion, Backus recalled: "The Lord God is a Sun [and] when any Soul is brought to behold his Glories, them eternal rays of Light and Love Shine down particularly upon him."[1] The miracle of such conversions, multiplied many thousand times, seemed to make other miracles possible, indeed likely. The millennial hopes of many surged; a major reformation of society, both political and moral, seemed within reach. Increased religious activity began to involve more women, children, and blacks, who had little if any stake in the established order. Public participation of women in churches became common, and, while female preachers did not become the rule, this at least represented a trend on which Mother Ann was later to capitalize. After all, it was recognized that God converted women in just the same way as He converted men.

With so much religious ferment involving so many Americans, it is hardly surprising that there was little agreement among those who sought change. Those who wished for immediate and drastic reform of the Congregational establishment began to look outside it for a new organization. The Separate movement within the Congregational church began in Connecticut in the 1740s and institutionalized many of the freedoms introduced during the Great Awakening. The Separates believed in lay ordination, majority rule by church members, freedom from ecclesiastical organization, and emphasized the importance of a converted clergy as opposed to a learned one. Pastors were reminded that they "hath no more power to Decide any case or controversy in the church than any private brother."[2]

Following hard on this schism in the Congregational ranks over organizational issues, arose one among the Separates over theology. A significant splinter group, called Separate-Baptists to distinguish them from the so-called Old Baptists of the Rhode Island region, grew in numbers and influence throughout the rest of the eighteenth century. United principally by their fight for exemption from religious taxes for the support of Congregationalism, the Separate-Baptists experienced doctrinal wrangles as well. Because of their belief that only adult members should be baptized, arguments over communion with proponents of infant baptism, and formal association with the Old Baptists dominated the 1750s and 1760s. In 1767, persuaded by a group of Philadelphia Baptists of the need for an over-arching Baptist organization in New England, the Separate-Baptists joined with the Old Baptists to form the Warren Association in Warren, Rhode Island. In uniting with their former foes to fight more effectively for Baptist rights, the Separate-Baptists shed most of the radical trappings of a schismatic sect and became, instead, part of an increasingly respectable denomination.

As a result of this transformation, the Separate-Baptists alienated many of their own radical adherents. One of the strains in Baptist theology that had long offended conservatives like Backus was perfectionism. A good Calvinist who believed in predestination found it hard to understand those who took Christ's words "Be ye perfect" seriously, yet such radicals kept reappearing.

In 1757, an unordained preacher named Ebenezer Ward persuaded a group of Baptists in the Attleborough region of Massachusetts to form a church on the grounds that their conversions had freed them from Satan's bondage and rendered them sinless. Many such groups advocated freedom from earthly marriage laws and recommended that their members seek spiritual soul mates. After permitting his daughter to cohabit with someone other than her husband, an Attleborough father expressed surprise when she became pregnant, "for they lay with the Bible between them."[3] Schismatics with similar beliefs interpreted

Christ's promise of eternal life literally and expected to live forever. Shadrach Ireland, of Harvard, Massachusetts, was one such convert. After his death, many of his disappointed followers found satisfaction of their perfectionist longings among the Shakers instead.

Not surprisingly, many Separate-Baptists found Connecticut and eastern Massachusetts rather restrictive, and sought new homes where the religious and social climate was more congenial to liberal Baptist beliefs. Seeking cheap land and freedom from the strict Congregational parish controls that were so distasteful to them, many emigrated to western Massachusetts and eastern New York in the 1750s and 1760s and took their radical tendencies with them. In the newly settled regions there were few learned clergymen, and in some towns Baptists even outnumbered Congregationalists. New ideas caught on rapidly in these areas, much to the dismay of conservatives from more tradition-bound locales.

Nathan Perkins, a Congregational minister from West Hartford, Connecticut, took a missionary tour through western Massachusetts and Vermont in 1789, finding to his horror "scarcely any sensible preaching . . . about one tenth part of ye state quakers and anabaptists—Episcopalians and universalists; & a ¼ deists." He professed to have discovered a singularly cooperative nature in these uncouth radicals that surprised him. "Woods," he decided, "make people love one another."[4]

Other ministers were equally discomfited by the ease with which new religious ideas gathered adherents. Jeremiah Hallock, a Congregationalist from Canton, Connecticut, opined in 1787: "It cuts me down to see the inconstancy of my people. They seem to be leaving me. . . . Every wind of doctrine tosseth them about."[5] During the 1770s and 1780s, interest in religion reached a peak almost as high as that attained in the 1740s. There were so many people at a "New Light" meeting in Oyster Bay, Long Island, in January 1773 that "they feared the Galleries would break."[6]

This cyclical revivalism, coupled with the revolutionary upheaval that seemed to many to presage the second coming, provided the arena in which the eight English Shakers arrived in the 1770s. Mother Ann's beliefs, derived partly from inspiration and partly from association with a small group of radical English Quakers, provided just what many New Englanders were searching for. Quaker pacifism and reliance on divine revelation to individual members were particularly welcome to Americans as much fatigued by war with England as by the pretensions of learned clergymen who often seemed to have forgotten the essentials of Christian life. Mother Ann indeed seemed to have received the further enlightenment they had long anticipated. Most important, she settled many thorny doctrinal problems permanently. She asserted that these "Shaking Quakers," so-called because of their charismatic worship practices, had received the power to live without sin. They followed in Christ's footsteps, forsaking the world and all its ways. Confession to one of God's witnesses cleansed the repentant sinner and marked his or her spiritual rebirth. The powerlessness attendant upon the Calvinist belief in predestination was gone forever.

True conversion was followed immediately by drastic and visible changes in lifestyle. According to the Shakers, the children of God were no longer to behave as the children of Adam. Private property was surrendered to the group so that all members might partake equally of their heritage on earth. Marriage also had no place among them. As Mother Ann pointed out: "You must forsake the marriage of the flesh or you cannot be married to the Lamb." [7] The only way to become perfect, she asserted, was to overcome one's carnal nature and return to an Edenic state of simplicity. Celibacy solved forever the problem of competition between love of God and love of family. As a Believer, love for biological relatives was superseded by love for all Christian Brothers and Sisters. All these concrete changes in lifestyle appealed tremendously to many newly converted Christians because subscription to them proved the authenticity of their conversions. Instead of seeking worldly success, the Believers joyfully surrendered the burdens and concerns of earthly life and concentrated on angelic values: purity, humility, peace, union, order. Their goal was to create a working heaven on earth.

Those who came to talk to Mother Ann and her English comrades at their new home in Niskeyuna, New York, near Albany, were generally impressed by what they found. An uneducated woman, with no pretensions about being a learned cleric, she told them simply and forcibly what they could do to remake their lives. Fatigued by the psychological strain of years of disillusioning revivals and petty doctrinal squabbles among all denominations, many found her certainty refreshing and comforting. Nor were potential converts pressured to accept what they did not yet understand.

Particularly appealing, no doubt, to the latent perfectionists among them, was the Shaker belief that Mother Ann represented the second embodiment of the Christ spirit who opened the door for all to experience a personal second coming. This most revolutionary element of Shaker theology thus elevated women to a truly equal spiritual position with men. Mother Ann embodied the second coming of the Christ spirit, and Holy Mother Wisdom represented the female nature of God.

The Shakers lived on the boundary between this world and the next. Spirits surrounded them, often delivering messages or "gifts" of song and movement. The differing light received by each individual was gratefully respected as a gift from God. All who wished could come and be saved, even in the spirit world after death. The message was hopeful, indeed revolutionary, partaking of the same belief in universal salvation that gave rise to such contemporary denominations as the Universalists. In accordance with the freedom of the time, all were free to interpret Mother Ann's message for themselves. Elder Benjamin Youngs told a new Believer: "We cannot believe alike in every respect; neither shall we with you. And those things you cannot see into, leave them, and embrace and unite with what you do believe is right." [8]

Most of those attracted to this new gospel came from the radical wing of the Separate-Baptists. In Shakerism, many strands of pietistic religion seemed united in one glorious millennial reformation. Marriage to the Lamb resolved problems concerning familial duties. Shaker mysticism appealed to those who had long believed in the power of revelation to individuals. The Believers' simplicity, brotherhood, and cooperation recalled the practices of the early Christian church and the original intent of the Puritan founders.

The vast majority of these early Shaker converts who confessed their sins and "took up their crosses against the flesh" in the 1780s came from families that had emigrated from traditionally nonconformist, usually Baptist strongholds in Rhode Island and eastern Massachusetts. Ezra Stiles, president of Yale, noted in his diary that the Shakers had made over four hundred converts by February of 1781. On visiting New Lebanon, New York, the new center of the Shaker church, he wrote: "I find these Shakers are almost to a man converts fr. the Rh. Isld. & Narragansett Baptists called there New Lights & Separates." [9]

Documentary evidence, though scanty, tends to confirm this assessment. An examination of the birth records of the New Lebanon Church Family shows that those "gathered" between 1787 and 1805 were overwhelmingly from these areas. Central and southern Connecticut claimed forty-one of the first generation, Rhode Island and eastern Massachusetts another fifty-three. [10] Together with many of their offspring, born in western Massachusetts and New York, these Baptists formed the core of the early Shaker church.

Some former Baptist Elders and deacons soon rose to positions of authority within the new sect. Joseph Meacham, Jr., one of Mother

Ann's successors, had been a Separate-Baptist minister in New Lebanon and had long been exposed to Baptist ecclesiastical organization.
Son of a Baptist minister of the same name from Enfield, Connecticut,
Meacham had grown up in the same swirling tide of doctrinal change
that had affected more conservative Baptists like Backus. Meacham's
father had adopted Separate views in 1753, and his church had been
reorganized as Separate-Baptist in 1757. Suspicious of the encroach-
ment of ecclesiastical organizations, he refused to join the Warren
Association in 1767 and fought for the repeal of a Massachusetts law
that prevented dissenting ministers from performing marriages.[11] It
is ironic that his son, as a Shaker, was to mastermind the establishment of a far more restrictive ecclesiastical structure than the Warren
Association.

Another early convert with a background as a New England clergy-
man was Samuel Johnson, a 1769 graduate of Yale. Perhaps the only
college graduate among the "first gathering," Johnson had been
brought up in the Durham, Connecticut, region and had undertaken a
mission with some of his Yale classmates to the Indians in upstate New
York during his undergraduate years. In November 1772, he was installed as pastor of the Congregational church in New Lebanon. Dismissed for unknown reasons in 1776, he continued to preach informally in Stockbridge, Massachusetts, until 1780, at which time he
joined the Shakers together with his wife and their four children. Although he never made the mark within the sect that Meacham did, he
subsequently rose to the rank of Family Elder.

By far the most notorious former Baptist minister to convert to
Shakerism was Valentine Rathbun, Sr., Meacham's counterpart in
Pittsfield, Massachusetts. At the request of some members of his congregation, who had heard peculiar reports of these "Shaking Quakers"
claiming to follow a female Messiah, Rathbun journeyed to Niskeyuna
to investigate. Upon his return, he called a meeting in a barn and declared to his eager audience: "I believe they are the people of God. . . .
I would as soon speak against the Holy Ghost as to speak against these
people; they sing the song of the redeemed."[12] Convinced, Rathbun
and most of his congregation converted. One family among them, so
numerous that the Shakers jokingly referred to them as the "royal family," was the Goodriches of Hancock, Massachusetts. In all, twenty-
four Goodriches joined the Hancock and New Lebanon communities
during the first gathering, many of whom were to figure as temporal
and spiritual leaders of the Society well into the nineteenth century.

Rathbun, however, fared less well. Though he understood that he
had been promised a position as an Elder, he was found unqualified.

When the appointment failed to materialize, he apostatized after just a few months. Soon thereafter, in 1781, he published "Some Brief Hints of a Religious Scheme . . . ," the first in what was to be a long line of exposés about the Shakers written by backsliders. Rathbun returned to his Baptist ministerial duties in Pittsfield, but his congregation recovered slowly from the defection to Shaker ranks. By 1786, its numbers had been reduced to twenty-four. By 1807, only sixteen new members had joined.[13]

Baptist losses in other regions of New England were significant as well, though not on the scale of the Pittsfield defection. Perfectionist Baptists in Harvard and Shirley, Massachusetts, formed two Shaker communities. Another was established in Enfield, Connecticut, the Meachams' home territory, and considerable inroads were made among the Free Will Baptists in New Hampshire and Maine, resulting in the foundation of four more societies. Not surprisingly, more conservative Baptists were vituperative in their attacks on the competition. Backus, following a 1782 visit to the New Lebanon community, alleged:

Their chief elders delight themselves much in feasting and drinking spiritous liquor. . . . They endeavor to enforce and propagate their scheme with a strange power, signs, and lying wonders. Some of them . . . have carried matters so far this year as for men and women to dance together entirely naked, to imitate the primitive state of perfection.[14]

James Manning, president of Baptist Rhode Island College (now Brown University), was shocked to learn in 1783 that "some carnal fruits . . . have inadvertently resulted from their chaste embraces."[15]

Such unpleasant tales appear to have originated among disaffected apostates like Rathbun. Some backsliders simply felt that the Shakers were well-intentioned, but hopelessly deluded. Others, more threatened because of the actual or potential loss of property or family members, were convinced that the Shaker leaders were purposely misleading as many converts as possible to enhance their own prestige and, at the same time, to line their own pockets. Rathbun, particularly, felt bitterness toward the Shakers because they had ensnared so many members of his own family. When Backus visited New Lebanon in 1782, two of Rathbun's brothers, one of his brothers-in-law, and four of his adult children still remained faithful. The rancor he bore the Believers is perhaps more understandable in light of this situation.

Other apostates, often with seeming relish, reported both indulgence in alcohol and nude dancing. Many sincere inquirers after truth were put off by these rumors and shied away from a full commitment to the sect. Thomas Brown, who joined the Watervliet, New York, community for a time in the early years of the nineteenth century, reported that Elder Hezekiah Rowley of the Gathering Order had confessed that dancing naked had indeed been introduced in the very early days of the sect's development as a "gift" to subdue the carnal nature.[16] In a work published in 1823, Brothers Calvin Green and Seth Wells provided at least vague substantiation of Brown's claim, explaining that, in the 1780s, because "the work was all new to those who embraced it, and the leaders few in number, and the work extensive, irregularities could not always be foreseen nor prevented."[17] It seems likely that such "gifts" had indeed been exercised for a time in the chaos and exuberant revelation of the early 1780s, but were quickly suppressed.

Whatever peculiarities new converts may have encountered, few were sufficiently disgusted to leave the sect. Judging by testimonies written for publication in the 1820s, early Shakers experienced the same elation and reforming zeal common to converts in other sects and denominations. Comstock Betts, member of a southwestern Connecticut family that had moved to Richmond, Massachusetts, in the early 1760s, went to Niskeyuna to visit Mother Ann when he was in his early twenties. What he heard there impressed him. Their "doctrines, which, though strange, appeared so consistent with truth and reason," also seemed to be "so much in harmony with the testimony of Jesus Christ," that Betts was all but won over. Indeed, many found a belief system that appealed so strongly both to reason and emotion hard to resist.

What stood in the way for Betts, at least at first, was the requirement of "hating and crucifying the carnal nature of the flesh." Betts recalled years later that, at age twenty-one, his "natural feelings at that time were very far from yielding obedience to this work." He concluded, however, that the narrow road the Shakers walked was the only one to salvation, and so he capitulated. He clearly felt that the way to heaven was not supposed to be easy, stating plainly: "I presume I never should have been one of this despised and persecuted people called Shakers if I could have found any other way short of this . . . in which I could have felt any real hope of acceptance with God."[18]

The stories of a large proportion of the first generation of Shakers are strikingly similar to that of Betts. Daniel Goodrich, Jr., perhaps because he was a few years younger than Betts at the time of his conversion in 1779, was even more strongly affected. On visiting Niskeyuna with his family, he participated in his first Shaker meeting. "Mother Ann and her little family," he later recalled, "all sat down and sung in such a solemn and heavenly manner that I felt as tho' I had got among the heavenly hosts, and had no right there."

Mother Ann told Goodrich about the liberating power of confession and the possibility of living a life free from sin as Christ had, and Daniel was convinced. Like Betts, he echoed rationalist sentiments in his justification of the Shaker way, asserting: "It has afforded me that salvation from sin which I never was able to find in all my labors and researches after what was called religion among mankind . . . and hence I have proved by actual experience that a religion which does not save the soul from sin . . . is not the religion of Christ." [19] In an America where deist "infidels" were applying the power of reason to the sphere of religion, such proof by "actual experience" was particularly valuable.

That Mother Ann, an illiterate blacksmith's daughter from the slums of Manchester, England, was able to give Betts and Goodrich and hundreds of others assurance of their salvation is in itself remarkable. She seems, indeed, to have possessed extraordinary power over people, both individually and in angry mobs. Following a well-established New England tradition, Mother Ann spent most of the years 1781 to 1783 in itinerant preaching throughout Massachusetts and Connecticut, wherever there were small groups of Believers. Mob violence broke out sporadically in many of the areas she visited, as opponents attempted to break up meetings and curtail the influx of converts into this peculiar new sect.

Understandably, unconverted Baptists found Shaker beliefs especially disturbing. Even though their insistence on celibacy and on communal ownership of property, a tenet then in its infancy, was incomprehensible to most people, there was no denying that some found such a way of life attractive. Statistics do not indicate how many families, like Rathbun's, were broken up by the new faith, but the number was certainly significant. Rathbun himself was noted as an enemy of the Believers, and was seen at the head of several mobs that harassed Mother Ann and the Elders in Richmond and Hancock.

One such band, which accosted them while they were worshiping at Daniel Goodrich's, met with more than they bargained for. Emboldened by the cudgels in the hands of his supporters, one man claimed to have proof that Mother Ann had come to America to escape prosecution for some crime, and asserted that her cropped ears were always kept covered by a cap for just this reason. Not in the least confounded, Mother Ann removed her cap and revealed two perfectly normal ears. She then turned the tables neatly on her persecutor, remarking: "The churning of milk bringeth forth butter, the wringing of the nose bringeth forth blood; run out your tongue as many times as you have told lies." In the words of two Sisters who observed this encounter: "He commenced running out his tongue as swift as a snake, and felt so ashamed that he left the house." [20] This embarrassment does not seem to have prevented continuing mob harassment protesting the Shaker presence, but the Society thrived on opposition because it knit new members more closely together in combination against the wicked World.

Mother Ann's obvious saintliness was proof enough of the truth of her teachings. She seems, indeed to have been endowed with a remarkable preaching ability. Daniel Goodrich, Jr., recalled that "she would often make the most stubborn and stout-hearted quiver and tremble." When she called on Believers to humble themselves before God, "she would often minister, in a few words, such feelings of sorrow and repentance as to make the whole assembly break forth into weeping. . . . At other times, when she perceived the people to be borne down with tribulation and sorrow, she would by a few words of comfort, and sometimes by singing a melodious and heavenly song, instantly fill the assembly with inexpressible joy." [21]

It was not difficult for the pious Christian of the day to acknowledge that a person with such obvious gifts was the chosen messenger of God. Her example provided the rule against which the behavior of others could be measured. She was remembered for providing "an eminent pattern of modesty, gentleness, kindness, temperance &c.," while at the same time bearing "a powerful and swift testimony against lust and uncleanness, lasciviousness, pride, intemperance, deceit, lieing, hypocrisy, idleness, sloth and all manner of evil." [22]

No character flaw or misdeed was too small to escape her attention. Before she elevated Calvin Harlow, later first Elder in the Hancock Ministry, to a position of authority, she required him to master a manual trade so that he might contribute equally with all Believers to the welfare of the Society. She deplored the waste of any of God's gifts, even going so far as to emphasize careful use of soap grease. When Elizur Goodrich (husband of Lucy Wright who was soon to join Joseph Meacham in the Lead Ministry) switched his plain Shaker coat for a scarlet one to escape harassment while in the World, she reproved him for deceit, and recommended that all Believers always remain faithful to their beliefs in every particular. [23]

Combined with these gifts, Mother Ann also seems to have possessed a lively sense of whimsy. On hearing Amos Rathbun's ecstatic and tuneful reaction to his own conversion, Mother Ann remarked to him cryptically: "Amos, thou shalt sing bass in heaven." [24] Once, after a long, hot journey, she refreshed herself with a slice of watermelon and proved to have quite a way with children. A shy youngster sidled up to her, and looked longingly at her watermelon, but claimed he didn't want any. At this, she responded: "God hates liars."[25] By responding in such a way, she exhibited both an evangelical concern with the sin of telling falsehoods and a canny understanding of the nature of childhood. She knew that measuring up to Christ-like standards of behavior was far from easy, and she was obviously sympathetic toward those who undertook to meet the challenge.

In the light of such evidence, it is not difficult to understand why the Shakers revered and loved Ann Lee. It is, however, impossible to determine how the sect would have developed under her direction after the initial revivalistic excitement had diminished. Perhaps fortunately for the Society's survival, the mantle of leadership was soon to pass to the shoulders of James Whittaker, one of Mother Ann's English companions, and subsequently to Joseph Meacham and Lucy Wright. Meacham and Wright were to organize the Shaker Society in ways unforeseen in the mid-1780s. Ann Lee was never to see an established Shaker village set apart from the outside world. She died in 1784, at the age of forty-eight, probably the victim of mob violence.[26] But the beliefs for which she gave her life have sustained the challenges and rigors of social change, and are experiencing a renaissance, both popular and scholarly.

2

A Sect of Some Continuance
(1784-1796)

When Ann Lee died in 1784, some perfectionists among her followers found this proof of her mortality disillusioning and left the Society. She had never claimed that she would live forever but, somehow, a few Shakers clung to the lingering hope that she might. After her death, all that remained were scattered memories. Her unifying example was gone. It was left to three of her followers—James Whittaker, Joseph Meacham, and Lucy Wright—to shape Mother Ann's teachings into a cohesive doctrine for the sect. Their focus was to be less on belief than on practice. Through their efforts, and in spite of considerable opposition, celibacy, communalism, separation from the World, confession of sins, and unquestioned obedience to anointed leaders were to become firmly established as the cornerstones of Shaker "gospel order."

The oral tradition of "Mother used to say . . ." was one of the major problems they encountered in their early efforts to codify Mother's words and embody them in durable institutions. Everyone had their own tales to tell about Mother's kindness, her gentleness, her testimony against lust and idleness, and sometimes, certainly, the stories differed. Sister Hannah Prescott, for example, remembered that while at Shirley, Massachusetts, "Mother had a particular gift to examine the children and search out their idols, consisting of childish toys, and testified that such things would shut out the gifts of God from their souls; that if children were kept from such things, and suitably instructed in the way of God by their parents, they would abound in the gifts of God, and grow up in the gospel." [1]

Sister Jennet Davis's story differs a little. She recalled that Mother Ann had exhibited a more tolerant attitude toward children and their toys, telling her followers that,

It needs great wisdom to bring up children. . . . You ought not to cross them unnecessarily; it makes them ill-natured—and little children do not know how to govern their natures. If your children get play things, or such things as you do not allow them to have, watch over them, and when they lay them down, you may take them and put them out of their sight; then they will forget them. You ought not to find fault with them for every little fault or childish notion, but when they are disobedient let them feel your severity, and let your word be law; and you never ought to speak to your children when you are in a passion, for if you do, you will put devils into them.[2]

These directives reveal a curiously ambivalent attitude toward children and suggest that the early Believers were not quite certain how to raise youngsters to remain in the faith, a problem that plagued their successors in the nineteenth century to an even greater degree.

Although the record reveals few of these discrepancies, it is probable that they were fairly common. Certainly there must have been differing opinions about the best way to proceed after Mother Ann's death. Any struggle for supremacy that may have developed among the early leaders, however, remains veiled. The mantle of authority seems to have passed fairly smoothly to the shoulders of James Whittaker, one of the earliest and most dedicated of Mother Ann's English converts. Although somewhat overshadowed by Mother Ann and her brother, William, who predeceased her by three months, Whittaker had made a name for himself as a brilliant preacher and indefatigable worker. At her death, most Believers who could have challenged him for the leadership of the sect, including Joseph Meacham, acknowledged him as their superior, or spiritual "Father."

Although he survived Mother Ann by only three years, Whittaker made substantial contributions to the form Shaker society was to take. He was particularly concerned about the need for a total separation from the carnality of the World. Interestingly, he shared with American evangelical preachers like Jonathan Edwards an obsession with the danger posed by man's sensual nature. When such men became "brides of Christ," they were forced to combine what were considered feminine virtues of passivity and humility in their spiritual lives with masculine virtues of strength and dominance in their temporal lives, and some found the two incompatible. One solution was to deny their masculinity in order to demonstrate their complete subjection to God. Edwards wrote, choosing his words with care: "There is the tongue and another member of the body that have a natural bridle, which is to signify to us the peculiar need we have to bridle and restrain those two members."[3]

Whittaker's language on this subject is even more graphic. In a letter written to his family in England in 1785, he boasted that the Shaker gospel had freed him from all "terrestrial connections," and especially from "effeminate desires." He claimed to have found "redemption from the bondage of corruption; which is that sordid propensity, or ardent desire of copulation with women."[4] When men of the World came to Whittaker asking advice about what they should do when tempted to gratify that "sordid propensity," he counseled them to pray. This, he assured them, would result in a "relaxation of that nature."[5] Doubtless Shakerism's insistence on the eradication of these carnal appetites appealed strongly to evangelical men like Whittaker. Control was easier for them when the possibilities for temptation were as severely circumscribed as would be natural in a celibate society.

There were other human tendencies, however, that Father James had trouble controlling effectively among his charges. Fanatics appeared who perhaps wished to dance naked in the woods, or live forever, or prepare for their imminent ascension into heaven. Both Mother Ann and Father James found them a problem. In Enfield, New Hampshire, soon after the Shaker gospel had been introduced among the Free Will Baptists in the region, several new Believers, "having more zeal than wisdom," began squandering their property in a very un-Shaker-like manner. They were evidently convinced that the physical end of the world was near and so felt no need to make any provision for successive generations. Mother Ann had reproved them sharply, exhibiting the canny concern with economic affairs that marked most early Shaker leaders. She told them to go home and improve their farms, plant orchards and the like—in other words, to plan for the next thousand years.[6]

Father James experienced similar difficulties with overzealous members during his three-year ministration. "The theme and motto of the day," as Brother Issac Youngs was to write some seventy-five years later, "was mortification and the cross, and separation from the world, without and within." Apparently, some converts found these strictures impossible to tolerate and fell away to the World. Some among those who remained went too far. They indulged in "excessive bodily hardships" to prove their faith, but when it came to a "real inward work of mortification in spirit, by obedience and submitting to order," they failed to come up to the mark.[7]

Some early Shakers also found it difficult to sever their ties to Worldly politics. When Brethren who had fought in the Revolutionary War converted to Shakerism and became pacifists, they voluntarily surrendered their pensions to a surprised federal government.[8] Their interest in the cause for which they had fought, however, did not disappear. During Shays's Rebellion, Father James had to speak pointedly to a few Shakers who had verbally taken sides with the rebels, warn-

ing: "Those who give way to a party spirit . . . have no part with
me. . . . The spirit of party is the spirit of the World." [9]

James Whittaker was the first of a long line of Shaker leaders to emphasize the paramount importance of strict obedience by the rank and
file members. It is possible that Mother Ann would have come to es-
pouse this position had she lived, but she seems to have been able to
deal with a scattered membership of diverse religious opinions with
greater flexibility than any of her successors. Sister Jemima Blanchard
of Harvard later remembered that Mother Ann had indeed taught that
Believers should seek union, as it was called, with the "leading gift" in
meeting, because "a body without a head is a monster." [10] The problem
with this system of organization, if indeed it can be called that, was the
nebulous character of a "leading gift," which could, and probably did,
change frequently.

Sister Jemima had reason to respect Mother Ann's gift for dealing
with different kinds of Shakers. Mother Ann knew that "some are of a
tender disposition and can be saved by mildness and charity. Others
must be saved by severity, and some will never be saved only by judgments." [11] She had treated Sister Jemima with gentleness and rarely reproved her for a fault, but Sister Sarah Robbins, of the same community, had instead experienced harshness at her hands. [12]

Mother Ann may have been able to carry off such a flexible and un-
structured leadership style, but Father James chose a different course.
He evidently recognized the need for organization in the infant sect
and knew that obedience was the key to its survival. In what may well
have been the earliest formulation of the doctrine that became one of
the cornerstones of Shaker society, Whittaker said to Brother Daniel
Goodrich, Jr. of the Hancock community: "Daniel, faith is a gift of
God; whenever a soul receives it, then his heaven or hell will begin—in
obedience heaven, in disobedience hell." [13]

Although Whittaker did not live long enough to implement fully
whatever plans he may have had for the organization of the sect, he
established a general pattern upon which his immediate successors
were to elaborate. His activities between 1785 and 1787 set precedents
that Meacham and Wright were to follow closely. In 1785, he was responsible for what the Shakers called the "withdrawal of the testimony" from the "World," which resulted in a severe curtailment of
missionary activity. He evidently felt that certain elements within the
Society were beginning to get out of hand, and a time of inward consolidation and regularization of doctrine was required before the gospel
could be spread again effectively. He was also responsible for the shift

of the spiritual and geographical center of the sect from Niskeyuna, New York, to New Lebanon, near the Massachusetts border, where the first Shaker meetinghouse was completed in 1786. In addition, the Maine and New Hampshire communities trace their roots to missionary visits made to those regions by Whittaker in 1785 and 1786, which strengthened the tradition of a Shaker traveling ministry.

Thus, although he cannot be given credit for the shape the Society was ultimately to take, Whittaker's contributions were significant. Observers in the outside world were beginning to notice his calming effect on the group. In 1786, Ezra Stiles reported in his diary that a Mr. Darling, who had just completed a visit to New Lebanon, judged "that after a revelation or two to lop off some impracticable Usages among them, they will settle down into a Sect of some continuance."[14] Whittaker's impact is clearly visible here, but after his death, the remainder of the task was left to Joseph Meacham and his colleagues in the first Lead Ministry, Lucy Wright and Henry Clough.

Meacham's assumption of command came as no surprise. Mother Ann had several times prophesied that he was to play a central role in the sect's development after her death. She called him "the wisest man that has been born of woman for six hundred years," and proclaimed that God had called him to serve as a "Father to all His people in America." She reiterated this message many times, telling Hannah Kendall of Harvard that Meacham was her "first born son in America," and telling Jonathan Slosson of New Lebanon: "Joseph is my first Bishop; he is my Apostle in the Ministry . . . what he does, I do."

Naturally, these prophecies were recalled during the troubled days of July 1787, when Whittaker died and left the Believers bereft of all the original English leaders. Mother Ann had, after all, been even more specific. She had said that Meacham would one day gather the church into order, but that she would not live to see it.[15] In the face of such an obvious preference, expressed again within days of her death, Meacham's principal competitors, his younger brother David and Calvin Harlow, acknowledged him as their spiritual Father.

Perhaps Mother Ann recognized that Joseph Meacham, alone of all the early converts, possessed the organizational skill required to unite the amorphous bands of Believers throughout the northeast into a religious society with a rigid hierarchy and formalized doctrines. The need for such order became increasingly evident in the years following the deaths of Mother Ann and Father James. Squabbles over beliefs proliferated. Some zealots in the group tried to assume too much authority and resented attempts at control. Mother Ann had been reluctant to reprove such members too strongly because she feared they would lose their enthusiasm and leave the sect. She once declared that it would be preferable for ten souls who had never heard the Shaker gospel to go to hell than it would be for even one soul who had heard it to be damned.[16] But while she may have been able to tolerate a measure of volatile and disruptive behavior, after her death the success of the Shaker sect depended increasingly on organization that would enable it to survive the initial decline of revivalistic fire.

By the time of Meacham's accession, even those chosen as Elders in the various regions where Shakers were numerous began to disagree about policy and vie with one another for supremacy. At Harvard, Massachusetts, Jeremiah Willard, as head of a household that had converted *en masse* to Shakerism, had assumed the role of Elder in that little Family. Willard sought only the young and able-bodied as new members because they could assist in raising the Family's economic standing, a policy in sharp contrast to that of Aaron Jewett, an Elder at the same community, who accepted any honest Believer into his Family.[17] Although such obvious selfishness as Willard's was condemned, there was no effective way to deal with such problems until Meacham constructed a hierarchy of Elders and Eldresses.

Father Joseph's first act as lead Elder proved a brilliant move for the future strength of the Society. He decided to elevate a woman to share authority with him, a step that came as a surprise to many. He was, however, merely putting into practice a principle stressed by Mother Ann. She had felt very strongly that men and women should share the administration of Christ's family; in fact, she had based her claim to authority on this premise when Meacham had questioned her in 1780 about the role of women in the church.[18] So when he chose Lucy Wright, the wife of a Richmond, Massachusetts, merchant, as first lead Eldress in the New Lebanon Ministry and gave her the honored title of "Mother," Meacham was merely doing what he thought Mother Ann had intended.

Lucy Wright had long been a favorite of Mother Ann's. Born in Pittsfield in 1760, she had managed to acquire an education described as "uncommon," and was known for being thoughtful and cautious. Just prior to the revival that sparked the growth of Shakerism, Lucy had married Elizur Goodrich, one of the Hancock "royal family," and they apparently lived an "uncommonly continent" life together, in spite of the marriage bond. In this regard, it is interesting to note that the couple had no children and that Lucy retained the use of her maiden name. At the outset of the revival, Goodrich immediately became engulfed by religious zeal, but his wife stood a little apart, unwilling to commit herself to anything without careful consideration. Both were among the first to visit Mother Ann at Niskeyuna, and Lucy's calm reserve did not go unnoticed. Mother Ann told Elizur, who had converted almost instantaneously, that gaining Lucy as a member would be the equivalent of gaining a nation.[19]

Gradually won over to the sect, in 1781 Wright moved to Niskeyuna at Mother Ann's request to take charge of the Sisters' affairs, another example of Mother Ann's knack for selecting colleagues whose varied talents would complement her own. Wright was so successful in organizing the temporal concerns of the women at Niskeyuna that Mother Ann, on her return in 1783 from her three-year missionary tour, recommended that all Sisters take her as their model. Joseph Meacham had evidently heard of her success and asked her to move to New Lebanon early in 1788, elevating her to "Mother" several months later.

Her primary task was to accomplish on a Societywide scale what she had so efficiently done for the Sisters at Niskeyuna, which was by that time called Watervliet. In the process, as her biographer, Brother Calvin Green, later recorded, she "had great prejudice to overcome, & many erroneous ideas & sentiments to correct . . . ," particularly about the proper spiritual relationship between gospel Brethren and Sisters.[20] Reuben Rathbun, an early backslider, was more forthright about the problems Wright encountered after her appointment. "As to their parents," he recalled, "it was doubtless without any difficulty they acknowledged Elder Joseph to be their father in the Gospel; but as to a mother, it was such a new thing and so unexpected that there was something of a labor before the matter was finished."[21]

While Mother Lucy was occupied overcoming these prejudices, Father Joseph was busy developing an overall organizational plan for the Society. His principal goal was to create a model for a durable and practical church order that would function effectively wherever Believers were gathered. It was crucial that the model work smoothly independent of the personalities of different leaders. It is said that Meacham "labored" and prayed so diligently for divine guidance on this matter that he lost complete track of time, and did not even know what day of the week it was.[22]

Meacham established the "gospel order" of the Shaker Society on two fundamental principles: 1) that "all true Church order and Law . . . is given by revelation. . . ." and 2) that "order and union are necessary for the health and prosperity of the Church."[23] In other words, the commands of anointed leaders could not be questioned because their instructions were divinely inspired. Anyone who disrupted the union and order of Christ's family by disagreeing with the Elders was, therefore, committing a sin. Obedience to acknowledged leaders thus became the mark of a good Shaker. Whatever early converts may have been taught about free will and the importance of individual interpretation of God's word was no longer appropriate. Meacham warned that the time had come for true Believers to abandon previous conceptions of their positions in the sect and concur with his own God-given understanding of their proper role or "lot."[24]

Meacham clearly viewed the "gathering of the Church," as it was called, as a process by which troublemakers could be culled, and by which a complete physical and ideological separation from the World could be effected. After creating a male/female Lead Ministry, with New Hampshire's Henry Clough and New Lebanon's Thankful Hamlin as assistants, he turned his attention to the construction of lower level echelons of government based on the same model. In August 1788 the first Shaker communal dwelling, the New Lebanon "Great House," was raised and David Darrow and Ruth Farrington installed there as Church Order Elder and Eldress. This "Church Order" was comprised of firmly committed Shakers who had completely severed their ties to the outside world. The remainder of the group was organized into two "outer courts," the first for those less advanced in spiritual understanding and more involved with the World, and the second for the elderly and infirm.

When he created this authority structure, Father Joseph might well have simultaneously rigidified behavioral standards and increased the harshness of discipline, but apparently he did not. In these early days of the "gathering," Shaker rules remained uncodified. Necessary instructions were conveyed verbally in meeting, and violations were met only with "gentle admonitions." Certain rules, however, trace their inception to Meacham's ministration, and became foundation stones of Shaker social life. Members were required to confess any and all sins before entering meeting, and even confess knowledge of another's unconfessed sin. A distinction was made between rumor-mongering to create ill feeling and simple reporting of sin in order to permit its eradication. Members were also instructed to maintain no "private union" with one another through correspondence or unnecessary touching or conversation.[25]

These regulations could easily have turned the Shaker Society into a near police state where spying and tattling were the rule, but Shaker emphasis on the importance of "union" prevented this development. Leaders constantly reminded the Believers that none of them were so holy that they should not seek the guidance and help of their fellow

Brothers and Sisters. Mother Lucy repeatedly expressed her concern about "union" or its absence, warning: "Remember, you cannot get to heaven alone, but you can be lost alone." [26]

The first Shaker institution developed to minimize factionalism was the so-called union meeting, which Father Joseph introduced in 1793. Recognizing that some official policy about the permissible degree of association between the sexes was necessary, Meacham decided that small group meetings held several times a week to discuss topics of general community interest would best foster the type of spiritual union he favored. Each Brother was paired with a Sister of similar age, and each union meeting was comprised of four or five pairs of different ages to provide a measure of community integration. Sisters looked after the clothing needs of the Brethren with whom they were paired, while the Brethren "in return did needful favors" for the Sisters, probably such chores as fixing equipment or hauling firewood.[27] Death, removal to another Family or community, or apostasy were generally the only reasons for a change in the composition of a union meeting.

It was hoped that small-scale union meetings and Family-size "laboring" (or general worship) meetings would so bind Shaker Families that jealousy and competition would be eliminated. Father Joseph had a hand in organizing laboring meetings as well, minimizing individual activity, and ritualizing movement into the set pattern dances so familiar to nineteenth-century visitors to Shaker villages. By always grouping the Believers for sleep, worship, work, and meals, Meacham hoped to mold them into a true family of Christ instead of a collection of primarily selfish individuals. Shakers who understood that their spiritual "travel" depended in large part on their degree of union to other members would always, Meacham felt, seek the good of the group before individual advancement.

Meacham's goal was to construct a spiritual government that best served the pursuit of union and order. Union meetings and obedience to anointed leaders bonded Believers on a religious plane, and "joint interest" or communal ownership of property accomplished the same result in the economic sphere. This new communalism, which in the nineteenth century came to be regarded as the sect's most important contribution to American social organization, arose more out of circumstance than ideological commitment.

Mother Ann and other early Shaker leaders shared with their Puritan predecessors many beliefs about the proper role of economics in religious life. The common seventeenth-century admonition to the Puritans that they were to live in but not for the world was still an important part of the late eighteenth-century Protestantism the Shakers inherited. The implication that godly life would somehow produce economic success still lingered, and the application of temporal terminology to spiritual affairs affected even Mother Ann, who counseled the early Shakers to "make the way of God your occupation; [it] is to be learned as much as a trade."[28]

James Whittaker was the first Shaker leader to hint at communal organization when he wrote to a Hancock Brother in 1782: "You have land enough to maintain three families or more, well improved." Whittaker went on to remind this Brother that failure to improve his land to its capacity might well result in its confiscation through an act of God.[29]

But it was Joseph Meacham who elaborated on Mother Ann's and Father James's concern with thrift and diligence by institutionalizing Shaker communalism. Father Joseph felt very strongly that money was a dangerous thing for the people of God to become involved with. To minimize this problem, he separated spiritual and temporal leadership in the late 1780s when he appointed David Meacham as the first Deacon of the New Lebanon Church Family. He instructed Meacham to "give all members of the Church an equal privilege, according to their abilities, to do good, as well as an equal privilege to receive according to their needs."[30] To carry out these instructions, Deacons and Deaconesses were appointed in every Family to superintend the operation of barns, fields, and workshops. As trade with the World developed in such items as brooms and garden seeds, the Deacons also introduced quality control because the leaders considered it vital that everything sold by Believers should be as perfect as possible.[31]

The establishment of a Deacons' "lot," as any group of leaders was termed, made equal distribution of limited resources possible. The early Shakers fought poverty as well as persecution. Many of those attracted to the gospel came from the "middling sort," and some had no property at all. Living conditions in the 1780s and 1790s were poor throughout the Society. At Watervliet, the Shakers concentrated on clearing land, planting, raising buildings, and establishing small industries, subsisting all the while on rice, milk, and bean porridge.[32] The situation at other villages was similar. Voluntary contributions of goods and property trickled in from the members, but this uncertainty made economic organization a must.

Most converts in the 1780s brought some property into the sect when they joined. The land donated by farmers in New Lebanon, Hancock, and elsewhere provided the core property on which those communities were built. Some new members possessed considerable estates; a few were even wealthy. The Talcotts of Hancock, in addition to significant quantities of livestock, rye, wheat, oats, cider, and cheese, contributed the first and perhaps the only silver spoons the community ever owned.[33] The Farringtons of New Lebanon were among the wealthiest converts, consecrating an estate valued at £678.0.5.[34]

More typical, however, were couples like Joshua and Lois Birch of Stonington, Connecticut, who joined the Hancock community in 1791. Their estate totaled £13.4.10., and included household furniture, sole leather, lumber, two yards of Dutch lace, half a pound of tea, and a paper of pins.[35] Other members of the same community added a variety of personal goods: Reuben Rathbun, a span of horses and a wagon; Stephen Slosson, a set of joiner's tools; Josiah Torrey, a two-year-old heifer; and Eliphalet Slosson, a small iron pot.[36] Many early converts still in their teens and twenties who had never established their own households brought in no "temporal interest" when they joined. The disparity of contributions made economic organization a necessity if Father Joseph's vision of equality of effort and reward was to be realized.

Potential disagreements over economic policy were minimized during this period by the overall homogeneity of the converts in the "first gathering." The New Lebanon Church Family, for example, was dominated by a handful of extended families, among whom the Goodriches, Darrows, Farringtons, and Meachams were perhaps the most influential. Over 75 percent of converts joining the Family between 1787 and 1790 were members of nuclear kin groups. The New Gloucester, Maine, community (later called Sabbathday Lake) witnessed a similar pattern, with the Briggs, Holmes, and Merrill clans contributing a total of seventeen adults and sixty-six minor children during the 1780s.[37]

The stability that these kinship networks provided was considerable, and was a key factor in the early success of the sect. The age distribution of members in the Families was also crucial. Most new converts were in their twenties, thirties, and forties—old enough to possess usable property and to have experienced lasting conversions. At New Lebanon, 64.7 percent of the Church Family's members in 1790 were between the ages of sixteen and thirty-nine. Yet, none were under seven and only fifty-four (17.9 percent) were under sixteen. While 1790 census returns are very scattered for the eastern communities, most of which had not yet been officially "gathered," figures for the year 1800 indicate that few youngsters were brought into the sect during its early years. In that year, there were only thirty-nine children under sixteen in all eleven communities, a mere 2.8 percent of the total population (see Appendix B.5). As a result, supervisional problems were few and older Shakers had little reason to resent a large number of members who were too young to have contributed to the Society's economic well-being.

While these demographic characteristics appear to have reduced serious dissension over the transition to communalism, Father Joseph quickly recognized the potential for problems. In 1795, First Order Shakers at New Lebanon signed their first written covenant, a document Meacham designed to protect the church from lawsuits by apostates. Signing this covenant supposedly made a member's consecration of property irrevocable, although backsliders were frequently given an equivalent amount of cash or goods at their departure. Some former Shakers, however, tried to sue the church for wages covering the time they had spent within the Society. Mother Lucy was forced to remind members: "You are not gathered into Gospel Order as Servants, but as heirs of all things . . . that the People of God possess . . . therefore to go to the inconsistency of demanding wages as hired Servants would be unjust & a violation of our professed Faith & sacred privilege." [38]

These stirrings of discontent failed to mar the general success of the system of temporal and spiritual government inaugurated by Father Joseph. Immediately after its establishment, he turned his attention for a time to theology. Few Shakers were skilled in this discipline in the late eighteenth century; indeed, it is likely that quite a number were illiterate. It is not possible to determine where and how Meacham acquired his expertise. He may merely have absorbed the rudiments of the subject from his father and his Baptist associates. At any rate, in the late 1780s, he appears to have decided that the time had come for a "reopening" of the Shaker gospel in the World. This time there were no three-year missionary tours, no fiery camp meetings, and no eye-catching spirit manifestations. For Worldly consumption, Meacham instead authored the first in a long line of Shaker theological publications, a modest pamphlet entitled *A Concise Statement of the Only True Church*.

Although no name appears on the title page, numerous Shakers credited Father Joseph with its authorship, especially since there were few other Believers alive at the time who possessed the skill to write such a treatise. In *A Concise Statement* Meacham told the Shaker version of Christian history consisting of a series of four divine dispensations to men: first to Abraham, then to Moses, Christ, and Mother Ann in succession. He hinted, in addition, at the glimmerings of a belief that made Shakerism one of the most hopeful of religions—that of conversion after death. Echoing contemporary Universalist sentiments, Meacham declared that "God was no respecter of persons but willing that all should come to the knowledge of the truth, and be saved."[39]

Although Meacham did establish the truly millennial nature of the Shaker sect in this publication, using Biblical arithmetic to claim that the Second Coming dated from Mother Ann's 1757 revelation from Christ about her mission, it is curious that he never once mentioned her by name. Nor did James Whittaker, in a letter to his family published in the same pamphlet, say one word about Ann Lee or even about a female leader. It seems likely that these omissions were made for the sake of the public Meacham hoped to reach, who perhaps would have had nothing to do with a sect that professed belief in a female Messiah. In theological manuscripts written for Shaker consumption, on the other hand, Meacham several times discoursed at length on the appropriateness of the appearance of Christ in a female form.[40]

Meacham thus seems to have been able to adjust his message to the needs and expectations of different audiences, Shaker or otherwise. The governmental system he established at New Lebanon between 1787 and 1790 was rigid enough to provide stability, yet flexible enough to allow change and progress. By insisting that every level in the sect's hierarchy be composed of at least two people, male and female, and in most cases up to four, Meacham made it impossible for a single leader to govern by mere whim. The importance of a single, dominant leader at the apex of the hierarchy should not, however, be dismissed. By the 1820s, when such leaders failed to appear, the system of mutual interdependence was to have serious consequences doubtless unforeseen by Father Joseph.

It appears that Meacham may have regarded the system he set up at New Lebanon as experimental. Brother John Warner implied in his history of the Harvard Bishopric that the New Lebanon pattern was applied to other communities only after its efficacy had been demonstrated there.[41] When Meacham discovered that the system worked, he decided to establish the same organizational structure wherever Shakers had collected into communities.

In 1787, Father Joseph and Mother Lucy had selected a group of Brethren and Sisters to serve as their ambassadors in the various regions where Believers were gathering. Travelers from the spiritual fount at New Lebanon held the sect together in the unsettled years of the late 1780s and early 1790s while the transition from scattered converts to settled communities was made. Between February 19, 1791 and August 17, 1792, for example, the Shakers at Harvard received thirty-four visitors from New Lebanon, including Father Joseph himself on one occasion, and his principal assistant, Henry Clough, on another.[42]

While New Lebanon and Watervliet, New York, were united in the First Bishopric under the direct supervision of the Lead Ministry, communities in other areas were combined into separate Bishoprics under the leadership of local Ministries that answered to the Lead Ministry directly. In 1790, Hancock and Tyringham, Massachusetts, and Enfield, Connecticut, were united in the Second Bishopric and placed in the charge of Calvin Harlow, an early convert to the gospel and a transplant from New Jersey, and Sarah Harrison, from a Hancock family most of which had joined the sect in the early 1780s.

The eastern Massachusetts communities at Harvard and Shirley were combined under the ministerial care of Eleazer Rand, a former indentured servant from Boston, and Hannah Kendall, daughter of a Woburn farmer who had converted with his family in the early 1780s. In 1792, the two New Hampshire communities, at Enfield and Canterbury, were placed in the care of Job Bishop of New Lebanon and Hannah Goodrich of Hancock. The following year, the two communities in Maine, at Alfred and New Gloucester, were given into the charge of John Barns of Alfred and Sarah Kendall, a natural sister of Hannah.

Of these eight, six had served in Meacham's "traveling ministry." They proved without exception more successful as leaders than the two who had not had the benefit of that experience—John Barns and Sarah Kendall. All eight were born between 1754 and 1763, making them between twenty-eight and thirty-six when they assumed their positions. It is possible that Father Joseph and Mother Lucy consciously selected Elders and Eldresses who could reasonably be expected to live long enough to entrench the New Lebanon governmental system firmly in the Bishoprics entrusted to them. The Hancock Bishopric suffered most in this regard, because Harlow died in 1795 and Harrison in 1796, but Hancock's proximity to New Lebanon made the appointment of successors comparatively easy. In New Hampshire, which many Believers regarded as traditionally the best governed Bishopric other than New Lebanon, the original Ministry members survived the longest, Goodrich dying in 1820 and Bishop in 1831.[43]

All four of these Bishopric Ministries were established in "gospel order" with the assistance of Henry Clough, Father Joseph's second-in-command. A native of Canterbury, New Hampshire, Clough had converted to Shakerism in 1782 after a distinguished local career as a Free

Will Baptist lay preacher. An itinerant Shaker preacher during Father James's ministration, he was called to New Lebanon in 1788 to assist Father Joseph in the gathering of the church there.

There seems to have been some feeling among Believers that Clough would have been a better choice than Bishop as senior Elder in the New Hampshire Ministry; indeed, Bishop himself thought so at first. When he traveled to New Hampshire in 1791 to gather the Believers there into gospel order, he encountered difficulties that sent him hurrying back to New Lebanon for guidance. Father Joseph sent him back in the company of Clough to straighten things out. Bishop was evidently depressed because he felt that he had been wrongfully appointed to a position Clough should have held. But, when Clough explained that he was needed more at New Lebanon than in New Hampshire, Bishop accepted his explanation and continued his journey alone. When he arrived at Canterbury, he was able to convince the Believers there that their local favorite was where he belonged.[44]

The Elders and Eldresses chosen by Meacham and Wright to establish the nine New England societies were selected because they exhibited the same qualities as the best of their followers: obedience, submissiveness, diligence, and humility. They do not appear to have been great risktakers. Meacham was interested in people who could carry out orders to the letter. John Warner of Harvard remembered that Father Eleazer Rand "was in no ways ostentatious for his own merit and careful not to commence any work, nor enter into any controversy beyond his comprehension."[45] Similarly, Father Job Bishop "was always very careful to acknowledge the lead placed in order before him whether old or young, and in a peculiar manner was extremely careful to pattern the gift and order of things in the Mother Church."[46]

While these leaders did indeed prove themselves faithful in carrying out the orders of the Lead Ministry, their attitude was far from plodding and lackluster. They possessed sufficient charismatic appeal to be attractive to their charges, but not enough to pose a challenge to their superiors. Many were excellent speakers, like Father Calvin Harlow, who cleverly played on his audience's desire to emulate the New Lebanon Believers, telling them in 1791 that the "brethren in the church at New Lebanon loved and esteemed each other, better than themselves, and strove to make each other happy," intimating that the Hancock Brethren had yet to achieve this state.[47] Leading by example was another of their strengths. All good Shaker leaders threw themselves into their temporal labor with an enthusiasm that inspired their followers. Sister Eunice Bathrick remarked about Mother Hannah

Kendall: "Nothing felt hard that she required us to do, for her presence lightened our burdens."[48]

In spite of the talents and commitment of these leaders, however, serious problems were on the horizon. Although Meacham was certain that his organizational plan was working and that the leaders he and Wright had selected to establish it throughout New England would ultimately accomplish their task successfully, he anticipated that the effort to found "gospel order" would, indeed, encounter some stumbling blocks. In 1795, he told the Elder Brethren at New Lebanon that he "foresaw a great shaking among the young." He was afraid that "there would be such a breaking that hardly two of them would be left together." Apparently, in an atypical error in judgment, Father Joseph had appointed two Elders to the Young People's Order who were guilty of "unfaithful and unwise conduct," and later fell away to the World. Under their governance, many of the young Brethren refused to submit themselves to good "order," became coarse and vulgar in their behavior and conversation, and even tried to imitate the ways of the World.[49] As a result, Meacham's prediction was fulfilled. In 1795 and 1796, the New Lebanon Church Family, which numbered approximately 180, lost twenty members through apostasy.[50] The apostasy rate in this Family reached 19.9 percent during the 1790s, a level not surpassed until the 1860s (see Appendix A.2). Other communities suffered similar difficulties. The Shirley Church Family lost ten of sixty-eight members between 1795 and 1800, and the Church Family at Harvard lost eighteen of ninety-four Believers between 1794 and 1796.[51]

As Joseph Meacham's health gradually worsened during this period, the task of attempting to stem the rising tide of backsliding fell to his assistant, Elder Henry Clough, who continued to visit all the New England communities and solidify local leaders in their positions. But Meacham never expected Clough to succeed him; that job was reserved for Mother Lucy Wright. In writing to her in 1796, shortly before his death, Meacham made this plain, saying: "Thou, tho' of the weaker sex, . . . will be the *Elder or first born* after my departure."[52]

Detractors in the outside world viewed the high apostasy rate and the death of Joseph Meacham as sure signs of the sect's imminent demise. In an article published in May 1797, the Shakers' old enemy, Valentine Rathbun, reported they were so desperate for converts that they were using his name to try to attract them, claiming he was friendly toward them. Rathbun fumed: "In all of which there is not the least colour of truth. . . . When I consider . . . the awful effects of that diabolical scheme in parting men and their wives, . . . in monopolizing wealth to themselves in the most fraudulent way, &c. I believe it to be

my duty to caution and warn people against such lying imposters."
Perhaps Rathbun assumed that Mother Lucy was far too weak a leader
to hold the sect together. Gleefully, he reported: "The Shakers in New-
lebanon and Hancock being on the decline, their old people being
dead and dying, and their young people leaving them, they are
brought to their last trial to maintain their ground."[53] But to the cha-
grin of ill-wishers like Rathbun, Mother Lucy proved more than equal
to the challenge.

3

Bait to Catch Good Gospel Fish

(1796-1821)

Because of his declining health, Father Joseph resigned in Lucy Wright's favor during the spring of 1796, and died in August of the same year. Although a few Believers hoped that Henry Clough would assume the principal duties of the Lead Ministry, Mother Lucy's appointment was acknowledged by the "spontaneous union" of the members and was "cordially and efficiently supported by Elder Henry Clough."[1] It is quite possible that without Clough's support, Wright would have found her transition to leadership far more difficult.

During her unprecedented twenty-five-year tenure, Mother Lucy focused her attention on internal organization and regulation as well as on efforts to attract converts. The population of the eastern communities increased markedly between 1800 and 1820; much of this increase was accounted for by the rising proportion of children and teenagers among the membership. This trend, coupled with a simultaneous decline in the proportion of adult members in the leadership pool, created a challenge that Mother Lucy and her successors were unable to meet satisfactorily. Much of Wright's time in office was devoted to establishing standards of behavior so that these new converts, often drawn as much by economic as by spiritual reasons, could learn to live pure Shaker lives, unsullied by the growing "worldly sense" she saw proliferating within the communities.

Yet when Mother Lucy assumed control of the sect, these difficulties were years away. She inherited a system of government firmly established in the hearts and minds of her followers. In the brief span of nine years, Father Joseph had fostered a union between faithful Believers so durable that even a rash of apostasies among the young caused no permanent disillusionment. Daniel Goodrich, Sr., of Hancock was so surprised to see such a number of "young and middle aged people laboring day and night, all in agreement, for the support and benefit of each other" that he decided it had to be the work of God.[2] Descriptions of the Believers in 1796 create an image of solemn, yet vigorous, dedication to the gospel cause. Brother Isaac Youngs recalled many years later: "They flinched at no cross, willingly endured all sufferings, privations and labors spiritual and temporal, and devoted their all."[3] Mother Lucy, however, found this apparently praiseworthy dedication a trifle too solemn.

Perhaps, after all, the apostasies among the young did have a lasting impact, amply demonstrating the need to continue to draw upon the World for converts.[4] By the turn of the century, Shakerism's well-organized radical Protestantism appealed to a significant number of evangelical Christians who were still searching for millennial perfection on earth. The sect became more acceptable in the eyes of some when they noticed that the charismatic features of its worship had been modified, and as they became familiar with the Believers' commitment to diligence and honesty through the variety of items increasingly available for sale in the World. Continuing waves of revivalism brought new converts to the faith during the years after Father Joseph's death.

To prepare for their integration into the Society, Mother Lucy instituted a few important changes in its organization. She felt very strongly in 1796 that the sect's condition was too "heavy" for zealous souls fresh from the sin-ridden world. "It was needful," she declared, "that the elemental Life in Zion should be modified so that infant Souls could partake and live thereby."[5] In 1799, therefore, Wright established a special "Gathering Order" for new members at New Lebanon under the leadership of Ebenezer Cooley, a veteran missionary of the early 1780s in eastern Massachusetts. In making this choice, Mother Lucy certainly knew that Cooley had early established a reputation for telling potential Believers just what they wanted to hear. A Baptist commentator complained that, while Cooley was preaching the Shaker gospel in New Hampshire in 1782, he had "made high pretensions to spiritual life and practical piety, shrewdly keeping in reserve, for a time, most of the objectionable features of his religion."[6] This experience served him well seventeen years later when the World began to exhibit renewed interest in the sect.

Among the first to confess their sins and join this new Gathering Order was the Wells family from Long Island. Their experience demonstrates the kin ties that often connected Believers with different surnames. In the fall of 1799, Seth Youngs Wells, a teacher at Hudson Academy, came to New Lebanon to visit his uncle, Benjamin Youngs, who had converted during the first gathering. Convinced of the truth of the Shaker gospel, Wells went home to Long Island and told his family of his wish to become a Shaker. He must have been extremely persuasive because both his parents and all nine of his siblings joined the Society and lived out their lives as Believers. In addition, at least ten other relations converted, four of whom later apostatized.

Another important accession in these years was Issachar Bates, a former Baptist minister who joined the Watervliet community in 1803 with his wife and seven children. Born in Hingham, Massachusetts, Bates had been raised as a Presbyterian. Profoundly affected by revivals in the 1780s, he began searching for the "true religion." After reluctantly entering the Baptist fold, he was licensed to preach in 1795, but remained discontented.

Always hoping that the next revival would give him permanent assurance of his salvation Bates hung on until 1801, but disillusionment had set in. He came to recognize that all revivals eventually "ended in flesh," and began to preach that salvation "was not among us, nor never would be in that way of going." In this state, he visited Elder Cooley at New Lebanon and confessed his sins after a discussion of little more than an hour, "for we did business quick, I eat quick & talked quick, heard quick and started home quick, for I was quickened."[7]

The years between 1800 and 1810 saw the return of extensive Shaker missionary activity. Local revivals in neighboring states frequently attracted the attention of the leaders at New Lebanon, and on many occasions two or three Brethren noted for their preaching ability were dispatched to spread the gospel. One such small revival began in Pittsford, Vermont, in 1801 when a strange light appeared over the roof of a house belonging to a man named James Wicker. In the spiritual upheaval that followed, many residents joined the Methodists, while others prayed that "God would send them something more, even if it came from the Shakers."[8]

The Believers at New Lebanon heard about the excitement in Pittsford because a neighbor of Wicker's, Justus Brewster, had written them to request guidance. Brewster was a Methodist but had failed to discover in that or in any other denomination, preachers who "had come out from the world, nor had manifested by example that they were living any better life than he did."[9] When Brothers Issachar Bates and Benjamin Youngs came to Pittsford, Brewster at last found Christians who proved their conviction by their lifestyle. He evidently agreed with his nine-year-old daughter, Sally, who decided that they "looked just like Jesus Christ."[10] Others in town were equally impressed with their appearance and their message; approximately twenty-five residents confessed their sins and moved to various Shaker communities, among others, the Brewsters to Hancock, the Copleys to New Lebanon, and the Wickers to Watervliet.

Often these new converts expressed the depth of their commitment to the gospel by missionary work among their relatives still living in the World. When Brothers Daniel Goodrich and Calvin Green set out to visit a woman named Mary Rust, they carried with them a letter from her daughter, Mary Boynton. A member of the Hancock community, Sister Mary begged her mother to maintain the degree of faith in Shaker principles she had already received and to strive for greater understanding. Apparently, Rust's husband was not a Believer, and she had become alarmed by the evil reports spread abroad about the Shakers. When the Brethren arrived to reassure her and to try to convince the family of the truth of Shaker tenets, Mary was nowhere to be found. Goodrich and Green lingered hopefully for several days, but she never reappeared. It seems likely that her family was suspicious of her attachment to the sect, and contrived to send her out of what they viewed as harm's way.[11]

Mary Rust was only one of a significant number of Believers during this period who were never able to move to a Shaker village because of family responsibilities. Indeed, Shaker growth during these years, already known to be impressive, may actually have been phenomenal if surviving records permitted the inclusion of converts living outside of established communities. The Shakers regarded these people as true Believers. Goodrich and Green reminded Mary Rust of this in a letter written shortly after their frustrating visit: "Remember, if thou art faithful in the cause of Christ, thou art a member of his body, and will be joined in spirit to the People of God, though never so distant in body."[12]

Converts more fortunate than Rust brought new life and vigor to the communities they joined, lightening the solemn, almost grim character that had disturbed Mother Lucy. The new Shakers of these years were better able than many of their seniors in the gospel to express their joy about being Believers. Much of the initial hard work of establishing the sect was over. Exultation was the response of many, like David Rowley, a cabinetmaker from Sharon, Connecticut, who converted in 1810. "I can say," he later wrote, "that I never have seen one moment since I set out in this blessed way but that I felt thankful for it; & can with confidence recommend it to all souls who are sick of the vain world & are seeking . . . a way of true life & imperishable love."[13]

This new confidence in the efficacy of the Shaker way, combined with the recognition of the need for converts, led directly to the most far-reaching Shaker missionary effort in what was then the western frontier. As a result, seven additional communities were founded; two in Kentucky, four in Ohio, and one in Indiana. The small ingatherings in the eastern societies between 1798 and 1802 had whetted the Believers' appetite for a more widespread "opening of the gospel." When news reached the east of the tremendous camp meetings taking place in the Cane Ridge section of Kentucky, excitement grew. Many members recalled that Mother Ann had once prophesied: "The next opening of the gospel will be in the south West, but I shall not live to see it." [14] By early 1804, most Shakers were convinced that the time had arrived.

While perhaps reluctant to sanction a missionary endeavor so far from the center of Shaker strength and order, Mother Lucy responded favorably to the ground swell of enthusiasm that arose among her followers. On New Year's Day in 1805, Brothers Issachar Bates, Benjamin Youngs, and John Meacham set out on foot for Ohio. After their journey, they worked initially at the home of Malcolm Worley in Turtle Creek, and began meeting with leaders of the local revival. Richard McNemar, an ordained Presbyterian minister and owner of considerable property in the region, was an early convert. His influence was such that most of the members of his congregation followed him into the sect.

In spite of this support by local leaders, however, Mother Lucy felt that the organization of the new communities should be entrusted to easterners. Accordingly, in July 1805, Elder David Darrow was dispatched from New Lebanon to oversee the gathering of the western Believers, and was joined the following April by Eldress Ruth Farrington and several other Brethren and Sisters. During the next ten years, as many as thirty eastern Believers were sent west to assume positions of authority.

As had been the case in the eastern societies twenty-five years earlier, living conditions were poor. Some eastern Shakers found the adjustment from the comparative prosperity of their old homes to the extreme poverty of their new environment difficult. Benjamin Youngs, while at Busro, Indiana, in 1810, wrote home: "We have planted a nursery—Plenty of Apples & cider by & by; I could easily drink three egg cups full of good cider this minute if I only had it. . . . I am already so tired & sick of this limy water." [15]

The expansion of Shakerism into Ohio and Kentucky created a backwash of excitement among the Shakers in the east. As the willingness of many to emigrate indicates, they were wholehearted in their support of the endeavor. Indeed, Calvin Green later asserted that he had never seen the Believers more in agreement. [16] Daniel Goodrich, Sr. expressed his commitment in a typically effusive letter to David Meacham in Ohio in 1806: "I have had great desire to Live for many years to hear and see what is Now manifested at Ohio and in adjacent places, for which my heart is Glad; I can truly say with confidence I feel more Interested in this Work . . . than I ever did in all the Kingdoms of this World." [17]

In the fall of 1807, Mother Lucy used this heightened enthusiasm as the basis for a small-scale revival among the eastern Believers, calling them to "wake up to God and come out of [their] Lethargy." She sent letters to all the societies warning that a further "increase in the gospel" was imminent and demanding that all purify themselves in preparation. She inveighed against "vain jesting, joking, obscene & filthy communication," and was particularly distraught over the increasing incidence of private conversations between Brethren and Sisters.[18] She also appears to have been concerned over the increasing level of friction between older and younger members, telling the Believers at Harvard: "If a man has labored and acquired an interest and then consecrates it . . . he does but give up all. Then the young who have nothing; and consecrate their time and talents . . . it may be said with equal propriety that they give up all." [19] As a result of this revival, there was great pressure to enliven worship meetings, to which Mother Lucy bowed, allowing the introduction of hymns in 1808 and anthems in 1812, many of which had western origins.

At about the same time, Mother Lucy inaugurated another effort to spread the Shaker gospel to a Worldly audience. The publishing campaign she initiated led to the appearance of five major works by Shaker authors in the next decade. Of central importance was Benjamin S. Youngs's *Testimony of Christ's Second Appearing*, which was first printed in Lebanon, Ohio, in 1808, and again two years later in Albany, New York. An impressive theological work, tracing the history of Christianity from Adam and Eve to Mother Ann, it created quite a stir in the World. Relying heavily on standard eighteenth-century theological works and Biblical references, the *Testimony* gave credence to Shaker principles among some intellectuals who had hitherto scoffed. The Shakers later reported the reaction of Thomas Jefferson, who had supposedly read the book three times. "I pronounce it," he is said to have concluded, "the best Church History that ever was written, and if its exegesis of Christian principles is maintained and sustained by a practical life, it is destined eventually to overthrow all other religions." [20]

The *Testimony* was well received among the less prominent as well. After reading it in her Lancaster, Ontario, home, Dolly DeWitt became so convinced of the truth of Shakerism that she talked her husband into joining with all eight of their children, six of whom converted on reaching adulthood. Although DeWitt's husband was later to apostatize, Brother Calvin Reed felt justified in rejoicing: "Thus was that book a bait to catch seven good Gospel fish."[21]

The *Testimony* penetrated even into the "wicked city" of New York, and made a good name for the Shakers there as well. An unidentified master combmaker owned a copy that was eagerly read by two of his apprentices. One of them, Richard Bushnell, came to New Lebanon in 1813, and confessed his sins, declaring himself to be sick of the frivolity of the World. Two years later, his fellow apprentice, Joseph Adams, arrived to inquire about Shakerism and ultimately joined. Then, in 1817, two of Richard's brothers from Saybrook, Connecticut, came to see him and discuss Shaker beliefs. One of them, Charles, became so taken with the faith that he returned to Saybrook, armed with more copies of the *Testimony* to spread the good news. He was instrumental in the conversion of his mother, who was too ill ever to move to a Shaker village; his sisters Patience, Martha, Sally, and Sophia; Sophia's husband, Gilbert Avery, Sr.; Avery's two children by his first wife who moved to the community at Enfield, Connecticut; and the two children of Gilbert and Sophia, Giles and Eliza, who moved with their parents to New Lebanon.[22] This again demonstrates the web of family and community relationships that connected many Believers, doubtless far more than can be determined from surviving records.

This atmosphere of religious enthusiasm in the first decades of the new century continued to bring significant numbers of converts into the Shaker fold. Between 1800 and 1820, the eleven eastern communities experienced an average increase in population of 42.5 percent. At Hancock and Watervliet in particular, the gains were impressive, as 184 and 116 new members joined these respective societies (see Appendix B.1). But this influx of converts was to strain the sect's governmental structure at one of its most vulnerable points.

To deal with these changing circumstances, Mother Lucy spent much of her time in office attempting to systematize standards of behavior. She placed tremendous emphasis on showing a unified and modest face to the outside world. In small ways, she tried to bring the Believers' behavior up-to-date, particularly in the area of language. She always used correct English and abhorred "clipped, or low, vulgar words, or expressions." She insisted that Believers never use nicknames or Worldly titles, such as "Mister" or "Miss," and rebuked them for abandoning the use of "Yea" and "Nay," the simple speech supposedly favored by the apostles. To remedy the "awkward mode of speaking" many members exhibited, Mother Lucy even established a special school in 1808 where they could learn to say "them" instead of "'em," "other" instead of "t'other," and "It will do" instead of "Twill does."[23] She was so concerned with what she saw as the backward ways of most Believers that in 1820 she appointed Brother Seth Wells as superintendent of Shaker schools and public writings. Largely due to his efforts, by midcentury Shaker schools were among the best in the northeast.

Mother Lucy was also responsible for the regularization of Shaker dress between 1805 and 1815. Brethren no longer wore the eighteenth-century style knee breeches, stocks, and waistcoats that had been the norm in the World when the Shakers first gathered into communities, and Sisters were required to abandon short gowns and stays. Shaker clothing became less and less fashionable, designed primarily for economy and uniformity, and possessing the added advantage of concealing the wearer's physique.[24] With Brethren adopting long, baggy trousers, and Sisters enveloped in long gowns, high collars, and neck handkerchiefs, their shapeless appearance was appropriate for a celibate society.

The pattern throughout the later years of Mother Lucy's ministration continued to be one of gradual rapprochement with the World and consolidation of Shaker doctrine and standards of behavior. Through a series of confrontations with the World over military service and the custody of property, the Shakers, even though they refrained from active involvement with federal and state governments, allowed themselves to become increasingly subject to their control. During the War of 1812, Shaker Brethren became subject to conscription, and some actually paid fines for refusing to serve. By intensive lobbying within the confines of the Worldly legislative system, however, leaders at New Lebanon were ultimately able to free their members from the draft on the grounds of religious conviction.

After the war, several apostates who had been unsuccessful in their attempts to recover property dedicated to the Shaker Society either by themselves or by family members, introduced a bill in the New York legislature requiring that all men wishing to join the Society surrender to their heirs title to all their property. Arguments on this bill were long and bitter, but ultimately the Believers won again. Both of these experiences taught otherworldly Shaker leaders how to use the institutions of this world to their political advantage.

These gestures of reaching out to the World and welcoming a large number of converts were not without negative consequences. As the Shakers increasingly abandoned their isolation from the outside world, some members gradually noticed a significant change in the atmosphere within the villages. Prosperous Believers of the 1810s and 1820s had more difficulty living in, but not for the world, than their predecessors. Mother Lucy upbraided the Shakers on many occasions for the growing "worldly sense" she saw infecting all Families and Orders. She complained that most members did not pay enough attention to spiritual things. They were "so engrossed in temporal business" that they could "hardly set time to think of [their] souls once a week." Mother Lucy apparently felt that this state of affairs was even beyond her control, for she commented plaintively in 1815: "The sense seems so drowned in temporal things that there can be but little sensation or desire for the gifts of God. . . . I sometimes feel I would be thankful with all my heart if the sense was so that it could be satisfied with less . . . of this world's treasures." [25]

A major ingathering from Savoy, Massachusetts, beginning in 1817, distracted the Believers, leaders and followers alike, from these nagging difficulties. "Having heard of a stir there," Brother Calvin Green traveled to Savoy to investigate, and successfully induced enough people to confess their sins that a small branch society, or "Young Believers' Order," was established there and remained active for several years. But controlling these small societies from New Lebanon was difficult. Believers at Savoy, whether native converts or imports from New Lebanon, were free from the more severe strictures that would have governed their lives at more solidly established Shaker villages, and they behaved accordingly. Ducks nested under the breakfast table and had to be shooed away; brash young Brethren paraded in dooryards clad only in their shirts; and some new members chatted and generally "supported union" with their "old mates" in a casual manner that would have horrified the Lead Ministry. [26] It is hardly surprising that Mother Lucy "felt a gift" in 1821, shortly before her death, to have the Savoy Believers liquidate their assets and move to settled communities like Hancock and New Lebanon. The Savoy adventure was the most successful eastern missionary effort during this period, resulting in the accession of some eighty Believers in all.

The Savoy Believers were not the only ones misbehaving. Members in long-established communities were beginning to cause trouble as well. Between 1805 and 1820, a new generation of Shakers grew to maturity who had never been through the crucible of a religious revival. They were mostly children of devoted converts, and grew to be Shakers perhaps as much out of habit as conviction. As early as 1811, Mother Lucy began taking steps that reveal her concern about the sect's spiritual welfare. In that year, she issued an order to terminate intercommunity visiting, except for Deacons or Ministry members traveling on business. [27] In 1820, she recalled most of the western missionaries, declaring that the time had come for the Believers in the west to bear their own leadership burdens. She knew that the Shakers had perhaps overextended themselves preaching and writing for the World while the foundation that was thought to be so solid was showing signs of stress.

Part of the problem was demographic. In founding their communities, early leaders had not developed institutions for the education and socialization of the young because they had few converts under age sixteen. By the early nineteenth century, however, that situation had changed markedly. Between 1800 and 1820, the proportion of members under sixteen in all the eastern communities had increased dramatically, from 2.8 percent to 19.8 percent (see Appendix B.5). Many of the adults showing an interest in the sect during these years were attracted solely by the promise of temporal security, as the Lead Ministry observed ruefully in 1817: "We could have a great many *loaf Believers* in this distressing time (especially children) if we were willing to take them—doubtless we could have enough to fill all our buildings and consume all our provisions, and by that time they would be willing to go somewhere else."[28]

The difficulties these trends entailed were numerous. Behavior suffered, as Mother Lucy commented when she observed that many members, especially the young, tried to "trample upon the laws of Zion" in order to "satisfy some inclination" in themselves.[29] Other leaders were disturbed as well. One New Lebanon Elder reported to a colleague in South Union, Kentucky:

We sometimes discover lurking about our peaceful habitation some little tory that would wish to betray our souls into the hands of our enemies. There are three or four scoundrels of this grade who are very pestiferous. They go by the names of Mr. Slug, Mrs. Lounge-about, Great I and Old Fret! It may be you have heard of them, & as we are fully authorized, we take the liberty to treat them with as much disrespect & neglect as we feel to. Doubtless, the young Believers under your care often experience much inconvenience from their intrusion, but time & due exercise of grace will deliver from their clutches.[30]

In spite of this Elder's hopeful conclusion, it had become painfully clear to many leaders and devout members that "time & due exercise of grace" were insufficient remedies. The need for codified, written rules was becoming increasingly acute.

Prior to 1821, any rules or general instructions that leaders at any level of the sect's hierarchy felt to be necessary were communicated verbally. In 1800, for example, the New Lebanon Church Family leaders decided to abandon the use of liquor except for medicinal purposes, but no written order was recorded.[31] Before 1810, Father Eleazer Rand and Mother Hannah Kendall taught the Harvard Shakers how devout

Brethren and Sisters behaved toward one another. Among other guidelines, they decreed that Brethren and Sisters should not address one another unnecessarily nor pass on stairs or in a doorway.[32] These and other verbal instructions from the early nineteenth century became integral parts of rule books written in subsequent decades. But these rules, scattered as they were and varying from village to village, were difficult to follow and even more difficult to remember. By the 1820s, it was no longer possible for leaders to rely wholly on the faith and consciences of Believers to guide them in their daily behavior; not all Shakers in this period were the best of Believers. Mother Lucy was indirectly responsible for the compilation of a rule book for these lukewarm Shakers, so they could know without doubt what was expected of them.

Called the *Millennial Laws*, this book of regulations was assembled by Brother Freegift Wells of Watervliet shortly before Mother Lucy's death in February 1821. Wells collected all the rules that could be recalled from the ministrations of Father Joseph and Mother Lucy and arranged them in categories: "Separation of the Sexes," "Orders pertaining to the Sabbath," "Orders on uniformity in certain acts of behavior," and the like. He showed the book to Mother Lucy, recommending that copies be distributed to all Shaker Families and read aloud to members in meeting. Surprisingly, Mother Lucy refused Wells's request. She was afraid that the act of recording Shaker rules would limit the freedom of successive leaders to change them as a result of divine revelation. She was also reluctant to have rule books spread so widely throughout the Society that the regulations contained in them would be familiarized, and therefore, less sacred. The possibility that some of the orders might leak to the World also dismayed her, so the project was temporarily abandoned.

In spite of her reluctance to write Shaker rules down, Mother Lucy continued to issue verbal instructions up to the end. On her death bed, she outlawed dogs from the Society, asserting: "They do not belong to Believers; they are unprofitable animals; they are a Temptation to young people, and must have great notice, or they are of little service. It is natural for people to be fond of Dogs, and use great freedom with them which is a loss to the Soul."[33] But after her death, and perhaps because of it, the *Millennial Laws* were transcribed many times over and copies dispatched to every Family in the Society. Instructions were given to have all members repeat the orders one by one in an annual meeting to ensure that no one could claim ignorance of the law. Thus, bereft of the last of their dominant spiritual Parents and removed one

step further from Mother Ann herself, the Lead Ministry substituted a
rule book in her stead.

The 1821 *Millennial Laws* dealt primarily with proper relations between members and with members' duties to leaders. "Tattling, tale-
bearing and backbiting" were outlawed and members were prohibited
from dredging up old grievances that had been confessed and put away
forever. If anyone became "overcome with anger" and spoke sharply
to a fellow Believer, confession was required before attendance at Family meeting. Although tattling for malicious purposes was forbidden,
members were encouraged to concern themselves actively with the
spiritual welfare of their colleagues. If any Shaker knew of another's
sin that had not been revealed to the Elders, it was that member's responsibility to confess it.[34] The *Millennial Laws* emphasized that the
burden of maintaining the purity of Zion had to be shared.

Another intriguing inclusion in the 1821 *Millennial Laws* was a list
of restrictions concerning alcohol. Apparently the 1800 decision of the
New Lebanon Church Family had not been emulated by Believers elsewhere in the Society. The *Millennial Laws* decreed that any member
drinking "so as to be disguised thereby" was banned from the ranks of
Family meeting until he or she had been restored by confession and
repentance. Members were to abstain from all "distilled spirits" on the
Sabbath except when heavy work in the barns, fields, or kitchen made
it admissible, but in these cases indulgence was only allowed in the
morning. It was, however, further established that no one was to consume spirits before breakfast.[35]

Despite the decree on drinking it is evident that the Shakers were no
more strangers to alcohol during this period than their Worldly neighbors. Family account books confirm this conclusion. During the year
1817, the New Lebanon Church Family expended $138.18 on pur-
chases of alcohol, or roughly 2 percent of its total outlay. For this sum,
its members obtained seventy-one gallons of rum, thirty-five and a half
gallons of gin, thirty-three gallons of brandy, and five gallons of wine.[36]
These figures fail to include whatever spirits may have been produced
within the Family, but even so, the Believers in this Family at least,
seem to have been moderate in their indulgence.

The tenor and specificity of this rule book is clear proof that the behavior it was designed to curb had become a serious problem within
the communities, despite the serene exterior exhibited to the outside
world. While Mother Lucy had not been directly responsible for its
creation, the thrust of her whole ministration had been regulatory. Her
commitment to missionary endeavors during the early years of the

nineteenth century brought hundreds of converts into the sect, and resulted in the foundation of seven new communities in the midwest. By
regularizing Shaker education, speech, dress, doctrine, and orders, she
created a uniform structure into which the zeal of these new members
could constructively be channeled. The *Millennial Laws*, which were
necessitated by her death, were designed to bolster the Society during
the growing pains of the next several decades.

4

Our Precious Good Elders

After Mother Lucy's death, the responsibility for maintaining Shaker order and union never again fell principally on the shoulders of a single individual—a change from previous practice that was to have far-reaching consequences in subsequent decades. These sacred leadership duties were assumed by scores of Elders and Eldresses, from those in charge of small Families of Young Believers, to the Lead Ministry at New Lebanon. The character of these leaders, their various skills, their reactions to crises, all affected the faith and commitment of their followers. As the proportion of young members (those most likely to be chosen as leaders) declined, the Society's system of self-government faced a serious challenge. Perhaps more than any other single factor within the Society, the quality of its leadership explains both Shaker success and failure in the nineteenth century.

The philosophy that informed the Shaker authority structure was not one of tyranny or oppression, as some early nineteenth-century apostates would have us believe. Shaker Elders and Eldresses did not seek power; if they had, they would never have been judged fit to exercise it. Meekness was the key: an understanding that they were chosen to serve God and His special people, not themselves. Good leaders were never to forget that they too were weak creatures, and only had the power to govern because they had been anointed by God. They tried to remember to

> Chide mildly the erring, entreat them with care
> Their natures are mortal, they need not despair
> We all have some frailty, we all are unwise
> And the Grace which redeems us must shine from the skies.[1]

Overall, Shaker leaders compiled a remarkably successful record. In the 1830s, Sister Elizabeth Lovegrove expressed the leaders' contribution to her own and other's success in the gospel this way:

Our precious good Elders like watchmen do stand
To help us press on to the promised land
They're faithful to strengthen the aged & youth
And teach us the way in meekness & truth.
Their zeal for the gospel no tongue can declare
The deep tribulation and suff'rings they bear
Their kind invitation is to everyone
To press for the Kingdom; be valiant and strong.[2]

Leaders were chosen to guide, instruct, exhort, and sympathize, and they required obedience. But the leaders as individuals had no special rights or privileges. Eldress Cassandana Goodrich of the Hancock Ministry reminded the Believers: "I have no natural right over you, neither have you any natural right over me. But where the gift of God is placed, there it must be supported and built up. You must all strive to get a right understanding, that it is the gift and order of God that is to be respected, and not the person."[3]

Every Shaker assumed individual responsibility for his or her own spiritual "travel." Believers could not relax and expect their Elders to secure salvation for them. Every member was expected to enter the contest "to make great crosses little crosses and little crosses none at all." Mother Hannah Kendall reminded them: "We make our own times so if the times feel hard, we must amend our ways and they will become easy. . . . I can tell you what is best for you but cannot *make* you do it."[4]

Although Shakerism was born in the 1780s, and was, therefore, co-eval with the American republic, most Believers held the democratic system in low esteem. Brother Seth Wells was particularly vehement in his comments about representative government, claiming that its most obvious creation was a "high flaming party spirit" that would have been fatal to Shaker union had the Believers sought to emulate it.[5] Brother Isaac Youngs, for his part, went so far as to acknowledge that God had given men wills of their own, but only to do His will, and not theirs.[6] Consequently, Shaker Brethren and Sisters had no official voice in the selection of the leaders that governed them.

Some members found this deliberate abridgment of what they regarded as a God-given right impossible to swallow and left the Society, grumbling about tyranny and slavery. Most Shakers went along with the system, believing with Seth Wells, that "the government of the Chh. in the ministerial institution [originates] from Divine Authority."[7] Anointed leaders at the lowest level of Shaker government, the Family, were appointed by their predecessors and confirmed in their positions by the Bishopric Ministry to whom they answered. The

Bishopric Ministries, in turn, were confirmed by the Lead Ministry at New Lebanon, and when gaps were created in that "lot" by death or poor health, the survivors selected an appropriate successor. The Lead Ministry had been appointed by its predecessors who, in their turn, had been appointed by Mother Ann. Thus, apostolic succession created a system of government fit for heaven. A vote given to each member would, the Shakers felt, cause dissension in God's kingdom. The system so painstakingly constructed would "soon tumble to pieces." [8]

There is some evidence that members were, to a certain extent, consulted about appointments in their own Families. It even appears that members occasionally voted on matters of general concern not involving the selection of leaders. A good example was the spate of "CAUCUS meetings" held at New Lebanon's Second Order in 1860 to resolve issues about the construction of a new Dwelling. Beginning in March of that year, the Brethren began meeting to discuss the material out of which the proposed Dwelling was to be built. They remained deadlocked for several months, with half favoring brick and half preferring clapboard. By May a formal bill had been drawn up and signed by the majority of the Family's members, asking the Ministry to agree to the use of stone (possibly a compromise), which they did several days later. [9] While it cannot be determined how frequent such meetings may have been, or indeed if they occurred only late in Shaker history, it is likely that members were informally consulted regarding many minor domestic issues.

In situations where Elders and Eldresses had to be replaced, however, the rank and file had no official input. Perhaps few Believers regretted this, feeling that those charged with the selection of leaders looked for the same qualities they preferred: humility, kindness, and meekness. Good followers were likely to make good leaders in the Shaker world. Brother David Parker of Canterbury remarked: "We cannot expect to govern or direct unless we can submit to be taught ourselves, and keep our union." [10] Parker emphasized the fact that all of the sect's leaders had superiors; even the Lead Ministry were responsible to God. Believers were likely to accept as leaders members who had distinguished themselves by their obedience.

Sometimes new Elders and Eldresses assumed spiritual names as a mark of their appointments. When Polly Landon of New Lebanon was elevated to the Lead Ministry, she took the name Ruth, out of respect for her predecessor, Ruth Hammond, who had retired because of poor health. Similarly, Stephen Markham became Henry, after Elder Henry Clough who had recently died, when he went to serve under Ebenezer Cooley in New Lebanon's Gathering Order in 1799. When Sally

Brewster entered the Hancock Ministry in 1835, she became Cassandana, after Cassandana Goodrich, her senior associate. Perhaps the acquisition of a spiritual name in these cases symbolized the absorption of the individual into the character of an anointed leader.

Typically, Elders and Eldresses moved up the ladder of the sect's domestic hierarchy before being appointed to a position of spiritual authority. Sister Rhoda Blake's experience at the New Lebanon Church Family was similar to that of other leaders. One of many children gathered into the Shaker fold as a result of the Savoy revival of 1817–1821, Sister Rhoda grew up in the newly established Children's Order and was appointed as a Family Deaconess in 1835, when she was twenty-six. She subsequently held the positions of Girls' Caretaker and Physician before being elevated to the Family Eldership in 1861. Members like Rhoda Blake were chosen for positions of spiritual responsibility because they had proven themselves devoted Shakers. The best of them shared characteristics with Mother Lucy Wright who was remembered for "practicing whatever she professed and taught as Principle. She was strictly punctual to observe and keep all the rules, Orders and Regulations of Gospel Order in Church relation." [11]

Rufus Bishop of New Lebanon was another member who exhibited the qualities desirable in an Elder, even as a teenager. Even then, he was known for being more devoted, more punctual, more diligent than any of his peers. His companions in the Boys' Order thought him a prig, and carried tales about him to their Elder. This unidentified Elder, "possessed of the same spirit of enmity and envy," believed these reports and subjected Bishop to constant reproof and public humiliation, claiming that he was "insubordinate." Demonstrating praiseworthy meekness, Bishop complained to no one and instead prayed for relief. In answer, Father Joseph Meacham sent him word that he had learned through revelation of his unfortunate situation, loved him for his restraint, and prophesied that he would one day stand as first Elder in the Society.[12] Meacham's prescience was proven in 1849, when Rufus succeeded Ebenezer Bishop as senior Elder in the Lead Ministry.

Bishop had reacted well to unfair treatment, proving that his primary concern was the good of the Society to which he belonged. Unfair treatment was sometimes deliberately meted out by leaders to test a member's faith and character. Hervey Elkins, who for fifteen years had been a member of the Senior Order at Enfield, New Hampshire, recalled: "It is common for the leaders to crowd down by humiliation, and withdraw patronage & attention from those whom they intend to ultimately promote to an official station, that such may learn how it seems to be slighted and humiliated." [13]

These tactics may have worked in the 1790s, when Bishop was young, but by the 1820s and 1830s, the internal situation in the communities was considerably different. As the century progressed, good leadership material became increasingly scarce, especially among the male ranks. More and more young Brethren were forsaking the Shaker way for the enticements of the World. Between 1801 and 1840, for example, the adult apostasy rate at the New Lebanon Church Family climbed from less than 3 percent to just over 9 percent, whereas the rate for males increased from just over 4 percent to roughly 16 percent (see Appendix A.2).

The effect of this trend on the selection of leaders was significant: the proportion of Brethren between the ages of twenty-five and forty-nine (the years when they were most likely to be chosen as Elders) dropped from 75.4 percent in 1800 to 17.3 percent in 1825. A similar, though less dangerous, trend developed among the women, the proportion of Sisters twenty-five to forty-nine dropping from 60.2 percent in 1800 to 29.5 percent in 1825 (see Appendix A.4).

Throughout the eastern communities, a similar trend was observable, as the overall proportion of Brethren aged twenty-six to forty-four fell from 36.8 percent in 1800 to 20.7 percent in 1820. Among the Sisters, a parallel situation developed, as the proportion of women in this age group dropped from 43.6 percent in 1800 to 24.5 percent in 1820 (see Appendix B.4). Because the number of leaders required to govern a Shaker community remained the same, the selection process became increasingly difficult as the number of members in their middle years declined.

The 1841 *Holy Orders of the Church*, received through inspiration from Father Joseph Meacham, for the first time included guidelines requiring a minimum age of forty for First Order Elders and Eldresses, and suggesting that they "shall have had a privilege of twenty, or twenty-five years in the gospel."[14] Sometimes, however, it proved impossible to satisfy these conditions. Once in a great while, members were selected for office in spite of their questionable records. Such a situation occurred in Maine in 1829, when a Brother named Paul Nowell, who had been less than successful as a Trustee, was appointed junior Elder of the Alfred North Family. In writing to New Lebanon to explain their choice, the Maine Ministry acknowledged that at first inspection it seemed a poor one, but went on to assure the Lead Ministry that "there was as free a united feeling throughout the Ministry, Elders, brethren and sisters as there ever was in any member we ever placed in any lot whatever." They then pointed out that "a person may be of that turn and disposition, if they are noticed a little, and they feel as tho' there was a little confidence plac'd in them, it will have a powerfull influence upon their minds to incourage them in the ways of welldoing." [15] Clearly, they hoped that Nowell would prove to be of that "turn and disposition," and was one of the few Shaker leaders appointed not so much because of what he had done but because of what he might do.

Most leaders recognized that some dislocation, some "disunion," would follow any major leadership change, or "sturing the Pudding," as Hancock's Elder Grove Wright called it.[16] When the Maine Ministry underwent a major reconstitution in 1830, the new members reported to the Harvard Ministry:

You know that such important changes are many times attended with serious consequences and is apt to cause party spirits . . . and if you should hear of some scatering from here, you need not think it strang . . . [for] you know by experiance when an evil spirit or root of bitterness springs up among a people many are likely to be defil'd therewith.[17]

Ideally, leadership changes were greeted with approbation, not dissatisfaction. Brother Seth Wells worked out on paper a masterful scenario whereby any member who found fault with an appointment would immediately be recognized by his fellows as ambitious and proud, thus rendering his opposition harmless. It was understood that the rest of the Believers would have no "union" with such a refractory colleague until his or her position had been renounced. Thus, while Shaker rules required that all appointments be confirmed by the "general approbation" of the rank and file, and members were granted the right to protest appointments if they felt they had "reasonable cause," few dared to disapprove. Wells boasted that cases of formal protest were very rare, because most members believed "that the Ministry and elders have the best opportunity to know & judge of the fitness and qualifications of the selected members . . . & if they are found unfaithful or unqualified upon trial, they will soon be removed." [18]

It appears, however, that Wells underestimated the extent to which rank and file members privately disagreed with leadership selections. While most Believers certainly did not voice their disapproval of any appointment very loudly, there is evidence that not every choice was viewed with favor. In 1865, when the Lead Ministry decided that a certain Eldress Abigail should be removed from her position as first Office Sister and replaced by Sister Sarah Ann Lewis, a Brother wrote in the Family *Farm Journal* that this was a "peculiar gift" which he hoped God would bless, implying that many members would not do so.[19] Ruth Landon, when she was first Eldress in the Lead Ministry earlier in the century, would have been horrified by this Brother's non-

chalant suspicion of a Ministerial "gift." In making her decisions
about appointments, she claimed that she never listened to the grumbling of the rank and file. She insisted that whenever she discovered
disagreement about an appointment she had made, she just went to
the members involved and told them they had no right to question the
gift of God. "She considered indulgence had been a great loss to this
people."[20]

It was not possible, however, for most Shaker leaders to follow Landon's example and justify their appointments simply by claiming the
authority of divine instruction. Rather than make leadership choices
they knew would be unpopular and cause "disunion," Elders preferred
to look for potential appointees from among the ranks of those whom
they knew were admired by their peers. When the Maine Ministry
needed a new junior Elder in 1833, their choice wavered between a
certain Brother Isaac and Brother Joseph Brackett. The New Hampshire Ministry, in Maine to give their advice on the matter, wrote to
New Lebanon explaining that Brackett had been selected because
many of the Brethren disliked Brother Isaac; they added that "he had
previously given them some occasion."[21]

Once in office, it was expected that Elders and Eldresses would continue to exhibit the same qualities of obedience and humility that had
led to their appointment. There was very little place in the Shaker
world for brash, bold, overly innovative leaders. Particularly at the
Family level, Elders and Eldresses concentrated their energies on maintaining the status quo. Father Joseph had decreed: "The Elders of families ought not to give any orders contrary to that which they have been
taught, nor alter the order of anything established before they came
into office, but by the counsel or liberty of the Ministry."[22]

Family Elders were always to maintain "union" with one another because the Shakers realized the potential danger of schisms within the
leadership. It was crucial that all four leaders of any Family present a
united front, whatever their private disagreements may have been. To
insure this, Family Elders at New Lebanon met together for half an
hour every evening right after supper to exchange information, discuss
the day's events, and plan what they were to say to the Family when it
assembled for meeting. Mother Lucy had been especially concerned
about possible "disunion" among the leaders at New Lebanon when
she was away and unable to act as a buffer. She advised: "Now you
must not get to be male & female while I am gone; you must keep your
union and be one."[23]

Relations between spiritual and temporal leaders within a Family
were carefully regulated as well. Deacons, Deaconesses, and Trustees

were to be obeyed "in their order," just as Elders and Eldresses were obeyed in theirs.[24] All leaders were reminded that no one should judge an issue which did not concern them, which was out of their "order." Elders were not to meddle in business affairs, and Trustees were to keep out of spiritual matters. When a Family member required something from a Deacon and failed to get satisfaction, he or she would then report the matter to the Elders, who in turn informed the Ministry. It was felt that the Ministry would be better able to "stir up" temporal leaders because they were free from the taint of possible favoritism.[25]

Because Family Elders knew the strengths, weaknesses, and eccentricities of the Believers in their charge, they certainly must have liked some members better than others. Ministry members, in contrast, existed on another level altogether. They ate, slept, and worked in quarters separate from the rank and file members, and their spiritual responsibility for several villages made constant travel a part of their lives. They knew no common members well enough to develop friendships and play favorites; their only contact with the rank and file was through the Family Elders.

Bishopric Ministries could not realistically be expected to keep track of all the details of a community's temporal and spiritual life. They did indeed establish general policies, but they relied on the judgment and specialized knowledge of the Family Elders in making their decisions. Elder Ebenezer Bishop of the New Lebanon Ministry established guidelines shortly after Mother Lucy's death to regulate the relationship between the Ministry and Family Elders, declaring that there should be a "perfect freedom" between them. He continued, "If the Ministry brought forward any gift, and [the Elders] felt that it would not quite do, [they] had the right to express [their] fears how it would operate; but still, if the Ministry after hearing what [they] had to say on the subject, should feel it best to have the thing as they proposed it, then for the Elders to unite."[26]

The most important duty of all Elders and Eldresses was that of hearing confession. From the sect's earliest days, confession had played an important role in the spiritual "travel" of all Believers, allowing them to forsake their sins and be reborn. Throughout Shaker history, members were expected to confess their sins several times a year, children to their Caretakers and adults to their Elders or Eldresses, depending on gender. Elder Rufus Bishop determined that it would be best to have flexible times for confession rather than a strict requirement that all members confess once a month. He hoped that the majority of adult Believers would have enough sense to know when and how often each of them needed to confess. He felt that members would feel freer to tell their Elders of wrongdoing if they did it voluntarily. Ideally, when Believers confessed their sins, "they ought to feel as though they were going to their best friends." [27]

In spite of this emphasis on harmony among the leaders, and between themselves and their charges, certain imbalances did develop within the sect's leadership structure. Although Elders and Eldresses were equal in theory, apparently gender did make a difference, especially to Worldly observers. Men dominate the Ministerial correspondence that survives; most Shaker patents were issued to men; male "Office Deacons" were commonly called "Trustees," but females of the same rank were referred to as "Office Sisters;" and Sisters were legally prohibited from holding property in trust for other members, at least until late in the nineteenth century. We know that Shaker Eldresses and Deaconesses have always been extremely important, particularly in the organization of domestic life, but they maintained a low profile as far as their public image was concerned, perhaps because the World found it difficult to deal with them.

Even within the Society, however, the role of female leaders was circumscribed. Women were regarded as the spiritual equals of men, but they exercised far less temporal authority than their male counterparts. Brother Calvin Green put it this way: "The female ought to have a correspondent & equal power in her sphere, with the male in his sphere." [28] The unexpressed qualifier of this proposition is the difference that existed between the male and female spheres. While Elders and Deacons were often involved in organizing the Sisters' kitchens, laundries, and other workplaces, Eldresses and Deaconesses only rarely made similar decisions affecting the Brethren.

Occasionally, though, when a female leader demonstrated extraordinary skill in temporal affairs, the Brethren at least listened to her advice. Mother Hannah Kendall was one such female leader. She possessed a "calculation in temporal concerns . . . as great in proportion as her gift . . . in the spiritual line." Whatever course she recommended was acted upon. Once, in the early years of the nineteenth century, she called the farmers together at Harvard and expressed a wish to have a particular piece of land cleared for sowing rye. Brother Levi Warner, who wondered what Mother Hannah could possibly have known about planting rye, demurred at first but finally gave in, "as it was Mother's mind," and "was glad that [he] did not say a word against it, for we never were more prosperous in any undertaking than we were in that." [29]

Surprisingly, Mother Lucy Wright, ostensibly the most important leader of either sex between 1796 and 1821, had more trouble than

Mother Hannah getting some of the Brethren to take her seriously. In the spring of 1814, she "felt a gift" to have a certain house that stood two miles east of the New Lebanon Meetinghouse taken down and re-erected half a mile below the Second Family near the carding mill. Everyone but Mother Lucy was skeptical about the benefit of such an undertaking, and so the work was postponed by the Deacons "for a more convenient season." But Wright was convinced that the divine direction was important even though she did not understand it fully herself. She continually urged the Deacons to get on with the job, even going to the site herself to assist in taking down the house. As it turned out, the house in its new location proved an ideal home for several families of Believers from Savoy that moved to New Lebanon two or three years later, and many members realized that Mother Lucy's gift had not been "peculiar" after all.[30]

It is difficult to picture Mother Lucy out on a hillside ripping out nails and tearing down walls, but clearly this was a case of doing a job herself if she wanted it done at all. The Deacons and other Brethren evidently wondered at her eccentricity and humored her because of her position in the sect. When her "gift," like Mother Hannah's canny understanding of farmland, proved beneficial, Shaker Brethren evinced a greater respect for the advice of their female leaders. Indeed, as the nineteenth century progressed and male membership declined, Eldresses and female Trustees exercised increasing influence.

Elders and Eldresses were able to maintain their authority because of the importance Father James and Father Joseph had attached to obedience as the sign of a true Believer. Although in a few isolated instances the leaders had difficulty exacting the obedience due them, the majority of Shakers did what they were told. Good Believers, they were instructed, did nothing "out of order." Brother Calvin Green reminded them: "God works by a system of mediation of his own appointed order . . . however splendid the talents, or however great the gifts of any, they can never gain their own order in the House of God . . . without acknowledging in their real feelings the true line of order before them."[31]

In the early years of the nineteenth century, however, before unquestioning obedience was the rule, the Elders sometimes had great difficulty convincing a refractory member of their divine infallibility. Thomas Brown, who tried diligently during this period to reconcile all his doubts about the sect, was one who found this doctrine impossible to accept. Originally he had been told that every Believer was free to follow the dictates of his own conscience. Elder Hezekiah Rowley had asserted: "The gospel does not bind creatures, but gives liberty to all religious acts. . . . We cannot direct or tell you what you must do. . . . Each one should act according to his own faith." [32]

As Brown drew closer to the Shaker gospel, he saw that the Elders had been humoring him, hoping to entice him into a fuller commitment to the faith. When he demurred, he found that some of his requests to preach in the outside world were being refused. Perplexed, he went to his friend, Brother Seth Wells, for advice. Wells made the new doctrine of unquestioning obedience plain, saying: "When [the Elders] counsel me to do anything, I do not wait to consult my own mind or feelings about it, for I believe they have the gift of God & therefore I go forth in obedience." [33]

But Brown remained unconvinced. This new belief in the infallibility of the Elders suggested papism to some. It was more important for men like Brown to follow their own consciences than to assist in the survival of a sect like the Shakers, which desperately needed such a doctrine to prevent the membership from splintering. It was perhaps inevitable that a few intelligent, independent members like Brown should become disillusioned and turn away, grumbling: "When I first came . . . I heard nothing of a ministration doctrine, or obedience as the only way of salvation. . . . The word of God, you told me, was in my own heart, not in what the elders said. Your gospel seems like a tunnel; the farther I travel in, the narrower it grows." [34]

Brown was, of course, quite right about the narrowness of Shaker doctrine as it developed in the early years of the nineteenth century. Everything in the Believers' lives evinced the godly "narrow track" that led to heaven. A multiplicity of rules, and the requirement that they be strictly obeyed, kept the feet of all members, devoted and halfhearted alike, planted firmly in that narrow way. One of the leaders' hardest tasks was to enforce all the orders produced by regulation-prone Ministries.

Mother Lucy Wright had been particularly devoted to the role that order played in the Shaker world. A few Believers complained that there were too many petty regulations, that not all members required such direction, and that the profusion of rules diluted individual commitment to the faith. Mother Lucy disagreed sharply, remarking: "Such ones, I have observed, make very little progress in the way of God, & are the very ones that need these orders which they so oppose. True Believers are able to see the necessity of Order, & it is their life & support, & none can travel without it." [35]

As order and obedience became more important to the survival of the Society, methods employed by the leaders to maintain them became more extreme. In Mother Ann's day, relations with the outside world had been fairly open in the hope that more converts would be attracted to the new gospel. But when Father James and Father Joseph took over, it became increasingly difficult for Believers to contact friends or relatives left behind in the World. Whittaker and Meacham came to fear that even brief conversations with "World's People" would corrupt the purity of a Shaker's faith.

In 1800, when a nonmember named Sarah Mosely tried to gain admittance to the New Lebanon community to see her sister, she was turned away. An apostate herself, Mosely traveled throughout the region collecting the testimony of others who had experienced similar treatment. According to Mosely, Sister Phebe Walker was prevented from seeing her brother Titus, and was forced to send him word that she claimed no relationship with him and never wanted to hear from him again, "which she lamented as much against her heart & said in tears that she would give anything to see him." As a result of her research, Mosely concluded of the Shakers that "many young people among them weary of their constraints would gladly quit them if they would have the free offer of protection by their friends out of the hearing of their superiors." [36]

Independent-minded Thomas Brown was subjected to even harsher treatment while he was agonizing over his decision whether or not to sign the sect's covenant. His Elders were tired of trying to reassure him; they wanted him to make up his mind once and for all, and were prepared to go to great lengths to bring this about. The Gathering Order Elders at Watervliet sent Brown to New Lebanon in 1804 with the hope that the Lead Ministry would have more luck with him. Once there, he was virtually imprisoned in what rank and file members jokingly called the "potter's shed," because that was where the Elders remolded the opinions of borderline members. He was prevented from leaving at will, and was allowed no visitors except Elders. The Lead Ministry hoped that a period of quiet meditation away from the bustle of a crowded Shaker village would confirm Brown in his original estimation of the Shakers, but this strategy backfired. Appalled by their high-handedness in so severely confining his activity, Brown became more disillusioned than ever and left the Society shortly thereafter. [37] Clearly, the leaders felt that the limited exercise of harsh measures such as these was justifiable in the battle to win souls to the gospel. Intellectuals like Brown were often a problem, because they felt they understood the tenets of Shakerism better than the Elders.

Less educated, more emotional members created their own difficulties. Shaker leaders had to strike a balance between too great a reliance on intellect and too great an indulgence in emotion. Because of the enormous Shaker dependence on inspiration and divine revelation, which could come to any member regardless of his or her position in the sect, there was a real danger of generating too much religious enthusiasm. Throughout the nineteenth century, Shaker leaders tried, with varying degrees of success, to keep a tight clamp on revelations among the rank and file. As a matter of policy, all inspired messages were subject to the Elders' approval. Any "gifts" received "out of union" were repudiated.

If this had not been the case, a rank and file member could have taken over temporal and/or spiritual control of a Family simply by claiming receipt of a communication from the spirit world directing him or her to do so. Elder Henry Clough had been one of the first leaders to inveigh against excessive reliance on inspiration. He had strongly disapproved of all "divinely inspired" instructions that "were not in union with the present gift. . . ." Cleverly, he reminded the Shakers that "souls were as liable to be led astray by disorderly spirits out of the body as by those in the body." [38] Mother Lucy had been equally concerned about what she perceived as a growing tendency to circumvent the sect's orders by claiming exemption from a higher authority. She taught the Believers "not to make a sign of everything," because, if they got carried away, "there could not a leaf move without its being a sign." [39]

The danger of spurious revelation was very real. To combat this, and other threats to their authority, Shaker leaders were accustomed to exercising their power in ways that seem out of keeping with their professions of meekness and humility. Their public image, which they endeavored to sustain even in personal diaries and correspondence, was one of leadership by example. Little is recorded in their own writings about unreasonable actions such as refusing permission for a member to communicate with relatives in the World or the virtual incarceration of wavering Believers. Hints of similar behavior appear only occasionally in private codes and shorthands.

Elder Thomas Damon, a Church Family Elder at Enfield, Connecticut, in the 1830s and 1840s, was later elevated to the Hancock Ministry, where he served until his death in 1880. While at Enfield, he devised a simple shorthand for use in his diary. Careful study has permitted this author to prepare clear texts not only of this initial system, but also of his later, more complex shorthand. Though Damon was no Samuel Pepys, his journals reveal heretofore hidden insights into the workings of a Shaker Family. Perhaps most intriguing is his entry for June 19, 1844: "Sabbath night. Examined S.B.'s [Sarah Burlingame's] room to find contraband articles. No success." [40] One must wonder how often such searches were conducted, and how normal it was for Family Elders to search Sisters' rooms. Without additional evidence, however, no definitive conclusions are possible.

There is no indication that a majority of Believers found searches, strict regulations, or even temporary incarcerations out of keeping with Shaker principles. Even in a Christian community, many recognized that ideal conditions were impossible to achieve. Rules were necessary, and the sect's leaders were occasionally required to employ extraordinary measures to enforce them. A few members became disillusioned, grumbled about tyranny, and perhaps apostatized, but most put up with things they could do nothing about, short of leaving the Society.

Most Elders and Eldresses exercised their great authority with considerable care in an effort to avoid giving undue offense to their charges, though a handful became corrupted by the immense power they held, or thought they held. Overzealous leaders were less common than overzealous members, but a few did surface, especially in the sect's early history. The unfortunate Thomas Brown encountered one such leader in the 1790s, an Elder named John Scott, who was so obsessed with sin that he sometimes used "uncouth & indecorous language" in trying to root it out.[41] Such excessive zeal was understandable in light of Scott's desire to eradicate sin, but some leaders, blinded by self-importance, descended to inadmissible depths in their behavior.

Hancock's Reuben Rathbun, a relative of the notorious Valentine, had been appointed as Church Family Elder by Father Calvin Harlow shortly before the latter's death in 1795. When Mother Sarah Harrison died the following year, Mother Lucy Wright and Elder Henry Clough elevated the Ministry's junior Elder, Nathaniel Deming, to the senior position. Rathbun objected violently to this move and refused to acknowledge Deming as his "lead." He resented Deming's youth (he was thirty), and had apparently aspired to the position himself. "Exalted spirits" such as his obviously ran in the family.

He protested the appointment through proper channels, but received no satisfaction from Wright and Clough, so he set out to create himself senior Ministry Elder "by self-appointment and subtlety." He suddenly became very friendly with the Young Believers, promising that if they supported him, "there was no need of living so strict, that they might live more after the fashions and customs of the world, . . . they need not take up so much cross to be saved." The extent of the division within the Family was further aggravated because Jonathan Southwick, junior Elder in the Church Family, supported Deming.

Wright and Clough suffered this situation to drag on for a time, allowing in effect, a joint leadership, hoping that Rathbun would come to his senses and realize that such an arrangement was unworkable. But he remained adamant, so Clough was finally dispatched to Hancock to straighten everything out. He assembled the Family and told them flatly that their spiritual condition was very dangerous and could no longer be tolerated. Each member was to make up his or her own mind and stick to that decision. He invited Elder Brother Jonathan Southwick and all who supported Deming to come and stand behind him on one side of the room. Rathbun's supporters then realized how few they were and many of them sheepishly sidled across the room to join their fellows, leaving Rathbun in such a state of embarrassment that he immediately capitulated and acknowledged Deming as his "lead." His position in the Family was so tenuous thereafter that Southwick was appointed to take over, and Rathbun left the sect within a year.[42]

It is interesting to note that Wright and Clough employed no overbearing authoritarian tactics in this situation, which would appear on the surface to have been far more damaging to the union of an entire Family than a few hidden contraband articles. Evidently Shaker leaders at the highest level were long-suffering in their dealings with junior Elders and Eldresses, more tolerant than they were of peccadilloes among the rank and file. Several examples of this tolerance appear in the correspondence of the Maine Ministry during the 1810s, 1820s, and 1830s. Elder John Barns, not usually referred to as "Father," had been appointed lead Elder there during the first gathering. Little is known of his tenure until he was removed from that position in 1815 and recalled to the New Lebanon Church Family. After a stay of four months, he asked to return to Alfred.[43] Perhaps he chafed at the close supervision to which he was subjected; perhaps he wanted to be closer to the scene of his former glory; perhaps he missed his former associates. It is impossible to say. At any rate, he returned to Maine, and soon began causing problems for his successors.

Evidently, Barns found it difficult to get used to his new, and unimportant, status in the Maine Bishopric. As early as February 1816, the Ministry was complaining to New Lebanon: "J.B. [is] very high and uncomfortable. . . . We feel he is insensable what the matter is. . . . J.B. has sum new doctrines and manners which he proposes to be cloathed with the faith of the Church in supporting, if we should believe all we here of such things we should believe the foundation of things is much changed."[44] In May, they reported: "As to J.B., our tribulation & labour increases of late, we have to keep a sharp look out to hear so many new gospels & they all come from Lebanon (he says) which he labours hard to preach among the members."[45]

Apparently some of the Maine Believers had become so accustomed to trusting and obeying Barns that they found it hard to transfer their allegiance to his successor. This tendency made governing next to impossible for the new Ministry. Disunion was rife. "If J.B. begot anything," the new leaders complained, "it was that Spirit which supports nothing but disorder. . . . Its language is this (viz.) their never will be any blessing as long as such an Elder stands, or such a deacon . . . &c. and even that the orders of the gospel is Superstition and the like . . . and likely when it gits so as to speak its own language more fully it will speak against the Ministry."[46]

One might well expect that such behavior would have been met with an order of excommunication, but apparently nothing was done. John Barns continued to cause trouble into the 1830s, at which time he seemed most interested in writing material for Worldly consumption that would discredit the sect's leadership. Although in his seventies, in 1831 he had "jest reason or mental faculties sufficiant to do evil. . . . [He] will slyly search every room, place, and cupboard to find pen, ink and paper, which we have for a long time deprived him of, and we have taken every measure in our power to put a stop to his spreding his trash, except confining him."[47] By this time, one would have expected that the limits of Ministry tolerance had been reached. The damage Barns had done to the Maine communities was severe, particularly in the unfortunate influence he exercised over the Young Believers, yet the leaders did little more than rescind his writing privileges. In the light of available evidence, their attitude is puzzling. When Barns died in January 1832, they can hardly have mourned unduly at his passing.

Maine's difficulties with John Barns were, however, atypical. The vast majority of Shaker leaders had a far more beneficial influence upon the rank and file Believers entrusted to their care. Held in reverence, many elicited responses like this from New Hampshire's Henry Blinn about Hancock's Isaac Augur: "His very presence speaks peace. We feel that we are always made better by meeting him."[48] These leaders stuck to their jobs in spite of illness or infirmity. Courage was a common characteristic, as was humor. Hancock's Elder Daniel Goodrich, Jr. was sixty-nine when he wrote in 1834: "Old age creeps on— my strength fails, but my spirit is as bright and lively as ever."[49]

Daniel's sister, Cassandana, perhaps the most influential Eldress in Hancock's history, exhibited similar dedication, though less humility. In writing to her sister, Molly, an Eldress at South Union, Kentucky, in

1826, Cassandana made no bones about her undoubted value to the Society. "I am all the time," she wrote, "digging, scratching, and weeding in this part of the vineyard where I am placed. I have old believers, young believers, youth, children & babes, which in their turn must be counselled, taught, nursed & dandled." [50] In another letter to her sister, written three years earlier, Eldress Cassandana dwelt on her extraordinary contributions to the well-being of her followers, commenting:

I often think considering my constitution it is almost a miracle that I have been able to visit the different Churches yearly and perform all my duties, which I have never failed of doing. Yet I think if I had not been blessed with a good degree of wisdom and ingenuity I could never have done it,—for although I have always been feeble, yet I have never been confined but very little, which I think is greatly owing to my care and prudence. I feel sometimes as if I was rather wearing out, but I think I prefer wearing out to rusting out. [51]

Goodrich obviously felt a certain glamor in her position as senior Ministry Eldress, and would have been upset if poor health had forced her to step down. Although often troubled by various ailments, she remained steadfastly in her position until death claimed her in 1848.

While some Elders and Eldresses were sensible of the lofty positions they held, few became so arrogant that they became poor leaders. Eldresses like Cassandana Goodrich were revered by their followers, who probably had no idea of how they expressed themselves in their correspondence. They only knew that their leaders "counselled, taught, nursed & dandled" well.

Service to God and His children was always uppermost in the minds of good leaders like the Goodriches, whatever they may have thought of themselves. Like their charges, they were always obedient to the "lead" placed before them "in order." When Sister Jerusha Smith of the New Lebanon Second Order was asked by the Lead Ministry to go to Watervliet for a time as a junior Eldress, she "cheerfully complied," although it was a "great cross" for her to leave home. But, like most other members chosen for positions of responsibility, she was "ever ready to do what is thought best for her" and she did "not care where she goes if she can only do a little good & no hurt." [52]

Because they lived in relative isolation from their followers, members of Bishopric Ministries looked to leaders in other Bishoprics for friendship and moral support. Ministries were required to travel to New Lebanon annually if possible to learn about new policies, and they generally planned to visit several other communities on their journeys. Aided by frequent visits and regular correspondence, warm friendships often developed between Elders and Eldresses in different Bishoprics. Elder Grove Wright of the Hancock Ministry and Elder

Grove Blanchard of the Harvard Ministry became such close friends that Believers throughout the northeast made frequent mention in their correspondence of everything the two Elder Groves did together. Between 1814, when Blanchard was elevated to the Ministry, and 1861, when Wright died, Blanchard made thirty-eight visits to the three communities in the Hancock Bishopric.[53] The number of corresponding journeys made by Wright is unknown but it was certainly significant. During these years, letters went back and forth, many of which have survived to provide an unusual insight into the character of these two Elders. It is clear that they knew each other very well. In an 1849 letter to Blanchard, Wright appended this message: "There is so much grease on this sheet that I feel ashamed to send, but you will make allowance knowing who it is from."[54]

Reading this series of letters helps to explain the influence that the best Shaker leaders exercised over their followers. Elder Grove Wright won the hearts of Believers with both his lively sense of humor and his steadfast dedication to Shaker principles. Born in Pittsfield in 1789, Wright was brought into the sect at the age of three when both his parents converted. When he was nine he was moved from Hancock to Tyringham, where the Boys' Order was thinly populated, and it was there he learned the benefits of Shaker life. Caught up in the internal revival that illuminated the eastern communities just after the opening of the gospel in Ohio, Wright later claimed: "I have never seen a moment that I felt willing to exchange my privilege among Believers for all the riches, honor, pleasures & vanity which is to be found in the world."[55]

His devotion and capacity to inspire dedication in others led to his 1818 elevation to the Hancock Ministry, where he served until poor health forced his retirement in 1860. His letters to Blanchard provide an excellent insight into his character. Despite his execrable handwriting and erratic spelling (his large "corispondance," though full of "cincere" and "wormest" feeling, usually requires a "miricle" to decipher its "dificult scrall"), Wright kept up letter-writing for many years as a vital link between friends separated by the exigencies of duty. Although afflicted with a crippling skin disease (erysipelas) throughout the latter part of his life, he managed to retain his sense of humor, even playfully referring to his ailment as the "old scratcher."[56] Erysipelas caused him to suffer chronic laryngitis, recurrent fever, and on at least one occasion caused several layers of skin on the insides of his hands to peel off, preventing him from working, which irritated him a good deal.[57]

As his health deteriorated, Wright was dragged reluctantly from seaside resort to health spa to mineral spring, all over the northeast, in the hope of extending his years of faithful service. At the urgent request of his charges, in 1860 he took up residence at a hotel in Saratoga Springs, New York, and delivered himself into the hands of doctors, but with little faith in their techniques. His skepticism was obvious in his letters home:

> The first week appear'd rather favorable for me, but after that, rather lost ground. The Dr. thought, however, that if I could stay 6 or 8 weeks, he could cure me up. He probably thought I had money enough to last about that length of time. . . . I went thro' with quite a diversity of treatment in the Water Cure line, and after the *Foments, & Baths, & dashes,* &c, the attendants would give me such a rubing that they nearly wore out the *hide* in some places where the boans were near the skin.[58]

All efforts to restore Wright's health failed, and the Lead Ministry reluctantly acceded to his request for removal from office in October 1860. Free from the burden of leadership for the first time in forty-two years, Elder Grove surrendered authority gladly, and felt "a most blessed releasment in the change."[59] He moved from the Meetinghouse into the Dwelling and took his place at the common dining table, visibly relieved. He died quietly the following April, much lamented, at the age of seventy-two.

One of the principal reasons for the tremendous influence that leaders like Grove Wright had over their followers was their expertise and willing participation in various temporal activities. All Shaker leaders were required to labor with their hands in some useful occupation. Wright was a cabinetmaker of note, who in his later years spent a great deal of time fashioning pails for sale in the World. Other items of his manufacture were the popular table swifts (or yarn winders), for which he machined, stained, and assembled the various parts.[60] Elder Grove Blanchard's activities during the year 1866 were hardly more glamorous, consisting as they did of: bagging garden seeds, cutting palm leaf for fans and table mats, splitting wood, cleaning stovepipes, and doctoring horses, along with many other similar tasks.[61]

Nor were Eldresses, even at the Ministry level, exempted from such lowly undertakings. The Shakers believed that work of all kinds was good for the soul, and that menial labor was especially useful in preventing Believers from getting above themselves. The participation of leaders in manual labor set an excellent example. They engaged in domestic chores of all kinds, usually in workshops separated from the rest of the community, doing whatever they could to be most useful. Eldress Cassandana Brewster, as senior Ministry Eldress at Hancock, spent much of her time in 1865 making aprons, nightgowns, and similar articles of apparel for herself and her colleagues. In typical Shaker fashion, she remade several old wash gowns by turning them upside down and inside out, and extended the life of an Elder's shirt by refacing the collar and adding new cuffs. She delightedly used a sewing machine for the first time in October of that year, and in November was carrying loads of firewood into the Meetinghouse.[62]

One of her companions in the Ministry, Elder Thomas Damon, was an equally good role model for the Hancock Believers. He was particularly noted for his ingenuity and ability to try his hand at any kind of job. A visitor to his shop described him in 1869 as a "universal genius & Mechanic," an accolade that certainly would have pleased him.[63] He is known to have developed or improved, among other things: a lathe for turning iron, a device for planing and edging table swift slats, a machine for matching floor boards, as well as apparatus for washing seeds, and another for counting seed papers as they were printed.[64] When called on, he could even provide dental services to members stricken with toothaches.[65]

Although such varied talents surely endeared him to his charges, who had the highest regard for his workmanship, it was Damon's spiritual leadership that impressed them most. Born in 1819 in Rhode Island, the birthplace of so many good Believers, Damon had been brought to the Enfield, Connecticut, community in 1827 when his parents, former members of a revivalist group called simply the "Christian Church," had converted. Once there, young Damon was impressed by the purity of Shaker life, which he learned was "merciful in its offers, yet it is humiliating in its means, whereby it purposes to bring low the lofty looks of man and reinstate him in union and favor with his Maker." Such a life appealed to him because, by it, he was able to achieve "that peaceful serenity of mind which falls to the lot of such only as walk uprightly before their God." [66]

Offspring of pious parents, with Shaker tenets rooted firmly in his soul, Damon grew to be one of the nineteenth century's most valuable Elders, serving first as Enfield's Church Family Elder, and then as an Elder in the Hancock Ministry for thirty-four years. His journals for the years between 1834 and 1861 fortunately survive. From deciphered shorthand passages, it is possible to see that he had his weaknesses. It may be that he had a slight weight problem, for he used shorthand to record a resolution to give up eating pie and cake, a regimen he maintained for more than a year. He also noticed the appearance of female visitors, although perhaps his principles should have precluded this. When a woman named Submit Hacker, a member of the staff of the Portland publication, *The Pleasure Boat*, visited Hancock in 1847, Damon used English to record her presence in the village, but added in shorthand: "She is a very pretty woman." [67] But despite his tendencies to put on weight or admire women of the World, Damon was unquestionably a good Elder, much loved and respected by his followers.

Such sterling characters abound in the history of the Shaker Society. Exemplifying the highest ideals of Shaker life, they had little interest in self-advancement, seeking only to serve God. Even when relieved of their duties, most were glad to hand their responsibilities over to younger, more energetic members. When Elder Hervey Eads was removed from office in 1844 and moved from South Union, Kentucky, to Union Village, Ohio, he confided to Brother Isaac Youngs:

> But think of travelling down instead of up, as some jocosely remark, how does it feel? I acknowledge to milk the cows, and play with the boys is a different operation entirely from that of sober preaching, but agrees rather too well with my natural disposition. . . . I want no more honor than what I deserve, I care but little what condition I am in, so that I can be useful. [68]

Shaker leaders, by tradition, led the same simple, humble lives as rank and file Believers. Mother Ann and Father James had always insisted that they be treated just like than any other member. Father James was remembered to have once complained when his favorite dish, buttered potatoes, was set before him two days in a row. [69] His successors carried on this tradition. Hervey Elkins had been especially impressed during his time as a Shaker with the "great humility and simplicity of life . . . practiced by the first Ministry. . . . They will not even (and this is good policy) allow themselves those expensive conveniences of life which are so common among the laity of their sect." [70]

In spite of these praiseworthy efforts, Shaker records reveal that these practices were not universal. Leaders in the higher echelons of Shaker government appear to have been surrounded by better quality goods than were their followers. [71] Although these small conveniences and luxuries came to them unbidden, and in no way recompensed them for the years of stress and poor health their responsibilities frequently entailed, a few (a very few) of their followers resented what they perceived to be the leaders' higher standard of living, greater freedom of movement, and overlarge authority.

Mother Lucy Wright had foreseen this development when she warned the Believers:

> If you give way to a Spirit of jealousy, & suffer yourselves to Judge your Elders, & feel against them on account of any cross, or gift of mortification which they may have administered for your good; or if you harbor a spirit of unreconciliation & are watching for iniquity, injustice, partiality & the like, you will have a hard row of it. [72]

Unfortunately, her admonition fell on increasingly deaf ears. By the middle of the nineteenth century, Shaker dependence on the outside world for converts and markets had increased substantially. More Believers, who perhaps had joined for reasons other than religious conviction, began to question the unlimited exercise of authority enjoyed by their superiors. As the proportion of these lukewarm members rose, dangerous ideas about democracy and participatory government surfaced as well. More and more Believers ceased to regard their Elders as the infallible appointees of God and began to view them as "but mortals like themselves." They began to feel that their leaders had to be, in some measure, held accountable for their actions.

This trend was observed with dismay by the leaders. Elder Freegift Wells noted sadly in 1855 that most members believed their leaders were "as liable to imbibe wrong ideas and inconsistent notions as any other class, & of course are not able to place that confidence in them which is necessary to enable them to find protection." The erosion of the power of Shaker leaders was very real during these years. Because of this, the rank and file found themselves "without a foundation to support them," and, as Elder Freegift concluded, "they must fall."[73] This dangerous situation developed during the 1830s and 1840s as a result of internal dissension over such issues as vegetarianism and divine revelation. But in spite of these threats to Shaker order and union, daily life in the villages maintained its placid, serene pace. The generally strong commitment and ability of the sect's leaders ensured that the Society would survive these upheavals, though with sharply diminished numbers and popularity.

5

How Can I Help Being Happy?

The rhythm of Shaker life was calm as work, worship, food, and sleep succeeded one another with predictable regularity. At the day-to-day level of existence, few rank and file members troubled themselves with the great issues that occasionally intruded upon the measured, heavenward progress of the Society. Only when innovation or controversy touched something that was a part of their daily lives, such as modifications in dress or diet, did the common membership rouse itself to interest and debate. Deeper questions of theology and spiritual progress, as well as unpleasant dealings with apostates, Worldly courts, and the like, were left in the usually capable hands of the anointed leaders.

The perspective of the average members was thus too narrow to enable them to discern the development of long-term trends or changes in the spiritual commitment of members or the encroachments of the World. Though Elders and Eldresses concerned themselves with issues affecting the spiritual welfare of hundreds of Believers, most ordinary Shakers worried instead about the health of livestock, the scholarship of children, the menu for dinner, the attendance at meeting, or the chance for rain on the day of a scheduled "ride out" or picnic. The lives of rank and file members revolved around their Families and their work. These concerns, as reflected in journals and daybooks, changed little during the first half of the nineteenth century. The small details of everyday life reveal the human side of Shaker experience and help remove Believers from the pedestal on which they have too often been placed by awestruck admirers of their artifacts.

Even in "heaven on earth," the inhabitants were undeniably human. Scattered diary entries reveal these qualities in ways that published testimonies and public confessions of faith cannot. In 1845, for example, "Mariah Lapsley spraint her foot while jumping under a douche bath." [1] Such evidence brings the average Shaker of the last century within the limits of our understanding. By examining manuscript records, it is possible to discover what sort of people were drawn to

Shakerism, what they thought of the sect after they had joined, why some of them left, and how those that remained dealt with a growing volume of petty annoyances and serious problems.

Shaker life was ideal for individuals who preferred the security of assured salvation, as well as temporal well-being and freedom from decision making. The sect appealed especially to awakened Christians recovering from the throes of revivalistic excitement who were seeking concrete ways to live up to their new commitment. One such convert was Eliza Barber, a widow from Middletown, Connecticut, who joined the New Lebanon community with her two small children in 1828. She confided to a hometown friend that the reality of Shaker life exceeded her expectations: "I have at length arrived at the place we have so often conversed about. I find it indeed in a spiritual sense a land flowing with milk and honey; such peace, such harmony and love I never saw before. I feel and can testify this is the way of God."[2]

Although Sister Eliza's reaction of general happiness was duplicated by hundreds of converts, it was also possible to find in Shakerism only those particular tenets and practices for which one was looking. Evangelical Christians made up by far the largest proportion of adult converts in the first half of the nineteenth century, but a share of deists, skeptics, and socialists crept in as well. One of these was Frederick W. Evans, an Englishman who had come to New York City in 1820 to establish a radical workingmen's paper with his brother, George. While searching for active socialist communities on which he planned to model his own communal enterprise, he visited New Lebanon and decided he could not hope to surpass the Shakers' success. He joined the sect in 1830, and wrote shortly thereafter to his brother about his early discussions with the New Lebanon Elders:

They soon discovered I was a *materialist*, although I did not design to let them know it so soon, but I found I could not keep up with them at all on any other ground. And, instead of being *horror-struck* as I expected, they congratulated me on being freed from all kinds of superstition. I asked them if their system was founded on the Bible. "No," they said, "on nothing but principles set in living scripture to those who believe in them in order to convert them, but to *you* who do not believe we can bring *reason* enough to prove our system true. . . ." I unfolded our system of morality—that virtue was happiness, vice misery and that the whole pursuit of man should be to make himself *happy* in this world. All this they said was the very object of their institution. "But I do not believe in any spiritual world, in no salvation, in no heaven, nor hell, nor Christ, nor God." "Salvation," said they, "is to be *happy here*, and when you are happy you are in heaven."[3]

While his background and interests were totally the reverse of converts like Eliza Barber, Evans agreed that the Shakers had indeed succeeded in establishing something like an earthly paradise. He invited his brother to "come here and see what you nor I never saw before, a *happy people*, a people divested of self, and acting on the broad principle of justice, equality, charity, love, not in theory, mind you, but in practice."[4] There was, however, an important difference between these two types of convert. Christian humility and infidel pursuit of happiness mixed poorly, as the Shakers discovered later in the century. Non-Christian Shakers such as Evans had very fixed ideas about how a new world should be built and governed, but Christians were more likely to go along with established practices. It was these latter conformists who found life as Shakers ideal. One such member, who had grown old in the faith, was asked by Elder Rufus Bishop how he always managed to be so cheerful. He supposedly replied: "Why I can't help it for I love the way of God and keep my union to my Elders, & the Elders keep their union to the Ministry, & the Ministry are joined to Heaven, & how can I help being happy?"[5]

Shakers like this elderly Brother *knew* they belonged to God's chosen people. During the sect's most successful years in the early nineteenth century, even occasional rashes of backslidings could not shake their faith. When ill-advised members sought the Worldly way, their remaining colleagues shook their heads sadly over such foolishness and usually remarked "good riddance" or "best to stay off."[6] Even death held no terror for devout Believers. If they had dutifully kept their feet on the Society's prescribed "narrow track," they were assured a place in the "mansions of rest" with Mother Ann and all former Shakers. Since heaven on earth was their home, the real heaven would not feel at all strange. Elder Henry Clough once remarked, "The change at death to Believers . . . [is] not more than the change from one order to another here."[7]

Non-Christian Shakers like Evans took little comfort in these promises of spiritual reward in another world, and sometimes chafed at the heavily Christian orientation of the sect. Many apostatized to pursue their search for earthly happiness elsewhere.[8] Other Believers, equally dissatisfied and perhaps suffering from a variety of mental or emotional illnesses, sought more tragic solutions, as the journals occasionally record. "Seth Youngs committed suicide . . . by cutting his throat with a knife."[9] "Elizabeth Hanford hung herself on an apple tree at the 2nd family while the family were in evening meeting."[10] Such incidents appear to have been rare, probably because most disillusioned members found the will to leave the sect and seek new lives in the World.

Because the Shaker Society was comprised of volunteers, we can only assume that the majority of members who died in the faith found something in its goals and structure to satisfy them for a lifetime. Of course there continued to be a high proportion of deeply committed Christians among the membership who had chosen Shakerism as the best way to serve God. Others were less spiritual and more complacent, like Brother Robert Wilcox of Tyringham, whom Pittsfield novelist Catherine Sedgwick met while visiting common friends in 1849. She discovered that he had none "of the angular, crusty, silent aspect of his yea and nay brethren," but found him instead to be "a man of no pretension whatever; but content in conscious mediocrity." She described him as a ". . . genial old man, and fifty years of abstinence from the world's pleasures has not made him forget or contemn them. He resembles the jolly friars of conventual life who never resist, and are therefore allowed to go without bits or reins, and in a very easy harness."

Brother Robert's philosophy of life was expressed in the phrase "What's the use?" When asked if he had found it hard to sever his ties to family members who had joined with him, he replied that he did not think of such situations as "crosses" because "what's the use?" When his son absconded with a young Sister, he refused to go after him and try to persuade him to return, for "what's the use?" This convenient and comfortable approach to life undoubtedly endeared Brother Robert to his Elders, who must certainly have found such an uncomplicated, unambitious member an asset. As a young married man he, together with his wife, had "felt a call to join the brethren," a decision Wilcox never regretted. He told Sedgwick: "I am perfectly content. I have enough to eat and drink—everything good after its kind, too—good clothes to wear, a warm bed to sleep in, and just as much work as I like and no more."[11] This combination of temporal and spiritual security was too congenial to be forsaken.

The group to which Believers like Wilcox owed primary allegiance was their Family. In each community, members were organized into Families that typically numbered between thirty and one hundred, and were governed by two Elders and two Eldresses. Each Family was named according to its geographic location relative to the central, or Church Family, as in West Family, Hill Family, and so on. An 1819 membership list of the Canterbury Church Family reveals the demographic composition of a typical Family during this period.[12] The Family had ninety-nine members, of whom forty-five (45.5 percent) were male, a proportion that would fall to dangerously low levels by the end of the century at Canterbury and throughout the sect. The Family was composed primarily of adolescents and members over the age of fifty, and included only six Brethren between the ages of twenty and forty.

Nearly one third of the members were under covenant age of twenty-one, posing supervisional problems for their Elders that worsened in succeeding decades as the proportion of youngsters in most of the eastern villages increased. Similar proportions characterized the other eastern communities. In 1820, 24.0 percent of the members at Hancock were less than sixteen; the proportions at Shirley and Sabbathday Lake were 23.8 percent and 28.1 percent respectively (see Appendix B.5). The percentage of children in Senior Order Families, where they were generally housed, was often higher.

Within a typical Shaker Family, members were often related by biological as well as by spiritual ties. Over half the original 1790 Hancock Church Family came from just five extended families: the Goodriches, the Talcotts, the Demings, the Cogswells, and the Collinses. In 1832, the New Lebanon First Order totaled eighty-one residents, thirty-six of whom (44.4 percent) shared a surname with a fellow Family member. As a result, spiritual ties between Believers were often grafted onto the natural bonds that had united many of them at the time of their conversion.

The close living quarters in typical Family Dwellings reinforced these associations. When New Lebanon's First Order moved into its new "Great House" in September 1832, sixteen "retiring rooms" were shared by the eighty-one Believers in the Family, or about five people to a room. The arrangement of members within the Dwelling is interesting because it provides a unique perspective of the relationships that developed within the Shaker Family structure.

Room #1 housed the two Family Deacons, aged fifty-eight and thirty-two, and their counterparts, the Deaconesses, aged fifty-four and twenty-eight, lived across the hall in Room #2. Four "aged brethren" (older than seventy) lived in Room #3 across the hall from nine "aged sisters" who shared Room #4. The two Elders (ages seventy-one and fifty-five), and the two Eldresses (ages sixty-eight and fifty-three), occupied Rooms #5 and #6. Rooms #7 and #8 were shared by five middle-aged Brethren and seven middle-aged Sisters. On the floor above, ages were generally more mixed, with a few teenagers scattered in each room under the supervision of one or two middle-aged members. Interestingly, it appears that occupation within the community may have had some influence on this arrangement, because two physicians were among the tenants of Room #7 and at least four woodworkers were among the occupants of Room #15. Without more detailed information about the Shakers' principal occupations it is impossible to be certain on this point.[13]

Such close quarters occasionally strained relationships among members living in the same room, but available evidence indicates that most Shakers coexisted peacefully. Sharing was always an important part of Shaker life. Believers living in the same room learned important practical lessons about Christian brotherhood. In promoting such union, the Family served one of the primary functions of Shaker life. Closely-knit, bound by ties of economics, religion, and affection, most Believers functioned extremely well within the Family system. Hancock's Church Family Elders exulted in its benefits in 1835. "Union—similarity of opinion and interest—unity of object are emphatically our strength, they with the sement of pure gospel love make us strong, and fill our minds with agreeable emotions." [14]

Even in Shaker Families, however, difficulties sometimes arose. Members who contributed less to the spiritual life of the group than their leaders felt desirable could pose a serious threat. Religious zeal, as the Shakers knew well, tends to diminish unless new stimuli continually appear. To provide such encouragement was part of the job of Shaker leaders. They often reminded their charges:

Don't let us depend on others for the gifts of God. . . . Don't let us be deceived, and think, "O, I have had a great privilege; I have took up many crosses and suffered many privations and am surely a good believer; and now I think I ought to rest a little, and let the younger orders fight the flesh and bear the burden instead of me." I tell you, brethren & sisters, there is no time to lay down your weapons. [15]

Living so closely it is not surprising that even sincere Shakers sometimes transgressed the letter, and even the spirit, of the laws of Zion. The temptation to gossip about real or supposed wrongdoing must have been great, and only constant admonition by the leaders held such tendencies in check. Hancock's senior Ministry Eldress, Cassandana Goodrich, was particularly aware of these possibilities, enjoining her followers to "bridle the tongue" because of the "loss and disunion [which] comes by speaking things that ought not to be spoken." [16] She advised them to mind their own business "and not do or say anything but what is true. And don't tell everything you hear. You may not always hear the truth. If you see anything wrong, go to your Elders and let it rest there." [17]

Almost as common as these exhortations were leaders' reminders that peace and quiet were characteristics of heaven that good Believers would do well to emulate. Mother Lucy had felt that good spirits thronged Shaker homes only when stillness reigned. [18] Elder Nathaniel Deming of Hancock had similarly remarked that behavior on consecrated ground had to be appropriate—no stamping feet, slamming doors, loud laughing and talking, or leaning against walls or banisters like the "children of the world." [19] But these, like all rules, were occasionally overlooked.

Elder Issachar Bates was one of three missionaries who had gone to Ohio in 1805 and who had remained there as a leader. He found the decibel level in his Watervliet Dwelling distressingly high, leading him to complain:

Now in this building . . . there are fifty-eight doors . . . [which] are passed and repassed more than two thousand times in a day—opened and shut either by those that have some fear and care, with softness, or by those that have neither fear nor care with a bang like a little sharp clap of thunder. . . . There are twenty-three fires . . . which will require at least two armfuls of wood . . . a day, either put carefully into a woodbox, or thrown without care or feeling . . . and make as many claps of wooden thunder as there are armfuls. . . . Last of all add to the music more than forty thousand steps in a day of brethren and sisters; . . . some with a little softness and care, others like horses on the barn floor in fly time. . . . And I want you to know that I am not so averse to noise as you may suppose. I love a necessary noise. I love to hear a grist mill, and a saw mill . . . I love to see and hear a beautiful brother or sister stepping across the room with a soft elastic step . . . but I hate to see or hear a heavy footed brother or sister thumping across the floor, co-lump, co-lump, co-lump, and when they get to the door not think whether . . . they are going into another room or into a field.[20]

Because of the frequency of leaders' complaints and reminders about such behavior problems, we can be fairly certain that Believers did indeed lean against banisters, throw piles of wood about, laugh and talk loudly, and sometimes gossip about the misdeeds of their colleagues. Peer opinion within the Society certainly exerted tremendous pressure on refractory members to conform to at least minimum standards of behavior. Periodic private confession to Family Elders and Eldresses cleared the air, and kept the leaders aware of the spiritual states and temporal activities of their charges. Though not often mentioned in Shaker manuscripts, such confessions provided much of the cement that kept the Family system from falling apart.

Sincere Believers, who were convinced that "nothing but a love of godliness must become riveted to the soul," more often went to their superiors to seek help with their own spiritual problems than to tattle about the misdeeds of others. Because most Shakers believed "that a harsh word spoken to one of their comrades, that an idle joke, a wanton look, a seductive word, an alluring thought, or a careless transgression of a petty counsel will pollute the habitation of God," their consciences were indeed highly developed. Hervey Elkins, who was in a position to appreciate this system of rule enforcement after having lived under it for fifteen years at Enfield, New Hampshire, remarked that the Shakers "are indeed liable to live an exceeding righteousness of which the worldly-minded have no spiritual conception."[21]

In spite of occasional lapses, the bonds of union that had so impressed Elkins were very real. Relationships between Believers in a Family unit seem to have been generally cooperative and friendly, even across gender lines. While most nineteenth-century commentators sneered at celibacy and its attendant regulations and lifestyle, at least one observer had the perception to notice that Shaker Brethren and Sisters got along very well. He remarked that relations between the sexes were "much less restricted than is generally supposed," and applauded "those affectionate friendships and pure platonic enjoyments that spring up under what the world perhaps falsely calls an overwhelming obstacle to earthly happiness."[22]

Though it is true that a strict division of labor was typically maintained so that men and women worked at separate tasks in different parts of the community, there were exceptions to this rule. Wherever heavy work was involved, Brethren were regularly assigned to assist the Sisters. A Family Deacon, fifty-nine-year-old Benjamin Lyon of New Lebanon, both picked apples and helped the kitchen Sisters make a batch of crackers in one year.[23] More surprising, because of his youth, was the 1835 assignment of sixteen-year-old Brother Elisha Blakeman to assist in the dairy for the summer. At the close of the season, he noted proudly that "our order" had made 2,043 pounds of butter and 2,474 pounds of cheese.[24] Obviously his help in the dairy had been to some purpose.

Beyond occasional cooperation in a working situation and periodic conversation across a five-foot gap in union meeting, relations between the sexes were in fact severely circumscribed by Shaker rules. Apparently these limits were overstepped by some members from time to time. Although the evidence is understandably scanty, Brethren and Sisters were known to maintain "particular union" on a one-to-one basis. Such conduct was, of course, frowned on, and constituted a sin that required confession. A cryptic reference in Sister Anna Dodgson's *Dye House Journal* in 1846 may well refer to such a relationship:

Tabitha's in great _____ on account of being deprived of the full opportunity of conversing with _____ O!!! Anna's in great _____ on account of Tabitha's seeing and knowing just how the matter stands _____ and the opportunity of conversing at this time is interrupted O!!![25]

Union meetings provided the only sanctioned opportunity for small groups of men and women to meet and get to know one another, and sometimes this privilege was misused. Hervey Elkins commented on what could occur:

An hour passes away very agreeably and even rapturously with those who there chance to meet with an especial favorite; succeeded soon however, when soft words, and kind, concentrated looks, become obvious to the jealous eye of a female espionage, by the agonies of a separation. For the tidings of such reciprocity, whether true or surmised, is sure before the lapse of many hours, to reach the ears of the elders; in which case, the one or the other party would be subsequently summoned to another circle of colloquy and union.[26]

Elkins had reason to regret the operation of this system of "female espionage." In fact, the bitter experience of one of his friends contributed to Elkins's own decision to leave the faith. He told the story of the love that developed between "Brother Urbino" and "Sister Ellina," an affection that both acknowledged but which neither would act on, owing to the depth of their commitment to the Society's tenets. Sadly, the looks that passed between them over a period of several years did not go unnoticed and their conduct, irreproachable as it seemed to Elkins, was reported to the Elders. Urbino and Ellina were summoned before their respective "leads," and cautioned to stay well away from each other if they hoped to overcome this test of their faith. Evidently, the leaders respected their continuing commitment to the Society, but other members of the Family treated them with "recriminations, arraignments, admonitions and menaces." A group of "mistaken women, substituting their rancor for religious aversion to evil," constantly made Ellina feel that she was a disgrace to her profession and made it impossible for her to live in the Family peaceably. The Elders determined to move her to another community, a decision to which she agreed only reluctantly. Elkins reported the result: "Grief ineffable, grief incommensurable, grief unconquered and unconquerable, entered then her breast, and rankled and festered and corroded her bosom till the day of her death," an event which occurred shortly after her arrival at her new home. Elkins concluded that she had died of a broken heart.[27]

The inability of the Enfield leaders to control the conduct of those Sisters who made Sister Ellina's life so miserable demonstrates the limits of their influence. Theoretically infallible, in practice leaders' decisions were often dictated by what they knew their followers would accept. Scattered references in the manuscript record force one to speculate about the day-to-day operation of other Shaker principles as well. Tension between the sexes existed alongside the spirit of cooperation. We have already seen the difficulty experienced by Mother Lucy

Wright in getting the Brethren at New Lebanon to take her seriously over the issue of moving a certain house. They clearly had limited respect for the judgment of a woman, even though she was the senior leader in the Society at the time.

Conversely, she advised the Sisters to be especially careful in living up to their faith so that they might set a good example for the Brethren. "You have a greater privilege than the brethren do; you are more gathered in & not so much exposed to gather lightness, & you ought to be faithful & labor to keep a good substance so that the brethren can feel that you have been faithful." [28]

Cooperation and cordiality may have been the hallmarks of relationships between Shaker Brethren and Sisters, but there were elements of dynamic tension as well, some of which could certainly have been traced to sexual differences. A measure of competition between the sexes existed, as both men and women evidently felt superior to each other in certain respects. Brethren were commonly held to be gifted in temporal matters, but Sisters were in general considered more spiritually-minded, a division that mirrored accepted notions in the World.

The closest friendships that developed among the Believers were naturally those that involved members of the same sex. Members who worked closely together over a span of years often became the best of comrades. When such relationships were disrupted by changing circumstances, the Believers involved were often desolated. When Sister Anna Dodgson's colleague in the Dye House, Mariah Lapsley, was moved to the weaving department after an association of ten years, Anna sadly confided to her journal:

This will I think be to me a long remembered day! My long loved companion Maria removes from me. . . . We have spent ten years happily together without being disturbed by strife jar or contention & I really believe we have both felt more for each other's comfort than our own. Such a friend and companion as Maria is to me I never shall forget to all Eternity. [29]

In many cases, firm friendships were formed between young and older members on a mentor/protégé basis. Children were a vital part of all Shaker communities, although not every Family had a Children's Order. Leaders felt that the best Shakers were made young, and in the early nineteenth century were pleased to accept into the Society a growing number of youngsters whose parents or guardians had decided to indenture their offspring to the Believers. After all, had not Mother Ann said, "Little children are nearer the kingdom of heaven than those who have grown to riper age." [30]

Yet this proto-Romantic view of the nature of children coexisted with the remnants of a more evangelical attitude about the necessity of disciplining children vigorously and early. The Shakers did not exactly express support for "breaking the will" of youngsters, but they strongly emphasized the development of personal discipline in their young members. While visiting Enfield, New Hampshire, in 1833, Brother Seth Wells, architect of the Shaker educational system, reminded the children there of "the importance of strict obedience and true submission to their Elders and caretakers, as the only means to enable them to be useful to themselves and others, and of securing to them their everlasting happiness."[31] This goal was pursued in both academic and manual education. The tremendous emphasis placed on being useful to the Society, however, may well have taken precedence over spiritual development. The Believers never created a spiritual atmosphere for the youngsters in their charge that successfully brought a majority of them to conversion as adults. Unfortunately for the future growth of the sect, the emphasis on dealing with children was practical and logistical rather than spiritual.

Housed separately from adults after the late 1820s, girls usually lived in a "Girls' Shop" in one Family, and boys resided in a "Boys' Shop" at another. A common schoolhouse was used by the girls for four months in the summer, and by the boys for an equivalent time in the winter. When out of school, children were integrated into the working life of the community, sometimes given large tasks as a group, and sometimes assigned in twos or threes to specific workshops. In the latter case, an older member often took the children under his or her wing and became a surrogate parent.

It was in this fashion that Brother Luther Copley of New Lebanon took charge of teenager Elisha Blakeman and inducted him into the woodworking trade. An ideal relationship between the two men prospered. When Copley died in 1851, Blakeman penned the following tribute in which he plainly revealed his respect and affection for the older man:

> He was indeed a lovely child,
> Of God & Wisdom meek and mild
> Of Mother's spirit he partook,
> And all he did was like a book
> Wherein his character may be
> Most clearly read of Luther C.
> A holy, honest, upright man,
> A child of God and Mother Ann.[32]

Believers like Copley provided their younger colleagues with appropriate role models and served as tangible proof that it was not impossible to live a good Shaker life. Perhaps their most important role was one not readily apparent in the written record—the provision of spiritual education by example. Those few young people who converted to Shakerism and lived out their lives as Believers seem to have done so largely because of the individual influence of older members like Copley, rather than as a result of any community-wide system of spiritual education.

Desirable behavior for Shakers of all ages, and especially for the young, is described in the first lines of a song that originated at the Harvard community: "I will learn while I'm young to curb well my tongue, my own business I also will mind." Even though the Shakers believed very strongly that children should be governed by love and good example, they were not averse to an occasional application of the rod, as Hervey Elkins recalled:

Prayer, supplication, persuasion and keen admonition constitute the only means used to incline the disposition and bend the will of those arriving to years of understanding and reason. I affirm, without bias for any principle but truth, that a stringent, religious law positively forbids any corporeal punishment whatever, except the use of small twigs applied to extremely contumacious children under a dozen years of age.[33]

Adult Believers assigned as teachers and caretakers were usually quite young themselves, typically in their twenties. Not all of them relished these duties, knowing full well that only a small proportion of their charges would choose to join the sect upon reaching adulthood. When William Calver opened the New Lebanon boys' school in November 1859, he made his feelings plain in the *School Journal*.

I had supposed the idea of my becoming a teacher had been entirely abandoned. It is true I attended the school last Winter for a few days . . . but having the principal burden of the seed business . . . my stay was necessarily short. Considering these things . . . I supposed I should not be called upon to shoulder the unenviable burden. However, in the midst of disappointment I commence school today.[34]

To prepare children for adulthood, preferably within the Society, the Shakers advocated a strong common school education. Brother Seth Wells, appointed superintendent of Shaker schools by Mother Lucy Wright, advised that only the bare necessities be taught. In his 1836 "Remarks on Learning and the use of Boks," he decreed: "Life is short at the longest, and ought not to be spent in acquiring any kind of knowledge which cannot be put to a good use. . . . Letter learning is useful in its place . . . but there is much useless learning in the world which only tends to clog the mind and sense, and shut the gifts of God out of the soul."[35]

Caretakers, those who had charge of children during out of school hours and whose responsibilities were usually year-round, had an even more demanding job than the teachers. Many members considered it something of a "cross" to be asked to fill such a position. In 1844, when he was twenty-five, Elisha Blakeman of New Lebanon was summoned before his Elders and, as he recorded in his journal, "I was . . . informed that it was the gift to have me take some burden and care of the boys!!!!!!!—this in many respects loaded down my boat to its last degree of capability of sailing on the ocean of time and unnumbered troubles some visible and some invisible."[36] Freed from the job just three months later, Blakeman exulted:

> I'm now released from the boys
> And from a deal of din and noise
> And John is left to rule the roost
> Without a second mate to boost
> My Elders gave me a good name
> So I do leave devoid of shame
> Ha ha he he how glad I be
> I've no more boys to trouble me.[37]

Given the importance attached to the conversion of youngsters raised within the Society, it is curious that the leaders should have so often assigned as teachers and caretakers young adults such as these, whose attitudes can hardly be described as enthusiastic. The spiritual example they provided their charges could not often have been beneficial.

Since the majority of their time was spent out of school, Shaker children concentrated on learning agricultural and craft skills that would contribute to their Family's welfare and prepare them for a productive adult life. Most boys learned early to help with farm and garden chores like haying and hoeing, as well as chopping wood and cutting ice in winter. Girls were trained to assist the Sisters in textile production and served their turns in the kitchen and laundry as well. All were expected to devote themselves fully to whatever work was assigned. Sometimes the tasks required were not what the children would have preferred, as was the case at New Lebanon in 1850 when "it [was] thot well by the request of E. to have the boys improve their leisure moments learning to knit."[38] Often the jobs assigned to youngsters were menial, but at least the tedium was relieved by a free and friendly association with fellow workers.

In their out-of-school hours Shaker children had regular chores, much like their counterparts in the outside world. In November 1853, Elisha Blakeman, who had been reinstalled as Boys' Caretaker, noted in his journal: "E. commenced cutting seed bags—Cut 3000 Onion size P.G. works in the shoe shop. G. Br. making mittings in the shoe shop for E. A.S. helps D.H. at the Barn. J. Calver works at the seed shop—all go to school. O.B. is given up to size [broom]corn. H.S. and W.R. doubling bags. The rest of the boys have chores—getting in wood &c."[39] Though activities at any one time may have been repetitious, children were given a variety of jobs as the seasons changed. In 1828, eleven-year-old Benjamin Gates of New Lebanon spent most of his time learning the tailoring business, but never to the exclusion of other employments. During the winter, for example, he also attended school and helped with daily tasks such as filling woodboxes. In the spring, he helped with the general cleaning of the dooryards, tagged sheep, weeded the onions, grafted apple trees, and worked in the medicinal garden. The summer months were occupied with berrying, washing sheep, haying, pulling flax, and helping in the blacksmith and wood shops. In the fall, he was employed in harvesting wild herbs, gathering butternuts and chestnuts, digging potatoes, picking apples, and butchering hogs.[40]

But life as a Shaker child was not all work. The Shakers knew the value of carefully planned recreation. Several times a year, children were taken by their caretakers on picnics or excursions called "ride outs." On one such occasion in 1847, Elisha Blakeman recorded: "Took myself and 11 Boys—a ride out to Lenox. . . . I spent $2 for the Boys out of the money we received for a lot of apples we sold. Bought 2 lbs. & ¾ of candy, peanuts 2 quarts & raisins 1 pound. figs 7 lbs. or nearly 1 keg."[41] In August 1851, he noted: "J.D. took P.S. & oldest boys to Whiting pond fishing and for pleasure—We catched it by the ears."[42]

Adults, too, were allowed to combine work and pleasure, especially in the summertime. An 1859 expedition of four Brethren from New Lebanon took a horse team and went out fishing, returning with their catch many hours later—a single fish.[43] In 1860, a Brother recorded in the Family *Farm Journal*, "Farmers cut the Orchard grass and take a swim on mountain pond."[44] But it was during berry picking season that adult Believers had the greatest opportunity to do useful work and have a little fun at the same time. The opportunity arose in August 1838, when two young Brethren accompanied four Sisters on such an outing. The Brethren were sixteen and nineteen years old, and the Sisters twenty, twenty-two, twenty-two, and forty-five, the latter probably added to the party as a chaperone. Given the youth of the group, it is not difficult to understand why all involved had such a wonderful time, as one later observed: "We catched a considerable fun in the course of the day about one thing and another such as the letter, the oven brush, the old man, the great dog that was whipped so terribly, the little black pigs which shone as a glass bottle and I don't know what all."[45] Although these references are incomprehensible today, the atmosphere of innocent enjoyment still shines through the written record.

Beyond their possible legal admission to the Society, young people contributed a leavening spirit to the solemnity that often pervaded the communities. The example of little children was always deemed of great value because the Shakers encouraged members of all ages to be childlike, that is simple and innocent. The zeal and energy typical of younger Believers provided a lesson to older members whose enthusiasm and vitality were perhaps in danger of waning. Mother Lucy had once warned elderly Believers that none of them could ever relax their efforts in the fight against their carnal natures, even if they had years of successful Shaker life to their credit. Using plain, almost harsh language, she scolded: "If any think their age will excuse them from serving God, their age will excuse them from the Kingdom of Heaven."[46]

The phrase "serving God" had many meanings for the Shakers. Formal worship, missionary activities, and the cultivation of various spiritual gifts were of course included, but most rank and file members worked out their salvation on a daily basis by laboring with their hands in some necessary occupation. Relations with fellow Believers were governed by Ministry-established rules, supervised by Family Elders through the mechanism of occasional confession, and revolved around the communal Dwelling. But Shaker life had its individualistic side as well. All members strove to pursue excellence—perfection—in their daily occupations. Attention to detail and exercise of manual skills in the service of the community taught the Believers important spiritual lessons. In the Dwellings and Meetinghouses of Shaker villages, communal devotion was plain, but in the various barns, fields, and workshops Believers were free to express their own individual commitment to the faith. Instead of the "we did this" or "we sang that" so often found in official Family records, individual work journals employed the personal pronoun—"I learned this" or "I made that." Without this special Shaker attitude toward individual accomplishment within an occupation, daily life for the Believers would have been far less fulfilling. The Shakers were convinced, like the Puritans before them, that "a man can show his religion as much in measuring onions as he can in singing Glory halalua."[47]

It is clear from surviving records that many Shakers thought first and foremost about their work, a tendency that caused some leaders to fear for the spirituality of the sect. When Sister Anna Dodgson was asked to write something in Mariah Lapsley's "specimen book," she turned to the issues uppermost in her mind at that moment. The result-

ing entry is almost conversational in tone and makes plain the role of
work in her daily life.

Maria says I have promised for two years to write in her specimen book &
have never done it. What shall I write next? Why you've wrote that too close to
the corner, I don't know what it is. We don't never shear our sheep in June.
There they are shearing our sheep in June. I wonder when we shall get our
kittle to color in. I wish we could have suck wood. Well, get Barny to bring it
in. I wonder when you'll fix that wool. I wonder when Eliza Ann is coming
to comb.[48]

Work was a common experience to all Shakers, old and young, leader
and follower alike, and provided an important ingredient in the Society's recipe for gospel union. Work was divided by gender along traditional lines, with Sisters doing the cooking, cleaning, textile production, dairying, and the like, and Brethren concentrating on farming
and various home industries like broom-making and blacksmithing.
No one was left out. Even a ninety-one-year-old Sister knit twelve pairs
of footings in 1860. One of her comrades, eighty-three and blind, contributed to the Family's welfare by knitting twelve pairs of stockings for
the Sisters, footing thirty-five pairs, and winding one hundred runs of
knitting yarn.[49]

An 1850 list of the principal occupations of New Lebanon's First
Order shows how the fifty-four Sisters and thirty-four Brethren there
provided for most of their own needs as a Family.[50] Sisters over sixty
tended to be seamstresses or menders, although a few were listed as
spinners or "tailoresses." Middle-aged women were physicians, weav-
ers, dairywomen, and soap and basket makers; women under thirty
produced items for sale such as cushions, chair mats, hats, and brushes.
Kitchen and laundry work was rotated among all the Sisters, usually
on a monthly schedule, and so was not listed. Not surprisingly, thirty-
seven of the fifty-four Sisters were listed in occupations involving the
production or care of clothing, and probably almost all of them spun
or mended at least part of their time. Within the textile industry, some
specialization existed with Sisters listed as quillers, jenny spinners, fine
linen spinners, combers, worsted spinners, and the like.

Among the Brethren a similar amount of work was done by fewer
people. Men over sixty were tailors, gardeners, or woodworkers of one
type or another. Middle-aged men were "mechanics," horse teamsters,
physicians, tanners, shoemakers, and many were listed with two or
three occupations, revealing the decline in male membership. Younger
Brethren, of whom there were distressingly few (only eight under age
forty), were assigned jobs as farmers—a general term that could have

described every Brother—ox teamsters, broom-makers, or simply had a "variety" of tasks.

If any members balked at this division of labor by sex, little evidence survives. Sister Rhoda Blake of New Lebanon did record that as a youngster she had developed "a love for a business life," and was greatly interested in the Brethren's pursuits. When the men were moving an old building in the 1820s to put up a new wash house at the Second Order, she wrote: "If there had been no distinction of sex I should have been in their midst pulling out nails . . . and carrying away stones or rubbish from the foundation in my apron."[51] Perhaps she merely wished to follow the example set by Mother Lucy on the occasion of another memorable house-moving some years earlier. At any rate, her "love for a business life" was doubtless satisfied in later years by her appointment as Family Deaconess.

One of the mechanisms that helped prevent boredom and may well have increased productivity within the Society was a complex system of job rotation. A Sister might be known primarily for her fine weaving, and might indeed be listed as a weaver for the purposes of the census, but she might also be an accomplished teacher, dairywoman, or physician, at the same time sharing in the usual Sisters' tasks of cooking and cleaning. A Brother might occupy himself most often in the Machine Shop, but he might be equally comfortable in the tin shop, the tannery, or the orchard, and would usually share with his Brethren the basic care of land and livestock. Particularly among the men, where many jobs were done by progressively fewer members, work rotations could become bewildering. A New Lebanon *Farm Journal* entry for April 14, 1860 explains:

Various changes have taken place today. Henry gives up the horse team to Frederic & moves into the joiner shop in Hiram's place, who moves into the mill room for a shop. Frederic gives up his ox team to David Lyall who leaves the Blacksmith shop which is filled by Wm. Trent who leaves the herb house to one of the first Order. . . . David Rea gives up the barn to Andrew Barrett. George Long goes to the farm & James Vail is Blacksmith. David Rea goes out to the farm etc.[52]

Luther Sargent, the census enumerator for part of Merrimack County, New Hampshire, in 1870, found these constant changes confusing, and was not at all sure how to describe the occupations of the Believers in the Canterbury community. He commented helplessly: "It was rather difficult to give the occupation of all—as perhaps one may be in the mill today, and on the farm tomorrow, and perhaps teaming the third day. I have done the best I could."[53]

Sometimes the Believers themselves were overwhelmed by their un-
ceasing revolutions through their Family's workshops and barns. By
the middle of the nineteenth century, it began to seem as though there
might not be enough hands to do all the necessary work. After the
1820s, hired help became increasingly important to the economic survival of the communities.[54] Brother Isaac Youngs of New Lebanon was
one who complained about the number of young members who were
leaving the sect, but then returned doggedly to his work, trying to accomplish more instead of less as he grew older and feebler. He was jus-
tifiably proud of the expertise he had acquired during his many years
of devoted service, and wrote in a jocular way about his fatigue:

> Of various kinds of work I've had
> Enough to make me sour or sad.
> Of Tayloring, Joinering, farming too,
> Almost all kinds that are to do,
> Blacksmithing, Tinkering, Mason work,
> When could I find time to shurk?
> Clock work, Jenny work, keeping school
> Enough to puzzle any fool!
> An endless list of chores and notions,
> To keep me in perpetual motion.[55]

Though Shaker tenets forbade jealousy and wrangling among members as unChristian, some vestiges of friendly competition did remain
to cheer the Believers in their never ending round of toil. The tendency
to brag about accomplishments was ever present, and caused problems
for leaders who wished to encourage productivity without creating divisive rivalry. Mother Hannah Kendall of Harvard was one of the first
to warn about the possible consequences of showing off, when in 1810
"she gave us good counsel in relation to bravado. She said that two
bushels of grain were enough to lift at once; . . . she said it was wrong
for us to try to outdo each other in such things."[56]

Without pride in their work, the Shakers could never have fashioned
artifacts of such enduring quality and appeal, but excessive pride was
frowned upon because the Believers recognized that no achievement
could exist without God's help. All members tried to make the work of
their hands fit for an earthly heaven and a certain measure of pride was
unavoidable. At age seventeen Elisha Blakeman was young enough to
allow his excitement over a new project to spill into his journal, exult-
ing: "I help build the mill. I presume that there ain't another mill to be
found in this state for sawing lumber so copious & snug-built as the
aforesaid one."[57]

Such exuberance was perhaps pardonable in one so young, but exhibitions of this nature by older members had to be controlled. Sister Thankful Goodrich once recalled an occasion when she was making caps and Mother Lucy came in to watch her at work. Seeing the excessive attention she was paying to so unimportant an activity, Mother Lucy remarked trenchantly:

> Thankful, if I should take as much pains & feel as much about the caps as you do, it would be a sin in me. It seems to me that you think every stitch you take must be perfect enough to enter the Kingdom of Heaven. I cannot feel as you do about these things. . . . I am willing that you should do your work well, but do not set your heart and fancy too much on these things.[58]

Dedication to work was expected of all Believers, but overzealousness in temporal endeavors was as much a sin as overzealousness in spiritual affairs.

There were, of course, some members who were less eager than others to prove their faith by hard work. During the winter months, the daily routine became tedious to some. Severe weather made outdoor work uncomfortable, and even getting from Dwelling to shop and back an unpleasant challenge. One New Lebanon Sister, who probably enjoyed the tasks of spring, summer, and fall in orchard and garden, found the bitter storms of February 1836 disheartening:

> It snows & blows & whisks around,
> And, oh!, how hateful is the sound—
> For we have heard it times enough,
> To make a christian snort & snuff![59]

Brother Elisha Blakeman, after fighting with his team to draw wood on a particularly blustery day in December 1837, longed for the comparative ease and comfort of his regular workshop:

> As I was riding on my sleigh,
> Upon the mountain high;
> A zero cold and windy day,
> Did cause the snow to fly.
> I wished myself within the shop,
> Where I could warm my toes;
> And apples eat all roasted hot
> Which pleasant summer grows.[60]

Sometimes bad weather was welcomed because it prevented demanding outdoor work. A New Lebanon *Farm Journal* entry from late June 1859 shows that the writer, at least, felt he deserved a rest from the fatigues of planting: "Pleasant weather indeed. Rain all day. Farmers loitering here and there."[61] As an excuse for an easy day, poor weather was perfect, but the Shakers had no patience with slackers.

Mother Ann had insisted that all Believers pull their own weight and contribute as much as possible to the general welfare. When a Sister named Molly Needham shirked her own sewing to do something for Mother Ann or one of the Elders, she was sharply reproved. Mother Ann upbraided her: "We sent for you to work for us, & you set others to work. Here, take your work, & do it yourself before you do anything for us."[62]

When Brother David Rea of the New Lebanon Second Order failed to keep up with the fence mending he had been assigned, one of his Brethren entered that information in the Family *Farm Journal* for all to read, and laced the entry heavily with sarcasm.

This summer Elder Brother Giles told David Rea to see to making fences about the farm & he cheerfully complied with his wishes by setting himself arduously to work & by his industry at all times he has contrived by magic to build two lengths of fence, each length I guess is 12 feet long & 3 boards high, but I will not be positive as to the length for I've not measured, but for fear that I might rob his majesty of honor. . . . He said that he has been a hard working man all his life & that he thinks it is no more than right that his name should appear once in a while in the family's records. Neither do I in relation to his faculty for making fences for he has quite a gift in that line.[63]

Even though avoiding work was unacceptable, complaining about it was quite popular. Unpleasant jobs had to be done by someone, and griping about them relieved the burden a little. Sister Anna Dodgson's *Dye House Journal* is sprinkled with entries where she evidently lost her temper after an unsuccessful day. On July 20, 1849, she recorded:

O Sorrow & joy Betsy Crossman, Mary Ann Mantle, Amy Reed have finished coloring blue wool, they began the 12th had 105 lb. & more than this had it all to wash over because Maria says we had such poor judgment & got the liquor too strong . . . & too hot I suppose, O Murder, every thing happens this awful year!!!!!![64]

An entry earlier the same year includes one phrase (spelled backwards) that is probably as close as a Shaker would come to swearing.

We commenced turning our yarn on the Buck and find our lye has been too strong?
d.e.l.i.o.p.s.s.f.e.i.h.c.r.e.k.d.n.a.h.t.e.k.c.o.p.[65]

Eighteen-forty-nine continued to be a difficult year for Sister Anna and her associates in the Dye House. Clearly she found her work there distasteful, but slogged on only out of a sense of duty. By the end of the summer her patience had worn thin, and she complained, "Today we go to the old poison dye house. . . . We are all in an awful snarl, Elizaette wants the kettle all the time and so do we, so we do everything but lay awake nights to contrive."[66]

Dodgson was not the only member honest enough to record dissatisfaction with an assigned task in a journal that might easily have been read by the Elders. Brother Henry DeWitt, for many years in charge of the shoe shop at the New Lebanon Church Family, wrote on the day of his transfer to another duty: "This morning I heard the sound of liberty! Liberty from the bondage of old boots and shoes, having spent 26 years at the business." [67] DeWitt preferred his work as a wheelwright and manufacturer of textile equipment, but shoes continually wore out whereas looms and spinning wheels did not.

Declining numbers put great stress on those Believers remaining in the Society to produce more in less time. Shaker adoption of Worldly technology did help to a degree, but the burden on the Brethren in particular increased throughout the nineteenth century. Temporal concerns began to overshadow spiritual ones for some members, especially those charged with providing for the basic needs of the community, and the press of daily business affected all. Brother Isaac Youngs, whose preoccupation with temporalities was far from rare, opined:

> All full of bus'ness night and day;
> With scarce a moment's time to play;
> I've work enough that's now on hand
> For 15 years for any man.
> I'm overrun with work and chores
> Upon the farm or within doors.
> Whichever way I turn my eyes
> Enough to fill me with surprise.
> How can I bear with such a plan?
> No time to be a gentleman!. . .
> As long as *working* is the cry
> How can I e'er find time to die? [68]

Shaker Deacons and Trustees were especially prone to neglect the spiritual side of their lives, and occasionally had to be reminded of this by the Elders. In 1825, after the Maine Ministry had received a letter from the Church Family Deacons at Harvard describing the particulars of a windmill they were interested in building, they responded querulously to the Harvard Ministry:

We scrabled round with all posable expidition . . . but behold when we come to open the letter, how great the disappointment not one drop of love could we geather from it. . . . It was ver well on the subject of the wind-mill, . . . but Deacons cannot live without a little love any better than any one else so they ought to be a little more spiritual. [69]

Shaker prosperity in the early decades of the nineteenth century had heightened members' expectations about the quality of Shaker life. Indeed, during those years, some converts joined primarily, if not solely, for economic reasons. Although the sect was stable enough to absorb a considerable influx of these new "lukewarm" members, by the 1820s their Worldly attitudes had begun to rub off on their more spiritual senior colleagues. Beginning in the second and third decades of the nineteenth century, the tone of Shaker life underwent a subtle change —so subtle that even a devout Believer like Elder Issachar Bates came to emphasize the temporal benefits of life within the Society over the spiritual ones.

> I've not a word to say, nor dare I breathe complaint,
> I live in God Almighty's day and call'd to be a saint,
> I've plenty that is good, to eat & drink & wear;
> I've decent clothes and wholesome food, enough & some to spare.
> My bed is soft & sweet, my room is nice & clean,
> No court on earth is kept more neat, for any King or Queen
> My brethren are my friends, my sisters kind to me,
> Whoever plows or knits or spins are all at work for me.
> Is this what Jesus meant, an hundredfold to give?
> Then I've the whole in present time, yea every day I live.
> Now this is surely gain, then where's my dreadful loss?
> I shall eternal life obtain, sure as I bear my cross.[70]

The face the Shakers showed to the outside world did not reveal this gradual change. Indeed, probably few members were aware of it, absorbed as they were in the exigencies of everyday life. Hervey Elkins, who also emphasized the physical over the spiritual rewards of Shaker life, concluded in his 1853 account of the sect: "A *true* Shaker, surrounded as he is with every physical blessing and denied by an order, stringent as straightness, of every physical curse, seems almost a new being—a being who lives in the brightness, splendor, and beatitude of heaven."[71] But in this proliferation of temporal blessings lay the seeds of the spiritual decline that plagued Shaker leaders throughout the middle years of the nineteenth century, as they struggled to reawaken the religious enthusiasm of their followers.

6

Numbers Are Not the Thing
for Us to Glory in
(1821-1837)

Even before Mother Lucy Wright's death in 1821, hints of a spiritual decline had already begun to appear. In spite of her efforts to regularize Shaker temporal life without rigidifying the life of the spirit, new attitudes had begun to creep into the Society. These were often introduced by a new group of converts who were increasingly drawn as much by the prospect of earthly security as by the promise of salvation, and who required more supervision and regulation than had their predecessors. Their lives disrupted by economic or personal upheaval, many came to the Shakers looking for a haven—for both themselves and their children. Many, especially the young among them, had never experienced a true conversion, so it is hardly surprising that their devotion to the sect was correspondingly tepid. Throughout the 1820s and 1830s, the eastern communities experienced escalating rates of apostasy and levels of internal dissension. The proportion of young members increased just as the size of the leadership pool was reaching a dangerously low level. By 1837, a crisis of significant magnitude had developed, sparking a pervasive Society-wide revival.

This decay of commitment was caused in part by the Shakers' changing economy. Their well-known integrity and devotion to perfectionism led them to fashion products of enduring quality and beauty, appreciated perhaps more today than when they were manufactured. In the nineteenth century, items such as garden seeds, flat brooms, wooden ware, and baskets brought "World's People" flocking to Shaker villages as eager customers. Every year, Brethren traveled as peddlers throughout the northeast leaving their manufactures on consignment at general stores. Shaker products were highly regarded and much sought after, but the prosperity these increased sales brought the Society was a mixed blessing.

The Society's neat, ordered villages of the 1810s and 1820s attracted as converts many individuals who, for one reason or another, had no wish or ability to make their own way in the World. Religious conviction was a small matter to some of them. They were perfectly willing to pay lip service to Shaker principles if by doing so they received food, shelter, and lifelong security. Historians of the sect have observed that this trend led to a significant decline in the members' level of religious enthusiasm.

It seems likely that as the novelty of the Shakers' doctrines declined, and the country surrounding their societies became more settled and civilized, the societies increasingly attracted persons seeking security and refuge, rather than theological certainty and ascetic activism. An increasing proportion of submissive and complaisant members may in part explain the slow atrophy of the culture of the sect, and the drift toward accommodation to the world which took place in the second half of the nineteenth century.[1]

The influx of these "lukewarm" Shakers began, however, well before 1850. As early as 1816 Mother Lucy had shown concern over the changing character of the Society's membership, and commented: "Numbers are not the thing for us to glory in, but purity and holiness. I do not feel any lack in numbers; the great lack I feel is in purity."[2] Many members began to worry that their millennial goals would be undermined by the growing unpopularity of their tenets. They began to wonder if the time were not right for another major missionary endeavor, much like the one of a decade earlier that had resulted in the establishment of seven communities in Ohio, Kentucky, and Indiana. In 1826, the New Hampshire Ministry broached the subject in a letter to New Lebanon: "There have but few come in of late, so that we think it is about time to send out more hunters to hunt them and fishers to fish them."[3]

In general, the Shakers tried not to concern themselves overmuch with the number of converts joining the sect nor with the number of disaffected members leaving for the World, but complete indifference was impossible. In their journals, they insisted, as did Sister Elizabeth Lovegrove, "We want no such scabby sheep in our flock."[4] But much work had to be done, and hands were desperately needed even if the hearts were less than devoted. The Lead Ministry noted this unfortunate situation in 1824, opining: "Believers have grown so charitable that they would gather in almost anything and everything."[5]

More and more converts were seeking the "narrow track" of Shaker life because they were facing seemingly insuperable difficulties in the outside world. Jesse Gause of Philadelphia lost his wife in childbirth in

1828, and was left with the care of three young children plus the new infant. In the absence of relatives, it was an understandable decision for him to move with his family to the Hancock community.[6] Unfortunately, Shaker life did not agree with him. He left with his children in 1831 and subsequently became a Mormon of some influence.[7]

Other families joined after immigrating to the United States from abroad, perhaps because of problems establishing themselves in their new country. William and Elizabeth Taylor may well have endured such an experience. They arrived in America from England in 1811 with their six children. During the next nine years they moved some twenty times before ultimately joining the Watervliet, New York, community in 1820. In their case as well, the adjustment to Shaker life proved far from easy. William and Elizabeth left Watervliet for Albany in 1822, returned to the Shakers in 1824, left again in 1827, and returned a second time in 1828, having had two more children during the intervening six years.[8] They chose to leave a third time in 1829, but Elizabeth returned in 1830 to beg the Watervliet Shakers to readmit both her and her husband, together with their youngest son. Her request was granted because the senior Taylors, "being aged could not live in Albany. It was agreed to take them as they had children in the society who were good believers."[9]

A significant proportion of the sect's membership in the early nineteenth century was comprised of minor children, the elderly, and handicapped individuals unable to support themselves in the World—a combination that strained the resources of all the communities. In 1825 at Watervliet, New York, forty-four members were reported to the overseers of the poor as being unable to support themselves, a figure that represented roughly 20 percent of the community's total population. This number included thirty "poor children" under the age of eleven, nine members over the age of sixty who were unable to work, and five handicapped adult members. None of these Believers had donated any property to the community upon joining.[10]

Scattered references in Shaker records tell a few tales of these unfortunate members, including Hannah and Elizabeth Train of the New Lebanon Church Family. On December 7, 1828, a Ministry member recorded: "I go to the 2nd Order to enquire after crazy H. Train—find them in bed, occasioned by H. keeping them up till midnight."[11] Eldress Asenath Clark wrote seven years later, "E. Train has been growing crazy sometime, & had to be confined yesterday—and about 12 o'clock last night she got out of the 2nd loft window and went to the meetinghouse & broke 3 lights of glass before she was detected."[12] There is, of course, no way to confirm the details of the Trains' afflictions, or indeed whether they were merely so dissatisfied with Shaker life that they expressed their opposition in these colorful and annoying ways. It seems more likely that they suffered from some type of mental illness, and were cared for by the Shakers in as kindly a way as possible. If such were the case, they would have been unlikely candidates for apostasy because they would have been unable to provide for their own needs.

Members unencumbered by such problems, and who found Shaker life too restrictive or unfulfilling, were always free to leave. If they had come to the faith seeking only temporal security, they were all the more likely to backslide, a tendency that did not escape the notice of Shaker leaders. In 1819, the Lead Ministry reported to the Ministry in Union Village, Ohio, about conditions in the east. "There has been a considerable number set out to obey the gospel within a few years in this part of the vineyard; some appear to be very good believers, and a great many more have pretended that are after nothing but the loaves and the fishes; but when they begin to feel the burning truth, they fall off like withered branches." [13]

Some of those who left found that survival on the outside could not be assured, as it had been within the sanctuary of a loving Shaker Family. Occasionally they crept back repentantly to seek "another privilege," as it was called. In 1832, a former Brother named John Mantle wrote to the Lead Ministry pleading to return to New Lebanon.

As I have left my all and forsook the only way and work of God for the expectation of taking some comfort in the world but alas there is no comfort for the wicked and so it has proved to me for I have not taken any comfort by day or by night but on the contrary it has been nothing but a scene of horror and guilt of conscience since I left and I humbly implore thy mercy if there is any to be felt for me. I will do anything that is the gift for me to do to obtain my union to the work of God for if I cannot regain my union in a measure I of all souls am the most miserable. I thought before I left that I was a traditionated Shaker but I find my gross error for there is no such thing as a traditionated Shaker. Do help me. Do help me. [14]

As was often the case, Mantle's impassioned plea did not fall on deaf ears. Shaker leaders were usually willing to give an apparently repentant backslider another chance. Brother John was permitted to return to his Shaker home in 1833. He had evidently learned a harsh lesson while in the World, and had become a devout member instead of a "traditionated Shaker"—a Believer of conviction instead of one of habit.

Sadly, John Mantle was the exception, not the rule. Although Shaker leaders generally permitted repentant apostates to return to the fold, they did not expect them to remain very long. In 1824, the Maine Ministry expressed this belief plainly in a letter to New Lebanon: "It is almost infalibal that all those who have had an opportunity to receive a planting of faith and turn aside and wallow in their corruptions and are received back they not abide long, and while they do stay they are poor dead sunken souls not fit company for the living soul."[15] This gloomy assessment was confirmed by dozens of examples. More typical than John Mantle was Bushnell Fitch of New Lebanon, who had joined the community in 1810 at the age of sixteen. He departed on July 7, 1815, returned the next day, left again in April 1816, returned in August of the same year, and left for the last time in 1817.[16]

It was customary for apostates to receive at their departure some amount of clothing and cash, perhaps with the tools of a trade they had learned while members. This practice drained the Society's resources considerably, but the Shakers were unwilling to release backsliders without the means to support themselves. Between 1816 and 1884, 134 apostates from the Watervliet, New York, community received cash and goods with a total value of $11,634.80, or $86.83 a person.[17] In spite of this generosity, many apostates left the faith soured and embittered, eager to expose to the unsympathetic eyes of the World any ill treatment they fancied they had received. In 1853 Hervey Elkins marveled at the gall of some of these backsliders, saying: "Although the Society usually refund, to such seceders as make a dedication of any property, the full amount dedicated, and give as a present a small sum of money and a complete wardrobe to each who have appropriated only their services, yet this munificence . . . seems only to engender backbitings and murmurs."[18]

One such seceder who dedicated her life to the destruction of the sect was Mary Dyer, a former member of the Enfield, New Hampshire, community. Perhaps the vituperative tone of her written attacks, first published in 1818, is somewhat understandable in light of her experience among the Shakers. Married to Joseph Dyer and mother of five children, she was surprised and upset by her husband's wish (sometime around 1810) to have the whole family join the Shakers. She consented to try the way of life for one year, and stipulated that if she wished to leave at the end of that time, the two youngest children be permitted to go with her.

After one year she determined to leave the community. Her husband, aided by the Elders, prevented her from even seeing any of her children, knowing that she would attempt to spirit them away from the village. She was ultimately forced to leave without even bidding her children farewell, and sought to revenge herself by writing books and pamphlets to discredit the Shakers in the eyes of their neighbors. In an 1825 pamphlet addressed to the Elders at New Lebanon, she made her motivation plain, pleading, "Give me my children, I ask no more."[19] She later petitioned the New Hampshire legislature to launch a formal investigation of the Shakers in the state to determine whether or not they were fit guardians of children, an issue that was finally decided in the Society's favor in 1849.

Thus for some thirty years Dyer was a vociferous spokesperson for Shaker apostates and others who sought to restrict the sect's activities. The leaders responded by asking Joseph Dyer to write a rebuttal to his wife's charges, which was published by the Society and circulated throughout New England. In 1819, Elder Nathaniel Deming of Hancock wrote to the Harvard Ministry: "We saw A very slanderous peace Published in A Boston Paper about the brethren in New hamshire stateing that Mary Dyer had unfolded their wickedness &c.—would it not be best to get the brethren at Canterbury to send some of Joseph Dyer's Pamphlets there if they have not done it."[20] It is evident that leaders throughout the Society considered Mary Dyer a significant threat to the sect, and kept themselves and one another constantly informed as to her movements. In 1826, the Hancock Ministry reported to Harvard: "Mary Dyer the *Abominable* is in these parts, she has crept over into Lebanon hollow and like a sitting goose or turkey-buzzard is brooding over her nest of lies, and generating them into life with her lascivious pen."[21]

Apostates such as Mary Dyer, who had real grievances and actively sought their redress, were fortunately rare. Even as strain increased within the Society during the 1810s and 1820s, many good Believers maintained the principles of the faith without faltering, and others of like character converted. Small-scale revivals continued periodically throughout the northeast. It was still fairly common for large families influenced by these upheavals to seek religious certainty among the Shakers. One of these was the Winchester family of Brimfield, Massachusetts, who joined the Harvard community in 1813. Parents Bathsheba and Benjamin developed into good Shakers, dying in the faith in 1841 and 1845 respectively. The progress of their nine children was less impressive, however. All four of their sons and three of their five daughters apostatized, another daughter having died at the age of fourteen. Thus from a family of eleven converts, only three were transformed into devout Believers, a proportion that became distressingly common in the first half of the nineteenth century.[22]

Beginning in the 1810s, children came to represent a growing proportion of members in most communities. In 1800, children under the age of sixteen comprised only 2.8 percent of the total population of the eastern communities. By 1820, the proportion had increased to 19.8 percent (see Appendix B.5). Although their presence did not necessarily presage the decline of the sect, these young people did pose a challenge to the creativity of the Society's leaders. Some technique for their spiritual education had to be devised, and it was here that the Lead Ministry failed most significantly in their efforts to secure the future of the sect.

As they grew up, those youngsters who remained Believers more out of habit than conviction exhibited behavior that became troublesome for the leaders. Relations between the sexes, although carefully supervised and subject to increasing regulation in this period, occasionally ripened into "carnal" love. Mother Lucy Wright had earlier expressed her concern about this possibility. "If souls are after the gospel, and travel in the way of God, there will be a kind tender feeling between Brethren and Sisters. On the other hand, if any are after the flesh *there* is the first place it shows itself." [23] To her dismay, she observed that more and more Believers were seeking to live "after the flesh."

Other leaders, too, were alarmed by the declining standards of behavior they witnessed in the members under their charge. About 1815, Mother Hannah Kendall of Harvard reproved the young Sisters there for walking about unnecessarily from building to building on the farm and "for putting [themselves] in the way of the Young Brethren to tempt and allure them." [24] In 1834, the New Lebanon Second Order Elders gathered the Family together and told them "that there is a gift . . . that is not to go and open the doors into Sisters lodging rooms, and set in candles but to set them down by the door and wrap at the door to awake them, and the Sisters are to fasten their doors that open directly into the rooms where they sleep." Given the deteriorating conditions within the Family, Brother Philemon Stewart decided that this was a "good regulation." [25]

The behavior Mother Lucy and these other leaders sought to curb had clearly become something of a problem. Although not commonplace, it was by no means rare in these years for Brothers and Sisters to fall in love and leave the sect to marry. Relationships such as these might begin quite innocently. As Brother Abijah Worster of Harvard testified in 1837, "The worst snare that Satan has to decoy souls from the way of God is to lead them into carnal fleshly affections. These affections are often created by sympathizing with each other in times of sickness and weakness. . . . When you are obliged to be together at such times, you ought to be as careful as you would be if you was at work among powder with fire." [26]

Brother Abijah's use of the gunpowder metaphor is interesting because it confirms a suspicion that students of the sect have long entertained. Even though the Shakers sought to lead angelic lives, they were human. Their natural inclinations were not wholly eliminated by conversion and confession, but had to be daily and hourly watched lest they resurface to entrap the unwary Believer. The description of a Shaker Family as an emotional powder keg is apt. On several occasions, the fires of affection between the sexes were ignited, and at least a few souls fell away to the World as a result.

In 1821, Brother John Deming of the Hancock Church Family, member of a family that had converted to Shakerism in the 1780s, abruptly left the Society. The surprise at his departure must have been great because he had been a good Believer for many years and was at least fifty years old. Before he left, he wrote a letter explaining the reasons for his decision to his Elders, two of whom (Nathaniel and William) were his natural brothers. Brother John's letter had, therefore, a poignant personal message.

As the awful period has come that I am forced by necessity to change my home, I tho't it would be unmanly to not give some reason why I do so. The truth is, that the vehement affection which I have to Minerva has undone me. I have had to struggle for life, but fondly hoped that some change would take place which would save my credit—Her excessive kindness still increased my disease, and tho' not a word passed between us for years, yet, had it not been for my age, I should have known what it was at the outset, but I could not think her inclined to one of my age. But a letter which I found in my pocket last fall opened to me the whole. It had no name to it, but I knew the hand, and warned her to do so no more: but being unwell, I went in to lay down, and she came in and sat on the bed and put her face to mine, and I flung my arm around her neck and kissed her! but nothing else took place at that time, neither have I ever gone any further since, but that has taken place a number of times where we met. . . . I proposed to her to confess it, but she said if I did she would quit immediately, and then I knew there would be no mercy for me; I know the shock is dreadful, but what can I do?—to stay here and be a curse is more so. O brethren and sisters instead of being stumbled take warning by my fall! O God! O God! what shall I do? [27]

Brother John evidently had no strong wish to leave the faith he had upheld for so long, but felt he would be a contaminating influence in the Family he loved so well. By his departure, he hoped to provide young Shakers in particular with a powerful example that might save them from similar fates.

Hancock was not the only community to suffer from such unfortunate occurrences. Two cases of fornication have been documented for this period, at least one of which resulted in pregnancy. The first of these occurred at the Shirley community in 1832, and was duly reported to the Lead Ministry.

One thing more we have to inform you of which was unexpected to us and we believe it is to all the church; a few weeks since, poor feeble Anna Wetherbee and William Clark junr. nearly at one time came to the Elders with a confeshion the same as the first Adam and Eve when in the garden, professed to be penitent, Wm. plead much for himself and she also plead for him, because she was first in the transgression (as she said) but expected her case might prove so that she could not stay,—but before the setting of the sun they were both carried away to the great astonishment of all the beholders, but so it is, and to see one who never had been known to be on the courting ground, and after having the privilege which Anna had, to fall out (unsuspected) in such a way is very mortifying to the honest believer.[28]

As matters developed, the "mortification" the Shirley Elders wrote of was felt even in New Lebanon in 1835. The members involved were Brother Theodore Long, aged twenty, and Sister Sally Thomas, aged thirty-six. Ministry Eldress Asenath Clark recorded the event in her journal, but in such cryptic language that the nature of their offense was omitted. On March 21 she wrote: "Jonathan Wood took Theodore Long this afternoon to help him on his way to his company in New York, the latter having violated the faith of believers by base conduct to that degree that he could not be held in union."[29]

Fortunately, Eldress Betsy Bates recorded the same incident in the Family journal with greater candor, exclaiming: "The most distressing thing was brought to light that ever was made known in the church. A young one made here in the Second Order by Theodore Long and Sally Thomas . . . Awful Awful Awful. Never did I think this would been our disgrace."[30] Thomas was sent away to relatives in Savoy, Massachusetts, but Long sent an intermediary to New Lebanon after only a week in the World asking that he be taken back "into union." Eldress Betsy recorded: "There has been a man here from Canaan, where Jonathan left Theodore, begging we would take Theodore again—says he would kill himself if it had not been for him with Laudenum & cried & sniveled & took on most dreadfully. said he wanted to come back."[31] Out of kindness the Elders allowed him to return, but were probably not surprised when he departed again in October. From Eldress Betsy's tone, it is clear that this incident, like the one at Shirley, was far from typical, but the fact that they occurred at all indicates a certain laxity in Shaker behavior during the years following Mother Lucy's death.

Although the cases of John Deming, Sally Thomas, Theodore Long, Anna Wetherbee, and William Clark were certainly not the norm, their existence proves that not all Shakers were able to avoid major sins, despite the Society's professed goal of perfection. Members were apt to be led astray, not only by their natural affections, but by their intellectual pretensions as well. Believers who looked to their own consciences for instruction and justification made poor Shakers. Many of these felt it acceptable to challenge the leaders' authority whenever they deemed it appropriate. This difficulty was compounded as fewer young people reared in the communities converted at legal age, and as fewer committed adults joined the sect, shrinking the pool of good potential leaders (see Appendixes A.2, A.4, and B.4). As a result, the quality of leadership throughout the Society declined, and the confidence of members in their superiors diminished rapidly.

A key element in this process was the inability of the Lead Ministry during these years to maintain the high standard of leadership established by Father Joseph Meacham and Mother Lucy Wright. Though Elders Ebenezer and Rufus Bishop and Eldresses Ruth Landon and Asenath Clark governed jointly from 1821 until 1848, this remarkable stability at the apex of the sect's hierarchy does not appear to have been a particular strength. The written record reveals curiously little about these four leaders—a gap which may be attributable to the fact that they exemplified Meacham and Wright's goals of consensus leadership and conservative maintenance of the status quo *too* well. As individuals, none were able to provide the progressive vision and imagination necessary to prevent stagnation. It is hardly surprising, therefore, that a significant number of Shakers had less faith in their leaders.

One member who was often at odds with his Elders was Brother Philemon Stewart of New Lebanon. A devoted Believer, he was convinced that in some minor temporal affairs at least his judgment merited attention. In the 1830s, he served as overseer of the gardens and was especially interested in preventing soil exhaustion through the introduction of modern composting techniques. For four years he manured the kitchen garden almost single-handedly, with no help from either the Elders or the Deacons. Evidently, they did not share his concern over land use or were perhaps reluctant to alter familiar agricultural practices. But Brother Philemon refused to give up his crusade. In 1834, he and Brother Nicholas Bennet dug, without formal permission, a lime kiln for composting purposes "so that those who have not yet got their eyes open to see it to be necessary, may have help to get them open'd. There is a portion that say that Nicholas and I run away with strange notions. . . . Be this as it may, let things go on in general for six years to come as they have for six years past, and my word for it, if we do not set down with thankful hearts to a table furnished with roast pertatoes and salt."[32] Brother Philemon was plainly puzzled by the leaders' position. They encouraged members to do their utmost for the community, but then discouraged initiative. The key to the Elders' reluctance may well lie in Stewart's own assessment of his conduct: "I have had to press beyond the general feeling. . . . Perhaps zeal may have carried me beyond what was wisdom."[33] Shaker leaders were of necessity cautious about paying too much attention to brash, confident young Believers like Stewart, because without such care they ran the risk of undermining their own authority.

Some Believers went even further than Stewart in flouting their leaders' wishes, although such occurrences appear to have been rare. Brother Henry Baker of the New Lebanon Second Family created quite a stir there in the late 1820s by his "disorderly and refractory manner" in meeting, his "profane, abusive and threatening language," his destruction of church property, his connections with troublesome apostates, his frequent encouragement of young Shakers to rebellion, as well as by his habitual drunkenness.[34] Two Sisters from his Family testified that he

attended to no regular order but would often make frivolous errands into our rooms we believe for the purpose of venting his malicious intentions, sometimes he would say well you must look out for yourselves for I am a-going to tear the house down. . . . We would sometimes ask him what he talked so for he would say he wanted to make them turn him out of doors for then he should have a good hook upon them. . . . He said if he could only break the covenant he could overthrow the Shaker principle easy enough.[35]

By making his intentions so widely known within the Family, Baker did indeed invite excommunication. In June 1828, his Elders informed him that a meeting was to be held at which the subject of his future in the Society was to be discussed. He refused to attend, so the decision was made to "have no more union with him," a virtual decree of banishment.

Another Brother who caused dissension within his Family was William Evans of the Canaan, New York, Lower Family. An Englishman, he had toured most of the eastern communities before joining the Canaan Family in 1834. One of the Sisters there later wrote a vehement denunciation of his conduct in her history of the Family, calling him

. . . an aspiring would-be gentleman, who supposed he was called to be a leader somewhere or at least he meant to be ministry if boldness art or intrigue would give him that position and had those elements been the requisite qualifications he would have succeeded. He would not work, but was very willing to lay out and give orders to those who would work. He would take the manners book and bolt into the sisters rooms and give instruction because he had discovered someone in the act of laughing. . . . Many times the meetings were broken up in consequence of his personal lectures. He wanted to go into the kitchen and teach the sisters to cook and bake and would have succeeded had not the sisters rose en masse and threatened to leave the premises . . . as the brethren had not the power or lacked the disposition to get rid of him the sisters undertook the job . . . Hannah Briant and Harriet Sellick took him by the collar and put him into the street and threw his clothes after him.[36]

To the sorrow of the Lead Ministry, it was not just a few individuals such as Henry Baker and William Evans who were beginning to cause serious problems in the early nineteenth century. Entire Families, indeed whole communities, were combating the spirit of rebellion and disobedience. The community in Alfred, Maine, proved particularly vulnerable, having found it difficult to purge the lingering poison of Elder John Barns's ministration. In 1831, the Maine Ministry complained in a letter to Harvard: "It has fallen to our lot to have trouble upon affliction, in this place from the beginning, I believe beyond any people that ever was called by the gospel in this day of Christ's second manifestation."[37]

The dissension in Maine had arisen over the refusal of a few influential members to submit to the authority of the Elders. In September 1830, the Lead Ministry took the unprecedented step of placing the Maine Bishopric under the supervisional care of the New Hampshire Ministry, evidently because they felt that the problems in Maine exceeded the abilities of the local leaders.[38] The next summer the New Hampshire Ministry traveled to Maine "to establish good order and regulation in things spiritual and temporal."[39] They detailed the difficulties they encountered in a letter to the Lead Ministry in August.

The opposit party are trying to hold their ground, and are trying to gather the youth and children by telling them the Ministry and Elders are not worth minding, they are no better than they are &c.—this is principally from the females of the opposit party—and that little slick heritick, Isaac Coffin, is their Minister.[40]

Not until the 1855 appointment of Brother Otis Sawyer to the Ministry did the Maine communities again receive an Elder of the quality that the devotion of their true Believers had long merited. In October 1859, the Lead Ministry recognized his salutary influence by removing the Maine Bishopric from the superintendence of New Hampshire.[41]

The Lower Family in Canaan, New York, suffered from internal dissension of a similar kind, though the causes were different. Founded in 1816, the Family was first governed by Elder James Farnham who was, as one of his charges later recalled, ". . . a good preacher of the word but was not so good a calculator in temporal things. His organ of mirthfulness was largely developed which imparted a sort of levity to his character which was not beneficial in a family composed of the class of members with as little faith as this was." Apparently, rank and file members in this Family had begun to notice and bewail the diminished spiritual commitment of new converts. The dwindling number of faithful Brethren had given the Sisters an unfortunate sense of superiority, as an anonymous Sister later observed: "During that dark period of the first ten years they would certainly have failed had it not been for the exertion of the sisters. This the sisters were fully aware of and the effect was not salutary. It had a tendency to create a sort of independence and rather overbearing spirit . . . that when the scum was cast off and replaced with respectable brethren, it was injurious to the union of the family." [42]

The strained atmosphere within this Family was exacerbated by a string of temporal catastrophes, beginning with a fire in 1827 that destroyed the Dwelling and all the clothing, furnishings, and provisions within. Fortunately a new Dwelling was already near completion. But to offset losses caused by the fire, the Sisters had to begin the next year frantically raising teasels (a plant used in woolen manufacturing) for sale. In 1832, in an effort to increase the Family's income, the Lower Family entered into a partnership with the Upper Family to produce herbs for sale. Brother Aaron Gilbert was the Upper Family member entrusted with the business, and when he left to marry a young Sister in 1834, he took with him all available assets. Not until the 1840s was the Lower Family able to begin its financial and spiritual recovery from this series of disasters, and by that time its membership had fallen through apostasy to approximately twenty. [43]

Even at communities more fortunate than these, Shaker leaders had begun to observe behavior in their followers that alarmed them, causing a few to fear for the continued survival of Shaker principles. As early as 1819, the Canterbury Ministry reported a condition to New Lebanon that was widespread throughout the eastern villages: "We are fully satisfied that this craving earthly sense is quite too prevalent among us." [44] The root of this worrisome "craving earthly sense" lay, of course, in Shaker prosperity, which had been coincident with an influx of less than devoted converts who brought with them new tastes and ideas.

As a matter of long established principle, the Shakers had never sought monetary gain, even for the specific purpose of spreading the gospel. The Society's economic relationship with the World had developed gradually out of its domestic industries. The Shakers refused to sell goods of inferior quality for exorbitant prices. Only such items as were simple and perfect enough for their own use were judged fit for sale to outsiders. Profit was an alien notion, at least at first. The New Hampshire Ministry reiterated this position in 1835:

We think there is danger of believers getting the spirit of the world, which is a spirit of speculation, and of running too far, and of losing the rectitude which we profess to stand in—therefore we feel careful and watchful, and it is our labor to keep within bounds, and be as much disconnected from the world as possible. . . . There has been several applications to our Trustees to take shares in Factories, Rail roads &c. but we have never felt any liberty or disposition to have the consecrated property put into either.[45]

By pursuing such a course the Shakers sought to avoid the temptations of the contemporary money-mad, risk-taking investment market, whose activities helped spark devastating financial panics in 1837 and 1839, depressions from which even the partially insulated Believers were not immune.

The Shakers preferred to engage in legitimate occupations that earned them a spiritual reward first. If a monetary profit developed, that was merely a by-product. They preached diligence and economy as religious tenets that were crucial in the struggle to attain a heavenly standard of conduct, not because their pursuit would lead to earthly rewards. A Shaker poet summarized these principles neatly in a verse intended for the Deacons' instruction:

> Ye retail dealers, temporal heads,
> Who're cumber'd with much serving,
> Keep tally with your Shaker creeds,
> The better part securing . . .
> Be teachers of economy,
> And practicers of prudence,
> Fair emblems of sweet charity,
> Examples too of goodness.
> Be wide awake in industry,
> Have due respect to neatness;
> Let farm, and shops, and dwellings be
> True models of completeness.[46]

Close attention to these tenets led the Shakers to produce manufactures of praiseworthy quality and durability. It is ironic that a Society so little concerned with worldly possessions should have, by its dedication to otherworldly principles, created a standard of living for its members that did not always serve its own best interests. By the early nineteenth century, the eastern Shakers were unquestionably better off than their predecessors one or two decades before. The New Lebanon

Church Family was so prosperous by this time that it could afford to send $16,415 in cash and goods to the infant communities in the west between 1805 and 1815.[47] Certainly enough must have remained to maintain the Believers at New Lebanon in reasonable comfort.

Shaker income was derived from the sale of various home manufactures that differed from village to village. A good indication of the variety that one community (probably New Lebanon) could produce is provided in the following advertisement placed by a Philadelphia merchant in 1834.

Gideon Cox has just received from the Shaker Settlement. . . . a LARGE assortment of HOUSEKEEPING ARTICLES, CEDAR WARE, &c., among which are the following—viz. Baskets, sieves, brooms, whisks, butter prints, curled maple tubs, buckets, and coolers, butter bowls and trays, Boston rocking-chairs (assorted sizes and colors, spring-seat, rush bottom, and cane), patent sheep-skin mats and rugs (assorted sizes and colors), chair cushions, kitchen tables, step-ladders, clothes horses (all sizes), clothes lines, clothes hampers and baskets, wash-boards, wash stands and benches, lemon-squeezers, wheel-barrows, rolling-pins, pin-boards, barrel covers, knife boxes, cradles, &c. ALSO, Shaker herbs, garden seeds, Shaker diaper (very superior kind, warranted all linen), thread spools, carpet hammers, sugar hammers, rocking-horses.[48]

So successful were Shaker products in finding a market that by the late 1830s, the Hancock Church Family was making more than $8,500 a year on garden seeds alone.[49] Income on this scale naturally permitted a higher standard of living than Shakers had heretofore enjoyed, although simplicity continued a hallmark of the Society. By themselves, these improved conditions were not necessarily dangerous to the commitment of devout members, but an improved quality of life attracted many who were less than devout. As detailed above, the number of children in the eastern communities rose throughout the nineteenth century, a trend that increased the need for outside income without contributing greatly to its accumulation.

As living standards improved in the outside world, tastes changed and became more sophisticated. The Shakers found themselves in the awkward position of having to compromise some of their established principles in order to retain their customers. They began to produce items for sale that were deemed too fancy or elegant for their own domestic use. By the 1830s, the New Lebanon Church Family Deaconesses were buying such goods as silk for basket trimming, "casamere and welvet" for emeries, and French merino for sale cushions.[50] While the Believers were handling such fancy stuffs in their manufacture of sale items, they were elevating their own tastes to a more Worldly level. Some began to wonder why their religious laws pro-

hibited them from enjoying the elegancies of life that they had begun
to produce for the satisfaction of "World's People." Perhaps uncon-
sciously they began expecting the quality of their temporal lives to rise
in proportion to the quality of their wares.

As the Shakers became increasingly known for their products rather
than their principles, relations with the World became more open and
friendly. Each side ceased to fear the other because of their mutually
beneficial business relationship. By 1831, four members of the New
Lebanon Church Family could take a trip to the Rhode Island shore
for their health (a novelty for the Shakers, but a practice that became
increasingly common as the century progressed).[51] The financial prosperity that made such excursions possible also created a vast improvement in the quality of life at home. In 1826, the Hancock Church Family was sufficiently well endowed to invest $10,000 in the construction
of its own specially designed round stone dairy barn, and just four
years later its members were treated to a spacious new Dwelling at an
estimated cost of $8,000.[52] These construction projects drained the
Family's coffers, but in such prosperous times the Trustees anticipated
little difficulty in replenishing them.

Future developments did not justify their optimism. Elevated tastes
and expectations, together with an increasing number of minimally
productive young members, required an ever increasing income. To assure that income, the Shakers turned with reluctance to the Worldly
patent system to guarantee their profits from certain inventions and
improvements. Prior to the 1820s the Shakers had patented few of
their products, believing that gifts from God should be freely shared.
By 1828 however, an accommodation had to be made. The Lead Ministry in that year permitted a group of western Brethren to patent a
steam-powered water works—a step that Brother Thomas Hammond
believed to be the first of its kind.[53] This decision was not, however,
greeted with universal approbation by the Society's membership. In
1834, Brother Philemon Stewart recorded in his journal a discussion
about the advisability of patenting Brother Luther Copley's new water
wheel design: "As to the propriety of this step some of the Older Believers very much question, especially if it is to be carried into the monopolizing scheme—as some conjecture it will be; of this matter I cannot judge."[54]

This disagreement over the issue of Shaker patents highlights the
growing financial difficulties that troubled many of the eastern communities beginning in the late 1820s. It seems clear that tastes, especially among the young, had begun to exceed income. In such an atmo-

sphere, it is hardly surprising that the role of the Trustees became increasingly important in this period. Most of them dealt very well with the increased demands placed upon them, strictly adhering to the rules laid down for their conduct.

> And ye who keep the porch without,
> And deal in filthy lucre,
> 'Tis wise in you to look about
> And see that thieves don't pilfer.
> So use the consecrated grant
> To benefit the loaners,
> Not meanly glut your selfish wants,—
> Think, others toil as owners . . .
> And since you're representative
> For Shakers near and yonder,
> Pray do not just occasion give
> For spite, reproach or slander.[55]

But to the dismay of the Lead Ministry, not all Trustees successfully resisted the power and temptation of their positions. In 1835, a major shockwave ran throughout the Society when the defalcation and departure of Nathan Sharp, first Trustee at Union Village, Ohio, became known. Eldress Asenath Clark noted while at Watervliet, New York, "Our tribulation and labors concerning the western believers are very heavy at this time."[56] Sharp's apostasy was the culmination of a trend that had been developing for many years. Increasing numbers of rank and file members had come to believe that their leaders were not infallible. They accordingly came to wish for a voice in their selection.

The general atmosphere in the Society from the time of Mother Lucy Wright's death in 1821 to the Panic of 1837 was marked by greater strain and dissension, although a solid base of true commitment survived. Young Believers in many communities were exhibiting waning interest in all facets of Shaker life, particularly in worship. Isaac Youngs later observed of the mid-1820s: "Various other manners and forms were introduced occasionally, having the effect to enliven the sense and make the worship feel new and interesting."[57] In spite of these modifications, interest among the young dwindled, and confidence in the leaders was seriously undermined in many communities.

As early as 1822, Elder Nathaniel Deming of Hancock was forced to reprove his followers for their independent and unruly attitude.

The orders of God are given for your salvation and protection. There is a center of union for you to gather to in order to travel aright; there is a head placed in this family, and whatever you do do it in order, consult their minds in relation to your outward affairs. Set not your hearts upon worldly objects, but let this be your labor, to keep a spiritual sense. Do not feel to be independent. This may be a hard saying to some, that we cannot go the length of the dooryard without liberty. People in nature are taught to yield a degree of subordination to their parents untill they become of age, and then they are at liberty to live independent. But it is not so with believers.[58]

The independence and disobedience that triggered Deming's comments surfaced at other villages as well, and was often mentioned in local leaders' correspondence with the Lead Ministry. The situation at Pleasant Hill, Kentucky, in the years after 1825 was so dangerous that it created tremendous uncertainty within the Society as a whole, and may have helped spark the internal revival that began shortly thereafter.[59] Certainly the events at Pleasant Hill were cause for grave concern in the east and may well have mirrored developments at other communities. Elder Benjamin Youngs reported in an 1828 letter to New Lebanon marked "Confidential":

The condition of P. Hill is not to be despaired of, although it is indeed deplorable to what it was 5 or 6 years ago. The Society then was strong handed, . . . industrious, wealthy and prosperous, but the concealed misery and misfortune was that they were very selfish, that they considered themselves superior in gifts and talents; in order and arrangements. . . . The aspiring to leads, and the heretical,—the fault finders and ism hunters found subjects aplenty to speculate, to reason and to debate upon. . . . Infidelity, pride, presumption, disorder and confusion took deep root—the contagion spread and grew into a plague. Scarcely an Elder or a Deacon but what became contaminated, or as they now call it "smoked." "Away with the Elders and Deacons but such as are of the people's own choosing" became the pretty general sense . . . "away with the Ministry, down with priestcraft—let the people be liberated from bondage and be free to judge and act for themselves.[60]

This independent tendency may well have been fostered by the triumph of Jacksonian democracy in the World, as well as by the increasing popularity of such nonreligious reform movements as Robert Owen's socialism. These new ideas were to a certain extent imported into the Society, a development that was of considerable concern to the Lead Ministry. In 1829, they issued a "Circular Epistle" that warned all the communities about the dangers of this preoccupation with the outside world:

Considering the extent to which the gospel has already been spread, the many and various characters that are included in the profession of our faith, the boasted light and liberty that at this age greatly abounds among mankind, and with which the sense and feelings of many who are admitted among us are very full, and considering that it is natural for such to desire to be teachers, and to mingle their treasures of worldly wisdom with the self-denying and mortifying doctrines of the cross—we would ask, what security have we against all fear of degeneracy on the side of popularity and a pretended increase?[61]

The problems outlined in this "epistle" helped to spark a brief internal revival that spread throughout the eastern communities beginning in the spring of 1827. It is difficult to determine whether or not the agitation for the democratization of Shaker government from below had any direct connection with this revival. It is clear that the Society was riddled with lukewarm members who were beginning to dilute the purity of Shaker beliefs. This real "baptism of fire," as Isaac Youngs called it, did have "the effect to purge out the unfaithful," and certainly derived some of its energy from the spate of evangelical revivals then current in the World, but the role of the leaders in directing the revival is problematical.[62] At any rate, its impact was beneficial.

Sister Elizabeth Lovegrove, asked by her Elders at New Lebanon to keep a journal of the revival, observed happily in April 1827:

> O what a change is now affected
> Humiliation does abound
> For great big I is now rejected
> Do pray for me is the general sound.[63]

Brother William Fitch was one of the lukewarm Believers who was brought to a fuller commitment to the faith as a result of this revival. In Family meeting he "stepped out and said he felt that he had been under the bufitings of satan, . . . that his greatest loss was in not being willing to receive admonitions when he realy needed it, that he had tried to crook and turn every way to make his Elders think that he was on good ground, when he knew he was not, he then kneeled down and heartily begged that all would pray for him."[64]

The spirit of the Believers in the eastern villages improved markedly during this revival, at times echoing in liveliness and fervor the days of the first gathering. In April, Sister Elizabeth recorded:

Each one sung what they felt the most gift in, and every song was full of love; David seemed to be devoted to helping the youth, for every time I saw him he had hold of some one or other of them by the hand leading them on to God; Isaac Youngs had little James in his arms with his little hands clinched fast round his neck marching round, he said that he felt very unwell and hardly able to come to meeting when he came, but now he felt like another creature.[65]

By diverting attention from the World and its spirit, the 1827 revival seemed for a brief period to eliminate the worries of the preceding decades. Reverend Moses Hallock of Canton, Connecticut, noted in July

1827: "The present year is, in many places, remarkable for revivals of religion. The hopeful converts within a few months in the county of Berkshire are at least fifteen hundred."[66] The revival among the Shakers encouraged some New Englanders, already seeking further light, to join the sect. In March 1827, the New Hampshire Ministry reported to New Lebanon:

As to the world of mankind around us . . . light and conviction increases, and many are much alarmed and say what is the matter, what is among the Shakers? Some say they believe the Millenial, or day of judgment has come or is near at hand—The way seems to be broke, they flock to our meetings to see and to hear the testimony, so that there is not room for believers to perform their worship. The world as well as believers both here and at Canterbury begin to talk about building larger Meetinghouses—As to the increase of believers, they gather as fast as we can protect and take care of them.[67]

The excitement was destined to wane, and as it did tensions within the Society resurfaced. In spite of the brief spiritual reawakening provided by the revival, the fundamental character of the membership had not been substantially altered. Moreover, it was difficult for many Believers to maintain their level of interest after the fervor had died down. The primary issue of unquestioning obedience to the leaders was still unresolved. Then, in the mid-1830s, a still more divisive issue arose that destroyed whatever superficial accord the 1827 revival had achieved.

At that time, some members became interested in the teachings of a dietary reformer by the name of Sylvester Graham who advocated a simple, meatless diet to control, among other things, sexual impulses in young men. The Shakers had only recently abandoned the practice of "dram drinking" and were perhaps ready for further renunciation of earthly pleasures.[68] Many younger Believers felt that God had decided to reveal new truths to the "World's People" that they would do well to emulate. Internal discussion of phrenology and the water cure system then popular in the outside world also became common. But food concerned every member, and evidently all felt free to express an opinion. Without clear divinely inspired instructions, or perhaps due to a difference of opinion among themselves, the Lead Ministry felt unsure about establishing any definite rules. Instead, decisions about diet were left up to the individual members, an unprecedented departure from previous practice. The inability of the Lead Ministry to determine an appropriate course of action in this case represents the first major failure for the Society's system of consensus government. The ensuing discussion raged for many years.

In the Society's early history, the Shakers had suffered from such extreme poverty that their tables were seldom fully laden. When more prosperous days arrived their diet improved, until food became one of their few bodily indulgences. By the 1830s, the Believers were eating very well indeed, as Brother Ephraim Prentiss, a Grahamite, scornfully recorded:

breakfast: beef, pork, mutton or fish, most generally fried with a plenty of grease, mostly hogs fat, with bread and potatoes—Next followed bread and butter and pies of various kinds from plain pumpkin to the high seasoned mince pie, cakes of different kinds, milk and butter toasts and pancakes drenched in butter were common things—But these various articles were given at different times for a change—Fish, clambs, chicken eggs, rich gravies, honey, all in their turn, and according to the season.

dinner: . . . the various kinds of animal food boiled, roasted, baked or fried, with vegetables as usual with other varieties—pickled cucumbers, peppers, rich applesauce, and various other condiments &c.

supper: . . . cold meat, bread, butter, cheese, milk and tea and more or less of the above-mentioned articles as condiments were brought on at every meal.[69]

A journal kept by Brother John DeWitt of New Lebanon records a typical meal: "The Brethren go to mowing in the swamp. And Elder Ebenezer, Deacon Stephen, Elder Sister, Lydia, Electa and Samantha go and carry their dinner to them, which was: bread and butter, pye, strawberry sauce, fried potatoes, fresh meat, stewed beans and green tea sweetened with loaf sugar provided by the Ministry."[70]

Seasonal treats that Prentiss described so disdainfully did much to enliven the comparative monotony of the Shaker diet. In winter, a typical Family would usually have two or three meals of fresh ocean fish; in spring, a few meals of shad from the Hudson River, with occasional meals of clams and oysters throughout the year. Once in a great while, Carolina sweet potatoes were served.[71] But the most festive day of the year as far as food was concerned occurred in early summer. "We have our yearly shortcake this morning, strawberries and milk for dinner and the remainder of the strawberry cake for supper."[72]

This ample and occasionally indulgent fare was typical throughout the country and helped make dyspepsia, or indigestion, a national complaint. In the 1830s many Americans involved in the temperance movement expanded their reforming efforts to include food as well as drink, hoping to modify national taste along more healthy lines. These reformers were concerned about the rapid pace of change in the United States during these years—change that seemed to undermine the traditional standards and social constraints provided by stable families, communities, and churches. As the nation began to feel the effects of industrialization and urbanization, many Americans moved away from these standards both geographically and spiritually. The temperance and dietary reform movements, among many others current at the time, were designed to internalize social constraints, especially among the young.

Sylvester Graham, an initiator of this movement and inventor of the original Graham cracker, was a Presbyterian minister and an agent for the Pennsylvania Temperance Society. After moving to Philadelphia in 1830, he expanded his standard temperance lectures to include advice on the "science of human life," a regimen that added sexual chastity and vegetarian diet to more traditional approaches. His prescribed diet abolished the use of such stimulants as tea and coffee and emphasized the use of coarsely ground and unbolted grains in baking. He asserted that "all kinds of stimulating and heating substances, high-seasoned food, rich dishes, the free use of flesh, and even the excess of aliment . . . increase the concupiscent excitability and sensibility of the genital organs."[73] He promised that all who adopted his program could "so subdue their sexual propensity, as to be able to abstain from connubial commerce, and preserve entire chastity of body, for several months in succession, without the least inconvenience."[74] The appeal such a promise must have had for young Shakers seeking ways to reduce sexual tension is obvious.

Graham's teachings were extremely popular throughout the northeast beginning in the early 1830s, and Grahamite boarding houses and hotels sprang up in many cities and rural health resorts. Certainly the Shakers could not have been wholly ignorant of his ideas, but it is impossible to determine when they first became seriously interested in adopting some of his practices. Shaker records indicate that Brother Garret K. Lawrence, a New Lebanon Church Family physician, was among the first to introduce Graham's ideas to the Society. By 1835, members of the Harvard community were already experimenting with some of his recommendations. Brother Philemon Stewart of New Lebanon reported in the fall of that year:

We weakly folks begin to talk about living an abstemious life, as what they do at Harvard, that is eat no meat, eat no grease of any kind, no cheese, have your milk half water. The principal food is bread made of wheat ground without bolting, your drink cold water, no use of tobacco in any way, I commenced this morning. Some of the Sisters have partly commenced, tho' a little afraid of it.[75]

The popularity of this new regimen is indicated by its frequent mention in the diaries and journals of the period. Giles Avery of New Lebanon recorded on September 7, 1835, "We have a reading meeting this evening. The subject is Graham's work on human life and health accompanied by prescribed dietetic regimen." On the 15th, he noted:

"There are quite a number added to the Graham list, or at least have forsaken their tea and coffee; there are 22 on the male side and half that number on the female side." [76] The new practices spread rapidly to other communities as well.

The New Hampshire Ministry reported to New Lebanon in January 1836 that their "communications relative to the use of animal food, dieting, temperance, economy &c." had gathered many adherents. "The effect is good," they wrote, "altho there has been some excitement, but as there is no command or compulsion in the case . . . there is no cause of complaint. However, this work of temperance progresses; as we understand there are between 30 and 40 in the Church who do not drink Tea, Coffee nor Chorkolate, but have become waterites. Graham bread & the like seem to be preferred by many, so there is already considerable saving in meat, cider, tea, coffee &c." [77]

In the fall of 1835, the Lead Ministry, unwilling to issue a blanket regulation either supporting or condemning the consumption of meat, had decided to let each member make up his or her own mind on the subject, a curious step given previous Shaker adherence to the principle of communal uniformity. On September 6, after having dismissed the children from the New Lebanon Church Family meeting, the Ministry decreed: "If some had a mind to try a little milder manner of diet to eat less meat and drink less tea not to have it split the union." [78] Sadly, their reluctance or inability to take a firm stand one way or the other encouraged all members to express their own ideas, a situation that steadily worsened during the mid-1830s and produced the very disunion the leaders had feared.

When Graham's ideas first became known within the Society, many young Shakers, especially among the Brethren, seized on them as a new sort of fad—one that might help defuse the sexual tension that was growing in every Family as the number of young Believers increased. Certainly some of the members who experimented with Grahamism were led to do so as a result of peer pressure. An entry in Brother Aaron Bill's journal for September 12, 1835 suggests such a situation.

There has been a book read in the family that was put out by one Graham upon dieting and some of the family are trying to follow him in part, ie to eat bran bread clear potatoe tomatoes &c. and drink milk and water but not tea meat nor butter but Oh how their mouths water to see the fine beefsteak come on and to see the faithful eat of the good of the land. [79]

After the initial exuberance had subsided, many members no doubt missed their fried doughnuts, broiled beefsteaks, and buttered pancakes and reverted to previous gustatory habits. By 1836 the number of dedicated Grahamites had begun to dwindle. As Brother John DeWitt recorded in his Memo Book: "June 20, 1836—23 of the Brethren has united themselves to the vegitable diet for a season. September 3, 1836—The Brethren has concluded to try the old manner of diet, eating meat &c." [80] The problems such indecisiveness caused were made plain in another entry: "It is concluded to have our tables set alike and to make no difference on account of such as wish to eat vegitable food. The change is made on account of the burden it brings upon the cooks to accommodate so many tastes." [81] In this regard, it is interesting to note that Sisters were less likely to adopt vegetarianism than Brethren, perhaps because they were less concerned about suppressing sexuality or realized the extra work that would follow if the regime were adopted.

Because the Lead Ministry had made no definitive decision about Grahamism, discussion among the Believers was rampant and led to tremendous disagreement. As Isaac Youngs later observed:

People have ran very wild on this subject, and are of two parties, going to great extremes in opposite directions; the one discarding all indulgence of appetite, or rich or delicious or high seasoned food, all flesh meat, all grease, butter &c. confining themselves to brown bread, or unbolted flour, and rejecting the whole train of variety, and sorts of animal food; the other observing no particular restriction, but to eat what suits best, unless they know by experience that it injures their health; saying their own appetite is their best rule and judge. [82]

Shaker opponents of Grahamism certainly were dubious about its areligious philosophy, its denigration of spiritual revelation, and its complete reliance on individual as opposed to community control. But perhaps the crux of the issue involved the origin, and not the substance of these new ideas. Had they sprung from within the Society, opposition would probably not have been so vocal. As one Shaker commentator noted: "It appears to be the prevailing sense of some, that it is a dishonor to Believers to receive instruction from those who are of the world. But I would ask, is it degrading to the dignity of a good Believer to receive virtuous instruction from the wisdom of the world, merely because the instructors are of the world? Are we not in daily practice of receiving from the world temporal benefits and useful improvements?" [83]

Perhaps the most harmful disagreement engendered by the Grahamite controversy developed in the Watervliet Church Family between Elder Freegift Wells and the Boys' Caretaker, Brother Ephraim Prentiss. Prentiss was one of the most avid and outspoken Grahamites within the Society, arguing that a vegetable diet had caused behavior changes in his youthful charges that would be an improvement for adult Believers as well. Before the dietary change, he claimed that the boys "were cross and peevish, could not bear with one another . . . were sickly

[and] very troublesome at night, talking in their sleep, restless, fever-ish, wanting a great deal of drink, much addicted to wetting their beds . . . young as they were, their stimulating food excited and brought into action those base propensities which boys of their age ought never to feel—In short, their venereal excitements and filthy indulgences caused me much tribulation." [84]

After Prentiss gradually weaned the boys from their diet of meat, grease, cheese, butter, and milk, he claimed a wonderful improvement in their attitude and behavior. "Their sores have healed up, their hu-mors have dried up and disappeared, their headaches have ceased, their fevers gone and their urinary weakness entirely cured; that fero-cious fighting spirit . . . seems to have entirely vanished away. . . . [I] found to my great satisfaction that the indulgence of those base pro-pensities . . . has entirely disappeared. . . . In short, they are the most peaceable and happy little company of boys I ever saw." [85] Prentiss at-tempted to use this evidence to lobby in his Family for a full commit-ment to Grahamism by all members, even carrying his case all the way to the Lead Ministry. But he lacked the support of a key individual: his Elder, Freegift Wells.

Wells was convinced that Prentiss was merely a fanatic trying to make a name for himself. He reasoned that since the Shakers had eaten animal food from the beginning, the practice should continue. After all, God presumably had ample reason for making animals fit for hu-man consumption. Wells assumed that any attempt by a rank and file member to change the way that Believers traditionally lived was the Devil's work, perpetrated by young Believers who obviously cared little for the Society's principles of humility and obedience. As he later wrote: "I was led into the knowledge of the doings of a certain care-taker of boys in this Family, who restrained his boys altogether beyond the bounds of reason, and would not suffer them to partake of food and nourishment which the Ministry and Elders desired and requested they might have. But he stuck to his Grahamism, to the loss of much union with the Ministry and Elders." [86]

Though this disagreement created a severe rift between Wells and Prentiss, it had a deleterious effect on other relationships within the sect as well. Some other members at New Lebanon also viewed Wells's position and his influence on Family life at Watervliet with scorn. Brother Garret Lawrence wrote to Brother Isaac Youngs in 1834 to warn him about the risks of prolonging his visit there.

I plainly see by your . . . bill of table fare that the good folks at Watervliet are still pursuing the same track that they have pursued for many a year. . . . I speak advisedly and as one who having had experience and you may depend upon the truth of what I say. Should you be sick or in distress they would spare no pains to throw their chains of kindness around you and thus take advantage of your helpless situation. Thus all around you looks fair, and like comfort and happiness, while sugar and fine flour and fish and *flesh* is heaped upon the table. . . . *But*, if you should once conclude to *stay there*, and should really probe their souls and discover their *real principles*, they would tell you to *crucify the flesh*. . . . Yea, you would even find the Elder who seems so mild and clever . . . to be an experienced *Miller* who knows how to turn the screws *as quietly*, till not a grain shall pass the grinders uncracked and all the bran is separate from the flour. And like enough he would so completely subdue you that even of your own accord you would sing about your golden chains. . . . But just return here to the mountains of Lebanon and listen to the happifying doctrines that are held forth.[87]

Wells himself was greatly alarmed at the inability of the Lead Ministry to deal effectively with this internal crisis. He criticized Elder Rufus Bishop in particular for his softheartedness. According to Wells, Elder Rufus "would not even kill a musqueto when they lit upon his hand, and went to sucking his blood, but would wait and let them fill their bellies, and then carefully brush them off. This remarkable sympathetic instinct rendered him very easy of access by ambitious fanatics."[88] The disunion at Watervliet was viewed by the Ministry with grave concern and ultimately both Wells and Prentiss were transferred to other communities.[89] But the source of the problem remained, and engendered debate and dissent within the sect well into the 1840s and beyond.

One of the advantages of vegetarianism found in at least a few accounts was the reduced cost of food, a consideration that perhaps weakened the opposition of some leaders who might otherwise have been skeptical. By the 1830s, both the nation and the Society were experiencing hard economic times. It was also a time of considerable illness, with cholera epidemics in Worldly cities and the death of many who had been among the first generation of converts to the faith. Younger Shakers suddenly began to realize that the "living witnesses" who had known Mother Ann were disappearing. In 1834, Elder Sister Olive Spencer and Sister Selah Draper of the New Lebanon Church Family died within a twenty-four hour period, the first time in twenty years that two deaths had occurred so close together.[90]

In addition, the weather during these years had been abysmal. On May 15, 1834, the thermometer had read 22° in the early morning, one inch of snow had fallen, and most of the fruit trees in the New Lebanon area had lost their blossoms. Similar storms had struck much of the northeast. It is likely that part of Grahamism's popularity during these years was directly connected to this and subsequent devastating harvests. In October 1834, Philemon Stewart prophesied:

We are like to know what it is to live a good degree lower as to our victuals, for there has been no fruit of any kind worth mentioning this season; our pork is also pretty much gone, and the Sisters think we shall have to eat our pertatoe without much fat. I understand by the Sisters that we have only 12 lb. of butter now before hand that has been laid down. And our milk is daily decreasing and will be very short thro' the winter.[91]

These hard times, and the declining standard of living they necessitated, led many lukewarm Believers to leave the faith seeking greater financial security in the World. During the late 1830s a large outflow of members shocked the faithful throughout the Society. Most of those who left were young men at the threshhold of their most productive years. The Society's tenets do not appear to have appealed more to women than men. The greater ease with which the latter could provide for themselves in the World doubtless accounts for much of the difference between the male and female apostasy rates. At New Lebanon in particular the problem was severe, as dozens of young members, usually Brethren, chose to leave. The apostasy rate in the Church Family as a whole reached 9.1 percent during the 1830s; the rate for the Brethren was 15.9 percent (see Appendix A.2).

In August 1835, Reuben Reed and Rufus Hinkley left for the World, the latter going to New York City to make a living enacting Shaker worship on the stage.[92] In September of the same year, Josephus Seeley and Israel Knight departed.[93] Family journals record similar events almost weekly during this period, with most writers expressing their concern very plainly. Elisha Blakeman commented in June 1836: "A poor LOST SOUL—Charles D. Knight made the fatal choice to abscond from us. He was about 17 years of age, just entering the youthful stage of life. awful!! awful!!! awful!!!!!!!!!!!"[94]

This stream of backsliders grew larger into the late 1830s, prompting Isaac Youngs to ask: "What in the name of reason does it mean that so many are going off nowadays???!!! Is there none of the younger part that will abide & be good for something—are we indeed unable to raise any children or youth among us?"[95] Because most of these apostates were young people who had donated nothing to the "joint interest," the cash and clothing given them at their departure represented a considerable drain on their Families' finances. A vicious circle developed: every apostasy diminished Family resources, lowering the standard of living for those remaining faithful, and inducing more members to leave.

Throughout the remainder of the 1830s, this grave situation continued. The growing season of 1837 was nearly as bad as that of 1834, as very dry weather followed torrential summer rains, in spite of the Shakers' prayers. By December, affairs at New Lebanon had reached such a critical state that the Church Family Deacons called a Family meeting to explain the position they found themselves in.

The long talked of hard times at length we have to feel quite seriously. Little or no sales for manufacture, grain extremely high $2 per bushel for wheat is common price. Corn & Rye accordingly. Money very scarce. Many failures in Banks on which we have taken money &c. &c. Therefore considering all these things, the Deacons wanted to come & inform the family how the case was, that there might be consideration in relation to getting unnecessary things.[96]

Just five days after this momentous meeting, Isaac Youngs returned from a visit to Watervliet, New York, bringing with him "many wonderful tidings of the celestial world."[97] The celebrated revival known as "Mother's Work" had begun, and at the most opportune time. At a time when earthly life was so beset with trials, the Shakers were forcibly reminded that their future lay in the spirit world. In the midst of their difficulties, they looked to heaven for relief, and plunged into a paroxysm of religious enthusiasm that rivaled the last decades of the eighteenth century in its intensity. Temporal cares were, for a time at least, put aside.

New Lebanon, New York, Second Family, circa 1880. This view shows a secondary road running between a series of workshops. These large, plain, well-built clapboard structures are typical of Shaker architecture.

Brother Charles Greaves (1828–1916) of New Lebanon, New York, with his woodworking tools. The beard Brother Charles exhibits is one example of the relaxation of Shaker rules during the last half of the nineteenth century. Before the 1880s, Brethren had been forbidden to grow beards, in spite of considerable lobbying in their favor on the part of rank and file members.

Courtesy of Hancock Shaker Village, Inc., Pittsfield, Massachusetts.

Elder Henry Blinn (1824–1905) of Canterbury, New Hampshire, with his bees. Elder Henry, who became a Believer at the age of fourteen, was known throughout the Society for his varied temporal skills. He served his community as author, editor, printer, teacher, botanist, dentist, blacksmith, woodworker, and cartographer. He also held the honored positions of Family and Ministry Elder.

Courtesy of The Shaker Museum, Old Chatham, New York, No. 6241.

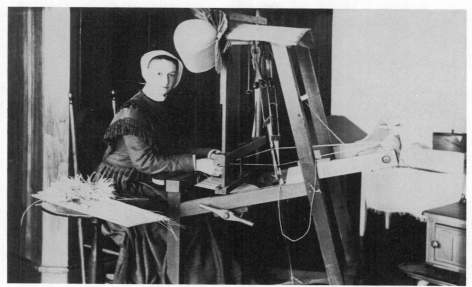

Sister Bertha Mansfield (1862–?) of Canterbury, New Hampshire, at her loom. Sister Bertha is weaving a uniquely Shaker "fabric" with a cotton warp and a weft composed of strips of poplar. This "poplar cloth" was fashioned by the Sisters into needle books and sewing boxes that commanded a ready market in the World.

Courtesy of private collection.

Brother Nehemiah White (1823–1887) of Canterbury, New Hampshire, with the boys he supervised as Caretaker. As Caretaker, Brother Nehemiah took charge of these boys both at work and at play, and may have had a hand in their education as well. If these boys were typical of the children brought up in Shaker villages, perhaps only one would convert on reaching adulthood.

Courtesy of Charles Thompson, Canterbury, New Hampshire.

The Shakers emphasized a strong common school education for the children placed in their care. Youngsters from the World also attended Shaker schools in many communities, so religious instruction was generally avoided. Innovative teaching aids, carefully selected Worldly textbooks, and dedicated instructors made Shaker schools among the best in the northeast.

Courtesy of The Shaker Museum, Old Chatham, N.Y., No. 4398.

Ironing room in the North Family laundry, New Lebanon, New York. Laundry work was rotated among all Sisters, typically on a monthly schedule, but involved other community members as well. Here young girls carry hot irons from the stove, and in the background, Brother Daniel Offord (1843–1911) presses flat pieces. Brethren were often assigned to assist Sisters with such heavy work.

Courtesy of The Shaker Museum, Old Chatham, New York, No. 7466.

Sisters Mary Hazard (1811–1899), Emma Neale (1847–1943), and Augusta Stone (1837–1909), of New Lebanon, New York, in one of the community's sewing rooms. Note the prominence of the sewing machine. Most of the eastern communities purchased such machines in the 1850s and 1860s, both to speed up clothing production and to assist in a variety of sales industries.

Courtesy of The Shaker Museum, Old Chatham, New York, No. 6651.

Sister Martha Burger (1853–1926) of New Lebanon, New York, tending the community's "Fancy Goods Store." In spite of internal opposition, most communities opened such souvenir shops beginning in the 1850s to cater to the increasing tourist trade. In such stores, visitors could purchase postcards, candy, pincushions, dolls, feather dusters, pen wipers, and sewing baskets.

Sisters Maria Doane (1833–1892), Elvira Hulett (1805–1895), and Sophia Helfrich (1834–?) of Hancock, Massachusetts, visiting Niagara Falls with Worldly friends. After 1850, increasing numbers of Believers traveled in the World and enjoyed leisure activities that had previously been forbidden.

Courtesy of Hancock Shaker Village, Inc., Pittsfield, Massachusetts.

Brother Rufus Crosman (1798–1891), Sister Dolly Sexton (1776–1884), and four unidentified children of the New Lebanon, New York, Church Family. By 1884, when this photograph was taken, the membership of the eastern villages was composed predominately of the elderly and the young.

Courtesy of Hancock Shaker Village, Pittsfield, Massachusetts.

The Sabbathday Lake, Maine, Church Family in meeting on September 20, 1885. This photograph, taken by the official photographer of the Poland Spring House, a well-known resort hotel near the community, is the only known depiction of an actual Shaker meeting. By this time, Shakers in most of the eastern villages had ceased the "laboring" or ritual dancing that had characterized their worship since the eighteenth century.

Collection of the United Society of Shakers, Sabbathday Lake, Maine.

7

Whirlwind, Earthquake and Fire
(1837-1844)

By the late 1830s, the Society had reached a level of spiritual, social, and economic crisis unparalleled in its history. The revival known as "Mother's Work" was a religious response to deeply felt insecurities, but also served crucial social and organizational needs as well. The excitement of "Mother's Work" was viewed by devout Believers as a necessary antidote to the insidious spiritual torpor that had crept into the Society beginning during the 1810s and 1820s. Giles Avery of New Lebanon complained in 1835, "We have meeting at home among ourselves and it is so dull that one would scarcely know whether we were trying to serve God or something else."[1]

The condition Avery lamented had several causes. The economic difficulties of the 1830s compounded demographic imbalances that had been developing for many years. Since the 1810s, the leadership pool in most communities had shrunk to dangerous levels (see Appendix B.4), but the number of leaders required remained constant. The quality of leadership therefore had declined noticeably. By the 1830s, problems such as those that affected the Maine Bishopric had become increasingly common. Even the Lead Ministry, since it lacked a single, dominant leader, had proven unable to deal with the Grahamite crisis effectively.

The growing proportion of children and young people in the villages during the 1820s and 1830s exacerbated these weaknesses. By 1830 the proportion of children under fifteen in the eastern communities had reached 15.2 percent, and the proportion of young adults aged fifteen to twenty-nine had increased even more dramatically to 26.7 percent (see Appendixes B.5 and C.1-C.11). Isaac Youngs concluded that the spiritual decay he observed in these years had arisen "in consequence of the ingathering of youth and children and those that had never known [Mother Ann] on earth, nor truly understood her gospel."[2]

It had become clear to most leaders by the late 1830s that an increasing number of members who had never experienced the crucible of a revival were undermining the purity of the faith. The solution was obvious. As Brother Thomas Hammond of Harvard asserted, "We should always need more or less of the whirlwind, earthquake and fire, as long as there was anything in us that was contrary to the order of God."[3] "Mother's Work" was to serve as this necessary agent of purification. The revival served two purposes that occasionally came into conflict. Leaders and many older members viewed it as a way to correct errant behavior and return to traditional spiritual standards, but young members typically seized upon its enthusiastic and charismatic features.

This new wave of spirit manifestations began in the Girls' Order at Watervliet, New York, a community badly riven by the vegetarian controversy several years earlier. As news of the "gifts" traveled from village to village, the interest among Believers quickly reached a fever pitch and manifestations spread rapidly. Sister Elizabeth Lovegrove of New Lebanon recorded in her *Dye House Journal* periodic reports of the progress of the "work." "Nov. 26, 1837—We attend to the reading of some remarkable visions seen by some of the Young believers at Watervliet, which was very interesting. Jan. 5, 1838—We receive inteligence from Watervliet that the visions continue. Jan. 6, 1838—Great anxiety about the visions, but no way at present to get any information."[4]

The immediate response of the New Lebanon Believers was overwhelmingly positive. Many had long been waiting for just such an awakening. For the first time in many years, physical "gifts" overwhelmed members outside of meetings, and with such regularity as to disrupt the prescribed daily routine. In 1838, the Lead Ministry reported this phenomenon in a letter to South Union:

Many have become Shakers indeed which in times past hardly deserved the name of a Shaker at all! But now they shake wherever they go; whether at work, or at Table! and sometimes their shaking is so violent that it is nearly impossible to get any food into their mouths, and they have to leave the table without eating. . . . It is truly a wonderful day. . . . Numbers who have been spiritually dead for many years, have been raised to life, and are now living souls in the house of God.[5]

Visions and messages from the spirit world, many from Mother Ann herself, inundated the Believers at Watervliet and New Lebanon during the winter of 1837–1838. As soon as knowledge of these goings-on reached other villages the gifts were quickly duplicated. In November 1837, Elder Grove Wright reported from Enfield, Connecticut:

I can truly say the brethren and sisters in this place have received and entered into the present gift beyond yea far beyond what I could have expected for the time. It truly appears like one of the greatest miracles to see and sense the change which has already been effected. Since the latter rains, and those refreshing showers from heaven descended, the drooping spirits have revived, and the withered plants spring up, and as it were, the dry forest begins to bud and blossom, and to leap for joy.[6]

By January 1838, the revival had spread to the communities in northern New England, as the New Hampshire Ministry reported to New Lebanon: "We perceive quite a change already in the sense and travel of Believers. They are more free, simple, watchful and obedient."[7] The revival had evidently reached all the eastern communities by early the next year, extending even to Groveland in western New York. In February 1839, the New Hampshire Ministry wrote the Groveland Ministry expressing their hopes for the future.

We are thankful to learn that the wonderful and marvelous work of God is so universal among the different Societies of Believers. From all the Societies as far as our knowledge extends we derive the same information; and if it has the same effect as with us, which we do not doubt, in strengthening the weak and confirming the strong, in establishing souls in Mother's gospel, and inculcating principles of humility, subordination and obedience, the good effect of this great and marvelous work will be seen, felt and realized by all Believers.[8]

How the various manifestations traveled from community to community is, of course, difficult to determine. Believers throughout the northeast were anxious to keep up with whatever was occurring at Watervliet and New Lebanon, which together comprised the first Bishopric under the direct control of the Lead Ministry. Whenever news of a new gift arrived from there, members were quick to emulate it. In a letter to Brother Seth Wells of New Lebanon, the New Hampshire Ministry may well have described just such a process. "The gifts of visions, turning, the great effusion of new songs and manners of labor have in a great measure subsided among us for the present, but the other gifts and graces abound. The same operations of bowing, jerking &c. &c. which we witnessed at New Lebanon now prevail among us."[9] It is readily understandable that the members at Canterbury should so quickly have aligned themselves with practices at New Lebanon. After all, news from that source was regarded as divine instruction.

Shaker leaders made the purpose of the revival no secret. Countless inspired messages, often received by instruments who were themselves leaders, informed the Believers just what was expected of them. Visionists at Hancock recorded in 1840:

Thus have her younger children, who never saw her face,
While she was in the body and moving in this place,
Receiv'd her pure instructions, monitions, and have heard,
As did her elder children, their precious Mother's word.[10]

The reaction was, at least at first, all that could have been hoped. Isaac Youngs, who dated the beginning of his "real travel heavenward" from 1837, later observed: "These gifts and exercises attracted great attention and captivated the feelings of the whole assembly. Those inclined to infidelity began to look with surprise and feel confounded in their natural wisdom. Evil workers were alarmed, they saw and felt something there which they feared would search them out."[11] Believers throughout the Society shared Youngs's conviction that the revival was indeed the work of God. The Church Family Elders at Sabbathday Lake, Maine, reported to their Ministry in January 1838: "We have been striving to persevere in the spirit and power of the revival, and we are still laboring to increase in it, and we have a very striking evidence that the present blessed gift is of God, because it serves to unite us more strongly together in the bonds of gospel Love & we can sensibly feel that we have found a measure of increase in love, in life, and in charity."[12]

Much to the delight of all Shakers, this fervor and activity engendered an increased interest in the sect on the part of outsiders. In January 1839, the New Hampshire Ministry reported that between sixty and seventy people had lately joined at Canterbury, and the Shirley and Harvard communities reported a combined increase of between thirty and forty members. In spite of the fact that most of these new members were children, the Shakers had high hopes that this influx would secure the Society's future.[13] This knowledge acted as a tonic for leaders and followers alike.

Many experienced a rekindling of their commitment. In 1843, Hancock's Elder Grove Wright testified:

In the late manifestations of the marvellous outpouring of the mighty power of God, displayed in diverse ways by means of God's own choosing, and extending thru out Zion on earth for some years past, I can truly say I am a full believer. I have been an eye, ear and heart feeling witness of the same in very many instances, and can truly bear witness that it can be no other than the mighty power of God, sent forth in mercy for the further increase of His Zion on earth.[14]

One of the members under his supervision, Brother George Wollison, was equally affected. "I have prayed with all my heart to be a partaker of the present gift. . . . Some may say, I guess George is going to be religious now, and so I am; for the judgments of God will soon come upon us if we do not wake up and labor for the power of God—this is my determination." [15]

By early 1838 the work of purification had begun, but only after it had received the full support of the Lead Ministry, comprised in these years of Elders Ebenezer and Rufus Bishop and Eldresses Ruth Landon and Asenath Clark. There is evidence that at least some members were surprised by the turn the revival took in the early months of 1838, after these leaders became actively involved in its supervision. Apparently, most Shakers expected the revival to follow a typical pattern, punctuated by physical "gifts," new songs, manners of worship, and a generally frenzied emotional atmosphere. Although these characteristics of the earliest phase of the revival did indeed survive, the tone of the messages and "gifts" changed markedly.

Isaac Youngs later recorded:

After a few months' suspense, the work . . . broke forth in the Church, tho' it came different from what was looked for. It came in solemn messages . . . in the name of our heavenly Parents, Christ and Mother. . . . The purport of the messages was that [they] had come to visit Zion and to search her as with candles, to show and point out her backslidings, and how she had greatly fallen from that perfect order in which she was first established. [16]

Both the time lapse between the beginning of the revival and these new manifestations, and the change in tone and purpose evinced therein, may well reflect the Lead Ministry's active efforts to contain and channel the excitement of the awakening—thereby inducing a closer adherence to the sect's rules and principles.

Many of these inspired messages simply reiterated tenets that had been part of the Shaker way for many years. It was hoped that familiar regulations, given added weight because of their reassertion through anointed mediums, would be more successful in maintaining gospel order than the *Millennial Laws* had been. Instrument Joseph Wicker, a Hancock Elder who had an obvious interest in modifying the unruly behavior of his charges, transmitted the following divinely-inspired counsel to them in September 1841.

Love not the ways of evil, Love not the carnal mind,
Love not to pick and cavil, Love not much fault to find;
Love not an idle spirit, Love not to fret and scold,
Love not to be from meeting, Love not to leave the fold.
Love not a boistrous spirit, Love not a noisy tread,
Love not a filthy union, Love not to slight your lead;
Love not to be a tattler, Love not to be unwise,
Love not a vile affection, Love not the least disguise. [17]

This lengthy catalog of transgressions effectively summarized the behavior problems that had been multiplying within the communities for
years, or presumably a spirit would not have issued such a warning.

The spirits who troubled to communicate with the Shakers during
the early days of the revival were often embarrassingly specific about
the misbehavior they observed. One of the earliest recorded visions
was seen by Sister Ann Maria Goff of Watervliet, New York, on October 24, 1837. She dreamed that she and Sister Elizaette Gibbs had
died and returned to their Family as spirits to find out if proper order
were being kept. What she saw horrified her.

It seemed to be retiring time, and the Sisters, some of them, stood in a huddle
together, talking and laughing, and putting their hands to the side of their
mouths, and winking at each other as though they had something private
going on. Elizaette brought her foot down heavy, and said, "You must keep
good retiring times, and you must not talk before kneeling in the morning nor
after kneeling at night." At which the Sisters seemed frightened hearing a voice
and seeing nothing.

Sister Ann Maria noted other departures from Shaker standards as
well: marring of stair railings, kneeling and praying with eyes open,
dirt in the kitchen and dining room, lying crooked in bed, going to bed
with lamps lit and stove doors open, and lying.[18]

The spirit of Mother Lucy Wright was a frequent visitor, and she too
was alarmed by the lax practices she witnessed throughout the Society.
In a lengthy message on February 12, 1839, her spirit sharply reproved
the Sisters for waste in the kitchen, dirt in the Dwelling, and for overall
"slack, careless, and extravagant sense and feeling . . . with regard to
temporal things." Of particular concern was the growing tendency to
take pride in personal possessions or appearance. Mother Lucy's spirit
railed:

I have seen some of these daughters standing a long time before their looking-
glasses prinking their caps and their handkerchiefs with lust in their hearts
saying such a one or such a one will notice me and think I look very handsome, I am sure some body will notice that my cap or some of my clothes look
better than the rest of the sisters do. And with this sense they have come into
meeting to undertake to worship God all plastered over with lust and pride,
triping along allmost afraid to stir lest they should muss their clothes or make
some motion that would not look quite so complete.[19]

Other misdemeanors observed and condemned by Mother Lucy's
spirit included excessively free conversation between Brethren and Sisters and levity at table. At the bottom of a page in a key message, an
instrument noted severely: "N.B. The Sisters are not to comb their
heads, wash their feet, smoke, or take snuff, or lay down in any part of

the kitchen." [20] When the spirit of Holy Mother Wisdom descended to earth through instruments, thorough inspections were required. In December 1841, a member recorded: "In the afternoon Holy Mother came to view us in our respective dwelling rooms. Nothing spoken but some signs given—appeared to examine every thing verry closely, looking into the cupboards and turning up the corner of the carpets &c." [21]

Another facet of Shaker daily life with which the leaders had become increasingly concerned was the growing "worldly sense" displayed by many members in their fondness for fancy and elegant articles acquired outside the community. Not surprisingly, this concern was reflected in early spirit messages as well. In 1841, Father Joseph Meacham's spirit dictated a new version of the *Millennial Laws* wherein he decreed: "Ye shall in no wise buy, or cause to be bought; nor bring into the Church . . . any new fashioned thing that has not been formerly and generally used, even to an inkstand or comb or a pair of suspenders without the full union and approbation of the Ministry and Elders." Father Joseph's spirit continued, "Ye shall purchase no crockery that has printing on it; no china ware, nor any superfluously cut glass ware." [22] The negative consequences of Shaker prosperity were more evident in these years, and the atmosphere of the revival was utilized by the leaders to combat the members' growing worldliness.

But the issue that concerned the leaders most was relations between the sexes, which had become distressingly familiar in the years following Mother Lucy's death in 1821. Proper deportment in the mixed union meetings was a topic that cropped up in countless inspired communications. Eldress Cassandana Goodrich of Hancock received the following counsel from the spirit of Mother Lucy in 1842:

Never, never my dear Daughters, speak in your union meetings or any where in the presence of your Brethren, of any thing pertaining to the unclean nature of the bruit creation in the multiplying of the species nor of any other filthy thing that may have a tendency to excite the nature of lust, but if there is any such thing introduced in conversation in your presence, labor to change the subject. [23]

The institution of the union meeting underwent severe scrutiny during these years because some leaders had come to believe that it encouraged intimate relationships between individual Brethren and Sisters. Through a spirit message in 1841, Holy Mother Wisdom introduced a new system of revolving participation in union meetings so that members would not be paired with one another for too long a time. This change was made, as Isaac Youngs later noted, because "a great por-

tion had not the grace sufficient . . . to make a right use of a near connection with the opposite sex." [24]

It is clear that "particular union" between members was becoming
increasingly common. As "Mother's Work" progressed, and the fervor
and interest of the Believers showed signs of waning, the inspired messages on this subject assumed an even more denunciatory tone. In the
late 1840s, Sister Paulina Bates of Watervliet, New York, received a
writing "gift" from Holy Mother Wisdom that led her to produce a
two volume work printed at Canterbury in 1849. In *The Divine Book
of Holy and Eternal Wisdom*, Holy Mother's spirit lambasted the
Shakers for their unholy behavior, demanding that they

. . . wash away these abominable pollutions from within the walls of my holy
Zion. . . . O my people! saith the Lord, how long will ye seek to be bastards in
my house? How long will ye seek to be inhabitants of my new earth, while
practicing the abominations of the inhabitants of the old earth? How long
shall I bear with mongrels in my kingdom, a mixture of the seed of malice with
the seed of love? [25]

The "abominations" mentioned are not fully described in this passage,
but hints elsewhere in the book point to possible sexual activities,
among many lesser transgressions. Early in the book, Holy Mother's
spirit addressed "O ye children of Zion, and ye sons of men" jointly,
fuming:

O ye seed of asps! ye fornicators of your own bodies! Ye that seek to cover
under a cloke of sanctity and outward uprightness the most base and vile
transactions, that which would cause the righteous soul to shudder and shrink
at the idea of committing. Deeds which you would tremble at the thought of
being made known to your fellows. [26]

A significant falling away from traditional Shaker standards had
reached crisis proportions by the late 1830s. Even if these later hints of
sexual misbehavior are ignored, it is certain that many Believers were
far from upholding the Society's original tenets. Cleanliness, simplicity
in belongings and attire, modesty in dealings with the opposite sex—
all of these attributes had become increasingly rare. "Mother's Work,"
which began spontaneously in 1837 in response to both internal and
external stresses, was redirected by the leaders beginning in 1838 to
purge the communities of halfhearted members. The Hancock Believers were informed of this intention in no uncertain terms by an instrument in 1841:

It is not the lukewarm that will gain the heavenly prize; but the valiant and
strong will overcome the powers of darkness, and conquer their enemies on
every hand. It is such, and such only, that will endure the furnace of Zion,

which is becoming hotter and hotter, and will so continue till everything is purged out that is filthy or unclean.[27]

Evidence that Shaker leaders consciously manipulated the events of the revival is understandably scanty, but what does exist is nevertheless compelling. Faced with internal and external difficulties of enormous magnitude, it is not surprising that they should have grasped the fervor of the awakening as an opportunity to remedy Zion's shortcomings. After all, such direction of "gifts" among the rank and file had always been one of the duties of Elders and Eldresses, and so the Lead Ministry's involvement in "Mother's Work" represented no departure from established practice. In the late 1830s and early 1840s, the spiritual and temporal condition of the Society was far more desperate than it had been for many years, prompting the leaders to initiate a policy that would establish their control over the manifestations.

Much of this control took the form of encouragement. A hint from an Elder or Eldress was usually sufficient to develop "gifts" in a member they had selected for that purpose. In 1841, the New Hampshire Ministry reported to New Lebanon about two young Brethren at Enfield who were being influenced in just this way.

They . . . were filled to overflowing with life, love, zeal and power, which they continue to keep, although they have not as yet been blessed with any inspired messages, notwithstanding we have encouraged them to labor to improve in this gift, and have given them our approbation to be free and improve in every good gift, which they are striving to do. We believe one or both of them will gain it.[28]

This passage reveals a new role for Shaker leaders that became increasingly precarious as "Mother's Work" progressed. The Elders had always been the ones to sanction or disallow "gifts" received by rank and file members, but "Mother's Work" changed the scale and function of revivalism within the sect. Earlier gifts had been intermittent and designed to increase emotional fervor, especially in worship, but the gifts of the 1830s and 1840s occurred continually and were designed primarily to correct behavior. The profusion of gifts during the revival's early years gave the leadership's role crucial importance. Some Elders and Eldresses were overtaken by spirits and became instruments themselves, but this activity was more typical of inexperienced members, those who were young either spiritually or chronologically and had yet to reach the inner circles of the Society's power structure.

The volume of spirit messages recorded in Family records during the earliest phase of "Mother's Work" is truly astonishing. In less than six months, instruments at Canterbury produced more than 450 manuscript pages of inspired messages for members of the Church Family, "some for consolation, some for edification, some for instruction, some for reproof, some for mortification, and some for simplicity &c."[29] In December 1841, a member commented in the New Lebanon *Church Order Journal*, "The week past and at the present time 8 or 10 individuals and times more are writing day and night for our Heavenly Parents and justified spirits."[30]

"Gifts" of music were equally common, as were new "manners of laboring" (or dancing) in meeting. So many gifts of these types were received that the leaders were quickly forced to restrict them. Giles Avery observed in January 1838:

Having been much exercised of late in learning new things, our meetings seemed more like conference meetings than anything else, accordingly the general feeling seems to be now (as we have nearly or quite learned all the new manners of laboring) to feel a gift in the various exercises and rob them of some of their formality.[31]

The leaders made such decisions concerning gifts more than once, but it is difficult to ascertain their frequency. They feared that too many gifts of one kind would surfeit the members and lead them to lose interest in the revival as a whole. As late as 1848, Philemon Stewart recorded: "We, the singers, were informed this evening by the Elders that the Ministry felt it would be best to cease having any more new exercise songs at present, until we have used those more that we have already been given."[32]

This abundance of manifestations is understandable given both the stress of the preceding decades, and the reverence in which the Shakers held inspired instruments. To be overtaken by a spirit was one of the most exciting things that could happen to a Believer, and marked that person as something of a celebrity in his or her Family, especially in the mid-nineteenth century when gifts had become increasingly rare. Many members would have agreed wholeheartedly with Brother Shadrach Hurlbert of Hancock who declared, "I have oft times felt as if I could crawl upon my hands and knees and lick the dust off the feet of those who had the power of God, if I could receive enough to move one finger."[33]

The potential threat posed by this attitude was twofold. Psychological pressure and the desire to participate actively in the revival induced members to receive gifts or to pretend that they had. Leaders were therefore forced into the awkward position of having to distinguish between true and false revelations. Most gifts received during "Mother's Work" originated with nonleaders, thereby dividing members' loyalties. Changing the loci of authority within the Society from the leaders to the instruments proved a very real problem as "Mother's Work" stretched into the 1840s. The difficulty of distinguishing between legitimate and counterfeit gifts created the possibility that instruments who had been disavowed by their leaders would surround themselves with similarly disaffected members and challenge traditional authority. As the revival spread throughout the Society, most Bishopric Ministries wrote to New Lebanon for advice on this matter. In June 1838, the Lead Ministry replied to South Union:

> In this extraordinary time of the outpouring of the spirit of Christ and of Mother it is all important that the Ministry and Elders keep their eyes open, and their spirits bright, so as to be able to distinguish clearly between the genuine spirit of Mother and that which is counterfeit; for we are sensible that young and inexperienced souls (as some of our visionists are) are liable to be inspired by an evil spirit and think it Mother or some good spirit.[34]

Leaders in other villages sought counsel as well, which came to some in the form of a divine communication. The New Hampshire Ministry wrote to New Lebanon in April 1839 to inform them of

> . . . a letter from the Alfred Ministry, by which it appears they have experienced great power, and have been exercised in various gifts of late, and they felt need of our counsel to regulate some, who it appears will be liable to run by their Lead if not checked. We answered this letter according to the best of our understanding, and will here copy a small portion of that letter. "Not long since one among us received the following special message from Father Job Bishop. . . . viz. *Let all gifts and revelations be brought into order, by making them known to their Elders and let every tongue throughout the Church be silent elsewhere.*"[35]

The tendency to "run by their Lead" was noticeable in many instruments, despite the leaders' supervision. One who appears to have done so was Philemon Stewart of New Lebanon, who had exhibited a tendency to argue with his superiors well before "Mother's Work" began. Events in 1837 and 1838 indicate that Stewart may have been using the excitement of the revival to carve out a position of authority within the community but outside the Eldership. Born in 1804, Stewart had been brought into the Society by his father seven years later, together with two brothers, Charles and Amos. When the revival began, Stewart was thirty-three years old. Although he had been in charge of the gardens at New Lebanon for a number of years, he had held no positions of spiritual responsibility. His existence on the fringes of the Shaker power structure may well have made him uncomfortable, particularly as his brother, Amos, was ascending the hierarchy as an Elder. As an instrument, however, Philemon rapidly became a force to be reckoned with.

His role during the early years of "Mother's Work" is suggested by Isaac Youngs's later observation: "The first messages were all given thro' a male Instrument, tho' in a general sense the females were much more gifted in outward operations and gifts."[36] This evidence does not prove that Stewart was the instrument in question, but other sources confirm this supposition. In April 1838, Brother Henry DeWitt wrote in his journal: "P.M. Meeting a Message was delivered by Mother Ann thro' Philemon Stewart which continued nearly two hours."[37] The next month, Giles Avery observed, "Much time spent by *Philemon* in delivering messages from *Mother*; indeed he has time to tend little else."[38] Whatever the impetus for Stewart's "gifts"—whether genuine or feigned—they certainly put him on center stage. For the first time he was in a commanding position within the sect, and his Elders, who had ignored him in the past, had no choice but to respect him. In September 1838, he was moved from the Second to the First Order at New Lebanon, and in December was made Boys' Caretaker. Certainly the prestige he had gained as an instrument was a factor in his subsequent advancement. Evidently, his rapid ascent up the sect's hierarchy was not greeted with universal approbation. An anonymous journalist recorded Stewart's progress in this rather cryptic fashion: "March 2, 1841—D. Boler leaves Elders. P. Stewart goes in. Nov. 26, 1842—P. Stewart leaves Eldership. (Joyful) April 20, 1843—P. Stewart G. Avery go Eastern Societies. Sept. 13, 1843—D. Boler to Canterbury after P. Stewart (wild). Jan. 30, 1844—P. Stewart Doctor (Trying to be one). Sept. 14, 1846—P. Stewart takes Grt. Garden."[39]

Philemon Stewart was not, however, the only instrument to become corrupted by the power newly bestowed upon him. In some communities, instruments became so self-important that they left the sect after disagreements with their superiors. Hancock suffered from at least one such apostasy; in 1842 the Eldresses there received a spirit message from Mother Lucy exonerating them for that case of renunciation:

Do not think beloved that ye were not directed by true Wisdom in anointing the instruments whom Mother had chosen to write the word of the Lord; because one proved a traitor it was not your fault nor the fault of the good spirits; for they strove hard to save her. And her writings were true, and the reason of her not feeling comfortable after she was spoken to concerning the sacredness of these writings was because she had done that which she knew made her unfit to handle these holy things, and rather than bow low enough to confess and repent of it, she chose to go to the world.[40]

Elder Frederick Evans of the New Lebanon North Family had also observed this unfortunate tendency in instruments, commenting many years later: "The mediums in the societies had given much trouble because they imagined themselves reformers, whereas they were only mouthpieces of spirits, and oftenest themselves of a low order of mind. They had to teach the mediums much, after the spirits had ceased to use them."[41]

Most Shakers, of course, believed that the gifts transmitted with the approval of the Lead Ministry were legitimate. Spiritual presents given in meeting were a special notification to the recipients that their struggles to live pure lives were appreciated. On Christmas Day in 1845, the members of the Hancock Second Family received a vast array of such gifts that were doubtless of greater value than more tangible presents: "bright silver crosses, bread and waters of life, large silver sacks, pitchers and bottles filled with never failing water, bright glorious crowns, beautiful stars from the Saviour, bundles of brooms from Brother George Washington, bowls of refining fire, and bundles of rods."[42] This proof of heavenly regard reinforced many members in their efforts to forsake the World, while at the same time providing them with some spiritual equivalents of the luxuries they were forbidden in this life.

Devout Believers yearned for such notice from the spirit world, and regarded the numerous gifts showered on the communities during the revival as tremendous blessings. They were taken very seriously. Mention of these gifts appears only rarely in the members' daybooks and journals, perhaps because many of them felt the subject was too sacred for these pedestrian written forms. When comments about gifts do appear, it is clear that Believers accepted them at face value. In February 1839, for example, Brother Benjamin Lyon of New Lebanon recorded: ". . . clean myself up go to Meeting have a presant from the spiritual world of a Transparent rule on foot long."[43]

Brother Robert Wilcox, though not a recipient himself, was equally convinced by the authenticity of spiritual gifts. While visiting the community at Watervliet, New York, he toured the orchard with a young Brother who was well-known as an instrument. At his departure, the young man gave Brother Robert something that he said was a white pear as a gift for a Tyringham Sister who was also a visionist. Brother Robert could not see the pear, but he insisted that he could feel its weight in his pocket as well as the slight warmth it exuded. When he returned home and went to give the pear to the Sister, she took it from his hand before he had a chance to explain what it was, remarking how kind it was of the young Brother at Watervliet to send her such a lovely white pear.[44]

As "Mother's Work" progressed, however, the nature of the gifts changed. Objects like pears and transparent rules continued to be received, together with new songs and manners of worship, but the manifestations increasingly took the form of written communications admonishing members for their unruly behavior. Between the spring of 1838 and the spring of 1840, the tone of these messages became, in Isaac Youngs's words, "more dignified, more weighty—more tending to be repulsive to common human feelings, more bordering on restraint, and designed to enforce strict Church order."[45] Holy Mother Wisdom's first communication to the Believers at New Lebanon was received in May 1840, followed by two personal visits, one in April and one in December 1841. Eighteen-forty-one also witnessed the establishment of the so-called sweeping gift, a physical and spiritual cleansing of the villages to prepare for some special occasion, such as Mother Ann's birthday or the visit of an important spirit.

Gifts like these served the leaders' goals: renewed commitment by the older members, return to traditional standards of behavior, and sincere interest and devotion on the part of young Believers. This last goal was pursued by maintaining the excitement of the revival long after it would have died a natural death. From the chronology recorded by Isaac Youngs, it appears that one or two major gifts were introduced every year with nearly clockwork regularity, suggesting that the reason for their appearance was the flagging enthusiasm of the members.[46] As the years advanced, the gifts became more and more outrageous and peculiar, or so some Shakers came to think. In 1841, the year of the first "sweeping gift," the Lead Ministry outlawed the use of tea, coffee, and pork throughout the Society, claiming the authority of a divine instruction. At least some rank and file members, and even a few leaders, doubted the wisdom and legitimacy of this particular gift. In 1842, manifestations in many of the communities were dominated by the appearance of Holy Mother Wisdom, Mother Ann, Eternal Father, and Christ. Meetings became so frenzied and gift-filled that visitors were appalled, and the Lead Ministry was forced to close them to the public. Eighteen-forty-two was also the year that the Lead Ministry decreed the establishment at each village of a sacred "feast ground" where outdoor meetings could be held from time to time. It was at this time as well that all the communities received new spiritual names. Hancock, for example, became the "City of Peace," and Harvard was renamed "Lovely Vineyard."[47]

Acceptance of various "gifts" was far from universal. David Lamson, a member of the Hancock East Family for a time during the 1840s, witnessed Christ's visit there through an instrument, Elder Joseph Wicker. When Wicker was unable to make an elderly deaf Brother hear and understand the words of comfort Christ had intended for him, Lamson concluded that the Lord was not present at all, "only Jo Wicker." [48]

In 1843, the Shakers printed for distribution in the World hundreds of copies of *The Sacred Roll and Book*, an inspired communication received by Brother Philemon Stewart. This book was intended to provide information about Shakerism to lost souls seeking truth. To that end, Shaker Elders sent copies to most of the foreign consuls in Boston for transmission to their governments. Little response was elicited.

Another gift received at about this time was called the "gift of fool." The New Lebanon *Church Order Journal* recorded in May 1842 an account of a meeting where this gift was administered.

Then we marched and the Saviour asked if we were ready to receive some further presents—yea—What do you want—no answer—"He said here is some fool don't you want some?" yea—The Elders received and dealt liberally with all and some began to eat and act foolish and he called us to silence saying here is some wine, drink this and you will act *querer* yet! So we drank freely and bondage, sorrow and trouble seemed to be gone. [49]

Then, in the fall of 1842, a gift was introduced especially for the young members. The hope was to encourage their participation in the conversion of unredeemed spirits who were seeking eternal rest through the Shaker gospel. Young Believers were instructed to surrender themselves to the influence of "unbelieving spirits"—Africans, native Americans, Chinese, Arabs, "Laplanders," and others. After the Believers performed some dance or other activity representative of a particular race or nationality, those unbelieving spirits would typically ask to be admitted as members. Perhaps by encouraging young, lukewarm Shakers to pantomime repeatedly the conversion of "heathen" spirits, the leaders expected the level of commitment to the faith to increase. This gift may well have been the Shaker response to the foreign and home missionary movements that involved so many young people in the World during this period. While this gift drew on a long-established Shaker belief in the ultimate conversion of the dead, many of the young members who became involved in it failed to take it seriously.

The meetings that these unbelieving spirits attended were more frenzied and lively than those of the late 1830s. In November 1842, a New Lebanon Elder recorded in the *Confidential Journal*:

Our Meeting last evening lasted until about half past one o'clock, the Negro spirits were acted out by all the young. . . . I believe in truth the Blacks have come, for in our Meetings the rank smell of a Negro is so strong that I have to take up a sound cross to come near one of them; their looks also much resembles the Affrican . . . and they blow bellowses, in full shape, like an Affrican; for they whistle, shrill and clear, almost like a steam Carr. [50]

Appearances by native American spirits were even more common than those by African souls. The scribe of the *Confidential Journal* noted in September 1842: "The Gift is for all the Younger part to labor to turn into Indians and Squaws, or in other words, to be wholly given up, and willing to act with the spirit of the Indian that Mother Ann has sent to be with them for a season." [51]

Apparently some Shakers were embarrassed when they discovered that they were expected to participate in these manifestations. In a book of orders intended for the children in the Society, Mother Lucy's spirit delivered instructions that could easily have been directed to the adult members as well: "You must never be ashamed of the blessed power of God which operates upon your bodies; you must love it, and always unite with it, and never strive against it." [52] Some young members, however, entered too wholeheartedly into the spirit of the gift and had to be reproved. "Last night, in our evening Meeting, we had a short, but powerful Message from Our Heavenly Father; This was in relation to the young gathering such a vain, light empty sense in respect to the Native spirits that had of late been sent among us." [53] The purpose of these gifts was twofold: maintaining the interest of the young, while at the same time inculcating in them the Shaker principles of obedience and humility.

Unfortunately, the increasingly peculiar nature of many of the gifts received after 1840 led some Believers to doubt their authenticity. Due to peer pressure, some members feigned these gifts in order to feel more a part of the group, and noticed that their superiors failed to detect the difference. Gifts such as taking in "unbelieving spirits" soon got out of control. The Elders, having encouraged young members to participate, found it hard to suppress the gift as its manifestations grew increasingly violent and distracting. Isaac Youngs later observed that this development did considerable damage to the revival as a whole.

This work was greatly calculated to lessen the value and solemnity of spiritual gifts and inspiration, and to give cavillers a fair chance to quibble, if they chose, and even to undertake to dissemble and counterfeit, and then turn and say there was nothing in it at all, and many among Believers have doubtless turned these things to their own hurt.

Although Youngs went on to assert that "it has not all hurt the sincere heart, nor shaken the faith of those who were well established in the work and gifts of God," the number of Believers who fit this description was evidently shrinking. [54] The revival, after all, had been intended more for wavering, partially committed members than for "those who were well established in the work and gifts of God."

Even a few leaders expressed doubts about some of the manifestations. In January 1845, the New Hampshire Ministry sent a letter to New Lebanon marked "Confidential" that described the reception various gifts had received in the Maine communities:

> Unbelief in the present manifestation is too prevalent. Even their former Elder Brother James Pote seems to have very little if any faith in the present work—in the Sacred Roll and Book, or in preparing the Sacred Feast Ground; and there is no doubt that some of the young have gathered weakness from him, Paul Nowell, and perhaps others.[55]

James Pote was not alone in his reservations. In an 1859 letter of complaint addressed to the Lead Ministry that rambled on for some one hundred and forty-five pages, Philemon Stewart revealed his long-standing grudge against Giles Avery.

> He [Giles Avery] also stated . . . that it was believed [by the Ministry and First Order Elders] that I had set myself up as the Lord's Prophet and he and the rest of the leaders in the Society had no faith in it. Neither had he any faith to believe that the writing and bringing forth of the Sacred Roll was dictated by any Angel, other than Philemon Stewart, and that was also the general feeling. . . . He also said he did not believe that the cutting off of swine's flesh, and many such like things in the Manifestation, was anything to be relied on . . . but if the Lead saw fit to establish any such regulation he would support it as he always had.[56]

The gift that sparked the greatest controversy in these years was undoubtedly the 1841 prohibition of pork, tea, and coffee. When the divine instruction was first made known, there was little to indicate the dissension it would engender. In November 1841, a New Lebanon Believer noted in the *Church Order Journal*, "The past week we have heared a new law from the Lord respecting swines flesh . . . it is pronounced cursed and unclean positively unfit for the children of Zion."[57] The writer recorded in this account that a period of ten years would be allowed for the total eradication of pork and pork products like lard.

These half-measures pleased neither the dedicated Grahamites nor the confirmed meat-eaters among the membership. Shaker dietary practice after 1841 was a curious mixture of traditional fare and Grahamite innovations. As Isaac Youngs later recorded: "Swines' flesh was entirely expunged from the table, and the people avoided all meat and fish kind on the sabbath, and also pretty much at suppers. Butter and bread and milk at the same meal have uniformly been avoided and also butter and cheese at one meal."[58] From Youngs's account, it appears that some measure of personal choice was still permitted on the issue of eating meat other than pork. The absence of a precise, inclusive, easily understood inspired message concerning diet made it difficult for the Shakers to reach a workable *modus vivendi*—a problem that had plagued the Society since 1835. As early as August 1842, hints appear in the New Lebanon Elders' *Confidential Journal* that dissension was developing. "There has been," the writer noted, "now within a year or two past, a great deal handed from the Heavens in respect to eating, which, in some cases, seems to be quite hard for all to get an understanding alike."[59]

Elder Freegift Wells of the Watervliet, New York, Church Family was one who failed to understand the importance of this gift. Recalled from Ohio in 1843, where he had again witnessed the devastating effects of disagreement over vegetarianism, Wells resisted all efforts by his superiors and followers alike to introduce even a partially Grahamite regime in his Family. He penned a lengthy piece in 1850 discussing the events of the preceding decade and clearly expressed his disbelief in the gift.

This veneration and sacred respect to my Parents in Zion, both visible and invisible, has not . . . in the least degree abated in my breast, until the late revolution which has extended thro' every branch among believers. . . . The severe shock which this revolution has brought to my mind and feelings . . . is beyond what I feel able to describe. I feel impelled by the most sacred obligations of duty to declare in the line of order my unshaken conviction that the Society of Believers in this place . . . are losing ground! Instead of moving forward in the work of purification and redemption . . . they are leavening back into unreconciliation to many requirements which . . . have been enjoined upon them. This has produced hardness of heart, blindness of mind, and unbelief in the genuine orders of God . . . which at the present time is so firmly seated and grounded in many that nothing . . . but a relinquishment by the Ministry of some of those restrictions . . . will ever enable them to come into the work of God.[60]

Wells objected so strongly to the Ministry's 1841 rules that he asked to be removed from office rather than have to enforce an order in which he had no faith. He was irate that the Ministry could demonstrate such a lack of respect for his judgment by ignoring his opinions. He later fumed: "And Why! after all this manifest disregard of my wisdom, and competency to discern between good and evil . . . I am still held in the place of first Elder of this Society is a problem which I am altogether unable to solve."[61]

According to his own account, Wells was not the only Believer that had no faith in the vegetarian gift. He claimed that he was merely the only one with sufficient position and courage to express his opposition publicly. He asserted: "There is a goodly number of Brethren and Sisters who, in many things are almost what they ought to be; yet, they dare not be honest, and let the Ministry know their secret feelings against the restrictions on diet for fear of losing their union thereby . . . but union preserved, or bought in this way will never answer my purpose—the price is too high." [62]

Other Shaker sources indicate that Wells was quite right when he claimed that the degree of opposition to the dietary regulations was far greater than the Lead Ministry were willing to admit. Although the gift banning tea, coffee, and pork was introduced in the fall of 1841, the Ministry were often forced to reiterate their position. In 1847, the scribe of the Elders' *Confidential Journal* at New Lebanon reported: "Positively decided by the Ministry never again to have pork admitted back into this family, altho there is quite an effort with some to palm much blame upon that movement; yet it is evident that a division of sentiment and feeling has produced more loss than everything else put together." [63] On September 27th of the same year, the Lead Ministry attended the Church Family meeting at New Lebanon "on account of the disaffected feelings that many have by reason of the restrictions brot forward in the late Manifestation, about leaving the use of swines flesh, tea, coffee, cider, Tobacco &c. . . . It seems to be a very trying time as to our meats and drinks, some wants Pork and some not, some wants tea and coffee and some not, but we must go together." [64]

Even as late as 1849, Believers in various communities were still not conforming to the regulation. Elder Thomas Damon of the Hancock Ministry recorded in February of that year, "Elder Grove went over to Lebanon *to see the Ministry in relation to* the Second Family's continuing *the use of pork*." [65] Apparently Freegift Wells's final conclusion about the vegetarian controversy was shared by many of his fellow Shakers: "I shall now enter upon the subject of purging out the swine —a measure which I fully believe has brought more loss of soul on believers as a body than anything else that has ever happened since the Society was first established." [66]

Elder Freegift developed an interesting theory about the origin of the vegetarian gift, evidenced by the opposition it engendered. Recognizing that young and inexperienced members were often prey to inspirational messages from evil spirits, he hypothesized that a former member named William Scales had inspired the gift in malice. Scales had converted when Mother Ann was alive and had hoped to succeed her. Failing in this attempt, he left the sect and devoted the rest of his life to undermining its success, even trying on one occasion to murder Father Joseph Meacham. Wells argued that the vegetarian gift received in 1841, and supposedly originating with Father William Lee, had ac-

tually been inspired by the spirit of William Scales in yet another attempt to destroy the sect. Scales's animosity to the Believers had been
so pronounced that Wells felt it was quite likely he might continue in
his efforts to create disunion by inspiring false messages from beyond
the grave.[67]

Wells first doubted the authenticity of this gift in the mid-1840s
when the Family pork supply at Watervliet failed to rot as an inspired
message had indicated it would.[68] He was thereby led to reevaluate the
content of other spirit communications and determined that as many
as half of them were spurious. "I once swallowed down without doubt-
ing every thing that came in the shape of a Message from the heavens
. . . but after a while I got confounded by receiving a Message in the
name of Mother Ann, which I knew was a positive lie. From that time I
found it necessary to be more on my guard."[69] It was the gift prohibit-
ing pork, tea, and coffee that concerned him most, as he wrote in
1850: "The Devil having been defeated in his plan of destroying the
union of God's people thro' Grahamism, his next stratagem was to
effect it thro' Inspiration."[70]

The first phase of the revival did have a beneficial impact despite an
undercurrent of doubt about the more peculiar revelations of "Mother's Work" and the swollen heads of a few instruments. The Believers
had been given a needed reminder in a time of trouble that their heavenly parents had not forsaken them. A timely recognition of some
problems in Zion was surely a healthy step. Leaders had long realized
that the future of the sect was uncertain unless a thorough work of
purification was undertaken. The Shakers were assured that such a purification would indeed take place. Holy Mother Wisdom promised
through Paulina Bates in *The Divine Book of Holy and Eternal Wisdom*: "Great shall be the ingathering of souls into my Zion, when my
people have become righteous, and are able to show forth a righteousness which will far surpass all other righteousness which was ever
made manifest in the children of men."[71]

By 1844, the fervor of the revival called "Mother's Work" had been
undermined by the undisciplined antics of some less than devout
young members, and had waned considerably. Perhaps the leaders realized that their sanction of partial vegetarianism and several other unpopular gifts had resulted in such disunion that a period of retrench-
ment was needed. Certainly the revival took a new turn after 1844.
During the next two years the Society was dominated by two apparently contradictory trends. Many Believers, disgusted by the excesses
of the revival or disillusioned about the legitimacy of some revelations,

left the faith. Those remaining faithful struggled to maintain their commitment, and remembered the promise of Holy Mother Wisdom in their plight. They saw the "purging of Zion" happening before their eyes and eagerly awaited the prophesied ingathering. Beginning in the mid-1840s, many Shakers looked hopefully to Millerism and Spiritualism as Worldly signs of that imminent ingathering.

8

Bad Fish Caught in the Gospel Net
(1844-1858)

Revivalistic excitement usually diminished naturally, and there is every indication that such was the case with the Shaker revival known as "Mother's Work." The spate of "gifts" and messages from the spirit world in 1837 and 1838 had provided a necessary distraction from temporal cares. By the early 1840s, however, the profusion of inspired rules and decrees had reached such a level that their effectiveness was proportionately reduced. The constant theme of these communications—that Zion had become sullied with sin and had to be purified—coupled with the peccadilloes that many messages dredged up and railed against, combined to undermine the faith of many Believers. Instruments recognized this problem, especially those who were also leaders, and repeatedly emphasized the critical importance of the revival. In 1841, the spirit of Christ spoke through Hancock Elder Joseph Wicker.

> I call on you to be resign'd
> To every gift I do you give;
> Nor ever be by *use* confin'd
> To any certain mode to live.
> But as my spirit does ordain,
> With that, O learn to be content,
> And never, never more complain
> Of any message to you sent.[1]

This refrain, however, fell on increasingly deaf ears. By the mid-1840s, the power of the revival had faded. Disillusioned, a significant number of Shakers, including some instruments, departed for the World. To fill the vacant places, Shaker leaders looked first to displaced children and then to two contemporary Worldly movements—Millerism and Spiritualism—as sources of new converts.

It is remarkable that the fervor of "Mother's Work" lasted as long as it did, considering the short life span of most revivals. But after six years of nearly continual excitement, the members were exhausted, and the leaders found it impossible to sustain a high level of enthusiasm. The 1841 gift banning pork and the 1842 gift of "taking in unbelieving spirits" had been so poorly received by the rank and file that it is hardly surprising that interest declined. Isaac Youngs reported that 1844 was "not so noted for extraordinary manifestations" as previous years. By 1845, the meetings at New Lebanon had calmed to such an extent that the Lead Ministry could reopen them to the public. Fewer gifts overcame members out of meeting, and most Families maintained the form, if not the spirit, of the gifts already introduced. Youngs recorded in 1846: "Went on the mount twice, and attended to the yearly appointment of sweeping and cleansing, tho' without any special external manifestations of spiritual influence." By 1848, he reported, "Considerable voluntary effort has been necessary to keep up a life of devotion."[2] The Lead Ministry became so exasperated by the "dull sense" they witnessed in meetings that in March 1847 they "appointed a Meeting at 6 o'clock, and such as did not feel truly thankful for the little simple gifts of God were desired to keep away. For it was their desire to have one good Meeting undisturbed by unbelievers."[3]

These observances of the late 1840s and early 1850s represented, in large part, an attempt to cling to the glorious Shaker past in the face of a new and uncertain future. With the death of an elderly member in January 1847 came a powerful reminder that many vital links to the first generation of Believers had been lost. As Philemon Stewart recorded: "Anna Hocknell Departed this life between 4 and 5 o'clock this morning at the Second Order. Anna was the last that was left with us who came from England with our first Parents; she was about 85 years of age."[4] The loss of these "first witnesses" created a spiritual void within the Society that the leaders desperately tried to fill by maintaining the excitement of the revival beyond the time when it would otherwise have subsided.

The so-called gift drawings, colorful records of visions received between 1841 and 1859 are perhaps the most celebrated remnants of the last phase of "Mother's Work." Many of these drawings of trees, baskets of fruit, wreaths of flowers, hearts, and leaves were intended as presents for elderly members and promised a heavenly reward for faithful service. Some were given to young members to encourage their perseverance in the gospel way. All were designed to remind the Believers that Mother Ann and other early leaders had not forsaken them in their time of trial, yet their individual nature represents an important shift away from the more public, community-oriented gifts of the earlier phase of the revival.[5]

By the mid-1840s, the possibility of influencing large numbers of members to purify themselves and their Families *en masse* had become unlikely. The hope of the leaders during these years was that selected individuals could yet be saved and transformed into true Believers—fit residents of a newly cleansed Zion. As the enthusiasm of most members dwindled, "Mother's Work" in a very real sense went underground and, by the 1850s had faded almost completely.

Some Shaker leaders felt that this diminished zeal had been caused by the very efforts of the Lead Ministry to maintain it. In 1845 they issued a new version of the 1821 *Millennial Laws* incorporating all the various instructions that had been received during "Mother's Work." Some members felt that the rules contained therein were trivial and therefore ridiculous. Elder Freegift Wells of Watervliet, New York, regarded this forced attempt to bring members into stricter adherence to "gospel order" as a tremendous error in judgment. He wrote in 1850: "I believe it is nearly . . . impossible to drive souls to Heaven by means that were never revealed till the late manifestation commenced. And I believe that whatever attempts are made in this line will cause more to jump into hell than it will help along in the road to heaven." [6]

Wells's assessment of the spiritual condition of Believers under his care during this period was overwhelmingly negative. He found that the establishment of myriad petty regulations had resulted in "a great increase of *unreconciliation—discouragement—rebellion—loss of confidence in the Lead—unbelief—self-indulgence—reaching after and gathering up the Philosophy and sciences of the World—Phrenology—Mesmerism and the like;—together with the misimprovement of time in useful Labor and setting bad examples in various ways.*" [7] Younger members, Wells concluded, had less respect for the dictates of their Elders as the number of "divinely inspired" rules proliferated. He noted that so many regulations were received during the early 1840s that it was impossible to remember all of them, thereby rendering adherence unfeasible. Though younger members blessed with good memories may have recalled these numerous instructions, they saw that many older Believers neglected some of them. As a result, they felt justified in following their seniors' example. [8]

The development of this trend gradually reduced Shaker order to something of a farce. It was especially a problem among the young because some of them had been embarrassed by the peculiar gifts received during the revival. As Wells noted sadly:

They hate order and government, and disregard it as far as they dare, which extends to a great length indeed. In our singing ranks, some who are endowed with first rate talents are but idle spectators, and stand with closed lips, and evident marks of uneasiness and disgust . . . and it would seem that almost every gospel requirement is hateful to their feelings; and they do not regard them at all from any principle of obedience, but only as eye servants, to prevent a fuss.[9]

Elder Grove Wright of Hancock observed the same tendency among at least some of his charges, writing in 1847: "As to the . . . young believers, there are a goodly number of them who appear to be a doing well and increasing in faith and good works, but there are some who seem to me like to prove *bad fish* caught in the Gospel net and have to be separated and cast away."[10]

The "bad fish" most lamented by the leaders were instruments who left for the World—they undermined whatever faith their fellows had had in the various spirit manifestations. As early as 1839 Isaac Youngs noted:

Shocking Apostasy! We learn this week that there has lately been a falling away at Hancock at the 2nd Family—the like of which has scarcely been known before. The particulars I have not learned but understand that 10 went away 4 males and 6 females—from another family, 4 or 5 went. They were chiefly between 15 and 22 years old. . . . Some that had been visionists went, Elizabeth Oaks for one.[11]

Such apostasies became increasingly common as efforts to prolong "Mother's Work" progressed. Brother John Allen of the New Lebanon Church Family departed in September 1846, reportedly because the "Ministry and Elders did not follow some inspired communications thro' him which [they] knew would be unprofitable."[12]

The correlation between such backslidings and the excesses of the revival is further demonstrated by another case that occurred at New Lebanon. Just eight days after Allen's departure, Philemon Stewart recorded in his garden journal: "Stephen Baker, the secret, the sly, and the abominably wicked has this day gone to the world a little before the time he intended. His great desire to my certain knowledge, was to remain untill he had ruined every Instrument and every young person that was in his power."[13]

The motivations behind this rash of backslidings were often complex, as demonstrated by the case of instrument John Allen. Admitted as a child in 1826, Allen was thirty at the time of his departure. He did not leave alone, however. Sister Betsy Ann Bennet, aged twenty-five, whom he subsequently married, Brother Derobigne Bennet, aged twenty-seven, and Sister Mary Wicks, aged twenty-eight and also a "visionist," all went with him. Bennet and Wicks also married once safely in the World, but these four did not find life there as pleasant as they had anticipated. Elder Rufus Bishop, reporting the findings of some members who had visited the foursome in order to settle accounts, commented:

> . . . their hell has already begun, for they reflect on themselves for the sad condition in which they have plunged themselves, & they accuse John Allen of being the instigator of the whole plan. They shed a flood of tears when too late. John was more braced for a time, but he finally bust forth in torrents. Poor Mary Wicks could hardly find words to express how awful it felt to her to lose her state of innocency which she had been brought up in. She said if someone would dig a hole in the ground & bury her therein it would be a heaven to her!!![14]

The secession of these four trusted members, all of whom had been brought into the Society as children, shocked the entire membership. According to Hancock's Elder Thomas Damon, their marriages were the first to be contracted at the New Lebanon Church Family—ironically, home of the most devoted Believers.[15] It is likely that the four planned their departure at a meeting where all were present; it may even have been a union meeting. One month later the Lead Ministry concluded "that the time had come for particular union to be abolished, and a general union to be substituted in its place, . . . it went into effect last sabbath."[16] Certainly this decision had some connection with this devastating quadruple apostasy.

Just as in the years preceding the revival, sexual attraction led many members to try the ways of the World. The departure of Allen and his companions was the most shocking, but it was by no means the last such occurrence. Shaker leaders had come to expect such developments, and usually recorded them routinely, such as Elder Thomas Damon did in 1854.

> June 8—Harvey Lyman left Hancock and went to Springfield.
> June 10—Mary Ann White left Enfield and went to Thompsonville.
> June 22—H. Lyman and Mary Ann White were tied together with the galling cords of wedlock.[17]

When a similar alliance was contracted in the same year between the junior Elder and a Sister at the Hancock East Family, the reaction of the Ministry was equally calm. Elder Grove Wright reported the event to the Harvard Ministry.

> He had long supported a *fleshly* union with a femail by the name of Silia Dempsy and they finally Rated out *completely*, and fell thro', and sank to rise no more. It will no doubt be much more surprising to those not intimately acquainted with Barnabas to hear of his *fall* than it was to those in the same family or society. The femail was one they took in when a little *Child* was now perhaps about 40. He could not have taken one who the family was so willing to get rid of as the one he took, of a verry uncomfortable, uneasy disposition, much like *himself*.[18]

Obviously, not all apostasies created the same furor as Allen's. In some cases, the Shakers were less than distraught by the departures of this period. When Brother Francis Sears left New Lebanon in 1847, Anna Dodgson was more pleased than anything else, observing: "Francis Sears got the fire maker to wake him in the morning at ½ past 3, and he set out on a long journey, nobody knows where and nobody cares." [19] In 1849, Eldress Wealthy Storer of the Hancock Ministry recorded another apostasy that she did not find overly distressing, "E. Linch went after strawberries and did not return." [20]

In general, good Believers tried to be philosophical about what they called the "purging of Zion." When Stephen Baker left New Lebanon in 1846, a leader commented in the Elders' *Confidential Journal*: "Stephen Baker has made up his mind to go, and we can say good riddance from bad rubbish, he, together with the rest that have gone have made us much trouble. Thus within the space of about one month eight have gone from this order to the world. They went out from us because they were not of us." [21] Other members reacted in a similar way, pitying the unfortunates who had left more than they pitied themselves for being forsaken. Brother Nicholas Bennet of New Lebanon remarked:

I have often been called to part with my companions that felt dear to me, and always as long as they remained among believers, I continued to wish for their prosperity, and felt anxious for their welfare, but as soon as they turned their backs and departed from the way of God, I buried them from the sympathy of my heart, as soon and as freely as I would bury a dead carcass from my sight. [22]

Not all Shakers, however, were able to deal with the economic and psychological impact of an apostasy rate that reached nearly 15 percent in the New Lebanon Church Family during the 1840s. By 1850, the proportion of members aged sixteen to twenty-nine (the years when they were most likely to leave the faith) had fallen to 21.7 percent in all the eastern communities (see Appendixes C.1-C.11). Certainly a high percentage of these 489 young Believers ultimately chose to apostatize. Given these figures, it is easy to understand why some members gave way to feelings of betrayal and disillusionment when their colleagues left the sect. When Allen, Wicks, and the two Bennets left New Lebanon in 1846, Anna Dodgson, who had grown up with the two Sisters, penned a poem of haunting poignancy in her *Dye House Journal*.

> Ah fond recollection comes stealing upon me,
> Unmindful the tears of affection do flow,
> As my heart wanders back to my former companions
> Who with me refused yet longer to go.

But ah! can it be that it will be eternal,
That this separation must always be made?
It will and it must, it can never be altered,
They've made their own choice and they cannot be saved . . .
O hear me my God for my soul is in anguish,
When but for a moment I take a review
Of the sorrow and grief and the sore tribulation,
That we have been called in times past to go thro'.
Could this be the end of these days of affliction,
I'd willingly live to be threescore and ten,
But my spirit does murmur when all the predictions
Do firmly declare it is but just begun.[23]

Nor was Sister Anna the only member to succumb to these lonely reflections. Elder Thomas Damon of Hancock reported to his friend, Elder George Wilcox of Enfield, Connecticut, in 1848: "On going into the wash room a few days ago, one of the Sisters who was to work there alone, mentioned to me what a lonesome feeling she had come across her that afternoon, and remarked that if all the folks were only here that had gone away in all these years, it need not be so, as she could then have help and company enough."[24]

The 1840s saw the incidence of apostasy peak and then decline slightly at many of the eastern communities (see Appendix A.2). Although this decline was short-lived, the remaining members tried to take heart and hoped that their days of tribulation were ending. In 1847, Philemon Stewart decided that the prophesied purging of Zion had been completed. "A heavy cloud of darkness resting in the hearts of false pretenders has surely by the Hand of God, within two years past, been purged from this part of the Church."[25] Anna Dodgson agreed, writing one year later:

But two years past had you foretold
What two years coming would unfold,
The change from sneaking here and there,
To get a flesh bit nice and rare,
For not one motion, act nor thought,
But's on the gospel anvil wrought,
And every one it seems to me,
A striving who the best can be.
The separation is complete,
Between the chaff and precious wheat.[26]

Even if Stewart and Dodgson had been correct in their optimistic assessments, the years of apostasies had exacted a toll which could not be lightly dismissed. Although fewer long-time members may have chosen to leave, overall apostasy rates remained high. At the New Lebanon Church Family, for example, while the overall apostasy rate did drop during the 1850s to 11.4 percent, it increased sharply in succeeding decades. Concurrently, the length of time that new members chose to remain in the faith continued to fall, averaging only 8.8 years for males and 9.6 years for females in the 1850s (see Appendixes A.2 and A.5). The total population of the eastern communities in 1860 was 2,060, down 15.1 percent from the peak reached just twenty years earlier. The situation among the Brethren was worse—the male population in 1860 was only 812, down 20.1 percent from the 1840 level (see Appendix B.1). The exigencies of everyday life surrounded members who remained faithful, and threatened to overwhelm them, as Stewart himself observed in 1847. "Business presses hard, but few hands to do it. May we again be blessed with numbers more righteous than those we have lost." [27]

The most damaging effect of these backslidings was not the departure of the individuals themselves, though their hands were certainly missed in the barns and workshops. Shaker leaders, in fact, were glad to have their rebellious spirits banished from the communities. By their sheer numbers alone, these seceders planted seeds of doubt in the minds of many hitherto devoted members. Those who remained in the Society began to wonder if the fault for the withdrawals lay wholly in the apostates themselves, as the leaders insisted, or at least partly in the faith they had chosen to abandon.

The high apostasy rates that had persisted in the eastern communities since the 1830s had drained Shaker resources at their most vulnerable point. So dire was the situation at some villages that it became difficult to find members to fill all necessary positions of responsibility. The crisis of leadership that had begun in the 1830s continued. By 1860, there were only 339 Sisters aged twenty-five to forty-nine, or just 27.2 percent of the total female population. Among the men, the situation was worse, with only 187 Brethren in this age group, or 23.0 percent of the male population (see Appendix B.4). Yet it was largely from this group that the leaders of the future would have to be selected. And, if these figures indicated problems for the future, the situation during the middle decades of the century was already serious. Estimating seven positions of authority each for males and females in every Family, and forty Families in all the eastern communities, then in 1850, 26.4 percent of all adult Sisters and 40.1 percent of all adult Brethren could be counted among the leadership. [28]

All levels of the Shaker hierarchy were affected. In 1848, the New Hampshire Ministry reported to New Lebanon about the condition of the community at Sabbathday Lake, Maine, whose Church Family was then struggling without a Trustee.

There are not members sufficient and able to do justice to the cause, in protecting, leading and governing the societies. What they will come to we cannot forsee. . . . Poor Elder Brother John Coffin, a feeble, sickly man, was obliged to go to Portland for their bread corn, taking with him a boy to help do the lifting . . . In that family with the exception of Elder Brother, there was only one brother between the ages of seventeen and sixty-four, and that one is subject to fits of insanity.[29]

To compound these difficulties, when the New Hampshire Ministry sought to replace Coffin with Brother Otis Sawyer, who had been serving elsewhere as a Trustee, Sawyer refused. He pleaded the press of temporal business, argued that there had been too many recent leadership changes in the Bishopric, and declared that he had no wish to serve in the same "lot" with the Elder Sisters then in office. The New Hampshire Ministry reported to the Lead Ministry:

. . . we could look upon him in no other Light, than as rejecting the gift. He finally said he would put office affairs into a condition by September next, so that . . . would be unobjectionable, and he would try to labor for a gift; but he keeps the power all in his own hands, for he would give no consent to give himself up to the gift of the Ministry.[30]

Even the Lead Ministry experienced staffing problems during these difficult years. The foursome of Elders Ebenezer and Rufus Bishop and Eldresses Ruth Landon and Asenath Clark, in office together since Mother Lucy's death in 1821, was broken up in 1848 by the death of Elder Ebenezer. During the next decade, seven new Elders and Eldresses were installed, effectively destroying whatever continuity the Lead Ministry had built up over the previous years.

This rapid turnover at the top level of the Shaker hierarchy was indirectly caused by the high apostasy rates that had plagued the Society for so long. Beginning in the 1820s, fewer and fewer members of leadership quality had chosen to remain in the faith, which led the leadership as a whole to age. When a leader died and had to be replaced, often the only members available were middle-aged or older, shortening their likely tenure in positions of authority. In 1852 alone, two such changes were required in the Lead Ministry after the deaths of Eldress Samantha Fairbanks in March and Elder Rufus Bishop in September. The problems that ensued were described in an October letter to the New Hampshire Ministry.

Now comes the spiritual part; O dear! what shall I say, I hardly know; it seems sometimes as tho we had got as much as one foot in the grave, and the other but just out, we have some pretty close times we may depend, but all in our little new formed lot have put their shoulders to the wheel so well that we make it go somehow, if it fails of going one way we try another and keep up tolerable good courage yet, hoping for better times ahead.[31]

The combination of a high apostasy rate and a weakened leadership in the 1840s and 1850s resulted in a marked change of attitude within the sect. Elder Freegift Wells concluded that the entire temper of the Society had been fundamentally altered. He found it difficult to maintain discipline among the young Believers in his care because they knew by example how easy it was to flee to the World and find friends among the growing legion of Shaker backsliders. As the nation began to recover from the Panic of 1837 and its subsequent depression, improving economic conditions also enticed some members to leave the faith. Wells complained in 1850:

I have known a time when going to the world seemed . . . like the most awful step that anyone could take. At such times souls would bear admonition and mortification. But in such a time as this, when going to the world seems but little more to some than to walk into another room, they are in no condition to bear much admonition or to be restricted beyond what they think is just.[32]

Wells was keenly aware that there were many "tottering souls" in Zion that had to be coddled, not driven to salvation.

Because other leaders recognized this as well, the methods they employed to maintain order and obedience changed subtly. By the late 1840s, Elders and Eldresses found that they had to be extremely careful in disciplining members if they hoped to save them for the gospel. They also realized that some modification of the severe restrictions from earlier years was needed if they hoped to stem the tide of apostasies. Wells's recommendation to the Lead Ministry that they relax some of the inspired regulations introduced during "Mother's Work" was heeded in due course. In the spring of 1855, liberty to use tea and coffee was restored.[33] The use of pork had already crept back into the communities, as Elder Thomas Damon noted in February 1854: "Commenced eating meat after an abstinence of more than 12 years, having quit the practice on the 5th of November 1841."[34]

Perhaps more than in any other period, the Elders were inclined to forgive transgressions that would earlier have led them to take serious action. Though their reaction to wrongdoing was the same as in previous years, their methods of dealing with it changed. Shaker leaders during this period were working from a position of weakness and both they and their charges knew it. The case of Brother Solomon Wollison of the Hancock East Family demonstrates this shift. Brother Solomon was a close friend of a Young Believer named David Lamson who had joined the community for a time in the early 1840s. Disillusioned by what he saw as the leaders' manipulation of gifts during "Mother's Work," Lamson left the faith and wrote a history of his stay among the Shakers that he published at his own expense in 1848.[35] When it appeared, the Hancock leaders were alarmed enough to consider publishing a testimony that Lamson had written while a member in which he declared belief in tenets that he disavowed in his book.[36] Hoping thus to discredit him, they gave the original testimony to one of the schoolteachers so that copies might be made. Wollison, concerned that his friend's reputation would suffer should the testimony reach the World, hired an outsider to steal the document from the Hancock schoolhouse.[37]

There is no record that the Elders took any disciplinary action as a result of this theft, although their correspondence reveals that they knew who was responsible. By the following year, however, the Ministry's patience had been exhausted. In June 1849, they convened a meeting to discuss Wollison's future in the Society. Present were the two Ministry Elders, the two East Family Elders, and eleven other Brethren, a number that guaranteed a fair hearing. In an earlier period, the Ministry might well have made a decision in such a case without summoning a meeting at all.

Wollison, who had more friends in the World than in the community, requested that some of them be permitted to attend this meeting as character witnesses, but his petition was denied. Since Wollison himself refused to be present under these conditions, those in attendance "unanimously agreed that the connection of said Wollison with the Society be dissolved."[38] The leaders' forbearance in dealing with such a troublesome Believer is remarkable. They had initially hoped that he would choose to leave of his own accord without having to be formally excommunicated. This not being the case, the leaders feared that Wollison would capitalize on his excommunication once in the World, claiming to be a hapless victim of Shaker harshness.

Although meetings of this kind had occurred earlier in Shaker history, their frequency increased during the mid-nineteenth century. A similar case developed at Watervliet, New York, in 1849. On March 5, Elder Freegift Wells summoned Brother Ransom Parks to a meeting of Brethren to answer charges of "disorderly and improper conduct" concerning a "pair of fine Boots then in making . . . with deep red Morocco tops, turned down about 3 inches, extravagantly stitched, . . . which thing or fashion was in nowise allowable in our Society." Parks was also accused of "unbecoming talk and harsh conversation and replies to the Elder Brother."

At the meeting the Brethren decided that Brother Ransom was "out of a proper gift of subordination and travel," and granted him a day free of work responsibilities to think over his sins and decide whether he wished to confess them and change his ways or leave the Family altogether. The next day, Parks knelt before his Elders and Brethren and confessed his sins, but the Brethren decided he was not sufficiently repentant, so he was given still more time. On March 8, Parks came to the Elders and told them that he had decided to leave the sect, a decision that the Brethren upheld at a meeting on March 14. Throughout these meetings, Elder Freegift later recorded, "nothing but the kindest of feelings were extended towards him, and not a harsh or rough word spoken by anyone, but on the contrary, all desired his comfort, prosperity, and happiness in the way and work of God."[39]

The most interesting feature of these meetings is their quasi-democratic nature. It is surely no accident that they first appear in Shaker records at the same time that many members had begun to agitate for a degree of democratization in the Society's government. As the leaders' authority was undermined by the Grahamite controversy and the unpopular gifts of "Mother's Work," they increasingly turned to such group conferences when difficult disciplinary decisions were required. Shaker leadership never wholly succumbed to the democratic spirit of nineteenth-century America, but significant steps were taken in that direction.

The weakening of Society leadership was merely one result of the rash of backslidings that continued throughout the 1840s and 1850s. Another was the realization that few new converts were likely to come from the adult ranks. Leaders such as Freegift Wells recognized that adults fresh from the freedom of the World naturally found it difficult to bear even minimal restraint. The Shakers of these years, therefore, hoped that the admission of large numbers of children, who could theoretically be trained from an early age to accept and profit by admonition, would offset declining adult conversions.

Six of the eleven eastern communities experienced small population increases between 1840 and 1860, and evidence indicates that many, if not most, of these new members were children. By 1860, children under age sixteen comprised 26.4 percent of the total population of the eastern communities, and in some villages the proportion exceeded 30 percent (see Appendix B.5). The proportion in many Senior Order Families, where children were typically housed, was often higher.

At the New Lebanon Church Family, for example, the proportion of children peaked in 1855 at 30.2 percent, and nearly 40 percent of the males in the Family were under sixteen (see Appendix A.7). Admission records for this Family reveal that prior to "Mother's Work" relatively few children were taken in, but during the years succeeding the revival the number rose dramatically. Between 1787 and 1830, only 182 children were admitted to this Family or 40.3 percent of total admissions. In the twenty years between 1841 and 1860, however, 211 children were admitted or 90.2 percent of new members (see Appendixes A.8 and A.9). In the face of a high adult apostasy rate, great efforts were made to keep these youngsters in the faith, but were met with limited success. Of the 173 boys admitted at New Lebanon between 1831 and 1870, only eleven died in the faith as adults (6.4 percent). Although more girls grew up to convert, only twenty-four of the 167 admitted in this period (14.4 percent) died in the faith (see Appendixes A.8 and A.9). Many of these potential members left by choice, but a large number were taken away by relatives or guardians. It was common for parents to indenture children to the Shakers and later change their minds and return, demanding loudly that their offspring be surrendered. Such situations occurred with greater frequency as the proportion of children living in the villages increased. Two representative incidents surfaced at New Lebanon and Hancock during the late 1840s.

In December 1846, as the New Lebanon Church Family was reeling from the shock of a single year high of fifteen apostasies, three boys were brought there to live by their father, William Pillow. They were promising children gratefully received into the Boys' Order, and quickly became contented there. Their mother, Ann, had also joined and took up residence at the New Lebanon North Family. The prospects for all four appeared excellent. Then, in July 1847, William Pillow returned to the village and threatened to break the indentures he had signed the previous year. He visited the community again in August, "all in a foam for his family."[40] The scene that ensued was by no means rare during these years. A scribe reported in the Family's *Domestic Journal*:

William Pillow is at our office today with a gang of associates. . . . They came determined to take Ann Pillow & the children. . . . After some conversation, William took Ann's bonnet and put it on her head and tied it, she seeming to make no resistance. He then took her by the hand and urged her forcibly out of the room, thro the hall. The man . . . and two women seized each of them one of the boys and were making for the door. Elder Daniel Boler being there stood in the passage and reprimanded them. Some of our sisters were also present, and resisted their hold of the boys who soon escaped. Ann also resisted, and in passing a door near which Samantha Fairbanks stood, seized hold of her and begged assistance. Hannah Ann Treadway being also present, they both held on to Ann, who shortly escaped from William's grasp. William and his company then gave it up, and after much abusive language and shameful conduct they all cleared away.[41]

In September, William Pillow, accompanied by a sheriff, returned triumphantly to the village and watched while his companion served Elder Daniel Boler with a writ of habeas corpus. Three days later, he had another writ served against Boler, Fairbanks, and two other Believers, alleging assault and battery during the altercation the preceding month. In spite of Shaker efforts to spirit the boys away to Enfield, Connecticut, Pillow discovered their whereabouts and seized them once more. The two youngest decided that they preferred to live with their father and were freely surrendered by the Shakers, but William, the eldest, expressed a wish to remain at New Lebanon. His father, however, took the issue to court, where the case dragged on until 1851. During the litigation, William, Jr., was not allowed to remain in his Shaker home. By the time the judge in the case decided in Pillow's favor, William and his brothers had lived so long in the World that none of them wished to return to the community.[42]

A similar incident occurred at Hancock in the same period. A man named John Irving joined the community with his wife and seven children in June 1847.[43] Soon thereafter, he departed with most of his family, leaving two daughters behind under indenture. Nothing was heard from him until April 11, 1851, when he burst into the Church Family dining room during dinner, accompanied by a sheriff from Pittsfield, and tried to take the girls away by force. One of the Ministry Eldresses described the scene this way.

Such a time was never witnessed by any of us. The girls resisted, screached, begged and cried with all their might, at the same time clinging to the Sisters with death like grasps, crying, do, O! do help me. I cannot go. I had rather die. O Father, father, how can you cause your children to feel such trouble; you brought us here, and you bound us here and promised you would never take us away. And now you will do it. O! you will have to suffer for this after you die you don't know how much. At this time the rest of the children and many of the Sisters were weeping aloud. And as resistance was out of the case, we did all in our power by way of pleading, entreating, and persuading, but all to no purpose. They forcibly took the children, and they went screaching and screaming through the village. This cruel scene lasted ¾ of an hour. The girls were good girls and much beloved by all. The eldest was 13 last September the youngest 9 last October. The Sheriff was surprised to hear them talk, and to see their love for their home and their friends here. He said after he got them to Pittsfield that he would not go through another such a scene for 50 dollars.[44]

The next day, however, the Shakers secured a writ upholding the legality of the indentures and the same sheriff was charged with returning the girls to the village. Justina, the eldest, arrived still clutching the Shaker cap that her father had tried to wrest from her and burn. In spite of the girls' expressed desire to remain among the Believers, their father took the issue to court where it remained undecided until 1852. He claimed that he had signed the indenture under duress and argued so persuasively that the girls had been detained against their wills that the case was ultimately decided in his favor. The Shakers were even required to pay the court costs. Justina, then in her late teens, died several years later of what was called "quick consumption," leading the Hancock Ministry to conclude that God was punishing her father for the forced removal of the children.[45]

Court battles such as these were commonplace in the 1840s and 1850s.[46] Indeed, some Believers grew disgusted because so many children were snatched from their Shaker homes just as they were reaching an age when they might begin making a meaningful economic and spiritual contribution. In 1865, after a couple named Sherman came to leave a seven-year-old and take away several older progeny, a New Lebanon Brother complained about what he called a "real money making scheme for Shakers to raise them up give them a good education board and clothe them till they get to be old enough to be of some benefit and then have them up and kick the bucket."[47]

Worldly parents of this period discovered that they could leave their children with the Shakers for brief periods while they reestablished themselves after economic or geographic dislocation. Even if they signed indentures, they knew that sympathetic Worldly judges were likely to decide custody cases in their favor. During the middle of the nineteenth century, Shaker communities increasingly became specialized institutions for the care of displaced minors, few of whom remained long enough to convert. Those who did often left the sect as young adults.

Afflicted by the departure of many adults who had joined during the excitement of "Mother's Work," and disappointed by the failure of their plan to augment Shaker membership by admitting large numbers of children, many Believers in the 1840s and 1850s turned hopefully instead to new religious activity in the World. Most promising as potential converts were the thousands of Millerites who, beginning in the 1830s, had begun to prepare for the imminent second appearance of Christ. Their founder was William Miller, a farmer from Low Hampton, New York, who had made a special study of the Bible in the late 1810s. By using information in key passages from the books of Daniel and Revelation, he had established to his own astonishment and satisfaction that Christ was due to reappear on earth during the year 1843. By the late 1830s, he was lecturing throughout the northeast foretelling the Lord's approach. Increasing numbers of Americans, alarmed by events in the World, listened with growing conviction. Miller wrote to a colleague in 1836 of his reception in Lansinburg, New York:

My lectures were well received in that place, and excited attention. The house was filled to overflowing for eight days in succession. . . . Infidels, deists, Universalists, and sectarians were all chained to their seats, in perfect silence, for hours—yes, days—to hear the old stammering man talk about the second coming of Christ.[48]

When the Adventist movement, as it was called, reached its peak of popularity in the early 1840s, it claimed approximately 50,000 adherents. Miller had lectured an estimated 4,000 times in 500 cities and towns, and was supported in his efforts by as many as 500 additional speakers. Perhaps 200 ministers had been converted to his teachings and at least 1,000 Adventist congregations had been established.[49] By 1843, when the great event was to take place, people throughout the country began making personal preparations to receive the Lord. An elderly Connecticut woman named Betsy Farnsworth supposedly acquired a new set of teeth and a green silk umbrella for the occasion, and David Parsons of Worcester, Massachusetts, reportedly painted and varnished his sleigh so that it would be ready if the Lord wished to ride in it.[50]

Even the Shakers, already living in the millennium, began to show an interest. In November 1842, Sister Margaret McGooden of Harvard received a gift in a dream and reported: "O Elder Brother! 'tis true, 'tis true, the Lord Almighty will surely visit the earth in 43, as the children of men have predicted, though not in the way they have laid out."[51] Some Believers began to expect that many of these hopeful Adventists would soon turn to them for satisfaction of their spiritual yearnings. In March 1843, the New Hampshire Ministry informed the Lead Ministry that "there seems to be more feeling and conviction manifested among the world of late than ever, partly owing to Miller excitement and the general depression in everything in Antichrist's Kingdom &c. &c. Souls do look toward Zion for something better than they now enjoy."[52] It is surely no accident that the spirit of Christ visited many Shaker villages in 1843, delivering messages of both warning and comfort. The inspiration for these visits may well have derived from the furor then present in the World.

As the year 1843 waned, Miller explained to his followers that they should not surrender their hopes. He had calculated that Christ would reappear sometime during the Jewish year 1843, which did not expire until March 21, 1844. When this day came and went without incident, Miller admitted that he had erred slightly in figuring the date of

Christ's crucifixion and a new date, October 22, 1844, was established for the beginning of the millennium. On this "Last Day," Millerites throughout the country met quietly in their homes and churches to pray and await their Lord. After a twenty-four hour vigil revealed that nothing had happened, the disillusionment was tremendous. Luther Boutelle, a Groton, Massachusetts, shoemaker reported:

The 22nd of October passed, making unspeakably sad the faithful and longing ones; but causing the unbelieving and wicked to rejoice. All was still. No *Advent Herald*; no meetings as formerly. Every one felt lonely, with hardly a desire to speak to any one. Still in the cold world! No deliverance—the Lord did not come! No words can express the feelings of disappointment of a true Adventist then.[53]

But millennial hopes die hard, and many Millerites simply decided that "there was to be a waiting time, a midnight before the Lord would come."[54] One group of Adventists maintained their faith so well that, under the name Seventh Day Adventists, they have become a major force in modern Christianity. But others, desiring "knowledge and sight" of God's kingdom rather than mere "faith and hope," turned to the Shakers who were already living in the millennium. Most influential among them was Enoch Jacobs, editor of the Adventist *Day Star*, a periodical which the Shakers received regularly. In 1846, he converted to Shakerism and joined the community at Whitewater, Ohio, together with some seventy fellow Adventists.[55] In August of that year, Jacobs traveled to New Lebanon to meet the Lead Ministry and tell them of his newfound faith.

Shakers in the eastern villages greeted Jacobs as the herald of a new ingathering, and listened eagerly as he told of Adventist interest in their beliefs and practices. By 1847, Shaker interest in the movement had increased to the point of active participation. In February, Isaac Youngs, Frederick Evans, and Giles Avery left New Lebanon to attend and speak before an Adventist conference in Enfield, Connecticut.[56] When they returned, the Believers enthusiastically heard their reports in meeting and carefully read their issues of the *Day Star*.[57]

Brothers Barnabas Sprague of Hancock and Philip Burlingame of Enfield, Connecticut, traveled to New York City and Long Island in May on a mission among Adventists there.[58] All these activities seemed to indicate that the long-promised ingathering was at hand. Spirit messages confirmed this supposition. In March 1848, "Mother Ann came and attended with us, and spake considerable to us, in a line to wake us up to be prepared for the increase of the gospel."[59]

The total number of Adventists who actually converted to the Shaker faith is unknown but it is estimated that as many as 200 joined the western communities. In the east, significant numbers joined at Harvard, Canterbury, and Enfield, New Hampshire.[60] Elder Thomas Damon reported in October 1849 that the Canterbury Gathering Order included fifty-five new members, forty women and fifteen men, half of whom were Adventists. He noted as well that nearly all the new male converts were Adventists, a trend that cheered Shakers who had for many years watched with concern as the ranks of the Brethren dwindled.[61]

The contemporary popularity of another religious group, the Spiritualists, further strengthened many Shakers in their conviction that the Society's days of declining membership were over. As Isaac Youngs observed, these developments "greatly attracted our attention . . . and they have been a source of consolation to us, inspiring us with hopes that God was opening a way for souls to be led thereby to the gospel, that Zion might be blest with an increase."[62] To many members, this movement seemed a logical extension of the spirit communications of "Mother's Work," a belief fostered by some Worldly mediums. In April 1851, Brother Jefferson White of Enfield, Connecticut, reported that Mother Ann's spirit was due to make an appearance among Spiritualists in Springfield, Massachusetts. He found nothing strange in this, concluding:

We have not the least doubt but what the work which is abroad is of God, and will spread far and wide. The messages of some are so near like those given to Believers . . . that we are constrained to say, if one is from a good source, so are both. Br. Philip says he does not see how believers can gainsay this work.[63]

As early as December 1849, Shakers throughout the northeast were noting with interest the activities of the soon-to-be-famous Fox sisters of Rochester, New York. A scribe recorded in the New Lebanon Church Family's *Domestic Journal*: "We heard in the Public Paper a remarkable story about a mysterious knocking at Rochester, which commenced two or three years ago. No natural cause can be discovered. It is confidently believed to be supernatural."[64] In 1850, Elders Richard Bushnell and Frederick Evans of the New Lebanon North Family visited Rochester to investigate these reports and returned to announce that spirits were indeed making themselves known there.[65] A company from New Lebanon went to Stratford, Connecticut, in September 1850 where a series of strange phenomena had been observed in the home of a Dr. Phelps. After returning home, Sister Jane Knight wrote a piece of doggerel in which she lamented the spirits' mischievousness, but observed hopefully that they seemed somewhat interested in certain Shaker publications.

> While we were sitting quiet there,
> A crash above doth reach the ear,
> A trunk is thrown and badly broken—
> Affording thus another token,
> That some unseen went in and out,
> Tossing whate'er they would about;
> The household thus is quite confused,—
> 'Tis vexing thus to be misused. . . .
> One day on hearing quite a clatter,
> I look'd around to learn the matter,
> What it all was I do not know,
> But a Millennial Church they throw,
> About the time of its arrival,
> Came the Kentucky Revival.
> Perhaps indeed the Spirit sees
> Much light contained in works like these.[66]

Some members felt that they were being passed over by the tide of spiritual progress and were alarmed that the spirits who had been increasingly deserting Shaker meetings were disporting themselves among "World's People." Before long, new kinds of spirit manifestations appeared in Shaker homes as well. In 1851, Elder Thomas Damon recorded:

May 17—Henry Gordon and Horace Cooley came to Enfield on a visit and to display the rapping process.
May 18—Henry and Horace visited the Church, North and West Families in the afternoon and had sittings—the raps were audible and quite intelligent.[67]

Believers at New Lebanon participated in similar gatherings. Elisha Blakeman noted in November 1851: "Last night and night before, we held circles around tables in taylors shop to wait on the spirits."[68] The impact of these events delighted leaders who had been sorrowfully observing the declining enthusiasm of many Believers under their care. The Hancock Ministry reported joyfully in an 1852 letter to New Lebanon:

It began in a very simple manner by moving material things, Tables, stands, chairs &c. with short but decisive communications. This so attracted the feelings of the young that they were easily led on to a real work of conviction and love to the gifts of God, which has produced a heart-searching work, and caused them to come to their Elders and there to confess their faults in honesty and humiliation, earnestly desiring the gifts of God.[69]

The leaders hoped that Spiritualism would prove as helpful in winning souls to the gospel as the slightly different spirit manifestations had been in the late 1830s. Elder Frederick Evans explained this to

William Hepworth Dixon when the latter visited New Lebanon in the 1860s. Dixon reported that "every great spiritual revival which has agitated America since his Church was planted has led to a new Society being founded on the principles of Mother Ann. . . . According to Elder Frederick, who is watching with a keen and pitying eye the vagaries of the new spiritualist movement in America, a nineteenth revival is now at hand, from the action of which he expects a considerable extension of his Church."[70] Eldress Cassandana Brewster of the Hancock Ministry agreed, telling Eldress Sally Loomis of Harvard in 1852, "The spirit rappers tell us the time is near when men shall acknowledge us as their pattern."[71]

Developments during the late 1850s further encouraged optimistic Shakers to expect hordes of new converts. Of particular interest was the establishment in Philadelphia of a small Shaker out-Family led by a black mystic named Rebecca Jackson. Under the nominal supervision of the Elders at Watervliet, New York, where she had lived for four years, Jackson recruited a small coterie of followers and gathered them into Shaker order beginning in 1851. She remained active in Philadelphia until 1857, spreading the Shaker gospel wherever she could find listeners.[72] Her involvement with evangelical religion in such an urban center was an early example of the urban revivalism that would be sparked by the Panic of 1857.

A similar panic twenty years earlier had touched off a wave of revivalism—the same type that had brought the Shakers converts since the late eighteenth century. Encouraged by Jackson's success in Philadelphia, Shaker leaders expected a similar influx of new members from America's urban areas, where a panic in 1857 had disrupted both economic and spiritual life. Using the new system of mass communication provided by the telegraph and penny newspapers, businessmen throughout the east allied themselves with one another and turned to evangelical religion as a panacea, a ritual cry to God for help.[73] Called the "Businessman's Revival," the fervor spread to rural areas as well.

The Freewill Baptists, who had started as a largely rural group in the late eighteenth century, founded organizations in New York City in 1849 and Boston in 1850. In 1857, their newspaper, the *Watchman and Reflector*, published an editorial to promote revivals throughout New England. The response was immediate. By March 1858, weeks of nightly meetings in Pittsfield, Massachusetts, had increased Baptist membership there to one of the highest per capita levels in the state.[74] It is not surprising that Shakers in the area should have viewed these developments as signs that their own ranks would soon be augmented. Their hopes were disappointed, however.

The time for rural, communal, celibate life had largely passed in a nation that was rapidly industrializing and increasingly urban. The image the Shakers had long enjoyed as a progressive, industrious, and sober sect was changing. They were being regarded more as a peculiar, if interesting, remnant of a previous era. Internal dissension and continuing leadership crises had, unfortunately, marred the peace and serenity that had attracted individuals tired of the World's bustle and excitement. As more apostates left the Society and told their tales in the outside world, fewer people considered converting. This connection was not lost on Elder Freegift Wells, who wrote in the 1850s:

Every now and then, one or more jumps overboard, and . . . succeed in reaching the shores of Babylon, where they publish all the jars and contentions, broils and animosities, and every other dishonorable thing which exists among us. This has a tendency to destroy the confidence that many have formerly had in us—Because by searching among many, they obtain satisfactory proof that not a few of these statements are facts. And instead of being a light to the world as we ought to be, our works reflect darkness—a shocking condition for the Zion of God to be in.[75]

Thus, despite the admission of hundreds of displaced minors, and the conversion of several hundred Millerites and a handful of Philadelphians, Shaker ranks never received the accession that had long been anticipated. In 1853, Brother Joseph Gilman wrote of the Alfred community, "The increase has proved hardly adequate to the diminution incident to death and apostasy."[76] His assessment was equally true of the other eastern villages. Data from decadal census schedules provides evidence of this situation. Total membership in the eastern communities had peaked in 1840 at 2,427, but this figure represented an increase of only 111 (4.8 percent) over the level of ten years earlier. In fact, the Society's membership had been nearly stagnant since 1830. Five of the eastern communities had reached their numerical zeniths by that year, and three more reached their highest membership levels in 1840 (see Appendix B.2). The traditional view that the sect maintained a high level of membership until at least the Civil War is manifestly incorrect.[77] The qualitative decline that had been marked by dissension and increasing apostasy rates in the 1820s was rapidly succeeded by a quantitative decline, first visible in the changing age structure of the communities, then in total membership figures.

By the 1850s most Believers recognized the seriousness of these developments. Eldress Cassandana Brewster was one who found these trends distressing, and wistfully recalled the promise that Zion would someday see a new generation of converts. In 1854, she wrote to the Harvard Ministry:

You must know we are surrounded with labor, tribulation and affliction. For what can be more grievous and heart rending than to have those whom we have placed confidence in prove traitors, and further do all in their power to destroy others. . . . we have often been told in days that are past that Zion would be purged and that some that we were not looking for would be swept out, and after this there would be an ingathering. The former we now realize, and the latter we believe is near at hand, for Zion is already bowed low and according to promise the time must be near when the Almighty will stretch forth his arm and raise Zion in her glory and beauty, and will turn the hearts of men to behold her brightness and splendor, and cause them to flock to her.[78]

Isaac Youngs similarly described the grim atmosphere in the sect during the late 1850s.

Much depression of spirit has been felt, and struggling thro' dark and gloomy prospects, on account of apostasies, lifelessness and backslidings of faithful members, and the scanty ingathering from without. There have been some efforts to open our testimony to the world . . . but there is such a stupidity of soul and absence of conviction for sin . . . that there is rarely one to be found who is willing to submit to the mortifying terms of the gospel. We gather in many children, but when they come to act for themselves, a large portion of them choose the flowery path of nature rather than the cross.[79]

The years after 1844, when the excitement of "Mother's Work" began to fade, saw a series of disappointments for Shaker leaders. Many Believers who had been attracted by the fervor of the revival left as soon as it showed signs of diminishing. Those who had been thought faithful, and who were looked upon as the next generation of leaders, often rebelled against the multiplicity of regulations introduced during the revival and also departed. Worldly religious developments that seemed to promise an ingathering in fact did little to increase either the quantity or quality of Shaker membership. The 1860s and 1870s would be dominated by the Believers' struggles to come to terms with these difficult circumstances. Bereft of the converts they had hoped to welcome, leaders were determined to uphold the purity of Shaker principles regardless of numbers. Committed followers remembered that their road to salvation had to be traveled alone. They were reassured by the belief that whatever happened in the World or within the Society, loving and protective spirits surrounded them. Although beset by temporal problems, good Shakers recalled that their eternal future was secure, and they were comforted.

9

A New Dress to Mother Ann's Gospel
(1858-1871)

When Millerism, Spiritualism, and the urban revivalism of the late 1850s failed to bring about the ingathering so long anticipated, Shaker leaders struggled to adjust to a more modest level of spiritual progress. This concern preoccupied the Elders far more than the future of the federal union fighting for survival at this time. Defiantly claiming the righteousness of Shaker principles in the face of Worldly disinterest, leaders throughout the Society strove to emphasize purity and upright behavior instead of numbers. Many of their followers, however, were disappointed that the promises given during "Mother's Work" had not been fulfilled, so they turned to more Worldly pursuits. As they traveled more in the World and as "World's People" came more often to visit and buy in the villages, there was a subtle but noticeable shift in the attitude of many Believers. Inexorably, as Shaker economic dependence on the World increased, the Society was invaded by Worldly tastes and ideas as well. The decade of the 1860s saw a materialistic interest proliferate within the communities, threatening, some leaders felt, to undermine the life of the spirit.

The leaders' initial reaction to the seemingly irreversible Shaker decline was marked by a determination to maintain the purity of the faith, regardless of developments in the World. As early as 1853, Elder Grove Wright rationalized the many apostasies he had witnessed in a letter to the Harvard Ministry. "But as you say, you had rather be less in numbers than to support sinners and evil workers. So say we, for they are but dead weights in the house of God. One honest true hearted soul is more to be prized than 500 such ones, for their salt has lost its savor if they ever had any." [1]

Elder Lorenzo Grosvenor of the Harvard Ministry agreed, although he could not hide his dismay at the situation. An Elder visiting from Ohio wrote of him in 1854:

He likes to preach as well as a hungry man loves to eat, and he is what might be called a right smart talker . . . thinks God is ready now, just now, today he is ready and there is no use in our procrastinating the work any longer to have the world better or more prepared than they now are. He said, we have been waiting these thirty years in the anticipation of an increase of numbers, and it is growing worse and worse all the time. And said with a sigh; I suppose I will have the satisfaction of going out of this world without seeing anything accomplished on this head.[2]

Elder Lorenzo's assessment was all too accurate. He recognized that the paths trod by the Believers and by the "World's People," which had sometimes seemed nearly parallel, were certainly diverging. He had seen promising Worldly movements such as Grahamism, Millerism, and Spiritualism fail to spark a widespread rebirth of interest in the sect. In an increasingly urban nation, where life had become more complex yet the solutions provided by evangelical religion were being rejected, the Shakers learned that they could no longer hope for large numbers of converts. This painful realization led some leaders to fear for the survival of the faith in any recognizable form.

Elder Thomas Damon believed that only among the older generation were Shaker tenets still upheld in their original purity. As these members died, the future seemed uncertain. Damon wrote in 1855:

We cannot contemplate the departure of those ancient worthies . . . without awakening unpleasant forebodings for the future. It is true that the foundation is laid, but unless the materials of which the superstructure is reared have sufficient strength and solidity in themselves to sustain the edifice, it will fall to the ground.[3]

There is a hint here that Damon knew changes would have to be made if younger members were to be kept in the fold.

One hopeful note was sounded by Elder Giles Avery of the Lead Ministry, who commented in 1861: "Another great source of weakness to many souls in Zion is the want of numbers. . . . Numbers, it is true, when united in righteousness, are the great fountain of strength . . . but the experiences of the human family have abundantly shown the fact that *individuals, single handed* [are] *more potent for victory than a host on the side of error.*" Perhaps Avery envisioned a Society purged of troublemakers by the emetic of disillusionment, reduced to a small core of devout Believers who could then set out to redeem the faith unhindered. He asserted that the most damaging developments contributing to the sect's decline had sprung from within—implying that the condition of the faith would soon improve if Believers would only ignore developments in the World and their own diminishing ranks, and concentrate instead on upholding Shaker principles in their own lives.[4]

But Avery knew that most of Zion's internal divisions could be traced to external sources. He noted in 1861 that "Believers are exposed universally to be somewhat influenced by those elements of disruption, disloyalty and weakness that are turning the outside world into confusion," and concluded, "we have found it vitally necessary in every place among Believers in the East, to revive the good old landmarks of Gospel principle and Order, in things both temporal and spiritual; to awaken resolution, and grow courage to press on in the Gospel path."[5] The most harmful Worldly influence, Avery decided, was the "modern materialistic spiritual infidelity [that] has introduced the idea that man has never fallen; and, when in a sinful state, is simply undeveloped; and, therefore, there is no sin in the world."[6]

Isaac Youngs, too, understood how exposure to Worldly ideas could sap a Shaker's commitment, noting with concern in 1860:

It is a day of great improvements in the world, a day of much free thinking and freedom of investigation, every man may judge for himself, &c.and this spirit, where there is so much freedom as now unavoidably exists between Believers and the world, insinuates itself powerfully among Believers, which is very injurious to their advancement in the gospel.[7]

Though Youngs did not specify the results of this regrettable contact with outsiders and their attitudes, other members were more forthright. Freegift Wells complained in 1864 that many Believers, anxious to attract new members as well as retain those already in the communities, were seeking to reduce the distance between Shaker principles and Worldly practices.

It seems that there are some Spiritualists among Believers that imagine that they can form & apply a *new dress* to Mother Ann's gospel—one that will feel much more agreeable and pleasant to a large portion of Believers at the present time, and far more inviting to the *Eye, Ear & Taste* of the World generally, who would then flock to our standard in large numbers, and fill our vacant ranks. And if this thing could be done to the satisfaction of its advocates, it would no longer be Mother Ann's gospel, and could no longer save one soul from sin. It would be like daubing a good Looking glass with Honey, that it might send forth a more Brilliant Reflection.[8]

According to recent research done by Louis J. Kern, the reformers Wells found so disdainful were also attempting to modify the Shaker principle of celibacy by advocating a type of "purified generation." This movement stirred dissension at most of the eastern communities in the mid-1860s, including New Lebanon, Watervliet, Hancock, Harvard, Canterbury, and Enfield, New Hampshire.[9] This ensuing upheaval may well have been responsible for the increased apostasy rates that plagued many of the villages in these years. At the New Lebanon Church Family, for example, the overall apostasy rate rose sharply from 11.4 percent in the 1850s to 24.8 percent in the 1860s, and the rate among the Brethren reached 35.8 percent (see Appendix A.2). Other villages suffered similar problems. By 1870, the Watervliet community's total population had dropped to just 196, down 35.5 percent from its 1840 peak. At Canterbury, the total population in 1870 was only 177, down 31.9 percent from its 1840 peak. The total population of all eleven eastern communities had dropped from 2,060 in 1860 to 1,444 in 1870, a 29.9 percent decline in just ten years (see Appendix B.1).

The severity of this decline made the leaders' task of maintaining pure belief and practice far more difficult. Though the effort to undermine the sect's commitment to celibacy did little to alter the Shaker lifestyle, other changes did occur in these years. It was impossible for the leaders to insulate their charges from developments in the World and, as a result, the Shakers of the mid-nineteenth century became increasingly like their Worldly neighbors. As the proportion of lukewarm members rose, and as the Society had to pander more and more to Worldly fashion in order to maintain its existence, Believers gradually became more sophisticated in their tastes and began surrounding themselves with little elegancies and fancy articles. When members traveled in the outside world to expand the sect's trading network, they were exposed to ideas foreign to Believers in earlier periods.

Americans were traveling as tourists during these years with a frequency and ease hitherto unknown. Aided by a nearly completed rail system, they eagerly explored the wonders of the natural landscape. A predominantly romantic aesthetic dictated outdoor excursions, and city-bound men marveled at the work of God's hand in nature. By also pursuing this fascination, the Shakers had much in common with their fellow countrymen. They admired the beauty and power of Mammoth Cave and Niagara Falls, and wrote in their voluminous travel journals descriptions full of the same romantic language found in the World. In such an account, a Sister could gush over "the most romantic scene my eyes ever beheld. Rocks of immense size, hanging over frightful precipices, others with large cavities by the hand of nature." [10] With her appreciation of this scene, this Sister exhibited an ideological perspective that would have puzzled her early nineteenth-century predecessors.

In their various travels, Shakers encountered sights that would have horrified the Believers of 1800. In 1847, when Elder Thomas Damon visited Hartford to buy some joiner's tools, he saw in the street "a procession of carriages (about 30 in number) containing wild animals, preceded by a gorgeous Roman chariot, literally covered with gold drawn by ten black horses." [11] He evidently gawked like any other bystander, feeling no incongruity between this lavish spectacle and his supposedly ascetic religious principles. In many Shaker journals of this period, such casual enjoyment of a Worldly pastime is commonplace. The Shakers of the 1850s and 1860s were permitting themselves entertainments that had never previously been allowed. Perhaps the leaders felt that with so few committed Believers willing to remain in the Society, contact with the outside world and its simpler pleasures could do little additional damage. Perhaps they tacitly sanctioned what they recognized they could not prevent.

An excellent record of a Shaker pleasure jaunt was kept by Sister Amelia Lyman of Enfield, Connecticut, who journeyed to the beach at Wickford, Rhode Island, with a party of colleagues in 1858. Her account reveals that the Shakers were learning to enjoy some of the temporal pleasures long denied them.

Aug. 20—A beautiful shore in the shape of a Halfmoon. The sea was very calm so we spent a little time in riding over the waves. It being a hot day, we spread our wet clothes on the rocks to dry, ate our dinner, travelled the beach, picked up a few shells. . . .

Aug. 25—. . . up to the knees in mud, seaweed and water after Quahogs. We stampt around till the water got almost to our necks and provision enough for breakfast when we went towards home. . . .

Aug. 26—The sea a little rougher than before but we never mind that, we jump in, the waves beat against us but we ride over them till well drenched in water both head and heels, and feeling the need of some dry clothing we went to the bedroom (as we called it)—a small place in the rocks which convenienced us very well.

Not wishing to neglect their spiritual responsibilities, Sister Amelia and her companions attended an Episcopal service on their first Sunday morning in Wickford, followed by a visit to the Baptist church the same afternoon. The next week, perhaps as a result of either curiosity or equity, they observed a Methodist service.[12]

While Believers like Sister Amelia and Elder Thomas were shopping in cities, luxuriating on beaches, and relaxing in a variety of health resorts like Saratoga Springs, New York, their Worldly neighbors were returning the favor by visiting Shaker villages. The 1860s saw a marked increase in the number of writers and journalists who came to the Shakers to find a story. What they found was an atmosphere of unhurried busyness, spiritual dedication, and a people who seemed to have no cares. William Hepworth Dixon, whose description of the New Lebanon community was published in his book *New America* in 1867, marveled:

No Dutch town has a neater aspect, no Moravian hamlet a softer hush. The streets are quiet, for here you have no grog-shop, no beer-house, no lock-up, no pound; of the dozen edifices rising about you . . . not one is either foul or noisy; and every building . . . has something of the air of a chapel. The paint is all fresh; the planks are all bright; the windows are all clean. A white sheen is on everything; a happy quiet reigns around. . . . Mount Lebanon strikes you as a place where it is always Sunday. . . . The people are like their village; soft in speech, demure in bearing, gentle in face; a people seeming to be at peace, not only with themselves, but with nature and with heaven.[13]

It is ironic that the serenity praised by Dixon was beginning to bore many young Shakers, who were increasingly attracted by Worldly values. Many older Believers were far from pleased when they saw flocks of "World's People" thronging to their peaceful homes. As early as 1850, Elder Freegift Wells had railed against the establishment of so-called fancy goods stores that were designed as souvenir shops for this stream of casual visitors. He claimed that these institutions were even more harmful to young members than the 1841 gift banning pork. He most deplored the influence that the stores' customers had on the Believers. He complained:

This fancy Store is a lure, hung out to draw the gentry, who come by Coach loads. . . . They will go into the Store and purchase a few articles, and then will seem to feel that they have purchased a right and we ought to let them go round wherever they please. . . . Thus they will stroll around in companies, generally highly dressed, males and females walking together with their arms locked, occasionally bobbing into the kitchen . . . where they can find some young females; they will then improve their chance by bringing on the subject of marrying, and wonder that such likely young women can content themselves to live as we do. . . . The frequent exhibitions on our walks, in our gardens and about among our buildings of groups of young men and women, gaily dressed, and their arms locked together, talking, tittering and laughing has a powerful tendency to fill the minds of young people with lustful sensations, and cause them to hunger and thirst after the vanities and gratifications of the world.[14]

Other "World's People" disrupted the daily routine of life in the villages as well—the hired men, who in ever increasing numbers had become a common sight in Shaker fields and workshops. Bereft of many young Brethren on whom they had relied for labor, Shaker leaders decided that it was better to hire outsiders to work the land than to let it lie idle. They hoped, of course, that soon an influx of converts would render this practice unnecessary. But by the 1860s, it was clear that this ingathering was unlikely to materialize and some leaders began wondering if they had not made a mistake. During "Mother Ann's Work," some discussion of this issue had arisen, and a few relevant inspired communications were received. At Canterbury, for example, an instrument revealed in 1841 that "Holy Mother cannot visit us in peace until all the hirelings are discharged. The Deacons have promised to discharge them this week." [15] Yet after the fervor of the revival waned, hired help appeared again in the communities. Many Believers found this compromising of their religious principles unsettling. Dixon noted in 1867 that "the chiefs at Mount Lebanon can see that this system of mixed labor, this throwing of the saint and sinner into common society, for the sake of gain, is foreign to the genius of the order." [16]

Thus by the 1860s, Shakers had traveled a good deal in the outside world, and "World's People," whether as tourists or employees, had begun to enter the communities with greater frequency—a trend that naturally accelerated the gradual modification of Shaker principles. Absorption of Worldly tastes and ideas came about slowly over a period of many years. Certainly the failure to attract large numbers of converts in the 1840s and 1850s led many members to look about them for ways to make their faith more palatable. Part of the problem was economic. By the middle of the century, America was becoming an important industrial power. The Shakers found it increasingly difficult to compete with mass-produced goods, hampered as they were by the small and ever diminishing number of Brethren. They began buying more staple goods like textiles from the World. Within the communities, they increasingly turned to industrial technology in an effort to salvage at least some of their economic base.

The Believers had, of course, never shunned modern technology as had some other separatist groups. Many devices developed by members were in use throughout the Society and some, like the flat broom, had become popular items in the World as well. Many Believers were inventors of note. Brother Hewitt Chandler of Sabbathday Lake patented a mowing machine in 1866, and Brothers Nicholas Briggs and Elijah Knowles of Canterbury patented an improved industrial washing machine in 1877. Other Shaker patents include: a folding stereoscope, a swivel foot for chair legs, broomcorn stripping and sorting machinery, a chimney cap, a green corn cutter, and a combined seeder and cultivator. Because Believers had patented few of their developments before 1830, this list is certainly incomplete. But as the nineteenth century progressed, even the ingenuity of the Shakers proved inadequate. Production methods became more complex, so pressure to adopt technological methods from the World increased.

Many of the machines bought from the World in the 1850s and 1860s were designed to reduce the manpower requirements of Shaker agriculture, on which their profitable herb and garden seed industries depended. Mowing machines were introduced at New Lebanon in 1857, and mechanized hay rakes in 1862.[17] The importance of the latter was plain to all members, one Brother commenting in the Family *Farm Journal*: "We try our new Rake it does up the work to our satisfaction it is equal to 12 men."[18]

In the workshops, too, complex machinery began to appear—so complex that its maintenance was occasionally beyond the capacity of the Brethren. In 1859, the New Lebanon Church Family purchased an Ericson hot air engine for use in their herb operation. Shortly after its installation, the manufacturer sent a representative from Schenectady to check up on it and make sure that the Brethren were operating it properly. One Brother extolled its efficiency, observing: "It has proved to be greatly superior to our old horse power. It runs with 100 lbs. of coal the Hydraulic and one of the lower presses at the same time. With our old power we could average 200 lbs. of herbs a day but now we can press 4 and 500 in the same time."[19]

Not surprisingly, most of the technological improvements introduced in the communities during this period were intended to reduce the Brethren's work load, but the Sisters were not wholly neglected. Since the finances of most Families were being augmented by the sale of items like baskets, fancy brooms, and sewing notions manufactured by the Sisters, the acquisition of mechanical aids for these industries was clearly justifiable. By 1849, knitting machines had been purchased for the Sisters at Enfield, New Hampshire.[20] By the mid-1850s, all the villages were obtaining sewing machines to assist in clothing production and the various sales industries.[21] In 1857, Sisters at New Lebanon were spending less time doing the Family laundry due to the introduction of a mechanical clothes wringer.[22] Most members were delighted when devices such as these lightened the drudgery of their daily occupations, and thought little of any possible economic or spiritual cost to the Society.

A few Shakers, however, objected strenuously to the expenditure of Family funds for machinery they felt was unnecessary or inappropriate. Philemon Stewart fumed in 1847: "Four Brethren have gone to Troy in the mud to see a Triphammer and a Horsepower for Threshing. O the poverty of Machinery, the breakdown of all people who engage largely in it. We might have had thousands to spend for the spreading and upbuilding of the gospel had it not been for this."[23] At least one other Believer agreed, complaining in 1858:

> Through virgin forests locomotives wail,
> And prairie flowers are crushed beneath the vail; . . .

And the swift lightning, once celestial fire,
Does drudgery now, in harness, on a wire;
While *patents* fill the air, beside the wave,
And dog us from the cradle to the grave.[24]

Obviously, these members lamented the transformation of their simple, rural, agricultural communities into noisy, smelly factories fighting to compete economically in a world mad for gain. They, at least, would have preferred that the Society sever its ties to the external economy insofar as was possible, produce its own cloth, grow its own food, and reestablish a way of life more in keeping with the simplicity of its original religious principles.

This concern about the evils of competition was shared by Believers like Isaac Youngs who observed in the Shakers of 1860 an unseemly desire to increase the number and quality of their personal belongings. He commented sadly:

Their condition as to the real value of their property or possessions, and the conveniences and luxuries of life, is now perhaps at a higher degree of attainment than at any time heretofore . . . The gain consists in continually accumulating buildings, furniture, machines, tools and articles of convenience or fancy . . . But the sense is continually aspiring after more, becoming more and more tasty about clothing, and articles of fancy, the use of high colors of paint, varnish &c., perhaps more than is virtuous or proper.[25]

It is impossible to determine whether this change came about as a result of a conscious desire to make Shakerism more acceptable to potential converts or simply because of a gradual change in Believers' tastes due to increased contact with the Worldly aesthetic of outsiders. Both processes may have been at work simultaneously. As the number of converts fell, it was less important to sustain an austere lifestyle in order to impress new members with the simplicity and humility required of Believers. Another important demographic shift was also at work. By 1870, nearly 30 percent of the membership of the eastern communities was over age sixty, a proportion that remained nearly constant through the remainder of the century (see Appendix B.5). In the World, by comparison, only 6.6 percent of the white population was over sixty in 1900.[26]

As the membership of the sect aged, the restrictions that had been necessary to discipline young members became increasingly superfluous. With nearly one hundred years of successful communal life behind them, the Shakers could feel secure in the knowledge that the minor temptations presented by worldly goods posed little threat to the commitment of a true Believer. The life of the spirit had, after all, always been paramount. Younger Shakers, and more progressive older members, saw no harm in the adoption of Worldly tastes, especially if these changes helped keep a few wavering members in the faith.

As early as the second half of the 1840s, personal journals reveal a more relaxed attitude toward the elegancies of life. Eldress Wealthy Storer of the Hancock Ministry noted in June 1849, "Barnabas Hinkley came over from Lebanon came to our shop and paid us a visit also gave each of us a bottle of Clogne." [27] In an earlier period, no devout Brother would have dreamed of giving such a present to an Eldress, nor would she have accepted it. But by 1849, the fear that an indulgence in perfumery might corrupt a good Believer's soul had largely vanished. Other hints of this attitudinal change appear in Family daybooks and letters throughout the 1850s and 1860s. Sister Sally Bushnell of Canaan, New York, casually mentioned that the Deaconesses' room had been repainted a light blue in 1857—a departure from the standard white. [28] The Hancock Ministry Eldresses, doubtless because of pressure from their charges, asked the Lead Ministry in 1867 about the propriety of installing purchased carpeting, willing personal possessions to other members, and the wearing of jewelry. [29] Looking glasses appeared everywhere in Family Dwellings, especially in the Sisters' retiring rooms, although their size and number had earlier been subject to strict regulation. [30] By 1874, even the Lead Ministry had succumbed to the new trend, and ordered wallpaper for their workshop. [31]

Everywhere in Shaker villages during this period the little conveniences of Worldly life were appearing. A great event took place at New Lebanon in 1866, when the First Order Dwelling was transformed by gas lighting, "quite a novel affair, and creates a great revolution in lights. The Brethren and Sisters seemed much animated and pleased." [32] Only a few older members, who had been raised to scorn the unending quest for bigger and better furnishings, opposed these innovations. In 1861, one Brother complained that "there is a great proclivity in this, our day, for fixing up matters very nice, and the varnish has to go on to the cupboards, drawers, &c. and the paint on to the floors, everything has to be so slick that a fly will slip up on it." [33]

This shift in the aesthetic taste of the majority of Believers was mirrored by a subtle ideological change. Older Believers struggled to uphold the standards of traditional Shaker life to which they had been accustomed in earlier years, and often bewailed the excessively indulgent character of their younger colleagues. Many older members exhibited what Daniel Patterson has called a "tempered resolve" to maintain their faith at all costs.[34] Brother Luther Wells was one member who complained about unruly behavior, declaring firmly in 1858, when he was eighty-five:

> Order is my life, my strength and peace.
> It paves the way for an endless increase,
> Its beauty I love! And keep it I will,
> And all gospel graces I will fulfill.
> Tho' idols appear to dazzle my eyes,
> I will not yield to their vanity and lies.
> Peace and good order shall be my aim,
> And will be while Luther Wells is my name.[35]

These sentiments had always been a vital part of the Shaker tradition, but by this period their appeal was evidently diminishing. Wells's hints about the appearance of dazzling "idols" suggest that many Believers did not share his intense commitment.

Not surprisingly, older Believers most often upheld traditional Shaker tenets in their original pristine simplicity. Some older members, unsure about the propriety of altering even minor practices, turned with renewed vigor to the life of the spirit, finding there a satisfaction they felt their younger fellows were missing. William Hepworth Dixon was surprised to find in 1867 that many older Shakers actually believed they were constantly surrounded by spirits. He commented in amazement that the Believers "live with the angels, and are more familiar . . . with the dead than the living. Sister Mary, who was sitting in my room not an hour ago, close to my hand, and leaning on this Bible . . . told me that the room was full of spirits; of beings as palpable, as audible to her, as my own figure and my own voice." [36] During this period many older Shakers were seeking and finding companionship with spirits who never deserted them, perhaps because they had been forsaken by so many of their flesh and blood comrades. In spite of the changes in the externalities of Shaker life, and in spite of the carpets, curtains, and cologne introduced by and for the young, the life of the spirit was far from dead.

Younger Believers, though still perhaps committed to fundamental Shaker beliefs, tempered them with a significant dose of Worldly values. By the 1860s, most had concluded that good Shakers need not deprive themselves of small material pleasures in order to secure greater spiritual ones. Young members were allowing themselves to enjoy life. They were not afraid, as some of their predecessors seem to have been, to be happy in their temporal as well as their spiritual lives. Dixon met one such Sister named Jane Knight, whose evident satisfaction with Shaker life impressed him. He observed, almost with surprise: "She is young, pretty, educated, rich; but she has given up the world and its delights; and if ever I saw a happy-looking damsel, it is Sister Jane." [37] There is no hint here of the grim countenances and sallow complexions that Worldly visitors often observed in Sisters of earlier periods. [38]

Young Brethren, too, exhibited the same cheerful appreciation of their lives. When the Scottish writer, David Macrae, visited the Hancock community in 1868, he interviewed twenty-six-year-old Brother Calvin Fairchild and was impressed by his

. . . singularly prepossessing appearance. There was a fine intellectuality about his fair handsome face; his blue eyes beamed with gentleness, and were not without a pleasant glimmer of half-suppressed merriment. He was just at the age when the passions of love and ambition burn most ardently; but one could see from the sweet serenity that showed itself in every look and tone and gesture of this young Shaker how completely the principles and life of the strange people to whom he belonged had permeated and subdued his whole nature. [39]

Fairchild was secure enough in his faith to joke with Macrae about celibacy; in fact, his sense of humor was quite strongly developed. He wrote in 1868: "Some people think it vulgar to laugh, but let such stand in life's gloomy shadows if they choose. As a *general* rule the best men and women laugh the most. Good, round, hearty, side-shaking laughter is health for everybody, for the dyspeptic it is life." [40] Believers like Knight and Fairchild were certainly good Shakers. They were merely modern ones, unafraid to accept new ideas and tastes from the World, and secure enough to enjoy their lives unabashedly.

Some young Believers, however, were embarrassed by what they regarded as the fussy, old-fashioned ways of their more traditional colleagues and were more avid than others in their pursuit of modernity. They turned eagerly to whatever was new to satisfy their longing for activity and change. The beard lobby that sprang up within the Society in the late 1850s provides an extreme example of this trend. Led by Brother Elisha Blakeman of New Lebanon, these Brethren argued that beards, heretofore prohibited, were more practical, healthy, and efficient than clean shaven faces. He wrote a lengthy pamphlet in 1858 addressed to the Lead Ministry in which he recommended that "all male adults among Believers . . . be required to wear the beard under the chin . . . specifying some given length over which it may not be suffered to grow, avoiding extremes either in length or in shortness; and that it be kept evenly trimmed, combed straight, well washed and in as good order as the *other hair* of *the same head*; and not like the world, where each man trims his beard as fancy dictates." Blakeman desired this change because he claimed that shaving was as much a luxury as smoking or drinking, and therefore, had no place among Believers. Although he disavowed any interest in Worldly fashion, Blakeman did support his plea by observing that certain other customs of the sect had been abandoned earlier in the century.

The work of God is an increasing work . . . but if we hang on to all the old customs, habits and ways of our Fore-Fathers, how is it to increase? Tight breeches, long stockings, shoe and kneebuckles, *seven* inch brim *beavers*, short gowns &c. have all been done away with, and things more economical and convenient have been adopted in their stead.[41]

Though repeatedly insisting that he would keep his arguments as brief as possible (he listed ninety-five), Blakeman came up with some very curious reasons for his support of beards. He claimed that the Sisters' obvious distaste for beards "may be the means of working in favor of those among them who are too apt to give place . . . to the 'lust of the eye' when viewing some heretofore smooth face belonging to our side of the house." He noted that God had given men facial hair for a reason, and that every time a man shaved he was contravening God's plan. He also estimated that the Society would save $13,000 in ten years by freeing an extra half hour each week when every Brother might be working instead of shaving. He further guessed that an additional $18,700 might be saved in a thousand years by the reduction of wear and tear on shirt collars. He also claimed that the Brethren's health would improve, citing the case of a railroad conductor who supposedly prevented his own death from bronchitis by allowing his beard to grow.[42]

As questionable as many of these arguments appear, Blakeman was surely in earnest. He knew that customs within the Society had previously been altered to conform more closely to ideals of simplicity and uniformity, and hoped to win a victory for the beard. He had forgotten, however, that these earlier policy changes had been imposed from above, not demanded from below. It is possible that the Lead Ministry were prejudiced against beards because they did not wish to ape another Worldly fashion. Whatever their inclination, they must have been disposed to ignore Blakeman's recommendation because of his attitude. He stated plainly early in his argument that it was "very natural (perhaps too much so) for me to investigate and pry into the why and wherefore certain *duties are required* and certain habits allowed among Believers, the virtue and propriety of which, not only myself, but many other persons among us question."[43]

Blakeman insisted that he would remain firm in the faith whatever the Ministry's decision. In 1872, however, he left New Lebanon and moved to New York City, no doubt bearded, and later published a book of riddles.[44] The Ministry apparently concluded that Blakeman's suggestion should not be implemented, because other Brethren took up the cause in his stead. Brother John M. Brown of New Lebanon requested in 1873 "the introduction of the beard in our United Society, in the name of Christianity, Physiology, and the public Sentiment, both within and without Zion."[45] News of the beard issue reached the World, and a *New York Times* writer reported in 1875:

It will be news to most people to learn that for some years past the doctrine of shaving has been the occasion of controversy in the various Shaker communities. The discussion has been as warm as any discussion conducted exclusively in the second person singular, and by casuists in broad-brimmed hats and poke-bonnets, could well be. Originating among the younger male Shakers, the heretical doctrine . . . speedily made perverts among the Shakeresses, certain of whom are understood to have declared that the enforced contemplation of shaved Shakers was an unnecessary and intolerable burden. The controversy finally assumed such proportions as to threaten a Shaker schism of . . . disastrous consequences. The courage with which the leading Shakers have dealt with this momentous question cannot be too highly praised. They have just held a convention in which the whole matter was discussed and a compromise agreed upon. It was felt by the orthodox party that inasmuch as the teachings of science and those of the sect were apparently at variance in respect to beards . . . it was therefore decided that all new Shakers should be required to abstain from shaving, while the present members should be free to wear beards, or to shave, as their consciences might dictate. Thus the danger of a schism was avoided. . . . But it is impossible to dismiss the fact that the Shaker beard, however soft and fleecy it may be, will prove the entering wedge which shall split Shakerism into fragments. Elder EVANS may yet live to see Shakers clothed in green trousers and purple neckties.[46]

By the 1880s, photographs of Brethren wearing beards were not uncommon, so this report was evidently accurate. The important lesson that the Believers learned from this agitation was that they could ultimately have their own way about issues of dress and personal possessions—if they were patient.

The other major issue that disrupted the Society in the late 1860s and early 1870s involved music. The Shakers had long incorporated vocal music into their worship but had always insisted that harmony and instrumental accompaniment were unnecessary embellishments. By the 1860s, however, many Believers had come to regard traditional Shaker worship and its attendant vocabulary as hopelessly old-fashioned. Florence Phelps, who grew up in the Canterbury community in the late nineteenth century, remembered that the young people of her day had been amused when older Believers spoke of the "fiery darts of the wicked" or the "beggarly elements of the World." When an elderly Sister attended a young people's meeting to teach them some of the songs and dances from her youth, the congregation laughed so much that the project had to be abandoned.[47] Young Believers such as these were behind the drive that began in the late 1860s to modernize Shaker music.

The question of the use of harmony and musical instruments was raised at least by 1868, for in that year a Canterbury Believer protested violently:

I have no doubt that the introduction of any worldly instrument into our meeting at this time, would banish every good Spirit from them, and would entirely destroy the spiritual gift of the meeting. Of course its tendency would be to make the *young* Worldly and draw *them* back into the flesh . . . That which comes from the *World* attracts to the *World*, and that which comes from the *heavens* attracts to the *heavens*. All true Godly progress and increase in Zion must come from within.[48]

This agitation had evidently started among the rank and file, causing the member above to complain about those who placed "mere intellectuality" above revelation. This anonymous Shaker continued:

When (if ever) the time arrives for musical instruments to be used in the worship of God, it will be manifest by a palpable revelation thro' the Ministry. . . . And when I see those who are most in union with the order of God . . . begin to feel intimations from the spirit world that the time has come for instruments of music to be introduced, I shall think it much more worthy of consideration by the Lead than if such intimations proceed from those who wish to remove the offense of the cross and make the gospel more agreeable to the carnal mind.[49]

To the dismay of Believers who shared this opinion, the movement to reform Shaker music gathered strength throughout the late 1860s and early 1870s. In March 1870, a New Lebanon schoolteacher decided: "The cultivation of the voice has been much neglected for many years past and our singing is very far from being what it should be. . . . It seems doubtful to me however if vocal music among us can be rendered really satisfactory without the assistance of some good instrument."[50] The Lead Ministry apparently concurred with this view, sanctioning the purchase of organs at about this time.

Members who continued to question the propriety of this change in policy tried to resign themselves to it. Philemon Stewart observed:

I will labor to bless the new fangles, and help what I can, tho' it may appear never so different from what I have practice in. . . . We know that it has been promised that finally Instruments of Music should again be restored to the Lord's People and if the present improvement and knowledge called for by the Lead in the Art and Gift of Singing is the Opening Wedge, . . . I shall not fight it, for I love to hear good Music too well for that.[51]

Stewart's mention of the Ministry's command to improve in "the art and gift of singing" is borne out by the frequent mention in journals of this period of various singing schools established throughout the Society. Giles Avery, for example, noted in 1874 that "singing schools are the prominent excitements of Shaker Village at Watervliet in these days."[52]

Another change instituted at about this time was the introduction of four-part vocal harmony, a move that culminated in the publication of two Shaker hymnals in which all the songs were written in parts. Believers who had accepted singing schools and organs with a minimum of fuss balked at this further innovation. Philemon Stewart remarked snidely in October 1870: "I believe there is now liberty to sing parted tunes in Worship . . . so we expect soon to hear the most *awful music*."[53] In February 1871, he was distressed to discover that his worst fears were realized. After attending a Family meeting, he opined:

I have just returned from one of the most confused, systematized Drills . . . that I have ever yet attended. The Leader of the Meeting wanted we should learn to sing and labor by the clicking strokes of a Machine . . . called a Metrinome, and we did so, I should think, to the heart's content of the most sanguine in expectation of great advancement. This is the way that some few think the work of the spirit of God is going to increase and gather souls to the Gospel. Fatal delusion.[54]

Stewart believed that the adoption of such precise, pseudoscientific methods reduced Shaker worship, traditionally governed solely by the free movement of the spirit, to a mechanical charade. Younger Believers, less astute, merely thought they were updating Shaker practices to conform to Worldly norms. Once this was accomplished, they expected to welcome numerous converts whose last vestiges of reluctance would have been eliminated by these progressive innovations.

These hopeful members were destined to be disappointed, as Stewart had anticipated. At least one Worldly observer found these Shaker efforts to put "a new dress to Mother Ann's gospel" ludicrous. Benjamin B. Davis, a Concord singing master employed by the Canterbury community, exhorted the Shakers there

to keep up the believers style, not try to imitate the fashions of the world &c. He often relates the pain he felt when attending our public meeting at the time the believers adopted, or attempted the singing of harmony. . . . Why, said he; it almost made me sick; and I would be obliged to leave the meeting and go home feeling so *sorry!* When you sing as Shakers ought to sing, there is something in your music that thrills one; makes a man feel as though he wanted to bow down his head, there is such a simple, earnest, religious feeling conveyed.[55]

Efforts by these young Believers to modernize the sect's image in their own eyes and those of the "World's People" masked a growing feeling of unease within the communities: an increasing level of tension between old and young, and between conservatives and progressives. A spirit of reform was indeed stirring, but there was a dark side to all this frenetic activity as well. Throughout this period there appeared to be little or no hope that people outside the sect would look with enough favor on its tenets and way of life to convert. The disappointment suffered after urban revivalism in the 1850s failed to encourage an influx of converts was exacerbated by the Shaker experience during the Civil War.

For four years, the nation was gripped by a fierce and bloody conflict that left little room for the consideration of such Shaker values as peace and humility. Though some members viewed the war as evidence of "a new era of more powerful shaking & revolutionary convulsions . . . which would progressively increase till it would convulse, shake & break down every system & institution of man's invention, civil, political & ecclesiastical" and lead to an extension of the Shaker millennium, this proved of little comfort.[56] Government demands for a census of all Brethren between the ages of eighteen and forty-five forced leaders throughout the Society to confront their acute manpower shortage. When written down in black and white, the figures were appalling.

Sabbathday Lake, Maine, reported only four Brethren in this age group, one of whom was chronically ill. Alfred reported seven Brethren, one a cripple; Shirley eight and Harvard four, of whom two were cripples and two partly blind. Canterbury listed twenty-four men in this age group, but counted one with a hernia, two who were blind in one eye, two with maimed hands, one with bad eyes, one subject to fits, two with weak lungs, one with a weak knee, and one partly insane. Enfield, New Hampshire, similarly reported twenty-three Brethren, one third of whom were exemptible due to physical disability.[57] Even if some allowance is made for possible exaggeration in these reports, the situation was grave indeed. By the mid-1860s, the Shakers were forced to the inescapable conclusion that some day, perhaps some day soon, there would be no more Brethren. The economic and spiritual impact of this grim realization was staggering.

A useful, though imperfect, measure of the level of stress within the Society in this period is provided by its suicide rate. Gaps in the record do not permit a thorough statistical survey of the rate of suicide within the sect throughout its history, but evidence suggests that it was rising during the 1850s and 1860s. Louis Kern has estimated that the 1830s and 1870s were the decades when the rate was highest at the New Lebanon community. For the years between 1833 and 1880, he has calculated a suicide rate of 0.125/492, or approximately three and a half times greater than the rate in New England between 1856 and 1880. He has also suggested that the incidence of mental illness and insanity had increased as the century progressed.[58]

Scattered Family records provide support for Kern's contentions. In 1858, Sister Sally Bushnell recorded in her journal that Sister Catherine Damph of Watervliet had killed herself by jumping out of a fifth story window.[59] A Canaan, New York, Sister named Betsy Scott, allegedly insane, stole a Brother's razor and cut her throat in 1863.[60] In 1869, a Sister at Watervliet named Maria Treadway drowned herself in the Family millpond.[61] But perhaps the most poignant record of such a tragedy appears in the journal of Brother Isaac Youngs of New Lebanon. A faithful Believer since childhood, he had been much distressed by the disunion and apostasy that had infected the Society beginning in the 1820s. He had nevertheless pursued his calling indefatigably, serving as community clockmaker, tailor, and scribe. Perhaps fatigue and overwork played a role in his development of what was certainly some type of senility or mental illness. He recorded in his journal in 1864:

I am very much out of health. I have very strange and wonderful experience in the night—there seems to be two of me—I am rational and irrational! I am wide awake and fast asleep—and no mortal knows the sorrows and sufferings I undergo.—O could I know why all this is so;—Some say it is all Hypo!—well, be it so;—who cares what name is attached, if it is really a disease; if it is really painful, if it be forced involuntarily on the patient—then it is a reality and the sufferer should be pitied and receive sympathy.[62]

Whatever his complaint, Youngs's condition steadily deteriorated, so that by the next year he required constant care and supervision. In August 1865, when one attendant left his room to search for a scheduled replacement, Youngs was said to have become convinced that the building was on fire, and jumped out of a fourth story window to his death.[63] Youngs's case may have been more sensational than many because of his importance to the Society, but his suicide was not atypical. It seems clear that the proportion of potentially suicidal and mentally and emotionally disturbed members rose significantly in these years, certainly the result of disillusionment and stress.

These instances of suicide; the efforts to introduce musical instruments, vocal harmony, and beards; the relaxation of regulations about architecture, furniture, and personal adornment—all these are evidence of the desperate Shaker search for relevance in a rapidly changing world. Perhaps in their eagerness to convince outsiders that their principles were still viable in an increasingly secular environment, young Shakers, and the group of progressive Elders and Eldresses who agreed with them, went too far. With the institution of various changes, they minimized the differences between themselves and the "World's People."

In the years following the Civil War, when some Americans were envious of Shaker villages for their peaceful isolation from the bustle of an urban, industrial, materialistic nation, the Shakers had become less easily identifiable. By departing from some of their traditional practices, they mollified a few wavering souls within the sect, but failed to attract many new members. At the New Lebanon Church Family, for example, admissions in the 1860s and 1870s dropped dramatically. Most of these converts were young, their average age near twelve years for males and fourteen years for females. Because members admitted during these years stayed in the community an average of only four to seven years, they failed to improve the demographic makeup of the Family (see Appendixes A.1, A.5, and A.6). Those adults who might have joined the Society for its religious beliefs were put off by the growing materialism visible in all the communities, and those who might have been pleased by this trend found the inflexibility of its fundamental tenets uncongenial.

Conservative members, who had been appalled by these developments, prophesied that dire consequences would befall the Shakers if they refused to renounce worldliness and return to their original practices of simplicity and self-denial. Philemon Stewart commented that the Believers had gone out of their way ever since the 1850s to contravene many of the regulations established during "Mother's Work." He complained in 1870 that they had "extended their trade and traffic four fold, if not more, and let in the world tenfold. . . . Hired Servants of the World seemingly are almost as thick round amongst us as those pretending to be Believers. . . . The love of Money, Popularity and Extravagance, with their dependence on their own natural wisdom, has been their Lead, guide and pursuit."[64] By the 1870s, some members felt that Shaker life had been so altered that it was in imminent danger of becoming wholly secularized. Disillusioned by the materialistic developments that had taken place, many conservative Believers feared for the future. In 1867, the spirit of Elder Rufus Bishop asked Brother Calvin Green:

> Cans't thou remember saying?
> Once on a time to me?
> That, tho' our Zion struggl'd
> A harder time would be?

In *Sixty, Sixty-One*! Yea,
Two! *Three* and Sixty *Four*!
Five, six and seven from thence to ten
Her suff'rings would be sore!

I've seen her vessels broken!
Her lovely garments *rent*!
While *lust, selfwill* and *grandeur*,
All found in her a Tent!
The Watchmen from her Borders,
Were heard to say aloud!
"Is Zion! blessed Zion?
Forsaken of her God?"
Nay, *truly*—but digressing!
From her most *sacred Laws*
Thus causing bitter anguish,
Thro' traitors to the *cause*![65]

Only among a small and ever diminishing core of Believers did the pure fire of spiritual life continue to burn. Their strength, however, was not proportional to their numbers. During the mid-1870s they would inaugurate a movement for broad reform within the Society, which, though not universally successful, helped to ensure that the Shaker gospel would survive into the twentieth century.

10

Plenty to Make the Brick—
Few to Build the Temple
(1871-1904)

As the centennial of Mother Ann's arrival in America approached, her followers faced a combination of serious and steadily worsening crises. Fundamental changes in the demographic composition of the eastern communities exacerbated economic and spiritual weaknesses that had been developing for many years. As the membership throughout the sect aged and became increasingly feminine, a small group of truly devoted Believers struggled to salvage those values that might still have relevance in a rapidly industrializing, secularizing World. But even among this faithful, committed group, a basic disagreement as to the course the Society should pursue prevented either progressives or conservatives from forging a healthy new consensus. By the beginning of the twentieth century, only a remnant of the faith's members and commitment survived.

As early as the 1870s, many Believers had begun to view the Society's situation with grave concern. In her New Lebanon *Tailoresses' Journal*, Sister Elizabeth Sidle observed sadly at the close of the year 1871: "Another year has *come* and *gone*, in which we've seen much sorrow. No thanks can we return while our destiny we learn—that we must be forsaken by loving friends, companions dear. This is truly heartrending."[1] Sister Elizabeth had good reason to be distressed. The apostasy rate at the New Lebanon Church Family peaked in the 1870s at an appalling 29.7 percent, and remained high for the rest of the century (see Appendix A.2). The situation at the other eastern communities was equally serious. By 1880, the total population had fallen to 1,178, down 51.5 percent from the peak in 1840. By 1900, the total population had again dropped precipitously, to just 644, down 73.5 percent from the 1840 level (see Appendix B.1). The impact of this numerical decline was staggering.

As in earlier years, most of those who left were young Brethren. In the 1870s alone, over 40 percent of the men in the New Lebanon Church Family chose the Worldly way. The danger of their example was plain, causing Philemon Stewart to exclaim in 1871:

Young Brethren going off in this way makes the young Sisters of their age and class feel extremely bad and Lonesome, but I pray God to comfort and bless them with wisdom and strength, to be more Wise than to follow their Example. We still have a pretty and agreeable set of Young Sisters, and I had rather die tomorrow than to have our Young People leave us, for who can bear to enter Eternity leaving no Spiritual Offspring on earth to build up the Zion of God.[2]

But even older Brethren were not immune to this apostasy fever. In 1872, Brother Elisha Blakeman, a devout if somewhat independent and troublesome member since 1834, finally decided to leave the faith. Philemon Stewart commented acerbically: "Elisha D. Blakeman in the First Order concluded to go and has gone to the World, where he can make and mend all kinds of Fiddles according to his own mind, and probably have a Woman to help him, when specially called for. What a shame for an old professed Shaker."[3]

This flood of backslidings was in no way mitigated by the conversion of new members. Such evidence as survives indicates that admissions were falling sharply at all of the eastern communities. Between 1861 and 1882, only fifteen new members joined the Harvard Gathering Order, six of them children.[4] At the New Lebanon Church Family, the prospects were similarly dismal. Of 110 youngsters admitted between 1871 and 1900, *not one* converted upon reaching adulthood (see Appendixes A.8 and A.9). In 1881, Sister Harriet Goodwin reported on the state of the Maine communities in a letter to Eldress Lydia Dole.

You ask as to the signs of ingathering in the northern reagon. I should think they were happy and contented, indifferent and sleepy. Have many children offered, some unborn up to 6 or 7 years of age, which we generally refuse. Have taken some older, which seem quite promising. Have received several male Adults since I have been in this place, but mostly for winter quarters, or loaves and fishes, ready to go when spring opens. As the women generally believe in obeying their husbands in preference to the gospel testimony about here I have but little hope for them.[5]

Moreover, even among those who did remain in the faith, there was a further decline in the standards of behavior. Philemon Stewart expressed misgivings about the conduct of some residents in his Dwelling in 1873.

Washington and Bozworth has moved the week past into the room against us. . . . After singing till half past 11 o'clock, over one hour and a half, the room was more like a noisy Bar Room than like a decent retiring Room. Sisters were there the whole of the time and a constant laugh and gabble by both. . . . If it is thus to continue, I shall be compelled to resort to my shop for any quiet or peace. Order seems all gone.[6]

Order thus deteriorated, and the level of commitment declined noticeably as well. Although he did not ultimately choose to leave the sect, the case of Brother John Cumings of Enfield, New Hampshire, reveals how the unsettled spiritual and economic conditions of these years could sap the devotion of formerly committed Shakers. A Church Family member and a Believer for twenty-eight years, Brother John had by the early 1870s become a vital part of the Enfield community's economic activities. A Family Deacon since 1856, as well as a mechanic, millwright, carpenter, carriage maker, and wheelwright, his varied talents and temporal dedication helped make up for the dearth of young Brethren in the Family. Then in 1873, he communicated shocking news to his sister, Rosetta, who was also a Believer.

I have hardly seen a day for two years but what I have wished myself away. And what shall I get for staying here—not one cent more than I should to have gone then. Is there any justice in turning one away with merely nothing who has spent 20 or 30 years of their best days and worked hard almost constantly—if so I cannot see it.[7]

Brother John had evidently reached a difficult decision under the influence of many conflicting loyalties. His brother, Enoch, once a Believer, had left the sect and moved to Michigan, where he was engaged in the lucrative broom corn business. Enoch often wrote to his brother in an effort to entice him away from the Shakers, whom he believed to be dwindling to rapid extinction. In 1871, he had written John:

I cannot imagine what earthly object you can have in staying there, and probably you have none, only you cannot get away. A more complete slave never existed down south than you are. . . . But we have given up all hopes of your ever leaving. Don't believe you have pluck enough left in you and hardly believe they can kick you away. I know they have lost all respect for you and only prize you for your labor. . . . Now Br., why is it so much harder for you than it was for me or others to break away from there. I know your affections are no stronger and certainly there is not so many to leave now as then—a few dried up Bachelors and Maids, and all the while growing less. . . .[8]

In 1872, Brother John had traveled to Ohio and Michigan on Shaker business, stopping to visit relatives along the way, and was impressed by their prosperity and independence. By the following year, the lures cast out to him by his family in the World, combined with his diminished belief in Shaker principles and practices, led him to a momentous decision. As he wrote to his sister, Rosetta:

I cannot reconcile myself to stay here any longer and I do not believe in some things that are done and said in our meetings. . . . for my part I am sick of such worship. We are told to labor for liberty and freedom and yet if we take one mite . . . we must be church mauled sure as day. We are told to labor for the power and gifts of God and what are they from? All I can see and feel now days it is nothing more nor less than a strong religious excitement and the best way to bring it on is to turn around and get dizzy and excited. . . . If they really were gifts from God why should they not be felt until you are drove to it by the Elders? Why is it that almost everything of a tangible form that has been given by Shaker inspiration for the last 25 years has proved false or unpracticable such as the holy ground, the Lord's Stone, drab jackets, hiring help, drinking tea and many other things I could mention.[9]

In spite of his dwindling faith, however, Brother John was ultimately unable to uproot himself from his Shaker home. Perhaps the economic depression that began in the World just as he had decided to leave dampened his hopes for financial gain or perhaps he merely remained because he knew he was needed. At any rate, he remained nominally faithful, and was appointed Church Family Trustee in 1882, a position he held until his death in 1911. His questionable devotion to the tenets of the Society, however, hardly distinguished him as an exemplary Believer. Many of his colleagues in the last third of the nineteenth century similarly exhibited diminished commitment to Shaker beliefs, even though they paid lip service to the sect's external practices.

John Cumings's decision to remain at Enfield alleviated the community's dire temporal situation to only a small degree. Due to the frequent and increasing apostasies of Brethren, the indifferent devotion of hired laborers, and the growing burden placed on a decreasing number of able-bodied Sisters, many of the eastern villages were approaching economic collapse. Partial membership and occupation records of the Watervliet community for 1850 and 1880 highlight this developing crisis. The 1850 list includes 101 adult males and 90 adult females engaged in forty-seven different occupations. The Brethren were listed holding twenty-seven different jobs, ranging from farmer, horticulturist, botanist, and herdsman, to painter, joiner, carpenter, schoolmaster, and physician. The Sisters were employed largely in housewifery, textile work, millinery, schoolteaching, and nursing. The 1880 list, however, includes only eleven adult Brethren and nineteen adult Sisters engaged in sixteen occupations, six for men and ten for women.[10]

This sharp decline in population and economic activity occurred at other eastern villages as well. Philemon Stewart lamented in 1871: "Zion's organizations in several places are very much reduced and broken and are trying to sell their property, and move, and help fill up some other Society. Tyringham is one place, Alfred and Gloucester, Maine are two other places, but whether they will make out to sell is yet to be proved."[11] The next year, the Lead Ministry reported to the Watervliet Elders about the unlikely prospects of their receiving financial aid from any other community.

Though some societies have been, and are such sufferers by fire and defalcation of Trustees that their ability to aid our Gospel Friends at the Valley is either destroyed or crippled immensely, yet these also deeply sympathize in feelings. The Harvard Society have lost largely by the Boston fire, and we do not look for them to do anything financially for Watervliet. The New Gloucester Society are so very miserably conditioned concerning a dwelling house, their old house being almost untenantable, and having no surplus funds on hand at all, we should not be willing to accept any aid from the Society there, and if Alfred could spare anything they should certainly contribute to the Gloucester society. Enfield, New Hampshire is certainly struggling under all the load they can possibly carry.[12]

These gloomy reports were confirmed by the 1875 decision to sell the Tyringham community and move the few Believers remaining there elsewhere. Once begun, this policy of closing villages and consolidating members continued throughout the remainder of the century and into the next.

By the 1870s and 1880s, these economic difficulties and membership problems seemed nearly irreversible, and set many Believers to speculating about the causes of their afflictions. In an undated pamphlet entitled "Shaker Land Limitation Laws" written sometime during the 1870s, Elder Frederick Evans announced: "The reason the Shakers are decreasing is that their best energies have been devoted to cultivating their lands and advancing their material prosperity. . . . We have just discovered that the idea of the desirability of the acquisition of land which we took from the world is wrong. . . . We must dispose of part of our farms and devote more time to missionary work."[13] Evans, a progressive member who hoped to bring Shaker tenets more forcefully before a needy World, thus construed the closing of villages and the selling of consecrated land a virtue—a disposal of encumbrances that would free Believers for the mission he envisioned.

Philemon Stewart, a conservative member who wished the sect to abandon what he called the "new fangles," agreed with Evans that materialism was at the root of the Society's decline. He admonished the sect's leaders in 1873 for the "thousands and thousands of Dollars spent for Extravagant Buildings that we do not need and are only a Curse to us now they are built, as we have no profitable use for them only to keep in repair, or to let go to destruction, as many are doing, a standing monument to our disgrace and disobedience."[14]

One Worldly observer, William Dean Howells, took a broader view of the causes for the sect's diminished popularity, and concluded:

There are several reasons for the present decrease, besides that decrease of the whole rural population. . . . The impulse of the age is towards a scientific, a sensuous, an aesthetic life. Men no longer remain on the lonely farms, or in the little towns where they were born . . . if they think of God, it is too often to despair of knowing him; while the age calls upon them to learn this, that, and the other, to get gain and live at ease, to buy pianos and pictures, and take books out of the circulating library.[15]

Howells's assessment was perceptive and accurate. The spiritual and economic atmosphere of the nation had indeed changed in the hundred years since Mother Ann had first opened her testimony. Remote rural communities, charismatic religion, and pietistic acceptance of life's mysteries no longer satisfied the majority of Americans. Progress—the search for intellectual knowledge and economic expansion—consumed the energies of more and more of the Believers' compatriots, and this fervor could not help but enter their minds and hearts as well. The land hunger and extravagance Evans and Stewart so deplored were merely symptoms of what Howells correctly saw as a much larger phenomenon—the "impulse of the age." Few Shakers, however, had the perspective to realize that the sect's problems extended beyond economic policy. Even fewer perceived that the roots of these difficulties had first appeared in the early decades of the nineteenth century. The need to find scapegoats for the Society's decline was widespread, and in this pursuit, Zion's leaders received a full measure of blame.

As early as 1868, an anonymous Shaker had bewailed the relaxation of former rules requiring simplicity of diet, dress, and surroundings, asserting: "The characteristics of the soldier are developed in tents and on hardtack, not in gilded parlors or rich oyster saloons and ice cream pantries. Therefore, it is our judgment that some fastings and mortifications of body are commensurate with the greatest good." [16] Conservative members who shared this opinion saw in the leaders' willingness to bow to pressure from the rank and file a spiritual weakness that did not bode well for the future of the sect.

Philemon Stewart, ever ready to criticize leaders who failed to look at things as he did, decided early in the 1870s that he had discovered the explanation for Zion's difficulties. He acknowledged that the Shakers were on the right track spiritually, but argued that they had failed to pursue the purifying gifts of "Mother's Work" to their logical and necessary conclusion. He went to the Lead Ministry in 1870 and asserted that "nine tenths of [Zion's] present diseases Physically speaking are the natural outgrowths of her improper modes of Cooking to pamper an improper and perverted habit and Appetite . . . it is utterly impossible for the true Gospel of Christ and of Mother now to open, and spread among mankind, only as it condemns and puts away Physical sins, as well as Spirit sins." Claiming that he had received a revelation to the effect that Believers must return to the strict regulations of the 1840s, Stewart produced for the Ministry more than one hundred pages of supporting arguments. As he subsequently recorded, their reaction was far from favorable. "After they had it some weeks, in consultation with the Elders in the Church, called me to their Shop, and Plainly told me they could not accept it as the Word of the Lord . . . they also desired I would cease writing anything more to them in the line of Inspiration, which I did." [17] His opposition to their liberal course, however, showed no signs of abating. In October 1871, he warned: "If the Leaders in Zion will not cease the use of Tobacco, Animal Flesh, Tea and Coffee, and all Spiritous, stimulating Drinks . . . their days as an Organized Body of the Lord's People are numbered." [18]

Stewart was certainly unfair in ascribing all of the Society's woes to the Ministry's unwillingness to force a return to the dietary strictures introduced during "Mother's Work," but he was correct in his perception that the sect's leaders were weaker than ever before. This development can be traced to demographic imbalances dating from the 1820s. Even though the leadership pool shrank (see Appendix B.4), the number of leaders required to fill the communities' many positions of responsibility remained the same. As early as 1845, for example, 20.8 percent of the members of the New Lebanon Church Family members were serving as Elders, Eldresses, Deacons, Deaconesses, Trustees, Office Sisters, or children's Caretakers. As the century progressed, and population levels in all the communities continued to fall, the situation worsened. By the late nineteenth century, as many as one fourth to one third of all adult Believers were holding some temporal or spiritual appointment.

As a result, the quality of those selected to fill positions of authority declined markedly, creating a vicious circle effect. As the quality of the leaders diminished, the likelihood that they would serve as appropriate role models and thereby convince capable young members to remain in the faith decreased. This further reduced the pool from which the next generation of leaders could be drawn. By the middle of the nineteenth century, barely enough acceptable Brethren and Sisters could be found to fill top posts within the Society. Elder Grove Wright of Hancock tried to joke about the situation in a letter to the Harvard Ministry in 1860.

We learn that there has been great changes at the East, also that in your Bishopric you have had a share of the same, but among us we are so *poor* that we have to keep along much as we have been for some time past. For if we should undertake to have changes, it would be much like the old Indian, who wanted to be like the white people, in the changing of victuals on his table, but as he lacked the different kinds; in order to imitate, he would call out "Succotash off," and then "Succotash on," and so keep reversing with the same dish.[19]

In succeeding decades, the leadership crisis described by Elder Grove worsened throughout the Society. The apostasy of trusted leaders, a rarity in the early years of the century, became more common. When Peter Greaves, a Deacon at the New Lebanon Church Family, apostatized in 1871, Philemon Stewart blamed the influence of Worldly liberal theology, opining:

It is lamentable that our Youngerly Leaders seem to think more of Beecher's Writings . . . than they do of our Heavenly Parents' teaching. . . . These kind of writings have been read for some time past Publicly in the First Order. . . . Is it not a little strange that well informed People, and Leaders too, do not yet seem to really understand that a generative ministration cannot strengthen anyone in the regenerative life.[20]

Stewart was not the only Believer to wonder at the increasing tendency of Shaker leaders to backslide to the World. Brother John Cumings complained of the situation at Enfield, New Hampshire, to his sister in 1873. "Since I have lived in the family there have been 12 different persons in the Elders order and 5 of them have left. Were they chosen by the gift of God? If so, I was able to choose better."[21] The condition of the other Enfield community, in Connecticut, was equally grave. In 1874, Elder Giles Avery reported: "Ministry all spend the day at the North family at Enfield, Ct., striving to bring to Gospel order the leading authorities in that place, who have now become divided, and the family lost, scattered, almost entirely annihilated."[22]

The departure of many leaders coupled with divisions among those who remained weakened the sect at one of its most vulnerable points. Economic and spiritual conditions during these years forced the Shakers to contravene one of their earliest and most fundamental regulations: the separation of temporal and spiritual authority. By the 1870s, Brethren were so scarce that many Bishopric Ministries had only one Elder, and many Family Elders had to do double duty as Deacons or Trustees. This mingling of spirit and flesh was not without negative consequences. Elder Frederick Evans and Brothers Levi Shaw and Henry Cantrell entered into a dubious partnership early in the 1870s with a Dr. Joseph Jones of Honesdale, Pennsylvania, who owned a lumber empire in that state and a steam sawmill in Windsor, New York. Shaw, whose earlier and subsequent investments included tracts of forest land in Michigan, apartment buildings in Chicago and Brooklyn, and gold mines in Colorado and the Yukon, proved no luckier with his associates in this business arrangement than in most of his other speculations. When the partnership with Jones was dissolved in 1876, the Shakers were left with 10,000 acres of timberland in what was ironically called Promised Land, Pennsylvania—a tract that they were able to sell only with difficulty and at a considerable loss.[23]

Other temporal leaders got into different kinds of trouble. Hancock's Church Family Trustee during these years was Brother Ira Lawson, who had joined the community in 1852 at the age of eighteen. When he was appointed Trustee in 1862, the Family was reportedly in debt for $2,000, but as a result of his "shrewd business acumen," by 1897 the community boasted $75,000 worth of such high grade securities as the Boston and Albany Railroad and Bell Telephone. But Brother Ira committed certain indiscretions too. In June 1871, when he was thirty-seven, he absconded with twenty-five-year-old Sister Eliza Van Valen. Intending to marry, the couple drove surreptitiously to Pittsfield and boarded a train for Albany, accompanied by a local Methodist minister. After stopping at one of the city's most opulent hotels, the minister began the service in one of its parlors. Midway through the ceremony, though, Lawson suddenly decided that he and Van Valen were making a terrible mistake. He is reported to have said later: "I was conscience stricken. I was terrified. I was speechless for a while. Right then and there in the parlor of that wonderful hotel, I decided to go no further in the path of wickedness and sin to which I had been so unwisely led by the tempter. I knew the marriage could not be undone, but it could remain unconsummated, and I determined it should be."

Eliza evidently felt that they had strayed too far from the Shaker way to be readmitted if they returned and confessed their sin, but Ira was willing to try. As a result, the Hancock Believers witnessed the strange sight of their colleagues returning to the fold after less than twenty-four hours of marriage. Penitent and humble, both were granted "another privilege." Lawson was reinstated as Trustee, and was also later elevated to the Ministry. He held these positions until his death in 1905. Sister Eliza, however, failed to rekindle her commitment to the faith and apostatized a second and final time in 1872.[24]

It is likely that Lawson was retained as Trustee and appointed an Elder in spite of his aberrant behavior because his business talent was indispensable to the Hancock community's survival. Perhaps the Elders also recognized that Lawson and Van Valen were not wholly at fault. The 1870 census records for the Hancock village reveal that they were two of only five Believers living in the Church Family Office. Because the other three were elderly Sisters, Lawson and Van Valen were probably thrown together more than would have been the case in an earlier period. Lawson eventually became one of the east's last powerful Elders, respected by all Believers, none of whom ever thereafter referred to his marriage escapade.

Lawson's peculiar apostasy and subsequent reinstatement highlight the shortage of qualified leaders that plagued the Society in the closing decades of the nineteenth century. The difficult task of simultaneously fulfilling the requirements of spiritual and temporal positions pushed many Elders to the brink of despair. In the early 1870s, after the apostasy of the New Lebanon East Family Trustee, Elder Giles Avery of the Lead Ministry was charged with the administration of the Family's financial affairs in addition to his other duties. When Elder Edward Chase, also of the East Family, departed for the World in 1871, he left behind a debt of $20,000. Philemon Stewart noted that "this of course brings a very heavy reaction in the minds and feelings of the people against Elder Giles . . . for leaving the Sacred Order of the Ministry and running into Speculation in a Temporal line." [25] Though this situation was clearly not Avery's fault, Shaker supervisory resources were being stretched to the limit, with predictable results. As Stewart observed: "It jars the Confidence, to the very center, in our Leaders." [26]

Rank and file members in these years could not fail to miss another weakness in their leaders—their often advanced age. In earlier decades, elderly, exhausted leaders had been permitted to retire when they felt that they could no longer carry out their duties at peak efficiency, but by the end of the nineteenth century there were few available replacements. The senility of Elders became an increasing problem. In an undated letter, Sister Emma Neale of New Lebanon described the condition of Elder Benjamin Gates: "He often does things whereof it is impossible for me to know of and when he is in trouble says I told you to watch me. Strange times these. There are plenty to make the brick— few O so few to build the temple." [27]

This worsening leadership crisis led many members to agitate for changes in the sect's governmental and financial organization. This movement received considerable support after the defalcation of Elder Edward Chase, a trend which Philemon Stewart observed in September 1871.

The Body of the Church is getting considerably waked up, after having their hard earnings squandered to the amount of Twenty Thousand Dollars by this

Concentration of Power all in the Hands of one or two. If the Body is of no use, and to bear no sway, in such profligate doings, why not knock it out of existence, and see whether the Head or Tail is of much account without a Body.[28]

As to the possible role of the "Body of the Church," Stewart had suggestions about this as well. After noting the recent apostasies of James Calver, a New Lebanon junior Elder, and Andrew Thompson, a Canterbury Elder and Deacon, he commented in November 1871: "I have proposed to appoint Committees on Various Subjects, Embracing in their turn all the Covenant Members, to Manage the Temporalities of the Church, also to Inspect the Books at the Office."[29]

Although Stewart's complaints and suggestions on other subjects often went unheeded, he was supported on this issue by many of his fellow members. Sometime during the 1870s, Elder Thomas Damon of Hancock authored a proposal entitled, "Considerations Illustrating the necessity of some revisions in the Direction and Management of Temporal Concerns." According to Damon, the Shakers had lost more than $200,000 in fifty years due to the mismanagement and apostasy of Trustees. This situation, he felt, had developed gradually, as the sect had become prosperous. In the eighteenth and early nineteenth centuries the Trustees had controlled such insignificant amounts of money that there was little temptation. But after the communities became firmly established and most industries were turning a handsome profit, some Trustees forgot the spiritual aspect of their jobs and concentrated instead on making more money. As spiritual issues and internal crises increasingly engrossed the attention of the Elders and Eldresses, they had less time and energy for the supervision of temporal leaders.

Rank and file members became more and more removed from the financial activities carried out in their names. Trustees regarded rank and file members as too ill-informed to understand the complexities of their jobs, and ceased to feel accountable, even to the Elders. Occasionally, as Damon observed sadly, Trustees had allocated financial resources for a "selfish or worldly purpose," simply because they knew they were unlikely to be caught. These investments, which were often unwise, undermined the faith of rank and file members, and as a result, they tended to lose interest in temporal activities because they no longer saw the visible fruits of their labor in community improvements. By the 1870s, these circumstances had produced a serious morale problem.

Changes proposed by Damon included the following: the institution of a "full and thorough system of book-keeping," an annual report to the Ministry by the Trustees of each Family, an annual report to Family members by the Trustees of all income and expenses, the appointment in each Family of a three-person Board of Directors to review finances on a quarterly basis, and the requirement that no Trustee sell or purchase land without the consent of the Family members. Damon also detailed several flaws in the Society's covenant that stood in need of revision.

The franchise of Covenant members are too vaguely expressed, so that the manner in which members give approbation to the appointments of Leading Authorities is not recognized; no sufficient provision for the modification or reorganization of society to meet the needs of the day we live in; no provision in our present covenant for females in the Order of Trustees to hold any money in their own names; an article should be embodied in the Covenant making direct provision for the expulsion of refractory or insubordinate members.[30]

These suggestions reveal that some progressive leaders were trying to come up with constructive ways of dealing with the behavior problems, leadership weaknesses, and economic irregularities that had been multiplying since the early decades of the century. An interesting part of this solution was the proposal to give more financial authority to female Trustees, a step dictated by demographic necessity. From 1800 to 1870 the adult male/female ratio in the eastern communities had remained relatively stable, hovering near 40:60.[31] After 1870 it had begun to drop noticeably though, reaching 34:66 by 1880, and 24:76 by 1900. In some communities, the ratio had fallen to less than 20:80 (see Appendix B.3). The necessity of transferring more temporal authority to the Sisters was obvious.

Another suggestion included in Damon's report was designed to redress the balance between spiritual and temporal leaders. Damon observed:

Elder *Thomas Damon* suggests an article in the Covenant . . . requiring a committee who shall be duly appointed to examine into the financial condition of every family in the Society once in three or six months, and take note of financial conditions and report to the Ministry, or, if Ministry constitute a part or all of this committee, to record the statistics of finances as found to exist in the Society. The same idea was suggested by Elder *Otis Sawyer*.[32]

Many of these reforms were introduced in Families and communities where the progressive party was dominant. As Anna White and Leila S. Taylor noted in 1904:

Following the plan already in successful operation in the Canterbury society, in January 1903, the business interests of the North Family were united; a treasurer was appointed from the sisters, a finance committee of brethren and sisters was chosen to meet monthly and decide all questions of business policy and one set of books was to be kept. Thus, without renouncing, in any degree, adherence to the Shaker principle of following an authorized leadership, the faithful, covenant-keeping members are more fully recognized, brought in closer touch with business operations and their influence and judgment accorded a larger place in the family politics.[33]

But the Canterbury community and the New Lebanon North Family were exceptions to the rule. In those environments, progressive leaders like Elder Henry Blinn and Eldress Antoinette Doolittle faced minimal opposition. Elsewhere in the Society, reform came slowly, if at all. The division between progressive and conservative leaders more often paralyzed both, leaving the rank and file bewildered.

Concern over purging the sect of materialism and revivifying spiritual commitment was, of course, shared by all Believers. Unfortunately, the selection of appropriate means to these ends proved to be a source of considerable disagreement. Progressive members, most vocally represented by Elder Frederick Evans of the New Lebanon North Family, sought to abandon some of the more antiquated beliefs and practices surviving from the eighteenth century, and concentrate instead on active missionary work to bring the more modern, socialist elements of the Shaker way before the World. Conservative members, championed by Elder Hervey Eads of South Union, Kentucky, advocated a stricter separation from the World and a return to traditional, ascetic Christian standards.

Concerned about the liberalizing tendencies he had witnessed throughout the Society, Elder Hervey traveled to the eastern communities in the mid-1870s in an effort to drum up support for his conservative program. Elder Frederick, however, was far from impressed, snorting:

As I see it, the Order of the Ministry is to him an Inquisition General, set for the correction and punishment of heretics who disrespect and disagree with his . . . theology. . . . The writer of this, on the contrary, was gathered to this Gospel wholly independent of all scriptures. . . . I highly prized the Scriptures whenever they sustained and confirmed my own views [but] whenever they conflicted with my opinions, I inferred that the writers did not understand the subject. . . . Shall we labor for and with the spirit of truth? When will the orthodox dam in Zion give way?[34]

Progressives like Evans were quick to point out that the danger to the Shaker way came not from theological liberalism but from internal moral decay combined with doctrinal rigidity. Evidently, some rank and file members had misinterpreted Eads's horror of liberal theology as support for the smaller, nontheological reforms they advocated— minor changes in Shaker lifestyle without significant changes in ideology. While Eads was still touring the eastern villages in 1875, Eldress Antoinette Doolittle, Evans's associate at the New Lebanon North

Family, complained that Eads's obsession with stamping out ideological heresy had so blinded him that he failed to see the sad decline in standards of behavior that had been accelerating since the early years of the century. She opined:

When I see individuals pleading for more self-indulgence and less self-denial, more social freedom between the sexes, for instrumental music and the cultivation of flowers, at the expense of other and more important duties, and who stand ready to grasp every fashion of the World, and plead for its adoption by Believers—always giving a sensible reason for the same, whether wearing the beards, throwing aside the plain Shaker cap and kerchief, and wearing long fringes on shawls and then manifest *great* concern, if there are any new ideas advanced in a theological point of view, lest *Mother's Gospel* will take damage, I am inclined to think there is a mistake somewhere.[35]

Eldress Antoinette was certainly right; there was indeed "a mistake somewhere." Conservative leaders like Eads and Elder Daniel Boler of the Lead Ministry and liberal leaders like Evans and Doolittle argued about which elements of Shaker theology should be reemphasized or reinterpreted, but rank and file members cared little for either position, concerning themselves instead with material things. Progressive leaders eventually came to dominate the sect's inner circles as their older, typically conservative colleagues died, and as a consequence their public activity on the Society's behalf increased. Beginning in the 1870s, progressive Shakerism was brought to the World's attention.

This transition from traditional to liberal attitudes among the majority of Shaker leaders occurred slowly over a period of several decades. During the mid-nineteenth century, Elder Frederick in particular had been viewed with some suspicion by leaders whose commitment derived largely from Shakerism's Christian tenets. In 1854, Elder Thomas Damon noted that "Elder William [Leonard of Harvard] had some theological notions to settle with Br. Frederick W. Evans which was a main cause of his leaving home. On some points there was an agreement, and in relation to others it was concluded not to agitate."[36] Twenty years later, at least some of these doubts survived, as Elder Giles Avery observed in March 1874: "Str. Anna comes over about Elder Frederick's peculiarities."[37]

By the 1870s, however, Sister Anna was the exception. "Elder Frederick's peculiarities" attracted increasing numbers of adherents. His desire to bring the Shaker gospel actively before the World, together with his obvious energy and devotion, seemed to promise the kind of ingathering foretold during "Mother's Work." Evans was never one to bewail the present condition of the sect by comparing it endlessly to the "good old days"; he was always concerned about moving into the

future. He had declared in 1853: "A sect looks back; a Church looks
forward. The highest aspirations of the former never ascend above the
measure of its founders, while those of the latter reach to God, by an
endless progression, through the means of continual revelation." [38] His
optimistic assessment of the power the Shaker example might assert in
the World appealed to members who had seen their beloved Society
dwindle in numbers and influence for decades, and who might otherwise have been wary of Evans's innovative doctrines. Evans defied the
distressing trends the sect's members had so long been forced to witness, and in 1869 declared: "The Shaker Order is the source and me-
dium of spiritual religious light to the world; the seed-bed of radical
truths; the fountain of progressive ideas." [39] In 1871, at the funeral of
Sister Mariette Moore of Canaan, New York, he reiterated these sentiments.

. . . the time [is] not far off when souls [will] be gathered to this gospel who
[will] readily unite with its precious truths for the Lord [is] causing a radical
change in the world of mankind which [is] breaking up their old theology and
producing in their hearts a thirst for greater truths both spiritually and
physically. [40]

The attraction of these positive statements at a time when the Society was experiencing internal upheaval is clear. Traditionalist leaders
had little to offer members but old solutions that had proven ineffec-
tive in the years after the Civil War. Many members felt that Evans's
program deserved a chance. By the late 1860s and early 1870s, Evans
had become the sect's *de facto* public spokesman, although he never
became a member of the Lead Ministry. This curious bifurcation in the
Society's authority structure did not go unnoticed by contemporary
observers. William Hepworth Dixon commented in 1867:

The chief elder . . . is Daniel Boler, who may be regarded as the Shaker bishop;
but the active power of the Society (as I fancy) lies with Elder Frederick, the
official preacher and expositor of Shaker doctrine. If the Shaker communities
should undergo any change in our day, through the coming in of other lights, I
fancy that the change will have to be brought about through him. Frederick is
a man of ideas, and men of ideas are dangerous persons in a Society which
affects to have adopted its final form. [41]

Although Dixon's assertion that the sect had "adopted its final form"
would have been denied by all Shaker leaders, Evans's progressive activism was unsettling to many of them.

Yet his reformist zeal and "ideas" heartened many rank and file Believers who had no wish to see the sect regarded as old-fashioned and
useless in a modern, industrial world. The liberal trends observed in
both the sect and the nation by William Dean Howells swept more and

more members into Evans's camp. In 1865, Sister Eunice Bathrick of Harvard copied in her commonplace book a contemporary poem that expressed the feelings of many Believers so desperate to feel relevant.

> If the salt have lost its savor, spake our Master, ages dead,
> Cast it out; 'tis fitted only for the rabble's feet to tread.
> So then old moss-grown traditions through the ages handed down,
> Full of savor in the old time, savorless to us have grown.
> Let us cast them from our churches to be trodden down of men,
> And a mine of newer virtue open to the world again . . .
> Worthy man's progressive wisdom, worthy man's immortal mind,
> Shall arise a glorious beacon for the guidance of mankind.
> Faith, we teach, must yield to knowledge; action supersedeth speech;
> And our hands must do a service that our prayers can never reach.[42]

This renewed desire to labor with both hands and minds for a new ingathering represented a major departure from the lethargic atmosphere of the 1850s and 1860s. As late as 1868, the Lead Ministry had complained of the members' spiritual torpor in a letter to the New Hampshire Ministry: ". . . some souls in Zion content themselves with a dull and stupid round of daily duties to get the bread of animal life, waiting for God to raise up other instruments as ministers of his saving Gospel grace."[43] In contrast to their predecessors, however, Believers of the 1870s and 1880s were eager to be active, a phenomenon the Lead Ministry reported with delight:

As an order of Ministry in Zion, having within the last two years visited every Society . . . , we have witnessed in every place an anxiety for the spread of the Testimony of the Gospel, for a resuscitation of Zion. . . . Cotemporary with this condition of feeling throughout Zion arises . . . a feeling in the world that Zion has a duty to do in manifesting her light to souls now sitting in darkness.[44]

Expressions of Zion's "duty" to the "World" took two forms in these years: active missionary work and the publication and distribution of a newspaper. The former broadened a long-standing Shaker tradition that had nearly vanished after early nineteenth-century successes in Ohio and Kentucky. In the late 1860s, the Union Village, Ohio, Shakers undertook a mission to Sweden (with little success), and in 1871, Elder Frederick Evans embarked on a speaking tour of England, bringing several children with him on his return.[45] Neither of these ventures resulted in the addition of substantial numbers of permanent converts, but the 1871 establishment at New Lebanon of a newspaper called *The Shaker* met with greater success, at least from an intellectual perspective.

Though the Shakers had previously published collections of testimonies and explanations of doctrine for a primarily Worldly audience, *The Shaker* (1871–1899) represented a significant departure from earlier practices. Because membership was so low (Shaker estimates for 1873 totaled 2,240), the Lead Ministry decided that "the press is the most efficient means of reaching the greatest number of persons with the least amount of expense and time."[46] The paper's purpose was twofold: to bring before sympathetic reformers in the World various Shaker tenets they might find congenial, and to reawaken missionary zeal within the communities themselves. The Lead Ministry made these objectives plain in February 1871, when they explained to the Watervliet Elders: "We would do all we can to stir up an interest in *The Shaker* and make a home as well as a foreign missionary. It will do good; we feel it; *we know it!*"[47]

There is some evidence that the initial impact of *The Shaker* was all that the Lead Ministry had hoped. In April 1871, four months after the appearance of the first issue, the Utica, New York, *Daily Bee* called it "a neat eight page paper, full of excellent sentiments and breathing a progressive spirit [that] gives evidence of an awakening among them, and kindles hope that this community will ere long change its customs and clothes, and annex itself to modern civilization."[48] Optimism waned somewhat in succeeding years, but *The Shaker* was welcomed eagerly by the Worldly reform community. Although the Lead Ministry had anticipated that circulation would reach 20,000 within the paper's first year of publication, they had every reason to be pleased with the 3,000 outsiders and over 2,000 Believers who avidly read each monthly issue.[49]

But even *The Shaker* quickly became a bone of contention within the Society. The paper's contributors and editors throughout its history were drawn almost exclusively from the sect's progressive wing, leading some conservative members to complain about its content. In February 1872, a furor arose over an article that had appeared in the January issue, as one New Lebanon Brother observed tersely: "J. M. Brown's 'Sentiments' in *The Shaker*, January No. 'Jesus a Sinner,' generally considered heterodox."[50] Philemon Stewart, traditionalist that he was, provided more details.

In the January No. of the Shaker, there was a piece headed Jesus a Siner . . . most of the members in the Church look upon it as rank infidelity and Herisy . . . will prove a death blow to the Shaker. I have written two sheets disproving it to go into the March number, but I do not expect they will put it in. The Paper is getting too Infidel, and too Aristocratic. Elder Giles and Elder Frederick Evans have engrossed much of its pages with such articles as favor . . . such kind of stuff.[51]

Throughout the remainder of the year, Stewart's opposition to *The Shaker* increased. In May, after his rebuttal of Brown's article was rejected for publication by the Ministry, Stewart complained: "As we all help support the expenses of the Shaker, one really had just as good a right to be heard in its columns as another."[52] He also had grave doubts that the typically urban readers reached by the paper would ever be willing to surrender their property and way of life to become Believers. He advocated instead a return to the rural missionary tours so successful in the sect's early years, and even traveled through central New York and Connecticut himself looking for potential converts. His reasons for supporting this old-fashioned technique were both financial and ideological:

I have never had any belief that Mother's true Gospel would ever be preached to take much effect in the Souls of People in any other way than in the most plain, humble, and homespun manner, and among the laboring, poorer classes, not among the Million Airs, City Speculators, Money Changers, Brokers, and High Hotel Boarders, but as this manner has been thoroughly tried and Thousands of Dollars expended for that purpose, I chuse to take an entire different Course, more in unison with the Manner that our First Parents planted it.[53]

In spite of the reservations of conservative members like Stewart, the pages of *The Shaker* continued to fill with liberal and reformist proposals and schemes, especially during the joint editorship of Frederick Evans and Antoinette Doolittle from January 1873 to December 1875. Scoffing at those traditionalist members who wished the sect would withdraw from progressivism and the World into a narrow cocoon of doctrinal rigidity, Evans thundered in April 1875:

This idea of sufficiency, carried out, would turn back the wheels of time and progress for two thousand years, and teach a savage life. Under its rod of iron we would not dare to say what we know to be true—because of self-adulated conservatism. Evolution is the key word of progress—the forerunner of the "good time coming." Her legitimate children are additions to genuine revelation.[54]

As support for Evans's progressive program increased among rank and file members in the last decades of the nineteenth century, life in the communities began to change subtly. Intellectual impulses, the increased age of the membership, and the diminished zeal and interest observable in every community led the Believers in the 1880s to abandon their ritual dance worship in favor of a less charismatic service of singing, reading from Scripture, and public "testifying." Because of pressure from the membership union meetings were changed as well— the emphasis shifted from the cultivation of the spirit to the expansion of the intellect. In 1884, Sister Amelia Calver of New Lebanon complained: "It seems a pity what with all the intelligence of the age, we have not time to devote one hour a week for mind culture, when the mind is what we must be measured by."[55] Although Shakers in earlier periods would have been horrified by the assertion that Believers should be judged by their minds rather than their souls, intellectual pursuits began to dominate the internal life of the villages in the 1880s. The effort to appear progressive and up-to-date to Worldly observers led many Elders to sanction singing and elocution lessons in these years, an innovation justified by Sisters Agnes Newton and Mabel Liscomb of Canterbury in 1885.

We are anxious to learn to speak, read and sing correctly, that we may better perform our Christian mission. Whenever opportunity is presented to speak or sing the testimony of Christ, in the perfection of its beauty, as manifested in the Second Appearing of the Christ Spirit, we would be able to do the same with souls and voices which give no uncertain sound, but are clothed with the culture and grace of the spirit.[56]

At New Lebanon, a so-called Family Union Circle of all interested members was substituted for the fragmented union meetings of previous years. In 1884, the list of topics covered by this group reveals how far the Shakers had departed from the traditions of the early nineteenth century: "Beauties of the Bible," "Proper Use of Irregular Verbs," "Mispronounced Words," "Notes on Ireland," "Essay on Prairie Dogs," "A Reading on the Benefits of Hot Water," "Postal Laws," "The Effects of Alcohol," "The Elk From Observation," and "Sieges and Battles and Such Stuff." In June of that year, after a meeting that included a twenty-minute address on "Gum Products," Sister Amelia Calver concluded: "Our little circle is quite an improvement over the sleepy dull union meeting where conversation was turned out by machinery which had no motive power but a rusted creaking crank."[57]

This social and intellectual modernization within the communities resulted at least in part from the sect's diminished popularity. Although progressive members like Evans, Doolittle, Avery, and Calver would hardly have admitted this in the late nineteenth century, their struggles to change the Society's image in the public mind had little permanent impact. As the sect's membership aged, the need for restrictive measures to indoctrinate and control new, youthful members was eliminated, perhaps leading some middle-aged and elderly members to relax their conservative tendencies and support modest progressive innovations. Even these updated elements of the Shaker lifestyle failed to keep wavering members in the faith or attract many new converts, and the Society gradually assumed a more tranquil attitude of mature old age. Wrangling between progressives and conservatives, so apparent in the 1870s, languished as most Believers seemed to accept an unspoken assumption that they would no longer agitate publicly on matters of belief or daily practice. Beginning in the 1880s and 1890s, the sect began to grow old more gracefully, trying to influence the World more by quiet example than by loud protestation.

The most noticeable features of this aging process were demographic. In the last third of the nineteenth century Shaker villages became visibly female dominated as the adult male/female ratio in most of the eastern communities dropped to approximately 30:70 (see Appendix B.3). Young people had dominated the sect's population in the middle decades of the century, but by the 1880s and 1890s they had been replaced by the elderly. By 1880, for example, members over sixty comprised more than 35 percent of the membership at the Watervliet, Hancock, Harvard, and Shirley villages (see Appendix B.5).

This shift significantly altered the tone of Shaker life. These older Believers were more willing than their juniors of the 1840s and 1850s to be patient and diligent in the task of perpetuating the faith. Their tranquil acceptance of the tribulations visited upon the Society was transmitted to those few of their younger colleagues who had remained faithful. After the mid-1870s many members, exhausted by the ideological controversies of the previous decade, broke through to a refreshing peace and serenity. In 1878, thirty-four-year-old Sister Julia Briggs of Canterbury rededicated herself to the responsibilities of bearing a pure witness to the World, telling Eldress Polly Reed:

I often say to myself, there is no turning back for me. I am called of God to the work of molding and remolding my life to his way. I would not be a marred vessel in the hands of the potter, unfit for the master's use. I would rather bear the cleansing, the confessing and the changing, till fashioned in the likeness of something better than the flesh is able to produce.[58]

The willingness to await God's time to revivify the sect was evident in many Believers during the last years of the nineteenth century. They remembered that in God's view the vagaries and difficulties of a decade or even five decades could vanish in an instant. By recalling this they returned to the kind of sweeping, millennial view of Christian history that had dominated Shaker thinking early in the sect's history. In 1891, Sister Sarah F. Wilson of Canterbury reminded Brother Alonzo G. Hollister of New Lebanon:

I can see no cause for discouragement to Believers because God's time has not come to bring an addition of numbers to our ranks. Could we hasten the ingathering before the grain is harvested and ground into meal to be made into bread for those who seek, would not loss of souls result? So I take the warning to garner carefully the lessons of Wisdom that in greater need I may have a treasure to impart.[59]

While this new assurance and tranquillity developed, the Shakers never surrendered their hope that the sect would soon experience a rebirth of popularity. In the 1890s, Believers at Union Village, Ohio, and New Lebanon inaugurated a new settlement plan pursued by thousands of other Americans seeking a warm, sunny retirement home. Between 1894 and 1898, these Shakers established two new communities in Georgia and Florida as places to which elderly members could move and live out their consecrated lives in a more salubrious climate than that offered by any of the northern villages. The southern climate was also intended to attract new members, and to revitalize the Society's troubled economy by diversifying its agricultural activities. All of these notions seemed sound initially, at least in light of the problems the sect had faced since the 1820s and 1830s. As population shifted away from the northeastern states, and as Shaker success in urban areas failed to materialize, a move to the expanding region of the southeast seemed eminently sensible.

The fate of the southern communities quickly proved that these expectations were foolish. Elder Joseph Slingerland of Ohio and three eastern Trustees toured Georgia and Florida in 1894 "to explore for land suitable for Believers to live on with a view to emigration thereto in the near future by some eastern Believers."[60] In 1897 and 1898, the Union Village Ministry, at Slingerland's suggestion, purchased the Altama and Hopeton plantations in Glynn County, Georgia, for $30,000; as well as 51,000 acres of undeveloped land in Pierce, Charleton, and Ware Counties; and the McKinnon estate of some 7,000 acres near White Oak in Camden County. These extravagant purchases soon proved a mistake, as the Shakers were forced to sell their Glynn County holdings and concentrate their Georgia efforts in the White Oak area. Even here, there were few local converts. The community never exceeded twenty members, most of them Ohio transplants. Slingerland's vision of grandeur evaporated rapidly—the White Oak community dwindled and was finally closed in 1902.[61]

The New Lebanon community sponsored a similar venture in Osceola County, Florida, and it appeared, at least at first, to be a greater success than these vastly overextended efforts to the north. Elder Benjamin Gates and Brothers Andrew Barrett and Charles Weed of New Lebanon visited the Narcoossee area near Ashton in 1894 and were favorably impressed both by its climate and its opportunities for economic development. Two years later, New Lebanon invested $94,500 in 7,046 acres and dispatched a small group of Believers to this new southern outpost.[62] The community never had more than ten or twelve members, but the interest it engendered among the Shakers in the northern villages was astonishing. In March 1896, aging Elder Abraham Perkins of Canterbury confided his hopes for the Florida experiment to Sister Corinna Bishop of New Lebanon.

Our relations and interest in Florida! I do hope that in that State may be found a place for a nucleus of souls to honor Zion. It is evident from reports that much strength, great deprivations, sacrifices and sufferings have been given, borne and expended, saying nothing of the draft from the purse required to furnish the meager comforts for those under the yoke. . . . While for them my sympathies are deep and my prayers go out, I cannot forget our people as a whole, our weeping Zion. . . . I turn to Florida. Our kind Sister Minerva gives us encouraging prospects of that flowery land. She describes their beautiful gardens, their flourishing fruit trees, their fields of potatoes now in blossom, and the beauty of ever blooming flowers. . . . Oh, I do so hope for their happiness, their prosperity, and their safe, permanent establishment of a protective and an orderly Zion home.[63]

Perkins's dream of Florida as the last, best hope for the sect evaporated quickly. Materialism, felt by many Believers to have been the bane of the northern communities, appeared in the south as well. Only a few months after it was established, Brother Andrew Barrett reported to Elder Joseph Holden of the Lead Ministry on worsening spiritual conditions at the new settlement, which had hopefully been named "Olive Branch":

In our meeting yesterday I gave in my testimony to strengthen what you said to me just before starting to *Florida.* "Go and be sure you build a spiritual household as well as the temporal." Dear Elder Joseph this bears more *weight* on my feelings than anything *else.* I fear at times we are not doing it. When I see the greed of money step in and engross our whole attention, I begin to think we have forgotten the primary object of our exit to Florida. . . . To me this was not intended as merely a *speculative scheme* for a quick and comfortable home with a good chance to make a few dollars. . . . If God is in it I don't believe he wants any such business.[64]

The futility of the Georgia and Florida experiments had become readily apparent when Eldresses Anna White and Leila S. Taylor of New Lebanon published *Shakerism: Its Meaning and Message* in 1904. Even in their moderate assessment of these resettlement efforts, White and Taylor revealed the division that had arisen among the members.

Much doubt was felt in many minds of the advisability of these moves. It was felt by many that concentration rather than scattering of force was demanded by the condition of the societies; that empty buildings and untilled fields in the north hardly called for new territories and the erection of new dwellings and store-houses in distant states. Others saw in the opening south opportunities for obtaining a livelihood with less outlay of strength, less waste of energy, than in the cold climate and on the rocky soil of the north. The experiments were tried without loss of union among those who differed in opinion. Perhaps it is too soon to say whether or not true wisdom prompted the last attempt.[65]

In spite of their disclaimer suggesting that there had been no "loss of union," White and Taylor clearly hinted that the efforts to establish new communities in the southeast had been mistakes that further undermined the members' already diminished faith in their leaders. The Florida settlement was indeed the "last attempt." By 1908, only five members remained. Then Brother Egbert Gillette and Sister Elizabeth Sears were arrested and charged in 1911 with the chloroform mercy killing of Sister Sadie Marchant, who had been in the final stages of tuberculosis. Although Sister Sadie had asked to be killed, and Brother Egbert and Sister Elizabeth were subsequently freed, the trial and attendant national publicity was the critical blow for the community—it was disbanded shortly thereafter.[66] As Brother Andrew Barrett had feared in 1896, "Olive Branch" failed to develop into a promised land for the remaining faithful and had proven instead "a huge Elephant on our hands to look after and eat its head off and finally die of the dry rot as some of our other great possessions have and are doing."[67]

The hopes and subsequent disappointments that characterized these southern endeavors did little to mitigate the disagreements between progressive and conservative members in the northern communities. Author William Hinds observed this division in 1902 and commented:

Important changes have . . . taken place in the internal character of Shakerism; its leaders are more liberal and tolerant than they were half a century ago; more ready to see good in other systems, and less prompt to condemn what does not accord with their own. It is also obvious that there is a growing party of progressives among the Shakers—men and women who, while firmly adhering to all the essentials of Shakerism, demand that non-essentials shall not stand in the way of genuine progress and culture. . . . Still it is natural that the more conservative should question the policy of the progressives. "I do not think," says one of their ablest thinkers and writers, in a recent letter, "we have gained anything by relaxing discipline, or letting down from the cross."[68]

While disunion remained, the progressive party grew proportionately stronger as older, typically conservative members died. White and Taylor's *Shakerism: Its Meaning and Message*, the last major Shaker public statement, was a substantially progressive manifesto. The authors, ideological heirs of Elder Frederick Evans who had died in 1893, asserted that the Believers had a vital contribution to make to twentieth-century America. They upheld the traditional belief that the Shakers possessed the power to live without sin, a power they felt was sadly lacking in the world around them. "The truth of this assertion," they observed

is upheld by the witness and experience of all those who sincerely came and who persistently continued through life in faithful adherence to this light; and it was no more real and convincing to those who thus confessed and received power to forsake sin, in the presence of Mother Ann's spiritually beautiful personality in 1780, than it is in 1904, to those who do the same work faithfully in the same way.[69]

Though White and Taylor argued that Shaker life in 1904 was little changed from what it had been in Mother Ann's day, they supported progressive departure from traditional beliefs and practices. Stressing Shaker success in communalism over its evangelical, Christian roots, they pointed to a long list of accomplishments that demonstrated Shaker relevance to the twentieth-century world, including: brotherhood of man, communism, rights of labor, sexual equality, protection of animals and children, pacifism, temperance, health food and sanitation, and personal freedom.[70] They felt that this shift in emphasis was necessary if Shaker influence in the World was to continue. They also supported certain democratic modifications of the sect's structure of government.

Has not the day arrived when that grand, divinely ordained theocracy, which united the spiritual man of earth to the heavens and to God, may, without endangering the structure, readjust its temporal relations? When the method of theocratic control in all the details of life . . . may give place to the broader freedom that belongs to men and women who have attained intellectual maturity? The man and woman of today . . . cannot be bound and shackled in swaddling clothes. . . . Give to . . . the faithful, covenant-keeping members, a voice in all the affairs of financial and temporal import. Grant them the intellectual freedom their development requires. Fit Shakerism to humanity today, as the Fathers and Mothers of the past fitted it to their age and time.[71]

Although this process of adjustment was never fully completed, largely due to dwindling numbers and to continued disagreements among the Believers, White and Taylor were convinced that the Shaker example would not go entirely unheeded. They were certain that the sect had a future.

A peculiar prophecy often referred to by Shaker historians is found in the seventy-second Psalm: "There shall be a handful of corn in the earth upon the top of the mountains, the fruit thereof shall shake like Lebanon, and they of the city shall flourish like grass of the earth." This handful of corn in the top of the mountains is to the spiritual eye of the Shaker beautifully fulfilled in the handful of true Believers at Mount Lebanon, the seed from which is to spring the harvest of redeemed humanity.[72]

For all their disagreements about doctrine and policy with conservative members such as Philemon Stewart, White and Taylor shared the vision of a saving remnant with him: a core of true Believers that would yet redeem the human race. Stewart had prophesied in 1873: "God's true work will never run out, tho' Zion's present Organizations will be mostly scattered and broken—yet a Remnant will be preserved who will willingly obey God's full requirements according to the day and age in which they live."[73] Such a remnant of Believers has survived, although withdrawn from the view of "World's People" until relatively recently. Their full story remains to be told.

Conclusion

Who were the Shakers? What was at the root of both their success and failure? Why do they command our attention? The answer to these questions is deceptively simple: the Shakers tried to be perfect.

The Shaker story is important because their system worked—in a specific time and place. Yet their appeal and influence have transcended the constraints of both. The Believers initiated a revolution that was both spiritual and temporal, radical and conservative. Their ideology and social structure were typically American in many ways, and the tale of their rise and fall reveals a great deal about nineteenth-century life.

Who were they? First and foremost, the Shakers were Christians, "Believers in Christ's Second Appearing." They shared evangelical, perfectionist roots with thousands of Americans, a fact which explains much of their popularity in the eighteenth and early nineteenth centuries. In their social and economic backgrounds, the early Believers were not unusual. Most were rural farmers and artisans with modest incomes who believed America was the hope of the world, the site of the long awaited millennium. But the revolution they supported was not a political one; they set out to rebuild human relationships. They created a religious and social system within which men and women were equal, the natural environment was respected and not exploited, and service to God and to others was a daily priority. For many, perhaps even most Believers, these goals were achieved.

The United Society of Believers in Christ's Second Appearing is widely recognized as America's most successful communal sect. More than twenty thousand, indeed probably many thousands more, Americans lived part of their lives as Shakers. Until the middle of the nineteenth century, eighteen villages flourished, two of which survive today. Why was the sect so successful?

The reasons for Shaker success are numerous, but it is mainly attributable to two factors: synthesis and adjustment. Early Shaker leaders possessed the rare ability to combine tradition and innovation in ideology, economics, and social structure. Puritan sense of community and reverence for labor, Enlightenment rationalism and respect for the individual, evangelical pietism and revelation, Romantic love of nature and pursuit of union among all creatures—all found a home in the

Shaker world. Celibacy satisfied evangelical longings for a total union with God, at the same time knitting Believers into newly defined Families whose bonds of gospel affection were eternal. At a time of severe cultural upheaval, the Shakers promised, and delivered, an enticing combination of temporal and spiritual security.

The Shakers also exhibited a remarkable ability to adjust to changing circumstances, either by altering their responses or by accepting what they could not change. Their belief in continual revelation helped to minimize the ossification of doctrine and practice. A willingness to learn from non-Believers and to accept the most beneficial and sensible of technological and ideological innovations developed in the World greatly lengthened the Society's years of prominence. But even with these considerable assets, the sect experienced a decline after the 1820s from which it has never recovered.

The United Society's decline was at first qualitative—a diminished level of commitment to traditional tenets—but was succeeded by a quantitative phase beginning in the 1840s. After that time, children and the elderly made up the greater part of the membership and the Shakers were increasingly viewed as a relic of ancient days, a relic for which other Americans felt nostalgia and curiosity, but little serious interest.

The reasons for the sect's decline were twofold: internal tension and external change. Even in their most successful and stable years, between 1800 and 1820, the Believers were poised on the brink of dissension. Dependent for both converts and markets on an ever changing World, leaders were unable to regulate successfully which new ideas and customs should be accepted and which rejected. The sect's very popularity during these years hastened its decline, as revivals in the World and economic stability in the communities brought hundreds of new members into the fold, many of them children who had never experienced conversions. These young people required increased supervision, straining leadership resources to the utmost. As a result, the traditional balance between regulation and order and rejuvenation and disorder had to be altered. Ritual increasingly replaced spontaneity as the century progressed, and the spiritual health of the Society suffered.

As these internal tensions developed, external conditions that had fostered the sect's growth changed markedly. After the 1840s, evangelical revivalism in the northeast diminished, greatly restricting opportunities for the Shakers to reach awakened, unsatisfied Christians. Urbanization, industrial development, and westward expansion removed more and more Americans from the pool of logical, potential converts, leaving the Believers in an ideological and economic backwater. Their response, after decades of despair and dissension over how best to rebuild the sect, has been patience. A few Shakers have maintained their faith into the twentieth century, even in the face of overwhelming odds.

Though the effort as a whole may have failed, and even this is by no means certain, many individual Believers have succeeded in the sect's more than 200-year history. The story of their struggles to be perfect, to build a working heaven on earth, has enduring value. Thousands of Believers learned crucial lessons about the world and humanity's place in it, lessons they were always willing to share. The ultimate example that the Shakers provided was in their efforts to change and restore human nature, as William Hepworth Dixon observed in 1867.

On being received into union, he no longer regards the earth as a spoil to be won, but as a pledge to be redeemed. By man it fell, by man it may be restored. Every one chosen of the Father has the privilege of aiding in this redemption; not only by the toil of his hands, by the contrivance of his brain, but by the sympathy of his soul; covering the world with verdure, filling the air with perfume, storing the granary with fruit. The spirit in which he puts his hand out is a new one to him. Hitherto, the earth has been his servant; now it is his partner.[1]

Although few Believers survive, this lesson of Christian dedication and cooperation may yet be learned.

Appendixes

Explanatory Note to Statistical Appendixes

The following collection of demographic data relative to the eleven Shaker communities in the northeastern United States represents the first major effort to undertake a broad statistical analysis of the Shakers. These figures were drawn from two sources, each of which has particular strengths and weaknesses.

Appendix A includes detailed data from membership records for the Church Family at New Lebanon, New York, and represents a significant sample size of 1,049 cases. This Family was selected for close study because its residents included both Senior Order adult members and children upon whom the Believers largely relied for future converts. New Lebanon was also the leading community within the sect and the headquarters of the Lead Ministry. Demographic data concerning this group of Shakers has, therefore, special significance. Unlike material drawn from manuscript census schedules, data is available for every year from the "gathering" of the Family on, and permits the compilation of apostasy rates, admission and persistence figures, and the average age of converts, as well as detailed analysis of the Children's Order. But Shaker membership records are incomplete and are heavily biased in favor of Senior Order Families. Conclusions that are made based on this data might not be applicable to other Families and communities.

Appendixes B and C, therefore, present data for *all* eleven of the eastern communities culled from manuscript census schedules (1790–1900). The benefit of this data is its inclusiveness. All Orders, all ages, all levels of commitment are represented. But census figures have drawbacks as well. Incremental changes within decades cannot be ascertained, nor can apostasy rates, admission or persistence figures, and average age of converts be calculated. Changes in enumeration categories from census to census lead to unavoidable imprecision in the definition of age groups. Wherever possible in the following tables, sixteen is regarded as the beginning of adulthood because the Shakers regarded it as such. At that age, a young Believer typically ceased formal schooling, assumed a full work load, and moved into the Family Dwelling. Full conversion, marked by signing the covenant, could come only after age twenty-one.

Taken together, these two sources provide demographic data that fundamentally alter the traditional picture drawn of the United Society. They demonstrate that the sect's numerical decline began as early as 1840, and prove that the rough estimates of total peak membership have been considerably exaggerated. More important, they reveal two key demographic weaknesses that developed in the 1810s and 1820s: a marked increase in the proportion of unconverted young members whose spiritual education had to be provided if they were to join the Society on reaching adulthood, and a serious drop in the proportion of members in the leadership pool. By 1820, the eastern communities as a whole had fewer than 25 percent of both their male and female members in the leadership pool. By the same date, the proportion of children under the age of sixteen was approaching 20 percent, and in fact, exceeded that level in six of the eleven eastern communities. Thus, the proportion of young people requiring temporal supervision and spiritual education was increasing, but the group from which their adult leaders and role models were drawn was declining. The overall quantitative decline that began after 1840 was presaged by demographic indicators that had shown themselves several decades earlier.

APPENDIX A
New Lebanon Church Family Demographic Characteristics

The following sources were used in the construction of this appendix: Isaac Youngs, "Names and Ages of Those Who have been gathered into the Church Since 1787 . . . , some additions by John M. Brown, 1870"; manuscript in Andrews Shaker Collection, Winterthur Museum, Winterthur, Delaware. Also Wallace Cathcart's 16,000+ Shaker name file in the Western Reserve Historical Society Shaker Collection, Cleveland, Ohio.

Tables 2 through 5 and Table 7 first appeared in Priscilla J. Brewer, "The Demographic Features of the Shaker Decline, 1787–1900," *Journal of Interdisciplinary History* 15:1 (Summer 1984) :31–52, and are reprinted here by permission.

TABLE A.1   Admissions to New Lebanon Church Family

Admitted	Males	Percentage	Females	Percentage	Total	Percentage
1787–1790	126	23.3	123	24.2	249	23.7
1791–1800	6	1.1	10	2.0	16	1.5
1801–1810	21	3.9	13	2.6	34	3.2
1811–1820	26	4.8	36	7.1	62	5.9
1821–1830	46	8.5	45	8.8	91	8.7
1831–1840	56	10.4	52	10.2	108	10.3
1841–1850	68	12.6	44	8.6	112	10.7
1851–1860	74	13.7	48	9.4	122	11.6
1861–1870	46	8.5	44	8.6	90	8.6
1871–1880	35	6.5	35	6.9	70	6.7
1881–1890	16	3.0	35	6.9	51	4.9
1891–1900	20	3.7	24	4.7	44	4.2
TOTAL	540	100.0	509	100.0	1049	100.0

TABLE A.2 Adult Apostasies in New Lebanon Church Family[a]

Decade	Males	Percentage[b]	Females	Percentage[b]	Total	Percentage[b]
1787–1790	5	4.0	1	0.8	6	2.4
1791–1800	25	28.1	13	12.7	38	19.9
1801–1810	3	4.2	1	1.1	4	2.5
1811–1820	7	8.2	4	3.9	11	5.9
1821–1830	7	6.4	1	0.8	8	3.3
1831–1840	22	15.9	4	2.7	26	9.1
1841–1850	33	22.0	14	8.3	47	14.8
1851–1860	22	16.2	9	6.6	31	11.4
1861–1870	39	35.8	22	16.1	61	24.8
1871–1880	25	42.4	21	21.9	46	29.7
1881–1890	12	29.3	24	28.9	36	29.0
1891–1900	10	33.3	15	26.8	25	29.1

[a]Those members who left the Family more than once have been counted only in their last year of departure.
[b]Percentage of decade's total population. Includes all members who lived in the Family for any part of the decade in question.

TABLE A.3 Adult Male/Female Ratio in
New Lebanon Church Family[a]

	Males		Females	
	Number	Percentage	Number	Percentage
1790	101	54.0	86	46.0
1795	88	49.7	89	50.3
1800	61	40.9	88	59.1
1805	60	41.7	84	58.3
1810	65	46.4	75	53.6
1815	58	43.9	74	56.1
1820	67	45.6	80	54.4
1825	69	44.8	85	55.2
1830	69	41.8	96	58.2
1835	77	43.0	102	57.0
1840	77	44.0	98	56.0
1845	81	45.3	98	54.7
1850	66	42.9	88	57.1
1855	61	42.7	82	57.3
1860	65	43.0	86	57.0
1865	59	39.9	89	60.1
1870	45	34.4	86	65.6
1875	28	29.8	66	70.2
1880	29	34.5	55	65.5
1885	19	27.9	49	72.1
1890	20	28.6	50	71.4
1895	15	28.3	38	71.7
1900	12	31.6	26	68.4

[a]Excluding all members under sixteen.

TABLE A.4   Leadership Resources in New Lebanon Church Family

	Males		Females	
	No. 25–49[a]	Percentage of Total	No. 25–49[a]	Percentage of Total
1790	60	48.8	54	45.8
1795	47	51.6	53	54.6
1800	46	75.4	53	60.2
1805	41	68.3	69	82.1
1810	29	42.6	50	64.1
1815	21	30.0	36	41.4
1820	21	28.0	32	34.0
1825	14	17.3	31	29.5
1830	20	22.0	28	24.8
1835	24	23.5	34	28.8
1840	21	19.8	44	35.5
1845	27	25.0	48	36.4
1850	26	26.5	40	34.5
1855	22	22.0	34	32.4
1860	20	21.7	33	31.1
1865	20	24.1	31	27.7
1870	14	24.1	27	27.0
1875	7	17.5	17	23.0
1880	5	11.9	17	23.0
1885	4	14.8	13	22.0
1890	4	16.0	9	15.8
1895	2	11.1	4	8.9
1900	2	13.3	3	9.7

[a]Of sixty-seven Church Family members chosen as Ministry or Family Elders and Eldresses between 1788 and 1861, fifty-five (82.0 percent) were between the ages of twenty-five and forty-nine.

TABLE A.5   Members' Persistence in New Lebanon Church Family[a]
(In years)

Admitted	Males	Females
1787–1790	21.9	27.9
1791–1800	32.5[b]	35.1
1801–1810	25.4	38.4
1811–1820	25.0	36.4
1821–1830	24.8	29.6
1831–1840	10.8	21.1
1841–1850	10.2	24.5
1851–1860	8.8	9.6
1861–1870	3.9	7.6
1871–1880	6.5	7.1
1881–1890	2.2	5.2
1891–1900	6.0	9.0

[a]Length of stay for each member was calculated to the nearest year. Those who remained in the Family less than one year were assigned values of zero. Males = 531, females = 505.
[b]This figure must be viewed with some reserve since only six males joined the Family in these years.

TABLE A.6   Average Age of New Members, New Lebanon Church Family
(In years)

Admitted	Males	Females
1787–1790	27.2	22.6
1791–1800	27.2	22.3
1801–1810	24.3	20.6
1811–1820	14.8	13.3
1821–1830	13.7	14.2
1831–1840	12.3	11.0
1841–1850	11.4	8.8
1851–1860	11.7	11.0
1861–1870	10.2	10.7
1871–1880	14.7	17.2
1881–1890	17.8	23.4
1891–1900	25.8	18.6

TABLE A.7   Age Group Distribution in New Lebanon Church Family

	Percentage of Males			Percentage of Females			Total Percentage		
	<16	16–59	≥60	<16	16–59	≥60	<16	16–59	≥60
1790	17.9	79.7	2.4	27.1	69.5	3.4	22.4	74.7	2.9
1795	3.3	92.3	4.4	8.2	86.6	5.2	5.8	89.4	4.8
1800	—	86.9	13.1	—	93.2	6.8	—	90.6	9.4
1805	—	85.0	15.0	—	94.0	6.0	—	90.3	9.7
1810	4.4	82.4	13.2	3.8	87.2	9.0	4.1	84.9	11.0
1815	17.1	64.3	18.6	14.9	73.6	11.5	15.9	69.4	14.7
1820	10.7	65.3	24.0	14.9	68.1	17.0	13.0	66.9	20.1
1825	14.8	58.0	27.2	19.0	60.0	21.0	17.2	59.1	23.7
1830	24.2	50.5	25.3	15.0	62.0	23.0	19.1	56.9	24.0
1835	24.5	50.0	25.5	13.6	60.1	26.3	18.6	55.5	25.9
1840	27.4	45.2	27.4	21.0	54.0	25.0	23.9	50.0	26.1
1845	25.0	52.7	22.3	25.8	50.7	23.5	25.4	51.7	22.9
1850	32.6	49.0	18.4	24.1	57.8	18.1	28.1	53.7	18.2
1855	39.0	47.0	14.0	21.9	62.9	15.2	30.2	55.2	14.6
1860	29.3	60.9	9.8	18.9	62.2	18.9	23.7	61.6	14.7
1865	28.9	54.2	16.9	20.5	59.8	19.7	24.1	57.4	18.5
1870	22.4	51.7	25.9	14.0	61.0	25.0	17.1	57.6	25.3
1875	30.0	40.0	30.0	10.8	50.0	39.2	17.5	46.5	36.0
1880	31.0	45.2	23.8	25.7	32.4	41.9	27.6	37.1	35.3
1885	29.6	22.2	48.2	16.9	37.3	45.8	20.9	32.6	46.5
1890	20.0	28.0	52.0	12.3	45.6	42.1	14.6	40.3	45.1
1895	16.7	38.9	44.4	15.5	35.6	48.9	15.9	36.5	47.6
1900	20.0	46.7	33.3	16.1	38.7	45.2	17.4	41.3	41.3

TABLE A.8   New Lebanon Children's Order, Females[a]
(N = 326)

Admitted	Apostatized	Taken[b]	Removed[c]	Died <16	Died in Faith
1787–1790	6	4	7	—	18
Percentage	17.2	11.4	20.0	—	51.4
1791–1800	1	—	—	—	1
Percentage	50.0	—	—	—	50.0
1801–1810	—	—	1	1	4
Percentage	—	—	16.7	16.7	66.6
1811–1820	1	5	1	1	18
Percentage	3.8	19.3	3.8	3.8	69.3
1821–1830	3	13	—	1	13
Percentage	10.0	43.3	—	3.4	43.3
1831–1840	10	15	—	6	10
Percentage	24.4	36.6	—	14.6	24.4
1841–1850	18	9	1	2	9
Percentage	46.2	23.1	2.6	5.0	23.1
1851–1860	18	21	2	1	4
Percentage	39.2	45.7	4.2	2.3	8.6
1861–1870	15	24	1	—	1
Percentage	36.6	58.6	2.4	—	2.4
1871–1880	10	17	—	—	—
Percentage	37.0	63.0	—	—	—
1881–1890	7	9	1	1	—
Percentage	38.8	50.0	5.6	5.6	—
1891–1900	8	7	—	—	—
Percentage	53.3	46.7	—	—	—
TOTAL	97	124	14	13	78
Percentage	29.8	38.0	4.3	4.0	23.9

[a]All members admitted when less than sixteen.

[b]By parents, other relatives, or guardians. All children leaving before the age of sixteen are assumed to have been taken away against their wills unless the record indicates otherwise.

[c]To other Shaker Families or communities.

TABLE A.9 New Lebanon Children's Order, Males[a]

(N = 352)

Admitted	Apostatized	Taken[b]	Removed[c]	Died <16	Died in Faith
1787–1790	11	2	5	—	9
Percentage	40.7	7.4	18.6	—	33.3
1791–1800	—	—	—	—	1
Percentage	—	—	—	—	100.0
1801–1810	2	—	—	—	4
Percentage	33.3	—	—	—	66.7
1811–1820	7	1	—	—	9
Percentage	41.2	5.9	—	—	52.9
1821–1830	17	3	3	—	9
Percentage	53.1	9.4	9.4	—	28.1
1831–1840	27	12	2	1	5
Percentage	57.4	25.6	4.3	2.1	10.6
1841–1850	22	28	4	—	4
Percentage	37.9	48.3	6.9	—	6.9
1851–1860	36	29	1	—	2
Percentage	52.9	42.6	1.6	—	2.9
1861–1870	17	28	—	1	—
Percentage	37.0	60.8	—	2.2	—
1871–1880	14	13	1	—	—
Percentage	50.0	46.4	3.6	—	—
1881–1890	3	10	—	—	—
Percentage	23.1	76.9	—	—	—
1891–1900	4	5	—	—	—
Percentage	44.4	55.5	—	—	—
TOTAL	160	131	16	2	43
Percentage	45.5	37.2	4.5	0.6	12.2

[a]All members admitted when less than sixteen.

[b]By parents, other relatives, or guardians. All children leaving before the age of sixteen are assumed to have been taken away against their wills unless the record indicates otherwise.

[c]To other Shaker Families or communities.

APPENDIX B
Eastern Communities' Demographic Characteristics

The tables in this appendix are based on data obtained from manuscript census schedules available on microfilm at the Federal Archives and Records Center, Waltham, Massachusetts.

TABLE B.I Total Population

	1790[a]			1800			1810		
	No. M	No. F	Total	No. M	No. F	Total	No. M	No. F	Total
New Lebanon	105	116	221	128	203	331	134	183	317
Watervliet	36	18	54	35	42	77	54	72	126
Hancock	32	62	94	62	71	133	62	116	178
Enfield, Conn.	25	21	46	55	74	129	72	87	159
Tyringham	6	12	18	23	30	53	32	37	69
Harvard	24	38	62	40	77	117	37	79	116
Shirley	16	27	43	23	50	73	27	51	78
Canterbury	—	—	—	47	67	114	85	90	175
Enfield, N.H.	—	—	—	71	76	147	62	72	134
Alfred	—	—	—	46	73	119	57	72	129
Sabbathday Lake	—	—	—	32	48	80	29	41	70
TOTAL	244	294	538	562	811	1373	651	900	1551

	1820			1830			1840		
New Lebanon	164	226	390	204	265	469	206	273	479
Watervliet	80	113	193	109	135	244	146	158	304
Hancock	135	182	317	149	189	338	124	185	309
Enfield, Conn.	91	105	196	94	119	213	79	96	175
Tyringham	45	47	92	40	44	84	33	43	76
Harvard	64	109	173	60	107	167	67	100	167
Shirley	35	49	84	23	46	69	23	47	70
Canterbury	88	130	218	96	140	236	103	157	260
Enfield, N.H.	—[b]	—[b]	—[b]	87	116	203	123	174	297
Alfred	68	86	154	67	91	158	64	90	154
Sabbathday Lake	51	88	139	45	90	135	48	88	136
TOTAL	821[b]	1135[b]	1956[b]	974	1342	2316	1016	1411	2427

TABLE B.I (*continued*)

	1850			1860			1870		
New Lebanon	216	275	491	239	311	550	140	208	348
Watervliet	122	152	274	129	161	290	96	100	196
Hancock	85	123	208	70	107	177	50	75	125
Enfield, Conn.	104	106	210	49	97	146	51	83	134
Tyringham	48	45	93	12	22	34	16	17	33
Harvard	68	110	178	36	71	107	27	56	83
Shirley	28	53	81	25	42	67	15	33	48
Canterbury	85	163	248	82	159	241	54	123	177
Enfield, N.H.	110	139	249	100	163	263	51	122	173
Alfred	40	76	116	29	53	82	17	45	62
Sabbathday Lake	36	65	101	41	62	103	23	42	65
TOTAL	942	1307	2249	812	1248	2060	540	904	1444

	1880			1900[d]		
New Lebanon	121	219	340	39	85	124
Watervliet	54	80	134	17	73	90
Hancock	27	54	81	2	41	43
Enfield, Conn.	38	64	102	28	57	85
Tyringham[c]	—	—	—	—	—	—
Harvard	15	39	54	14	25	39
Shirley	11	29	40	4	8	12
Canterbury	38	120	158	17	89	106
Enfield, N.H.	39	105	144	11	57	68
Alfred	18	37	55	9	28	37
Sabbathday Lake	21	49	70	12	29	41
TOTAL	382	796	1178	153	492	645

[a]These are partial figures as the "gathering" of the eastern communities was just beginning at the time of this enumeration.
[b]Data for Grafton County, N.H., missing from census enumeration schedules.
[c]Community closed in 1875.
[d]No data available from 1890 census.

TABLE B.2   Peak Population

	1820	1830	1840	1850	1860
New Lebanon	390	469	479	491	550*[b]
Watervliet	193	244	304*	274	290
Hancock	317	338*	309	208	177
Enfield, Conn.	196	213*	175	210	146
Tyringham	92	84	76	93*	34
Harvard	173	167	167	178*	107
Shirley	84*	69	70	81	67
Canterbury	218	236	260*	248	241
Enfield, N.H.	—[a]	203	297*	249	263
Alfred	154	158*	154	116	82
Sabbathday Lake	139*	135	136	101	103
TOTAL	1956[a]	2316	2427*	2249	2060

[a]Data for Grafton County, N.H., missing from census enumeration schedules.
[b]Asterisks indicate the year in which peak population occurred.

TABLE B.3   Adult Male/Female Ratio[a]

	1800				1810				1820			
	No. M	%	No. F	%	No. M	%	No. F	%	No. M	%	No. F	%
New Lebanon	128	38.7	203	61.3	118	42.0	163	58.0	142	43.3	186	56.7
Watervliet	32	43.8	41	56.2	45	41.7	63	58.3	70	40.9	101	59.1
Hancock	59	46.5	68	53.5	48	31.6	104	68.4	99	41.3	141	58.7
Enfield, Conn.	55	42.6	74	57.4	59	44.4	74	55.6	65	44.5	81	55.5
Tyringham	20	41.7	28	58.3	27	47.4	30	52.6	37	50.7	36	49.3
Harvard	39	33.6	77	66.4	27	28.1	69	71.9	51	37.8	84	62.2
Shirley	23	31.5	50	68.5	19	30.6	43	69.4	26	26.3	73	73.7
Canterbury	47	41.2	67	58.8	68	44.4	85	55.6	69	38.5	110	61.5
Enfield, N.H.	71	51.1	68	48.9	51	43.2	67	56.8	—[b]	—[b]	—[b]	—[b]
Alfred	44	37.9	72	62.1	44	39.6	67	60.4	57	43.5	74	56.5
Sabbathday Lake	26	38.2	42	61.8	24	40.7	35	59.3	36	36.0	64	64.0
TOTAL	544	40.8	790	59.2	530	39.8	800	60.2	652	40.7	950	59.3

	1830[c]				1840[c]				1850			
	No. M	%	No. F	%	No. M	%	No. F	%	No. M	%	No. F	%
New Lebanon	172	42.5	233	57.5	154	39.9	232	60.1	168	41.1	241	58.9
Watervliet	96	44.0	122	56.0	105	45.9	124	54.1	96	44.0	122	56.0
Hancock	119	43.6	154	56.4	94	38.1	153	61.9	56	37.1	95	62.9
Enfield, Conn.	77	43.3	101	56.7	60	43.8	77	56.2	77	49.0	80	51.0
Tyringham	33	47.1	37	52.9	26	44.8	32	55.2	30	50.0	30	50.0
Harvard	48	33.8	94	66.2	49	35.3	90	64.7	56	37.6	93	62.4
Shirley	20	35.7	36	64.3	15	28.3	38	71.7	23	33.3	46	66.7
Canterbury	86	41.7	120	58.3	74	37.2	125	62.8	58	30.7	131	69.3
Enfield, N.H.	78	43.6	101	56.4	89	40.1	133	59.9	72	40.4	106	59.6
Alfred	54	42.2	74	57.8	47	38.2	76	61.8	34	35.4	62	64.6
Sabbathday Lake	36	33.0	73	67.0	39	33.6	77	66.4	25	31.6	54	68.4
TOTAL	819	41.7	1145	58.3	752	39.4	1157	60.6	695	39.6	1060	60.4

	1860				1870				1880			
New Lebanon	171	42.3	233	57.7	117	38.6	186	61.4	95	36.0	169	64.0
Watervliet	83	44.1	105	55.9	74	47.7	81	52.3	47	44.3	59	55.7
Hancock	47	36.7	81	63.3	37	39.8	56	60.2	23	37.1	39	62.9
Enfield, Conn.	39	35.1	72	64.9	30	36.6	52	63.4	24	38.1	39	61.9
Tyringham	10	35.7	18	64.3	14	48.3	15	51.7	—d	—d	—d	—d
Harvard	27	30.7	61	69.3	21	30.4	48	69.6	13	28.3	33	71.7
Shirley	20	39.2	31	60.8	13	33.3	26	66.7	11	32.4	23	67.6
Canterbury	64	32.8	131	67.2	42	30.4	96	69.6	28	22.2	98	77.8
Enfield, N.H.	62	32.8	127	67.2	35	27.1	94	72.9	29	27.1	78	72.9
Alfred	23	35.9	41	64.1	15	32.6	31	67.4	14	34.1	27	65.9
Sabbathday Lake	27	38.6	43	61.4	20	35.1	37	64.9	21	38.9	33	61.1
TOTAL	573	37.8	943	62.2	418	36.7	722	63.3	305	33.8	598	66.2

	1900[e]			
New Lebanon	35	33.0	71	67.0
Watervliet	15	21.7	54	78.3
Hancock	2	7.4	25	92.6
Enfield, Conn.	18	32.7	37	67.3
Tyringham[d]	—	—	—	—
Harvard	12	37.5	20	62.5
Shirley	4	33.3	8	66.7
Canterbury	10	11.6	76	88.4
Enfield, N.H.	8	15.4	44	84.6
Alfred	5	20.8	19	79.2
Sabbathday Lake	8	26.7	22	73.3
TOTAL	117	23.7	376	76.3

[a] Excludes all members less than sixteen.
[b] Data for Grafton County, N.H., missing from census enumeration schedules.
[c] Because of census enumeration categories, these figures include all members over fourteen.
[d] Community closed in 1875.
[e] No data available from 1890 census.

TABLE B.4 Leadership Resources[a]

	1800[b]				1810[b]			
	No. M	Percentage of Total	No. F	Percentage of Total	No. M	Percentage of Total	No. F	Percentage of Total
New Lebanon	57	44.5	80	39.4	44	32.8	102	55.7
Watervliet	10	28.6	21	53.8	23	42.6	31	43.1
Hancock	30	48.4	38	53.5	11	17.7	42	36.2
Enfield, Conn.	16	29.1	30	40.5	37	51.4	43	49.4
Tyringham	9	39.1	9	30.0	11	34.4	13	35.1
Harvard	15	37.5	29	37.7	6	16.2	19	24.1
Shirley	5	20.8	28	56.0	3	11.1	10	19.6
Canterbury	28	59.6	42	62.7	37	43.5	39	44.8
Enfield, N.H.	12	19.4	31	46.3	29	46.8	39	54.2
Alfred	20	43.5	31	42.5	17	29.8	29	40.3
Sabbathday Lake	5	15.6	11	22.9	11	37.9	19	46.3
TOTAL	207	36.8	350	43.6	229	35.2	386	43.0

	1820[b]				1830[b]			
	No. M	Percentage of Total	No. F	Percentage of Total	No. M	Percentage of Total	No. F	Percentage of Total
New Lebanon	40	24.4	52	23.0	48	23.5	63	23.8
Watervliet	20	25.0	46	40.7	37	33.9	37	27.4
Hancock	30	22.2	40	22.0	34	22.8	29	15.3
Enfield, Conn.	9	9.9	10	9.5	24	25.5	20	16.8
Tyringham	10	22.2	14	29.8	5	12.5	9	20.5
Harvard	7	10.9	21	19.3	11	18.3	18	16.8
Shirley	2	5.7	7	14.3	2	8.7	3	6.5
Canterbury	24	27.3	31	23.8	19	19.8	26	18.6
Enfield, N.H.	—[c]	—[c]	—[c]	—[c]	14	19.4	26	22.4
Alfred	16	23.5	30	34.9	13	19.4	26	28.6
Sabbathday Lake	12	23.5	27	30.7	13	27.1	26	29.5
TOTAL	170	20.7	278	24.5	220	22.6	283	21.1

	1840[d]				1850			
New Lebanon	49	23.8	80	29.3	65	30.1	107	38.9
Watervliet	33	22.6	35	22.0	43	35.2	52	34.2
Hancock	30	24.2	56	30.3	17	20.0	40	32.5
Enfield, Conn.	16	20.3	20	20.8	26	25.0	29	27.4
Tyringham	6	18.2	10	23.3	10	20.8	9	20.0
Harvard	15	22.4	24	24.0	26	38.2	43	39.1
Shirley	6	26.1	8	17.0	10	35.7	19	35.8
Canterbury	14	13.6	33	21.0	28	31.5	53	32.5
Enfield, N.H.	22	17.9	46	26.4	25	22.7	40	28.8
Alfred	12	30.0	17	22.4	7	24.1	12	22.6
Sabbathday Lake	8	16.7	19	21.6	7	19.4	23	35.4
TOTAL	211	20.8	348	24.6	264	27.9	427	32.7

	1860				1870			
New Lebanon	54	22.6	90	28.9	33	23.6	62	44.3
Watervliet	18	14.0	33	20.5	20	20.8	15	15.0
Hancock	13	18.6	24	22.4	9	18.0	14	18.7
Enfield, Conn.	16	32.7	18	18.6	6	11.8	21	25.3
Tyringham	4	33.3	5	22.7	4	25.0	7	41.2
Harvard	9	25.0	19	26.8	6	22.2	8	14.3
Shirley	8	32.0	15	35.7	5	33.3	8	24.2
Canterbury	26	31.7	56	35.2	16	29.6	39	31.7
Enfield, N.H.	23	23.0	53	32.5	12	23.5	37	30.3
Alfred	7	24.1	12	22.6	5	29.4	7	15.6
Sabbathday Lake	9	22.0	14	22.6	6	26.1	7	16.7
TOTAL	187	23.0	339	27.2	122	22.6	225	24.9

	1880				1900[f]			
New Lebanon	37	30.6	62	28.3	13	33.3	18	21.2
Watervliet	17	31.5	20	25.0	3	17.6	11	15.1
Hancock	5	18.5	12	22.2	0	0.0	8	19.5
Enfield, Conn.	4	10.5	12	18.8	2	7.1	11	19.3
Tyringham[e]	—	—	—	—	—	—	—	—
Harvard	3	20.0	3	7.7	6	42.9	3	13.6
Shirley	0	0.0	9	31.0	2	50.0	3	37.5
Canterbury	10	26.3	38	31.7	1	5.9	21	23.6
Enfield, N.H.	8	20.5	31	29.5	0	0.0	13	22.8
Alfred	3	16.7	9	24.3	1	11.1	11	36.7
Sabbathday Lake	8	38.1	10	20.4	2	16.7	10	34.5
TOTAL	95	24.9	206	25.9	30	19.6	109	22.2

[a]Includes all members aged twenty-five to forty-nine, the age group from which the majority of leaders were drawn. At the New Lebanon Church Family, for example, of sixty-seven members chosen as Ministry or Family Elders or Eldresses between 1788 and 1861, fifty-five (82.0 percent) were between the ages of twenty-five and forty-nine.

[b]Because of census enumeration categories, these figures include all members aged twenty-six to forty-four.

[c]Data for Grafton County, N.H., missing from census enumeration schedules.

[d]Because of census enumeration categories, these figures include all members aged thirty to forty-nine, thus slightly underestimating the size of the leadership pool.

[e]Community closed in 1875.

[f]No data available from 1890 census.

TABLE B.5 Age Group Distribution
(Percentage)

	Males			Females			Total		
	<16	16–44	≥45[b]	<16	16–44	≥45[b]	<16	16–44	≥45[b]
1800[a]									
New Lebanon	—	64.8	35.2	—	68.0	32.0	—	66.8	33.2
Watervliet	8.6	74.3	17.1	2.4	80.9	16.7	5.2	77.9	16.9
Hancock	4.8	59.7	35.5	4.2	71.8	24.0	4.5	66.2	29.3
Enfield, Conn.	—	78.2	21.8	—	71.6	28.4	—	74.4	25.6
Tyringham	13.0	43.5	43.5	6.7	56.6	36.7	9.4	51.0	39.6
Harvard	2.5	52.5	45.0	—	58.4	41.6	0.9	56.4	42.7
Shirley	—	52.2	47.8	—	80.0	20.0	—	71.2	28.8
Canterbury	—	85.1	14.9	—	83.6	16.4	—	84.2	15.8
Enfield, N.H.	—	67.6	32.4	10.5	72.4	17.1	6.2	73.6	20.2
Alfred	4.3	58.7	37.0	1.4	80.8	17.8	2.5	72.3	25.2
Sabbathday Lake	18.8	43.7	37.5	12.5	64.6	22.9	15.0	56.2	28.8
TOTAL	3.2	64.2	32.6	2.6	71.4	26.0	2.8	68.5	28.7
1810									
New Lebanon	11.9	43.3	44.8	10.9	60.7	28.4	11.4	53.3	35.3
Watervliet	16.7	57.4	25.9	12.5	70.8	16.7	14.3	65.1	20.6
Hancock	22.6	24.2	53.2	10.3	46.6	43.1	14.6	38.8	46.6
Enfield, Conn.	18.1	61.1	20.8	14.9	56.4	28.7	16.4	58.4	25.2
Tyringham	15.6	43.8	40.6	18.9	46.0	35.1	17.4	44.9	37.7
Harvard	27.0	29.8	43.2	12.7	36.7	50.6	17.2	34.5	48.3
Shirley	29.6	14.8	55.6	15.7	19.6	64.7	20.5	18.0	61.5
Canterbury	20.0	49.4	30.6	5.6	58.8	35.6	12.6	54.3	33.1
Enfield, N.H.	17.7	46.8	35.5	6.9	54.2	38.9	11.9	50.8	37.3
Alfred	15.8	40.3	43.9	6.9	67.5	25.6	10.9	44.1	45.0
Sabbathday Lake	17.2	48.3	34.5	14.6	51.3	34.1	15.7	50.0	34.3
TOTAL	18.0	43.8	38.2	11.1	52.0	36.9	14.0	48.5	37.5

TABLE B.5 *(continued)*

	Males			Females			Total		
	<16	16–44	≥45[b]	<16	16–44	≥45[b]	<16	16–44	≥45[b]
1820									
New Lebanon	13.4	41.5	45.1	17.7	46.0	36.3	15.9	44.1	40.0
Watervliet	12.5	47.5	40.0	10.6	59.3	30.1	11.4	54.4	34.2
Hancock	26.7	34.8	38.5	22.0	35.7	42.3	24.0	35.6	40.4
Enfield, Conn.	28.6	29.6	41.8	22.9	24.7	52.4	25.5	27.1	47.4
Tyringham	17.7	40.1	42.2	23.4	44.7	31.9	20.7	52.1	27.2
Harvard	20.3	43.8	35.9	22.9	35.8	41.3	22.0	38.7	39.3
Shirley	25.7	37.2	37.1	22.4	28.6	49.0	23.8	32.2	44.0
Canterbury	21.6	48.9	29.5	15.4	48.4	36.2	17.9	48.6	33.5
Enfield, N.H.	—[c]	—[c]	—[c]	—[c]	—[c]	—[c]	—[c]	—[c]	—[c]
Alfred	16.2	41.2	42.6	14.0	47.6	38.4	14.9	44.8	40.3
Sabbathday Lake	29.4	39.2	31.4	27.3	43.2	29.5	28.1	41.7	30.2
TOTAL	20.6	40.2	39.2	19.3	42.1	38.6	19.8	41.3	38.9
	<15[d]	15–59	≥60	<15[d]	15–59	≥60	<15[d]	15–59	≥60
1830									
New Lebanon	15.7	66.7	17.6	12.1	70.9	17.0	13.6	69.1	17.3
Watervliet	11.9	67.9	20.2	9.6	72.6	17.8	10.7	70.4	18.9
Hancock	20.1	55.7	24.2	18.5	60.9	20.6	19.4	58.2	22.4
Enfield, Conn.	18.1	74.5	7.4	15.1	68.1	16.8	16.4	70.9	12.7
Tyringham	17.5	67.5	15.0	15.9	68.2	15.9	16.7	67.8	15.5
Harvard	20.0	61.7	18.3	12.1	63.6	24.3	15.0	62.8	22.2
Shirley	13.0	47.9	39.1	21.7	50.0	28.3	18.8	49.3	31.9
Canterbury	10.4	68.8	20.8	14.3	70.0	15.7	12.7	69.5	17.8
Enfield, N.H.	10.3	71.3	18.4	12.9	69.9	17.2	11.8	70.5	17.7
Alfred	19.4	56.7	23.9	18.7	59.3	22.0	19.0	58.2	22.8
Sabbathday Lake	20.0	55.6	24.4	18.9	67.8	13.3	19.3	63.7	17.0
TOTAL	15.9	64.6	19.5	14.7	66.8	18.5	15.2	65.8	19.0

1840

	<16	16–59	≥60	<16	16–59	≥60	<16	16–59	≥60
New Lebanon	25.2	55.4	19.4	15.0	62.7	22.3	19.4	59.5	21.1
Watervliet	28.1	52.7	19.2	22.0	62.9	15.1	24.9	58.1	17.0
Hancock	24.2	48.4	27.4	17.3	52.4	30.3	20.1	50.8	29.1
Enfield, Conn.	24.1	58.2	17.7	19.8	46.9	33.3	21.7	52.0	26.3
Tyringham	21.2	51.5	27.3	25.6	46.5	27.9	23.7	48.7	27.6
Harvard	26.9	58.2	14.9	10.0	64.0	26.0	16.8	61.6	21.6
Shirley	34.8	43.5	21.7	19.1	46.9	34.0	24.3	45.7	30.0
Canterbury	28.2	50.4	21.4	20.4	54.1	25.5	23.5	52.7	23.8
Enfield, N.H.	27.6	52.1	20.3	23.6	60.3	16.1	25.3	56.9	17.8
Alfred	26.6	57.8	15.6	15.6	58.8	25.6	20.1	58.5	21.4
Sabbathday Lake	18.8	56.2	25.0	12.5	63.6	23.9	14.7	61.0	24.3
TOTAL	26.0	53.4	20.6	18.1	57.9	24.0	21.4	56.0	22.6

1850

	<16	16–59	≥60	<16	16–59	≥60	<16	16–59	≥60
New Lebanon	22.2	56.0	21.8	12.4	63.6	24.0	16.7	60.3	23.0
Watervliet	21.3	58.2	20.5	19.7	56.6	23.7	20.4	57.3	22.3
Hancock	34.1	43.5	22.4	22.8	52.0	25.2	27.4	48.6	24.0
Enfield, Conn.	26.0	49.0	25.0	24.5	47.2	28.3	25.2	48.1	26.7
Tyringham	37.5	45.8	16.7	33.3	40.0	26.7	35.5	43.0	21.5
Harvard	17.6	63.3	19.1	15.5	59.0	25.5	16.3	60.7	23.0
Shirley	17.9	71.4	10.7	13.2	60.4	26.4	14.8	64.2	21.0
Canterbury	31.8	54.1	14.1	19.6	65.1	15.3	23.8	61.3	14.9
Enfield, N.H.	34.5	51.9	13.6	23.7	61.2	15.1	28.5	57.1	14.4
Alfred	15.0	57.5	27.5	18.4	48.7	32.9	17.2	51.8	31.0
Sabbathday Lake	30.6	44.4	25.0	16.9	58.5	24.6	21.8	53.4	24.8
TOTAL	26.2	53.8	20.0	18.9	57.8	23.3	22.0	56.1	21.9

TABLE B.5 (continued)

	Males			Females			Total		
	<16	16–59	≥60	<16	16–59	≥60	<16	16–59	≥60
1860									
New Lebanon	28.5	53.9	17.6	25.1	55.3	19.6	26.5	54.8	18.7
Watervliet	35.7	41.8	22.5	34.8	43.5	21.7	35.2	42.7	22.1
Hancock	32.9	40.0	27.1	24.3	47.7	28.0	27.7	44.6	27.7
Enfield, Conn.	20.4	49.0	30.6	25.8	46.4	27.8	24.0	47.2	28.8
Tyringham	16.7	50.0	33.3	18.2	63.6	18.2	17.6	58.9	23.5
Harvard	25.0	41.7	33.3	14.1	56.3	29.6	17.8	51.4	30.8
Shirley	20.0	60.0	20.0	26.2	57.1	16.7	23.9	58.2	17.9
Canterbury	22.0	63.4	14.6	17.6	67.3	15.1	19.1	66.0	14.9
Enfield, N.H.	38.0	50.0	12.0	22.1	63.8	14.1	28.1	58.6	13.3
Alfred	20.7	62.1	17.2	22.6	47.2	30.2	22.0	52.4	25.6
Sabbathday Lake	34.1	46.4	19.5	30.6	50.0	19.4	32.0	48.6	19.4
TOTAL	29.4	50.5	20.1	24.5	54.7	20.8	26.4	53.1	20.5
1870									
New Lebanon	16.4	53.6	30.0	10.6	61.5	27.9	12.9	58.4	28.7
Watervliet	22.9	45.8	31.3	19.0	50.0	31.0	20.9	48.0	31.1
Hancock	26.0	40.0	34.0	25.3	38.7	36.0	25.6	39.2	35.2
Enfield, Conn.	41.2	45.1	13.7	37.3	42.2	20.5	38.8	43.3	17.9
Tyringham	12.5	68.7	18.8	11.8	52.9	35.3	12.1	60.6	27.3
Harvard	22.2	33.4	44.4	14.3	35.7	50.0	16.9	34.9	48.2
Shirley	13.3	60.0	26.7	21.2	54.6	24.2	18.8	56.2	25.0
Canterbury	22.2	61.1	16.7	22.0	61.7	16.3	22.0	61.6	16.4
Enfield, N.H.	31.4	43.1	25.5	23.0	55.7	21.3	25.4	52.1	22.5
Alfred	11.8	58.8	29.4	31.1	42.2	26.7	25.8	46.8	27.4
Sabbathday Lake	13.0	60.9	26.1	11.9	50.0	38.1	12.3	53.9	33.8
TOTAL	22.6	50.0	27.4	20.1	52.4	27.5	21.1	51.4	27.5

1880

New Lebanon	21.5	52.9	25.6	22.8	48.9	28.3	22.4	50.2	27.4
Watervliet	13.0	46.3	40.7	26.3	42.4	31.3	20.9	44.0	35.1
Hancock	14.8	44.5	40.7	27.8	37.0	35.2	23.5	39.5	37.0
Enfield, Conn.	36.8	29.0	34.2	39.1	39.0	21.9	38.2	35.3	26.5
Tyringham	—	—	—	—	—	—	—	—	—
Harvard	13.3	40.0	46.7	15.4	30.8	53.8	14.8	33.3	51.9
Shirley	0.0	36.4	63.6	20.7	44.8	34.5	15.0	42.5	42.5
Canterbury	26.3	65.8	7.9	18.3	60.9	20.8	20.3	62.0	17.7
Enfield, N.H.	25.6	43.6	30.8	25.7	46.7	27.6	25.7	45.8	28.5
Alfred	22.2	38.9	38.9	27.0	54.1	18.9	25.5	49.0	25.5
Sabbathday Lake	0.0	57.1	42.9	32.7	38.7	28.6	22.9	44.2	32.9
TOTAL	20.2	47.9	31.9	24.9	50.6	24.5	23.3	49.8	26.9

1900[f]

New Lebanon	10.3	58.9	30.8	16.5	44.7	38.8	14.5	49.2	36.3
Watervliet	11.8	41.1	47.1	26.0	52.1	21.9	23.3	50.0	26.7
Hancock	0.0	50.0	50.0	39.0	36.6	24.4	37.2	37.2	25.6
Enfield, Conn.	35.7	28.6	35.7	35.1	47.4	17.5	35.3	41.2	23.5
Tyringham[e]	—	—	—	—	—	—	—	—	—
Harvard	14.3	50.0	35.7	20.0	60.0	20.0	17.9	56.5	25.6
Shirley	0.0	75.0	25.0	0.0	50.0	50.0	0.0	58.3	41.7
Canterbury	41.2	35.3	23.5	14.6	60.7	24.7	18.9	56.6	24.5
Enfield, N.H.	27.3	27.2	45.5	22.8	47.4	29.8	23.5	44.1	32.4
Alfred	44.4	22.3	33.3	32.1	53.6	14.3	35.1	46.0	18.9
Sabbathday Lake	33.3	50.0	16.7	24.1	62.1	13.8	26.8	58.6	14.6
TOTAL	23.5	43.2	33.3	23.6	50.9	25.5	23.6	49.1	27.3

[a] 1790 census enumeration categories too broad to permit age group distribution analysis.
[b] 1800, 1810, and 1820 census enumeration categories include all individuals over forty-four in one age group, thus overestimating the percentage of "elderly" members.
[c] Data for Grafton County, N.H., missing from census enumeration schedules.
[d] 1830 and 1840 census enumeration categories include all individuals under fifteen in one age group, thus underestimating the percentage of children.
[e] Community closed in 1875.
[f] No data available from 1890 census.

Census Data for Eastern Communities, 1790–1900

The tables in this appendix are based on data obtained from manuscript census schedules available on microfilm at the Federal Archives and Records Center, Waltham, Massachusetts.

TABLE C.1 New Lebanon, New York
(Eight families, including two in Canaan, N.Y.)

		<16	≥16	Total				
1790	Males	80	25	105				
	Females			116				

		<10	10–15	16–25	26–44	≥45	Total	
1800	Males	—	—	26	57	45	128	
	Females	—	—	58	80	65	203	
1810	Males	7	9	14	44	60	134	
	Females	8	12	9	102	52	183	
1820	Males	5	17	28	40	74	164	
	Females	17	23	52	52	82	226	

		<15	15–19	20–29	30–39	40–49	50–59	≥60	Total
1830	Males	32	23	37	26	22	28	36	204
	Females	32	30	49	42	21	46	45	265
1840	Males	52	29	21	28	21	15	40	206
	Females	41	23	48	43	37	20	61	273

		<16	16–29	30–39	40–49	50–59	≥60	Total
1850	Males	48	50	20	28	23	47	216
	Females	34	50	46	40	39	66	275
1860	Males	68	56	23	25	25	42	239
	Females	78	66	24	45	37	61	311
1870	Males	23	33	11	17	14	42	140
	Females	22	59	21	22	26	58	208
1880	Males	26	22	14	12	16	31	121
	Females	50	40	27	20	20	62	219
1900	Males	4	8	3	7	5	12	39
	Females	14	13	5	8	12	33	85

TABLE C.2   Watervliet, New York

(Four families)

	<16	≥16	Total
1790			
Males	27	9	36
Females			18

	<10	10–15	16–25	26–44	≥45	Total
1800						
Males	1	2	16	10	6	35
Females	—	1	13	21	7	42
1810						
Males	3	6	8	23	14	54
Females	4	5	20	31	12	72
1820						
Males	5	5	18	20	32	80
Females	2	10	21	46	34	113

	<15	15–19	20–29	30–39	40–49	50–59	≥60	Total
1830								
Males	13	9	13	18	19	15	22	109
Females	13	20	23	20	17	18	24	135
1840								
Males	41	16	19	21	12	9	28	146
Females	35	23	24	18	17	17	24	158

	<16	16–29	30–39	40–49	50–59	≥60	Total
1850							
Males	26	17	16	18	20	25	122
Females	30	28	21	20	17	36	152
1860							
Males	46	22	2	13	17	29	129
Females	56	21	8	20	21	35	161
1870							
Males	22	21	4	8	11	30	96
Females	19	29	3	6	12	31	100
1880							
Males	7	7	7	7	4	22	54
Females	21	13	13	3	5	25	80
1900							
Males	2	2	1	1	3	8	17
Females	19	21	6	2	9	16	73

Appendix C

TABLE C.3   Hancock, Massachusetts

(Six families, including two in West Pittsfield, Mass.)

	<16	≥16	Total
1790			
Males	21	11	32
Females			62

	<10	10–15	16–25	26–44	≥45	Total
1800						
Males	1	2	7	30	22	62
Females	2	1	13	38	17	71
1810						
Males	7	7	4	11	33	62
Females	8	4	12	42	50	116
1820						
Males	18	18	17	30	52	135
Females	12	28	25	40	77	182

	<15	15–19	20–29	30–39	40–49	50–59	≥60	Total
1830								
Males	30	10	22	20	14	17	36	149
Females	35	16	33	16	13	37	39	189
1840								
Males	30	9	12	17	13	9	34	124
Females	32	10	21	32	24	10	56	185

	<16	16–29	30–39	40–49	50–59	≥60	Total
1850							
Males	29	9	8	8	12	19	85
Females	28	15	11	25	13	31	123
1860							
Males	23	12	4	7	5	19	70
Females	26	17	6	10	18	30	107
1870							
Males	13	5	6	3	6	17	50
Females	19	10	11	2	6	27	75
1880							
Males	4	2	2	3	5	11	27
Females	15	6	3	9	2	19	54
1900							
Males	—	—	—	—	1	1	2
Females	16	11	2	—	2	10	41

TABLE C.4 Enfield, Connecticut
(Five families)

	<16	≥16	Total					
1790								
Males	10	15	25					
Females			21					

	<10	10–15	16–25	26–44	≥45	Total		
1800								
Males	—	—	27	16	12	55		
Females	—	—	23	30	21	74		
1810								
Males	7	6	7	37	15	72		
Females	8	5	6	43	25	87		
1820								
Males	8	18	18	9	38	91		
Females	10	14	16	10	55	105		

	<15	15–19	20–29	30–39	40–49	50–59	≥60	Total
1830								
Males	17	18	8	11	13	20	7	94
Females	18	8	26	8	12	27	20	119
1840								
Males	19	5	10	8	8	15	14	79
Females	19	5	6	8	12	14	32	96

	<16	16–29	30–39	40–49	50–59	≥60	Total	
1850								
Males	27	22	14	8	7	26	104	
Females	26	24	11	8	7	30	106	
1860								
Males	10	7	4	8	5	15	49	
Females	25	20	5	8	12	27	97	
1870								
Males	21	8	3	2	10	7	51	
Females	31	13	6	10	6	17	83	
1880								
Males	14	3	1	3	4	13	38	
Females	25	9	4	6	6	14	64	
1900								
Males	10	5	1	1	1	10	28	
Females	20	13	2	6	6	10	57	

Appendix C

TABLE C.5   Tyringham, Massachusetts
(Two families)

	<16	≥16	Total
1790			
Males	5	1	6
Females			12

	<10	10–15	16–25	26–44	≥45	Total
1800						
Males	2	1	1	9	10	23
Females	—	2	8	9	11	30
1810						
Males	2	3	3	11	13	32
Females	5	2	4	13	13	37
1820						
Males	1	7	8	10	19	45
Females	6	5	7	14	15	47

	<15	15–19	20–29	30–39	40–49	50–59	≥60	Total
1830								
Males	7	6	7	3	2	9	6	40
Females	7	6	10	3	6	5	7	44
1840								
Males	7	5	2	3	3	4	9	33
Females	11	1	4	8	2	5	12	43

	<16	16–29	30–39	40–49	50–59	≥60	Total
1850							
Males	18	14	3	2	3	8	48
Females	15	10	1	7	—	12	45
1860							
Males	2	2	1	2	1	4	12
Females	4	7	2	2	3	4	22
1870							
Males	2	4	1	3	3	3	16
Females	2	2	5	1	1	6	17
1880							
Males			COMMUNITY CLOSED 1875				
Females							
1900							
Males							
Females							

TABLE C.6   Harvard, Massachusetts
(Four families)

	<16	≥16	Total
1790			
Males	17	7	24
Females			38

	<10	10–15	16–25	26–44	≥45	Total
1800						
Males	—	1	6	15	18	40
Females	—	—	16	29	32	77
1810						
Males	4	6	5	6	16	37
Females	5	5	10	19	40	79
1820						
Males	1	12	21	7	23	64
Females	13	12	18	21	45	109

	<15	15–19	20–29	30–39	40–49	50–59	≥60	Total
1830								
Males	12	6	15	8	3	5	11	60
Females	13	15	23	7	11	12	26	107
1840								
Males	18	11	10	11	4	3	10	67
Females	10	6	22	19	5	12	26	100

	<16	16–29	30–39	40–49	50–59	≥60	Total
1850							
Males	12	17	9	11	6	13	68
Females	17	14	15	23	13	28	110
1860							
Males	9	3	4	4	4	12	36
Females	10	7	7	10	16	21	71
1870							
Males	6	1	2	4	2	12	27
Females	8	8	—	7	5	28	56
1880							
Males	2	1	1	2	2	7	15
Females	6	4	1	1	6	21	39
1900							
Males	2	5	1	1	—	5	14
Females	5	5	2	1	7	5	25

TABLE C.7   Shirley, Massachusetts
(Three families)

	<16	≥16	Total
1790			
Males	12	4	16
Females			27

	<10	10–15	16–25	26–44	≥45	Total
1800						
Males	—	—	7	5	11	23
Females	—	—	12	28	10	50
1810						
Males	7	1	1	3	15	27
Females	6	2	—	10	33	51
1820						
Males	1	8	11	2	13	35
Females	—	11	7	7	24	49

	<15	15–19	20–29	30–39	40–49	50–59	≥60	Total
1830								
Males	3	1	5	1	1	3	9	23
Females	10	4	6	—	3	10	13	46
1840								
Males	8	—	3	5	1	1	5	23
Females	9	2	7	6	2	5	16	47

	<16	16–29	30–39	40–49	50–59	≥60	Total
1850							
Males	5	9	3	5	3	3	28
Females	7	15	7	8	2	14	53
1860							
Males	5	5	2	4	4	5	25
Females	11	7	3	10	4	7	42
1870							
Males	2	—	1	4	4	4	15
Females	7	5	5	2	6	8	33
1880							
Males	—	2	—	—	2	7	11
Females	6	8	2	2	1	10	29
1900							
Males	—	1	1	—	1	1	4
Females	—	—	1	2	1	4	8

TABLE C.8   Canterbury, New Hampshire
(Two families)

	<16	≥16	Total
1790			
Males	NOT YET GATHERED		
Females	NOT YET GATHERED		

	<10	10−15	16−25	26−44	≥45	Total
1800						
Males	—	—	12	28	7	47
Females	—	—	14	42	11	67
1810						
Males	9	8	5	37	26	85
Females	1	4	14	39	32	90
1820						
Males	6	13	19	24	26	88
Females	7	13	32	31	47	130

	<15	15−19	20−29	30−39	40−49	50−59	≥60	Total
1830								
Males	10	16	15	7	12	16	20	96
Females	20	20	21	17	9	31	22	140
1840								
Males	29	11	18	9	5	9	22	103
Females	32	13	30	20	13	9	40	157

	<16	16−29	30−39	40−49	50−59	≥60	Total
1850							
Males	27	17	12	10	7	12	85
Females	32	49	22	18	17	25	163
1860							
Males	18	23	12	10	7	12	82
Females	28	45	23	19	20	24	159
1870							
Males	12	17	3	9	4	9	54
Females	27	34	15	14	13	20	123
1880							
Males	10	9	4	3	9	3	38
Females	22	29	19	9	16	25	120
1900							
Males	7	4	—	1	1	4	17
Females	13	29	8	4	13	22	89

TABLE C.9   Enfield, New Hampshire
(Three families)

	<16	≥16	Total
1790			
Males	NOT YET GATHERED		
Females	NOT YET GATHERED		

	<10	10–15	16–25	26–44	≥45	Total
1800						
Males	—	—	36	12	23	71
Females	—	8	23	32	13	76
1810						
Males	4	7	—	29	22	62
Females	2	3	—	39	28	72
1820						
Males	NO DATA FOR GRAFTON COUNTY, N.H.					
Females	NO DATA FOR GRAFTON COUNTY, N.H.					

	<15	15–19	20–29	30–39	40–49	50–59	≥60	Total
1830								
Males	9	11	19	3	11	18	16	87
Females	15	10	27	14	12	18	20	116
1840								
Males	34	10	20	18	4	12	25	123
Females	41	21	26	32	14	12	28	174

	<16	16–29	30–39	40–49	50–59	≥60	Total
1850							
Males	38	36	7	9	5	15	110
Females	33	46	14	16	9	21	139
1860							
Males	38	24	9	8	9	12	100
Females	36	42	19	20	23	23	163
1870							
Males	16	6	4	7	5	13	51
Females	28	30	12	14	12	26	122
1880							
Males	10	3	3	5	6	12	39
Females	27	14	14	11	10	29	105
1900							
Males	3	2	—	—	1	5	11
Females	13	7	5	6	9	17	57

TABLE C.10   Alfred, Maine
(Three families)

	<16	≥16	Total
1790			
Males	NOT YET GATHERED		
Females	NOT YET GATHERED		

	<10	10–15	16–25	26–44	≥45	Total
1800						
Males	—	2	7	20	17	46
Females	—	1	28	31	13	73
1810						
Males	7	2	6	17	25	57
Females	2	3	5	29	33	72
1820						
Males	3	8	12	16	29	68
Females	1	11	11	30	33	86

	<15	15–19	20–29	30–39	40–49	50–59	≥60	Total
1830								
Males	13	9	9	5	8	7	16	67
Females	17	6	11	10	16	11	20	91
1840								
Males	17	8	8	7	5	9	10	64
Females	14	8	13	8	9	15	23	90

	<16	16–29	30–39	40–49	50–59	≥60	Total
1850							
Males	6	10	5	3	5	11	40
Females	14	16	6	7	8	25	76
1860							
Males	6	10	1	5	2	5	29
Females	12	8	3	6	8	16	53
1870							
Males	2	5	1	1	3	5	17
Females	14	9	2	3	5	12	45
1880							
Males	4	3	1	1	2	7	18
Females	10	9	5	2	4	7	37
1900							
Males	4	—	1	—	1	3	9
Females	9	9	5	1	—	4	28

Appendix C

TABLE C.11 Sabbathday Lake, Maine
(Three families)

	<16	≥16	Total
1790			
Males	NOT YET GATHERED		
Females	NOT YET GATHERED		

	<10	10–15	16–25	26–44	≥45	Total
1800						
Males	—	6	9	5	12	32
Females	—	6	20	11	11	48
1810						
Males	2	3	3	11	10	29
Females	—	6	2	19	14	41
1820						
Males	7	8	8	12	16	51
Females	6	18	11	27	26	88

	<15	15–19	20–29	30–39	40–49	50–59	≥60	Total
1830								
Males	9	2	4	5	8	6	11	45
Females	17	8	11	10	16	16	12	90
1840								
Males	9	8	8	4	4	3	12	48
Females	11	10	14	12	7	13	21	88

	<16	16–29	30–39	40–49	50–59	≥60	Total
1850							
Males	11	8	4	1	3	9	36
Females	11	13	6	14	5	16	65
1860							
Males	14	10	2	4	3	8	41
Females	19	8	6	5	12	12	62
1870							
Males	3	5	4	1	4	6	23
Females	5	9	2	4	6	16	42
1880							
Males	—	4	2	3	3	9	21
Females	16	10	3	1	5	14	49
1900							
Males	4	3	—	1	2	2	12
Females	7	8	3	6	1	4	29

Notes

Preface

1. Constance Rourke, "The Shakers," in *The Roots of American Culture*, ed. Van Wyck Brooks (New York, 1942), pp. 195–237; Marguerite Melcher, *The Shaker Adventure* (Princeton, N.J., 1941); Edward Deming Andrews, *The People Called Shakers* (New York, 1953); and Henri Desroche, *The American Shakers: From Neo-Christianity to Presocialism*, trans. and ed. John K. Savacool (Amherst, Mass., 1971; originally published in 1955).

2. Rourke, "The Shakers," p. 197.

3. John M. Whitworth, *God's Blueprints: A Sociological Study of Three Utopian Sects* (London, 1975); Louis J. Kern, *An Ordered Love: Sex Roles and Sexuality in Victorian American Communes—the Shakers, the Mormons, and the Oneida Community* (Chapel Hill, N.C., 1981); Lawrence Foster, *Religion and Sexuality: Three American Communal Experiments of the Nineteenth Century* (New York, 1981); and Stephen A. Marini, *Radical Sects of Revolutionary New England* (Cambridge, Mass., 1982). Another useful comparative study of utopian communities and the law is Carol Weisbrod, *Boundaries of Utopia* (New York, 1980).

4. Edward Deming and Faith Andrews, *Work and Worship : The Economic Order of the Shakers* (New York, 1974); June Sprigg, *By Shaker Hands* (New York, 1975); and Dolores Hayden, *Seven American Utopias: The Architecture of Communitarian Socialism, 1790–1975* (Cambridge, Mass., 1976).

Studies of particular aspects of Shaker material culture include: Edward Deming Andrews, *The Community Industries of the Shakers* (Albany, N.Y., 1933); Beverly Gordon, *Shaker Textile Arts* (Hanover, N.H., 1980); Robert F.W. Meader, *An Illustrated Guide to Shaker Furniture* (New York, 1972); William Lassiter, *Shaker Architecture* (New York, 1966); and Amy Bess Miller and Persis Fuller, *The Best of Shaker Cooking* (New York, 1970).

5. Caroline B. Piercy, *The Valley of God's Pleasure* (New York, 1951); Edward R. Horgan, *The Shaker Holy Land: A Community Portrait* (Harvard, Mass., 1982); Daniel W. Patterson, *The Shaker Spiritual* (Princeton, N.J., 1979); Daniel W. Patterson, *Gift Drawing and Gift Song* (Sabbathday Lake, Maine, 1983); Diane Sasson, *The Shaker Spiritual Narrative* (Knoxville, Tenn., 1983); Flo Morse, *The Shakers and the World's People* (New York, 1980); D'Ann Campbell, "Women's Life in Utopia: The Shaker Experiment in Sexual Equality Reappraised, 1810–1860," *New England Quarterly* 51 (1978), pp. 23–38; and William Sims Bainbridge, "Shaker Demographics 1840–1900: An Example of the Use of U.S. Census Enumeration Schedules," *Journal for the Scientific Study of Religion* 21 (1982), pp. 352–65.

Other useful community studies are: Julia Neal, *By Their Fruits: The Story of Shakerism in South Union, Kentucky* (Chapel Hill, N.C., 1947) and Dorothy M. Filley, *Recapturing Wisdom's Valley: The Watervliet Shaker Heritage* (Albany, N.Y., 1975). Recent studies of Mother Rebecca Jackson's small community of black Shakers include: Jean Humez, ed., *Gifts of Power: The Writings of Rebecca Jackson, Black Visionary, Shaker Eldress* (Amherst, Mass., 1981), and Richard E. Williams, *Called and Chosen: The Story of Mother Rebecca Jackson and the Philadelphia Shakers* (Metuchen, N.J., 1981).

Chapter 1. Scarcely Any Sensible Preaching

1. Isaac Backus, quoted by William G. McLoughlin, *Isaac Backus and the American Pietistic Tradition* (Boston, 1971), p. 1. I am indebted as well to Dr. McLoughlin's enlightening analysis of revivalism in *Revivals, Awakenings and Reform* (Chicago, 1978).

2. Isaac Backus, from articles drawn up at the foundation of the Separate Church in Titicut, Connecticut. Quoted by McLoughlin, *Backus*, p. 43.

3. Quoted by McLoughlin, *Backus*, p. 97.

4. Nathan Perkins, *A Narrative of a Tour Through the State of Vermont from April 27 to June 12, 1789* (Rutland, Vt., 1964), pp. 25–27.

5. Quoted by Cyrus Yale, *The Godly Pastor. Life of the Rev. Jeremiah Hallock of Canton, Connecticut* (New York, 1866), p. 86.

6. Molly Cooper, *The Diary of Mary Cooper: Life on a Long Island Farm, 1768–1773*, ed. Field Horne (Oyster Bay, N.Y., 1981), p. 47.

7. Quoted by Anna White and Leila S. Taylor, *Shakerism: Its Meaning and Message* (Columbus, Ohio, 1904), p. 41.

8. Thomas Brown, *An Account of the People Called Shakers* (Troy, N.Y., 1812), p. 31.

9. Ezra Stiles, *The Literary Diary of Ezra Stiles*, 3 vols. (New York, 1901), III, p. 243.

10. Compiled from Isaac N. Youngs, *Names and Ages of those who have been gathered into the church . . .* (New Lebanon, N.Y., 1787–1854). Manuscript in Hancock Shaker Village Library, Pittsfield, Mass. (hereafter HSV).

11. McLoughlin, *New England Dissent*, 2 vols. (Cambridge, Mass., 1971), I, p. 437.

12. As remembered by Thankful Goodrich in *Writings of Deacon Daniel Goodrich*, comp. Alonzo G. Hollister. Manuscript in Andrews Collection, Winterthur Museum, Winterthur, Del., SA 799.1, pp. 119–20 (hereafter Andrews Collection).

13. Stephen Wright, comp., *History of the Shaftsbury Baptist Association* (Troy, N.Y., 1853), p. 19.

14. Quoted by McLoughlin, *Backus*, p. 183.

15. Quoted by McLoughlin, *Backus*, p. 183.

16. Brown, *An Account*, pp. 173–74.

17. Calvin Green and Seth Y. Wells, *A Summary View of the Millennial Church or United Society of Believers, Commonly Called Shakers, Comprising the Rise, Progress and Practical Order of the Society Together with the General Principles of Their Faith and Testimony* (Albany, N.Y., 1823), p. 18.

18. "Testimony" of Comstock Betts, Feb. 16, 1827 in Seth Y. Wells and Calvin Green, *Testimonies Concerning the Character and Ministry of Mother Ann Lee and the First Witnesses of the Gospel of Christ's Second Appearing; Given by Some of the Aged Brethren and Sisters of the United Society* (Albany, N.Y., 1827), p. 131.

19. "Testimony" of Daniel Goodrich, Jr., in *Testimonies* (1827), pp. 125–31.

20. "Testimony" of Rebecca and Mary Clark in *Book of the Busy Hours*, comp. Alonzo G. Hollister (New Lebanon, N.Y., 1877), HSV.

21. "Testimony" of Daniel Goodrich, Jr., in *Testimonies* (1827), p. 131.

22. "Testimony" of Jonathan Southwick, 1827. Manuscript in Western Reserve Historical Society Shaker Collection, Cleveland, Ohio, VI A 4 (hereafter WRHS).

23. Letter of Rufus Bishop, copied in WRHS IV B 37, pp. 159–60.

24. "Testimony" of Amos Rathbun, Sr., in *Writings of Deacon Daniel Goodrich*, pp. 121–23.

25. "Testimony" of Nathan Holland, n.p., n.d., WRHS IV B 37, p. 158.

26. When Mother Ann's remains were exhumed at Watervliet, N.Y., in 1835 for removal to a new site, it was discovered that she had sustained a fractured skull. Shaker legend ascribed this injury to the occasion on which a mob in Petersham, Massachusetts, dragged her down a set of stairs feet first. See manuscript #9764 at Shaker Museum, Old Chatham, N.Y., (hereafter Shaker Museum).

Chapter 2. A Sect of Some Continuance

1. "Testimony" of Hannah Prescott, n.p., n.d., WRHS IV A 11.

2. "Testimony" of Jennet Davis, n.p., n.d., WRHS IV A 11.

3. Jonathan Edwards, *Images or Shadows of Divine Things*, ed. Perry Miller (New Haven, 1948), p. 90. I am indebted to Philip Greven's analysis of the evangelicals and their concern over sexuality. See Philip Greven, *The Protestant Temperament* (New York, 1977), pp. 24−32.

4. James Whittaker, Letter to his "natural relations," 1785. Published in [Joseph Meacham], *A Concise Statement of the Principles of the Only True Church, according to the Gospel of the Present Appearance of Christ. As held to and Practiced upon by the True Followers of the Living Saviour, at New Lebanon, &c. Together with a Letter from James Whittaker, Minister of the Gospel in this Day of Christ's Second Appearing—to his Natural Relations in England* (Bennington, Vt., 1790), pp. 18−20.

5. Recalled by John Warner in *Testimonies of the Life, Character, Revelations and Doctrines of Mother Ann Lee and the Elders With Her . . .* , eds. Rufus Bishop and Seth Y. Wells, 2nd edition (Albany, N.Y., 1888), pp. 290−91.

6. In *Testimonies* (1888), p. 209.

7. Isaac N. Youngs, *Concise View of the Church of God and of Christ on Earth Having Its Foundation In the Faith of Christ's First and Second Appearing* (New Lebanon, N.Y., 1856−1860), Andrews Collection, SA 760, pp. 21−23.

8. "Testimony" of Amos Buttrick, Harvard, Mass., c. 1792, WRHS I A 7.

9. Quoted in *Testimonies* (1888), p. 290.

10. "Testimony" of Jemima Blanchard in *Testimonies and Wise Sayings, Counsel and Instruction of Mother Ann and the Elders . . .* , comp. Eunice Bathrick, Harvard, Mass., 1869, WRHS VI B 10−13, pp. 80−81.

11. Quoted by Bathrick, comp., *Testimonies*, p. 65.

12. In Bathrick, comp., *Testimonies*, p. 103.

13. Letter of James Whittaker to Daniel Goodrich, Jr., n.d., WRHS VI A 11.

14. Stiles, *Literary Diary*, III, p. 226.

15. *Testimonies* (1888), pp. 171−85, passim.

16. Ann Lee, quoted by Bathrick, comp., *Testimonies*, p. 125.

17. In Bathrick, comp., *Testimonies*, pp. 67−68.

18. *Testimonies* (1888), pp. 16−17.

19. Calvin Green, "Biographic Memoir of the Life, Character & Important Events in the Ministration of Mother Lucy Wright" (New Lebanon, N.Y., 1861), WRHS VI B 27, pp. 6−9.

20. Green, "Biographic Memoir," pp. 16−17.

21. Reuben Rathbun, *Reasons Offered For Leaving the Shakers* (Pittsfield, Mass., 1800), p. 9.

22. Recalled by Abijah Worster in Bathrick, comp., *Testimonies*, p. 111.

23. Rufus Bishop, comp., *A Collection of the Writings of Father Joseph Meacham Respecting Church Order and Government* (New Lebanon, N.Y., 1850), WRHS VII B 59, pp. 1−2.

24. Bishop, comp., *Collection of Writings*, p. 28.

25. Youngs, *Concise View*, pp. 50−52.

26. In Bathrick, comp., *Testimonies*, pp. 230−34.

27. Youngs, *Concise View*, pp. 184−85.

28. In Bathrick, comp., *Testimonies*, p. 109.

29. Letter of James Whittaker to unidentified Brother at Hancock, Mass., 1782, WRHS IV A 11.

30. Letter of Joseph Meacham to David Meacham, in Bishop, comp., *Collection of Writings*, p. 33.

31. Letter of Calvin Harlow to Daniel Goodrich, Sr., 1792, in Hollister, comp., *Book of the Busy Hours*.

32. "Testimony" of Jonathan Clark, 1788, in Hollister, comp., *Writings of Deacon Daniel Goodrich*, pp. 64−65. Cf. "testimony" of Rebecca Clark, Hancock, Mass., 1854, in Hollister, comp., *Book of the Busy Hours*.

33. *Record Book* (Hancock, Mass., Church Family, 1788−1815), Shaker

Museum, #10,804, Dec. 21, 1790. Total value of James Talcott's estate = £38.7.6.

34. *Brethren's Journal of Domestic Occurrences* (New Lebanon, N.Y., 1790–1860), WRHS V B 63–71, June 1793.

35. *Record Book* (Hancock, Mass., Church Family), Jan. 15, 1791.

36. *Record Book* (Hancock, Mass., Church Family), Apr. 10, 1789 to Dec.25, 1790.

37. Stephen A. Marini, *Radical Sects of Revolutionary New England* (Cambridge, Mass., 1982), p. 100.

38. Quoted in Hollister, comp., *Writings of Deacon Daniel Goodrich*, p.81.

39. [Meacham], *Concise Statement*, p. 14.

40. See Bishop, comp., *Collection of Writings*, passim.

41. John Warner, "A Short Account of the birth, character, and ministration of Father Eleazer and Mother Hannah" (Harvard, Mass., 1824), WRHS VI B 7, p. 20.

42. Florinda Sears, comp., "List of Visitors" (Harvard, Mass., 1791–1879), WRHS V B 58.

43. Calvin Green wrote in 1860: "No society has been established more permanently upon the foundational principles and order of the Church . . . at New Lebanon . . . or has maintained its standing and number any better . . . as those over which Father Job presided."

"Biography of Elder Henry Clough" (New Lebanon, N.Y., 1860), WRHS VI B 24, p. 34.

44. Green, "Biography," pp. 8–32, passim.

45. Warner, "Short Account," p. 11.

46. Green, "Biography," p. 34.

47. Recalled by Daniel Goodrich, Sr., Feb. 2, 1791, in Hollister, comp., *Book of the Busy Hours*.

48. In Bathrick, comp., *Testimonies*, pp. 297–98.

49. Green, "Biography," pp. 46–47.

50. Compiled from Youngs, *Names and Ages*, HSV.

51. Statistics for Shirley, Mass., compiled from William H. Wetherbee, *A Book Containing the Records of the Church . . . Shirley, Massachusetts* (1844), Shaker Museum, #10,803. Statistics for Harvard, Mass., compiled from Thomas Hammond, *Harvard Church Family Record* (1791–1853) in Harvard, Massachusetts, Shaker Church Records, 1790–1875, American Antiquarian Society, Worcester, Mass.

52. In Bishop, comp., *Collection of Writings*, p. 91.

53. Valentine Rathbun, "About the Shakers," *The New Star*, #5 (May 9, 1797), pp. 45–46.

Chapter 3. Bait to Catch Good Gospel Fish

1. Green, "Biographic Memoir," p. 25.

2. "Testimony" of Daniel Goodrich, Sr., in Hollister, comp., *Book of the Busy Hours*.

3. Green, "Biographic Memoir," p. 22.

4. See Green, "Biographic Memoir," pp. 26–27 regarding the state of the Society from 1798 to 1800: "The Church began to travel for a new birth of children. There seemed to be a universal labor and earnest prayer to God for an opening of the Gospel and there was scarcely a member that did not appear willing to spend and be spent for that glorious purpose."

5. Green, "Biographic Memoir," pp. 48–49.

6. I. D. Stewart, *The History of the Free Will Baptists* (Dover, N.H., 1862), p. 111.

7. Issachar Bates, *Sketch of the Life and Experience of Issachar Bates, Sr.* (New Lebanon, N.Y., 1832–1836), Andrews Collection, SA 779, p. 43.

8. Issachar Bates, *Sketch*, pp. 45–46.

9. "Testimony" of Cassandana Brewster in Hollister, comp., *Book of Remembrance*, WRHS VII B 109, p. 34.

10. "Testimony" of Cassandana Brewster, Hancock, Mass., n.d., Andrews Collection, SA 1548.

11. Letter of Mary Boynton to Mary Rust, c. 1810, Andrews Collection, SA 1220.

12. Letter of Daniel Goodrich and Calvin Green to Mary Rust, c. 1810, Andrews Collection, SA 1220.

13. Elisha D. Blakeman, "Religious Experience of David Rowley" (New Lebanon, N.Y., 1854), Andrews Collection, SA 1077, p. 104.

14. "Testimony" of Jemima Blanchard in Bathrick, comp., Testimonies, p. 85.

15. Letter of Benjamin S. Youngs to Molly Goodrich, Feb. 10, 1811, WRHS IV A 19.

16. Green, "Biographic Memoir," p. 38.

17. Letter of Daniel Goodrich, Sr. to David Meacham, Oct. 10, 1806, WRHS IV A 19.

18. Warner, "Short Account," pp. 15–18.

19. Warner, "Short Account," p. 20.

20. Quoted by White and Taylor, Shakerism, p. 321. In her 1977 bibliography of works by and about the Shakers, Mary L. Richmond noted that Brother Richard McNemar included Jefferson's name on a list of recipients of the 1823 edition, but she failed to locate documentation of Jefferson's appraisal of the Testimony. Mary L. Richmond, Shaker Literature: A Bibliography, 2 vols. (Hanover, N.H., 1977), II, #1471.

21. Calvin Reed, "Autobiography" (New Lebanon, N.Y., n.d.), WRHS VI B 29, p. 121.

22. Reed, "Autobiography," pp. 129–35.

23. See Green, "Biographic Memoir," pp. 82–83, and Bathrick, comp., Testimonies, pp. 41–42.

24. Youngs, Concise View, pp. 304–30, passim.

25. Green, "Biographic Memoir," pp. 88–94.

26. Calvin Green, Journal of a Trip to Savoy (New Lebanon, N.Y., 1821), WRHS V B 90, Aug. 15–16, 1821.

27. Hammond, Harvard Church Family Record, Apr. 27, 1811.

28. Letter of Ministry New Lebanon to Ministry Union Village, Feb. 22, 1817, WRHS IV A 33.

29. Bathrick, comp., Testimonies, p. 227.

30. Letter of unidentified New Lebanon Church Family Elder to Second Order Elders at South Union, Kentucky, Aug. 23, 1813. Quoted by White and Taylor, Shakerism, p. 134.

31. Domestic Journal of Important Occurrences (New Lebanon, N.Y., 1780–1860), WRHS V B 60–61, Sept. 1, 1800.

32. Bathrick, comp., Testimonies, p. 49.

33. Green, "Biographic Memoir," p. 123.

34. New Lebanon Ministry, Milenial Laws, or Gospel statutes and ordinances adapted to the day of Christ's second Appearing (New Lebanon, N.Y., 1821), WRHS I B 37.

35. Milenial Laws (1821).

36. Account Book (New Lebanon, N.Y., Church Family, 1817–1829), HSV, 1817, passim.

Chapter 4. Our Precious Good Elders

1. Unidentified Elder, Journal (Hancock, Mass., Second Family, 1829–1845), Andrews Collection, SA 783.

2. Elizabeth Lovegrove, Journal (New Lebanon, N.Y., 1827), WRHS V B 93.

3. "Testimony" of Cassandana Brewster in Hollister, comp., Writings of Deacon Daniel Goodrich, p. 80.

4. Warner, "Short Account," pp. 38–40.

5. Seth Y. Wells, "Testimony," Watervliet, N.Y., n.d., WRHS I A 8.

6. Isaac N. Youngs, "Address to

Believers at Harvard, Mass.," Nov. 21 1852, in Bathrick, comp., Visions, Spirit Communications, Religious Experience, Narrative Pieces, Poems and Sketches from Different Authors (Harvard, Mass., 1850–1865), Andrews Collection, SA 1077, p. 118.

7. Wells, "Testimony," Watervliet, N.Y., n.d., WRHS I A 8.

8. Hammond, Harvard Church Family Record, July 2, 1825.

9. Farm Journal (New Lebanon, N.Y., Second Order, 1858–1867), HSV.

10. David Parker, "Remarks at the Close of Evening School," Canterbury, N.H., Mar. 18, 1833, WRHS IV A 4.

11. Green, "Biographic Memoir," p. 77.

12. Green, "Biographic Memoir," pp. 85–87.

13. Hervey Elkins, *Fifteen Years in the Senior Order of Shakers* (Hanover, N.H., 1853), p. 22.

14. New Lebanon Ministry, *The Holy Orders of the Church, Written by Father Joseph* (New Lebanon, N.Y., 1841), Andrews Collection, SA 750.

15. Letter of Ministry Alfred to Ministry New Lebanon, Feb. 17, 1829, WRHS IV A 1.

16. Letter of Grove Wright to Grove Blanchard, May 25, 1852, WRHS IV A 19.

17. Letter of Ministry Alfred to Ministry Harvard, Sept. 29, 1830, WRHS IV A 2.

18. Wells, "Testimony," Watervliet, N.Y., n.d., WRHS I A 8.

19. *Farm Journal*, Mar. 20, 1865.

20. Hammond, comp., *Sayings of Mother Ann and the first Elders, taken from Abijah Worster* (Harvard, Mass., n.d.), WRHS VII B 22, p. 65.

21. Letter of Ministry Canterbury to Ministry New Lebanon, Aug. 24, 1833, WRHS IV A 4.

22. Bishop, comp., *Collection of Writings*, p. 3.

23. Hammond, comp., *Sayings of Mother Ann*, pp. 84–86.

24. Green, "Biography," p. 94.

25. Hammond, comp., *Sayings of Mother Ann*, pp. 36–37.

26. Hammond, comp., *Sayings of Mother Ann*, p. 35.

27. Rufus Bishop, quoted by Hammond, comp., *Sayings of Mother Ann*, pp. 38–39.

28. Green, "Biographic Memoir," pp. 18–19.

29. Bathrick, comp., *Testimonies*, pp. 292–93.

30. *History of Canaan, New York, Lower Family* (Canaan, N.Y., n.d.), WRHS V B 84.

31. Green, "Biography," p. 35.

32. Brown, *An Account*, pp. 50–51.

33. Wells, quoted by Brown in *An Account*, p. 55.

34. Brown, *An Account*, pp. 209–10.

35. Green, "Biographic Memoir," p. 116.

36. Sarah Mosely, "Affidavit," March 22, 1800, WRHS I A 6.

37. Brown, *An Account*, p. 258.

38. Green, "Biography," p. 94.

39. "Testimony" of Beulah Cooper in Bathrick, comp., *Testimonies*, p. 41.

40. Thomas Damon, *Journal* (Enfield, Conn., 1834–1845), Andrews Collection, SA 774.

41. Brown, *An Account*, p. 43.

42. Green, "Biography," pp. 55–58.

43. *Domestic Journal of Important Occurrences*, Oct. 12, 1815.

44. Letter of Ministry Alfred to Ministry New Lebanon, Feb. 12, 1816, WRHS IV A 1.

45. Letter of Ministry Alfred to Ministry New Lebanon, May 4, 1816, WRHS IV A 1.

46. Letter of Ministry Alfred to Ministry New Lebanon, Sept. 7, 1816, WRHS IV A 1.

47. Letter of Ministry Alfred to Ministry New Lebanon, Jan. 25, 1831, WRHS IV A 2.

48. Henry C. Blinn, *Journal of a Trip to Kentucky, 1873*, excerpted in *Shaker Quarterly*, vol. 5, #2 (Summer 1965), p. 39.

49. Letter of Daniel Goodrich, Jr. to Ministry Harvard, Mar. 19, 1834, WRHS IV A 19.

50. Letter of Cassandana Goodrich to Molly Goodrich, Aug. 30, 1826, in Hollister, comp., *Copies of Various Letters*, WRHS IV B 35.

51. Letter of Cassandana Goodrich to Molly Goodrich, Apr. 25, 1823, in Hollister, comp., *Copies of Various Letters*.

52. *Farm Journal*, Nov. 20, 1859.

53. *Record of Travels of the Harvard Ministry* (Harvard, Mass., 1791–1880), WRHS V B 59.

54. Letter of Grove Wright to Grove Blanchard, Dec. 22, 1849, WRHS IV A 19.

55. "Testimony" of Grove Wright in Hollister, comp., *Autobiography of the Saints*, WRHS VI B 37, p. 352.

56. Letter of Grove Wright to Grove Blanchard, Mar. 23, 1852, WRHS IV A 20.

57. Letter of Grove Wright to Grove Blanchard, Feb. 24, 1852, WRHS IV A 20.

58. Letter of Grove Wright to Grove Blanchard, Aug. 19, 1860, WRHS IV A 20.

59. Letter of Grove Wright to Grove Blanchard, Nov. 1, 1860, WRHS IV A 20.

60. Grove Wright, *Diary* (Hancock, Mass., 1854), Andrews Collection, SA 792, passim.

61. Grove Blanchard, *Diary* (Harvard, Mass., 1866), HSV, passim.

62. Cassandana Brewster, *Diary* (Hancock, Mass., 1865), Andrews Collection, SA 795, passim.

63. *Kentucky Ministry Travel Journal* (July 1869), WRHS V B 228.

64. See Damon, *Memoranda* (Hancock, Mass., 1846–1860), Shaker Museum, #13,357. Cf. Wright, *Diary*, Aug. 7, 1854.

65. Brewster, *Diary*, Oct. 30, 1865.

66. Damon, "Testimony," Enfield, Conn., 1843, WRHS VI A 2.

67. Damon, *Memoranda*, Dec. 9, 1846 and Oct. 19, 1847.

68. Letter of Hervey Eads to Isaac N. Youngs, Dec. 6, 1844, in Bathrick, comp., *A Second Book Copied from Br. Alonzo G. Hollister's Manuscripts, Copied for Elder John Cloutman* (Harvard, Mass., 1874), Andrews Collection, SA 805.

69. Jemima Blanchard, "Testimony," Harvard, Mass., n.d., in Hollister, comp., *Book of Remembrance*, WRHS VII B 107, p. 26.

70. Elkins, *Fifteen Years*, p. 22.

71. Several particularly well-made artifacts in the collection of Hancock Shaker Village, Inc. are labeled "Ministry," including a potty chair and an apple basket. The existence of such items may indicate that members gave their leaders articles of especially high quality as tokens of respect and affection. In addition, an entry in John DeWitt's *Memo Book* (WRHS V B 92, Sept. 1, 1835) mentions as a special treat taken to Brethren in the hay field tea sweetened with "loaf sugar provided by the Ministry." As molasses, maple products, and brown sugar were more typical, this may indicate that Ministry members were permitted such luxuries as white sugar.

72. Lucy Wright, quoted by Green, "Biographic Memoir," p. 132.

73. Freegift Wells, "Various Protests Regarding Rules" (Watervliet, N.Y., n.d.), WRHS VII B 270a.

Chapter 5. How Can I Help Being Happy?

1. Elizabeth Lovegrove and Anna Dodgson, *Dye House Journal* (New Lebanon, N.Y., 1837–1855), Andrews Collection, SA 817, July 11, 1845. This journal was evidently kept by Lovegrove from 1837 until approximately 1842 and was then taken over by Dodgson.

2. Letter of Eliza Barber to Elizabeth Sizer, Mar. 21, 1828, WRHS IV A 33.

3. Letter of Frederick W. Evans to George H. Evans, June 11, 1830, WRHS IV A 36.

4. Letter of Evans to George H. Evans, June 11, 1830, WRHS IV A 36.

5. Quoted by Wealthy Storer, *Journal* (Hancock, Mass., 1846–1854), Andrews Collection, SA 789, June 15, 1851.

6. Calvin Green, *Journal* (New Lebanon, N.Y., 1811–1822), WRHS V B 80, Sept. 8 and 28, 1816.

7. Green, "Biography," p. 76.

8. For a full account of one such member, see Priscilla J. Brewer, "Emerson, Lane and the Shakers: A Case of Converging Ideologies," *New England Quarterly*, 55 (1982), pp. 254–75.

9. *Domestic Journal of Important Occurrences*, Sept. 20, 1815.

10. *Domestic Journal of Important Occurrences*, Mar. 28, 1838.

11. Catherine M. Sedgwick, "Magnetism Among the Shakers," *Berkshire Culturist and Weekly Family Gazette* 2 (May 16, 1849), pp. 157–58.

12. Membership list (Canterbury, N.H., Church Family, Oct. 29, 1819), WRHS III A 2. The adult male/female ratio of the New Lebanon Church Family in 1820 was 45.6 : 54.4; 13 percent of its members were under sixteen, and 20.1 percent over fifty-nine (see Appendixes A.3 and A.7).

13. *Domestic Journal of Important Occurrences*, Sept. 5, 1832.

14. Letter of Church Family Elders Hancock to Ministry Harvard, Oct. 14, 1835, WRHS IV A 19.

15. Rebecca Clark quoting William Deming in Hollister, comp., *Writings of Deacon Daniel Goodrich*, pp. 127–28.

16. Cassandana Goodrich, quoted by Hollister, comp., *Writings of Deacon Daniel Goodrich*, p. 77.

17. Cassandana Goodrich, quoted by Hollister, comp., *Writings of Deacon Daniel Goodrich*, p. 92.

18. Betsy Bates, *Words of Mother Lucy* (New Lebanon, N.Y., n.d.), WRHS VII B 61.

19. Nathaniel Deming, quoted by Hollister, comp., *Writings of Deacon Daniel Goodrich*, pp. 73–74.

20. Issachar Bates, *Sketch*, pp. 126–30.

21. Elkins, *Fifteen Years*, p. 20.

22. "The Shakers at Niskeyuna," *Boston Palladium*, Aug. 20, 1829. Quoted in mixed copies of letters, WRHS IV B 35.

23. Benjamin Lyon, *A Journal of Domestic Events* (New Lebanon, N.Y., 1839–1840), Andrews Collection, SA 1031, Jan. 12, 1839 and July 30, 1839. Lyon is identified as a Family Deacon in the entry for Oct. 13, 1839.

24. Blakeman, *Daily Journal* (New Lebanon, N.Y., 1834–1840), WRHS V B 131, Apr. 13, 1835.

25. Lovegrove and Dodgson, *Dye House Journal*, Aug. 19, 1846. In the original, the blanks are filled with undecipherable pen marks that are clearly not a shorthand or code.

26. Elkins, *Fifteen Years*, p. 26.

27. Elkins, *Fifteen Years*, pp. 112–19, passim.

28. Green, "Biographic Memoir," p. 131.

29. Lovegrove and Dodgson, *Dye House Journal*, Aug. 5, 1854.

30. Ann Lee, quoted in *Testimonies* (1888), p. 216.

31. Letter of Ministry Canterbury to Ministry New Lebanon, Feb. 16, 1833, WRHS IV A 12.

32. Blakeman, *Boys' Journal of Work* (New Lebanon, N.Y., 1844–1865), WRHS V B 137, Apr. 1851.

33. Elkins, *Fifteen Years*, pp. 30–31.

34. William Calver et al., *School Journal* (New Lebanon, N.Y., 1852–1887), HSV, Nov. 8, 1858. This journal was kept by many different teachers: William Calver, Henry Hollister, Calvin Reed, James Calver, Peter Greaves, and Emma J. Neale.

35. Seth Y. Wells, "Remarks on Learning and the use of Boks" (New Lebanon, N.Y., Mar. 10, 1836), Andrews Collection, SA 770.

36. Blakeman, *Boys' Journal of Work*, Sept. 2, 1844.

37. Blakeman, *Boys' Journal of Work*, Nov. 20, 1844.

38. Blakeman, *Boys' Journal of Work*, Mar. 12, 1850.

39. Blakeman, *Boys' Journal of Work*, Nov. 23, 1853.

40. Benjamin Gates, *A Day Book or Journal of Work and Various Things* (New Lebanon, N.Y., 1827–1838), Andrews Collection, SA 1030, 1828, passim.

41. Blakeman, *Boys' Journal of Work*, Sept. 3, 1847.

42. Blakeman, *Boys' Journal of Work*, Aug. 8, 1851.

43. *Farm Journal*, June 6, 1859.

44. *Farm Journal*, June 27, 1860.

45. Blakeman, *Daily Journal*, Aug. 24, 1838.

46. Green, "Biographic Memoir," May 19, 1816.

47. Unidentified Elder, *Journal*, Hancock, Mass., Second Family, n.d.

48. Lovegrove and Dodgson, *Dye House Journal*, June 23, 1849.

49. *Book of Measurements of Brethren* (New Lebanon, N.Y., 1868–1880), WRHS III A 8.

50. *Brethren's Journal of Domestic Occurrences*, Jan. 1850.

51. Rhoda Blake, "A Sketch of the Life and Experience of Rhoda Blake" (New Lebanon, N.Y., 1864), Andrews Collection, SA 780.

52. *Farm Journal*, Apr. 14, 1860.

53. Census enumeration schedule for Canterbury, Merrimack County, N.H., 1870, p. 9.

54. The earliest located references to the regular hiring of farm laborers appear in an unidentified *Account Book* (New Lebanon, N.Y., 1817–1829), HSV, 1824 and 1826, passim.

55. Youngs, "Autobiography in Verse" (New Lebanon, N.Y., 1837), Andrews Collection, SA 818.

56. Warner, "Short Account," p. 27.

57. Blakeman, *Daily Journal*, Mar. 19, 1836.

58. Green, "Biographic Memoir," p. 124.

59. John DeWitt, *Memo Book* (New Lebanon, N.Y.), WRHS V B 92, Feb. 28, 1836.

60. Blakeman, *Daily Journal*, Dec. 1837.

61. *Farm Journal*, June 25, 1859.

62. Bathrick, comp., *Testimonies*, p. 138.

63. *Farm Journal*, Nov. 3, 1859.

64. Lovegrove and Dodgson, *Dye House Journal*, July 20, 1849.

65. Lovegrove and Dodgson, *Dye House Journal*, Apr. 7, 1849.

66. Lovegrove and Dodgson, *Dye House Journal*, Sept. 5, 1849.

67. Henry DeWitt, *Journal* (New Lebanon, N.Y., 1827–1867), WRHS V B 97, Oct. 30, 1852.

68. Youngs, "Autobiography."

69. Letter of Ministry Alfred to Ministry Harvard, Sept. 12, 1825, WRHS IV A 1.

70. Issachar Bates, "My Feelings" in *Sketch*.

71. Elkins, *Fifteen Years*, pp. 26–27.

Chapter 6. Numbers Are Not the Thing for Us to Glory in

1. Whitworth, *God's Blueprints*, p. 40.

2. Quoted by Green, "Biographic Memoir," p. 91.

3. Letter of Ministry Canterbury to Ministry New Lebanon, Jan. 18, 1826, WRHS IV A 3.

4. Lovegrove, *Journal*, June 8, 1827.

5. Letter of Ministry New Lebanon to Ministry Harvard, 1824, in Hammond, comp., *Sayings of Mother Ann*, p. 63.

6. Calvin Green, *Journal of a Trip to Philadelphia* (New Lebanon, N.Y., 1828), WRHS V B 98.

7. Piercy, *Valley of God's Pleasure*, p. 94. In a letter from Elder Matthew Houston of North Union, Ohio, to Elder Seth Wells at New Lebanon, dated Aug. 1832 (WRHS), Gause is referred to in these terms: "Jess Gaines [sic] of Hancock was also here of late; he is a Mormon, second to the prophet, Joseph Smith. We hope he will not return and bother us further." Gause severed his connection with the Mormons in 1832.

8. *Brethren's Journal of Domestic Occurrences*, Dec. 21, 1858.

9. *Domestic Journal of Important Occurrences*, Jan. 2, 1830.

10. "Report to the Overseers of the Poor" (Watervliet, N.Y., 1825); typescript in New York State Library, Albany, N.Y., A2903. According to the 1820 census, the Watervliet community's population totaled 193 members. By 1830, it had increased to 244. Assuming an 1825 population of approximately 219, then 20.1 percent of the members in 1825 were listed in this report. The five handicapped adults were: Harriet Hosford, fifty, subject to fits; Hannah Salisbury, fifty, deaf and dumb; Eunice Robbins, forty, "lunatic"; Clarissa Buckingham, fifty, "infirm"; and Emily Owen, eighteen, one of whose hands had been maimed by a cotton machine.

11. *Ministry Daybook* (New Lebanon, N.Y., 1815–1829), WRHS V B 85, Dec. 7, 1828. Hannah Train lived on at New Lebanon until her death in 1842.

12. Asenath Clark, *Ministerial Journal* (Watervliet and New Lebanon, N.Y.), copy HSV, Feb. 25, 1835. Elizabeth Train had served as an Office Sister, but was removed in 1816. She never again held any position of either domestic or spiritual responsibility, but lived out her life as a Shaker, dying in 1865.

13. Letter of Ministry New Lebanon to Ministry Union Village, July 1819, WRHS IV A 33.

14. Letter of John Mantle to Ministry New Lebanon, July 14, 1832, WRHS IV A 36. Mantle remained in the faith until his death in 1861 at the age of eighty-one.

15. Letter of Ministry Alfred to Ministry New Lebanon, Sept. 11, 1824, WRHS IV A 1.

16. Youngs, *Names and Ages*, passim.

17. "Inventory or Catalogue of Articles

of Clothing &c. Delivered to those who have left our Society" (Watervliet, N.Y., 1816–1884), WRHS II B 98.

18. Elkins, *Fifteen Years*, p. 21.

19. Quoted by Richmond, *Shaker Literature*, Vol. I, p. 537. Mary Dyer's publications included: *A Brief Statement of the Sufferings of Mary Dyer* (1818), *A Portraiture of Shakerism* (1822), "Review of the Portraiture of Shakerism" (1824), and *The Rise and Progress of the Serpent from the Garden of Eden* (1847). After the New Hampshire legislature granted her a divorce in 1829, Dyer returned to the use of her maiden name, Marshall.

20. Letter of Nathaniel Deming to Ministry Harvard, Mar. 27, 1819, WRHS IV A 19.

21. Letter of Ministry Hancock to Ministry Harvard, Mar. 27, 1826, WRHS IV A 19.

22. Grove Blanchard, *Names of those gathered into the Church* (Harvard, Mass., 1791–1860), Andrews Collection, SA 803.

23. Quoted by Betsy Bates, *Words of Mother Lucy*.

24. Bathrick, comp., *Testimonies*, pp. 285–86.

25. Philemon Stewart, *Daily Journal* (New Lebanon, N.Y., 1834–1836), WRHS V B 130, Dec. 31, 1834.

26. Bathrick, comp., *Testimonies*, pp. 347–49.

27. Quoted by Patterson, *Shaker Spiritual*, pp. 439–40. Sister Minerva's identity is uncertain, but she was probably Minerva Seaton, a member of the Hancock Church Family who signed the Senior Order covenant on May 13, 1821, at the age of twenty-one or twenty-two. She also left the sect at some point, although the date of her departure is not known. Descendants of John Deming, Jr., reported in a conversation with the author during the summer of 1981 that Deming and Seaton had later married.

28. Letter of Ministry Harvard to Ministry New Lebanon, Aug. 3, 1832, WRHS IV A 23.

29. Clark, *Ministerial Journal*, Mar. 21, 1835.

30. Betsy Bates, *Journal of Daily Events* (New Lebanon, N.Y., 1833–1835), WRHS V B 128, Mar. 21, 1835.

31. Betsy Bates, *Journal*, Mar. 31, 1835.

32. Stewart, *Daily Journal*, Nov. 7, 1834.

33. Stewart, *Daily Journal*, Nov. 5, 1834.

34. "Instructions Concerning Church Order" (New Lebanon, N.Y., n.d.), WRHS I A 10.

35. "Testimony" of Deborah Wheaton and Anna Davis (New Lebanon, N.Y., n.d.), Andrews Collection, SA 829.

36. *History of Canaan, New York, Lower Family*, n.d.

37. Letter of Ministry Alfred to Ministry Harvard, Jan. 21, 1831, WRHS IV A 21.

38. Giles B. Avery, *Book of Records* (New Lebanon, N.Y., n.d.), HSV.

39. Letter of Ministry Canterbury to Ministry New Lebanon, Oct. 15, 1831, WRHS IV A 12.

40. Letter of Ministry Canterbury to Ministry New Lebanon, Aug. 10, 1831, WRHS IV A 4.

41. Avery, *Book of Records*.

42. *History of Canaan, New York, Lower Family*, n.d.

43. *History of Canaan, New York, Lower Family*, n.d.

44. Letter of Ministry Canterbury to Ministry New Lebanon, Feb. 19, 1819, WRHS IV A 3.

45. Letter of Ministry Canterbury to Ministry New Lebanon, Oct. 2, 1835, WRHS IV A 4.

46. Robert Fowle et al., "Plain Dealing With Square Work" (Canterbury, N.H., 1847), WRHS X B 1. The other authors of this poem were Ephraim Dennett, Marcia Hastings, and Mira Bean.

47. List of contributions from various communities, c. 1810–1820, WRHS II A 17. Other communities contributed as well, the size of their donations perhaps indicating their relative degree of prosperity. Between 1805 and 1812, Canterbury sent $3,750 west, but Enfield, N.H., contributed only $1,375. In the period from 1805 to 1818, Hancock contributed $2,157.58. Between 1805 and 1806, Enfield, Conn., donated $851.88.

48. *The Pennsylvanian*, Oct. 4, 1834. Copy in Andrews Collection.

49. *Daybook* (Hancock, Mass., Church Family, 1837–1913), HSV.

50. *A Journal Kept by the Deaconesses at the Office* (New Lebanon, N.Y., 1830–1836), Andrews Collection, SA 894, Jan. 1, 1834 and Jan. 1836.

51. *Domestic Journal of Important Occurrences*, New Lebanon, N.Y., July 7, 1831.

52. Letter of William Deming to Benjamin S. Youngs, Jan. 12, 1832, WRHS IV A 19.

53. In Hammond, comp., *Sayings of Mother Ann*, p. 89.

54. Stewart, *Daily Journal*, Apr. 26, 1834.

55. Fowle et al., "Plain Dealing With Square Work."

56. Clark, *Ministerial Journal*, Oct. 28, 1835.

57. Youngs, *Concise View*, pp. 89–90.

58. Quoted in an anonymous letter from Enfield, Conn., Apr. 28, 1822, WRHS IV A 11.

59. Whitworth, *God's Blueprints*, p. 47. Whitworth claims that the members clamoring for a role in the selection of their leaders were all recent converts who had previously been adherents of Robert Owen, the English socialist.

60. Letter of Benjamin S. Youngs to Ministry New Lebanon, Sept. 8, 1828, WRHS IV B 35.

61. New Lebanon Ministry, "Circular Epistle," Sept. 1, 1829, WRHS IV A 35.

62. Youngs, *Concise View*, p. 94.

63. Lovegrove, *Journal*, Apr. 10, 1827.

64. Lovegrove, *Journal*, Apr. 10, 1827.

65. Lovegrove, *Journal*, Apr. 16, 1827.

66. Quoted by Yale, *Godly Pastor*, p. 366. Berkshire County, Massachusetts, had a long history of evangelical revivalism in the eighteenth and nineteenth centuries. Two Shaker communities, at Hancock and Tyringham, were within its borders.

67. Letter of Ministry Canterbury to Ministry New Lebanon, Mar. 13, 1827, WRHS IV A 11.

68. See New Lebanon Ministry, "Circular on Intemperance," 1827, Andrews Collection, SA 772. Cf. various letters: Ministry Canterbury to Ministry New Lebanon, Jan. 13, 1828, WRHS IV A 3; Ministry Alfred to Ministry New Lebanon, Feb. 27, 1827, WRHS IV A 1; and Ministry Hancock to Ministry New Lebanon, Mar. 31, 1827, WRHS IV A 19.

69. Ephraim Prentiss, "Report of Interesting Experience with the Boys of whom he was Caretaker" (Watervliet, N.Y., 1835–1837), WRHS VII B 258.

70 John DeWitt, *Memo Book*, Sept. 1, 1835.

71. Youngs, *Concise View*, pp. 294–95.

72. John DeWitt, *Memo Book*, July 1, 1835.

73. Sylvester Graham, *A Lecture to Young Men, On Chastity, intended also for the serious consideration of parents and guardians* (Providence, R.I., 1834), pp. 45–47. Quoted by Stephen Nissenbaum, *Sex, Diet, and Debility in Jacksonian America: Sylvester Graham and Health Reform* (Westport, Conn., 1980), p. 106.

74. Graham, *Chastity*, pp. 79–81. Quoted by Nissenbaum, *Sex, Diet, and Debility*, p. 32.

75. Stewart, *Daily Journal*, Sept. 6, 1835.

76. Giles B. Avery, *Journal* (New Lebanon, N.Y., 1832–1881), WRHS V B 104–126, Sept. 7 and 15, 1835.

77. Letter of Ministry Canterbury to Ministry New Lebanon, Jan. 20, 1836, WRHS IV A 4.

78. Betsy Bates, *Journal of Daily Events*, Sept. 6, 1835.

79. Aaron Bill, *A Journal or Day Book* (New Lebanon, N.Y., 1834–1840), WRHS V B 132.

80. John DeWitt, *Memo Book*, June 20, 1836.

81. John DeWitt, *Memo Book*, Dec. 8, 1836.

82. Youngs, *Concise View*, pp. 299–302.

83. "Treatise on Simple Diet" (n.p., n.d.), WRHS VII B 289.

84. Prentiss, "Report."

85. Prentiss, "Report."

86. Freegift Wells, *Notebook #4* (Watervliet, N.Y., c. 1855), WRHS VII B 270, p. 11.

87. Letter of Garret K. Lawrence to Isaac N. Youngs, May 14, 1834, WRHS IV A 36.

88. Wells, *Notebook #4*, pp. 8–9.

89. Wells was sent to Union Village, Ohio, as first Elder in March 1836,

returning east in 1843. Prentiss was moved to Sabbathday Lake, Maine, at an undetermined time prior to 1851. See Avery, *Journal*, Mar. 21, 1836; Franklin Barber and Philemon Stewart, *A Journal of Garden Accounts Commencing July 27th, 1840* (New Lebanon, N.Y.), HSV, July 29, 1843; and *A Journal of Domestic Events and Transactions* (New Lebanon, N.Y.) HSV, April 1, 1851.

90. Stewart, *Daily Journal*, Mar. 23, 1834.

91. Stewart, *Daily Journal*, May 15 and Oct. 24, 1834.

92. Stewart, *Daily Journal*, Dec. 29, 1835.

93. Gates, *Day Book*, Sept. 23, 1835.

94. Blakeman, *Daily Journal*, June 17, 1836.

95. Isaac N. Youngs, *Personal Journal* (New Lebanon, N.Y., 1837–1857), Shaker Museum, #10,509, Mar. 24, 1837.

96. Avery, *Journal*, Dec. 17, 1837.

97. Avery, *Journal*, Dec. 22, 1837.

Chapter 7. Whirlwind, Earthquake and Fire

1. Avery, *Journal*, Sept. 6, 1835.

2. Youngs, *Concise View*, p. 112.

3. Hammond, *Harvard Church Family Record*, p. 73.

4. Lovegrove and Dodgson, *Dye House Journal*, Nov. 26, 1837 and Jan. 5–6, 1838.

5. Letter of Ministry New Lebanon to Ministry South Union, June 20, 1838, WRHS IV B 36.

6. Letter of Grove Wright to Ministry New Lebanon, Nov. 16, 1837. Quoted in a letter from Ministry New Lebanon to Ministry South Union, Dec. 13, 1837, WRHS IV A 12.

7. Letter of Ministry Canterbury to Ministry New Lebanon, Jan. 29, 1838, WRHS IV A 4.

8. Letter of Ministry Canterbury to Ministry Groveland, Feb. 18, 1839, WRHS IV A 12.

9. Letter of Ministry Canterbury to Seth Y. Wells, Aug. 25, 1838, WRHS IV A 4.

10. "A Record of Messages and Communications given by Divine Inspiration in the Church at Hancock Commencing in 1840" (Hancock, Mass., Church Family, 1840–1845), Andrews Collection, SA 1066.

11. Youngs, *Concise View*, p. 101.

12. Letter of Church Family Elders Sabbathday Lake to Ministry Alfred, Jan. 14, 1838, WRHS IV A 4.

13. Letter of Ministry Canterbury to Ministry New Lebanon, Jan. 28, 1839, WRHS IV A 4.

14. "Testimony" of Grove Wright in Hollister, comp., *Autobiography of the Saints*, p. 153.

15. Quoted in "Record of Messages," p. 7.

16. Youngs, *Concise View*, pp. 110–11.

17. In "Record of Messages," p. 89.

18. In Bathrick, comp., *Second Book*, pp. 250–51.

19. "Orders Given by Mother Lucy" (Hancock, Mass., 1839–1842), Andrews Collection, SA 748, Feb. 12, 1839.

20. "Mother's Pure Teaching" (Hancock, Mass., 1841–1845), WRHS I B 82.

21. *Church Order Journal* (New Lebanon, N.Y., 1841–1846), WRHS V B 135, Dec. 29, 1841.

22. New Lebanon Ministry, *The Holy Orders of the Church, Written by Father Joseph* (New Lebanon, N.Y., Feb. 18, 1841), Andrews Collection, SA 750.

23. "Orders Given by Mother Lucy."

24. Youngs, *Concise View*, pp. 187–95, passim.

25. Paulina Bates, *The Divine Book of Holy and Eternal Wisdom*, 2 vols. (Canterbury, N.H., 1849), Vol. I, p. 113.

26. Paulina Bates, *Divine Book*, Vol. I, p. 35.

27. "Record of Messages," p. 83.

28. Letter of Ministry Canterbury to Ministry New Lebanon, Feb. 10, 1841, WRHS IV A 5.

29. Letter of Ministry Canterbury to Ministry New Lebanon, Feb. 10, 1841, WRHS IV A 5.

30. *Church Order Journal*, Dec. 25, 1841.

31. Avery, *Journal*, Jan. 14, 1838.

32. Barber and Stewart, *Journal of Garden Accounts*, Jan. 30, 1849. The first scribe in this journal was Franklin Barber, the second George Allen. Stewart took over the task after Allen apostatized in 1846.

33. "Record of Messages," p. 36.

34. Letter of Ministry New Lebanon to Ministry South Union, June 20, 1838, WRHS IV B 36.

35. Letter of Ministry Canterbury to Ministry New Lebanon, Apr. 15, 1839, WRHS IV A 4. Youngs, *Concise View*, pp. 105–6, confirms that this was a general policy.

36. Youngs, *Concise View*, p. 121.

37. Henry DeWitt, *Journal*, Apr. 22, 1838.

38. Avery, *Journal*, May 14, 1838.

39. *Journal of Remarkable Events* (New Lebanon, N.Y., 1841–1846), WRHS III B 13.

40. "Orders Given by Mother Lucy," Feb. 18, 1842.

41. Quoted by Charles Nordhoff, *Communistic Societies of the United States* (1875; reprint New York, 1966), p. 158.

42. "Record of Messages," pp. 34–36.

43. Lyon, *Journal*, Feb. 16, 1839.

44. Sedgwick, "Magnetism Among the Shakers," p. 159.

45. Youngs, *Concise View*, p. 126.

46. Youngs, *Concise View*, pp. 134–60, passim.

47. The spiritual names of the other communities were: New Lebanon—"Holy Mount," Watervliet, N.Y.—"Wisdom's Valley," Tyringham—"City of Love," Enfield, Conn.—"City of Union," Shirley—"Pleasant Garden," Canterbury—"Holy Ground," Enfield, N.H.—"Chosen Vale," Alfred—"Holy Land," Sabbathday Lake—"Chosen Land," Groveland—"Union Branch," Union Village—"Wisdom's Paradise," North Union—"Valley of God's Pleasure," Whitewater—"Lonely Plain of Tribulation," Watervliet, Ohio—"Vale of Peace," South Union—"Jasper Valley," and Pleasant Hill—"Holy Sinai Plains."

48. David Lamson, *Two Years' Experience Among the Shakers* (West Boylston, Mass., 1848), p. 101.

49. *Church Order Journal*, May 22, 1842.

50. Philemon Stewart and Daniel Crosman, *A Confidential Journal Kept in the Elders' Lot* (New Lebanon, N.Y., First Order, 1842–1881), WRHS V B 136, Nov. 11, 1842.

51. Stewart and Crosman, *Confidential Journal*, Oct. 2, 1842.

52. *A Book of Orders given by Mother Lucy for all that belong to the Children's Order* (New Lebanon, N.Y., 1840–1842), Andrews Collection, SA 756.

53. Stewart and Crosman, *Confidential Journal*, Oct. 2, 1842.

54. Youngs, *Concise View*, pp. 163–64.

55. Letter of Ministry Canterbury to Ministry New Lebanon, Jan. 1, 1845, WRHS IV A 5.

56. Letter of Philemon Stewart to Ministry New Lebanon, Feb. 14, 1859, WRHS IV A 42, pp. 1–2.

57. *Church Order Journal*, Nov. 27, 1841.

58. Youngs, *Concise View*, pp. 291–92.

59. Stewart and Crosman, *Confidential Journal*, Aug. 8, 1842.

60. Freegift Wells, "A Series of Remarks Showing the power of the Adversary in leading honest souls astray through the influence of inspired Messages. Or a Lamentation because the beauty of Zion hath faded, and Her Light become dim" (Watervliet, N.Y., 1850), WRHS VII B 266, pp. 1–2.

61. Wells, *Notebooks #5 and #6* (Watervliet, N.Y., 1855–1856), WRHS VII B 270a, p. 41.

62. Wells, *Notebooks #5 and #6*, p. 18.

63. Stewart and Crosman, *Confidential Journal*, Sept. 21, 1847.

64. Barber and Stewart, *Journal of Garden Accounts*, Sept. 28, 1847.

65. Damon, *Memoranda*, Feb. 1849. The underlined words are written in a personal shorthand devised by Damon in 1844–1845.

66. Wells, "Series of Remarks," pp. 8–9.

67. Wells, *Notebooks #5 and #6*, pp. 26–28.

68. Wells, "Series of Remarks," p. 18.

69. Wells, "Series of Remarks," pp. 16–17.

70. Wells, "Series of Remarks," p. 9.

71. Paulina Bates, *Divine Book*, Vol. I, p. 8.

Chapter 8. Bad Fish Caught in the Gospel Net

1. In "Record of Messages," p. 87.
2. Youngs, *Concise View*, pp. 161–72, passim.
3. Barber and Stewart, *Journal of Garden Accounts*, Mar. 1, 1847.
4. Barber and Stewart, *Journal of Garden Accounts*, Jan. 25, 1847.
5. Patterson, *Gift Drawing and Gift Song*, pp. 41–42.
6. Wells, "Series of Remarks," p. 40.
7. Wells, *Notebook #4*, pp. 14–15.
8. Wells, "Series of Remarks," p. 46.
9. Wells, *Notebooks #5 and #6*, pp. 68–69.
10. Letter of Grove Wright to Ministry Harvard, Aug. 28, 1847, WRHS IV A 10.
11. Youngs, *Personal Journal*, Oct. 30, 1839.
12. Rufus Bishop, *A Daily Journal of Passing Events* (New Lebanon, N.Y., 1839–1850), 2 vols., Shaker Manuscript Collection, New York Public Library, New York, N.Y., p. 273. Quoted by Patterson, *Shaker Spiritual*, p. 322.
13. Barber and Stewart, *Journal of Garden Accounts*, Sept. 18, 1846.
14. Bishop, *Daily Journal of Passing Events*, Sept. 12, 1846. Quoted by Patterson, *Gift Drawing*, p. 86.
15. Damon, *Memoranda*, Sept. 10, 1846.
16. Stewart and Crosman, *Confidential Journal*, Oct. 11, 1846.
17. Damon, *Memoranda*, June 1854.
18. Letter of Grove Wright to Ministry Harvard, June 5, 1854, WRHS IV A 20. Interestingly, the 1870 census lists a Celia Sprague, aged fifty-eight, as a member of the Hancock East Family. Marriage had evidently failed to satisfy this backslider, leading her to return to the Society, perhaps after the death or desertion of her husband.
19. Lovegrove and Dodgson, *Dye House Journal*, Aug. 25, 1847.
20. Storer, *Journal*, July 6, 1849.
21. Stewart and Crosman, *Confidential Journal*, Sept. 14, 1846.
22. Quoted in Polly Reed, comp., *Book of Miscellaneous Writings* (New Lebanon, N.Y., 1847–1864), Andrews Collection, SA 1261.
23. Lovegrove and Dodgson, *Dye House Journal*, Sept. 30, 1846.

24. Letter of Thomas Damon to George Wilcox, Apr. 1, 1848, WRHS IV A 19.
25. Barber and Stewart, *Journal of Garden Accounts*, Sept. 19, 1847.
26. Lovegrove and Dodgson, *Dye House Journal*, Sept. 1848.
27. Barber and Stewart, *Journal of Garden Accounts*, Sept. 14, 1847.
28. These figures are estimates, and may well understate the extent of the leadership crisis in this period. Many older leaders "retired" from their positions, but demographic data necessitated the inclusion of all adult members. The typical Family required two Elders, two Eldresses, two Deacons, two Deaconesses, two Trustees, two Office Sisters, one Boys' Caretaker, and one Girls' Caretaker.
29. Letter of Ministry Canterbury to Ministry New Lebanon, Nov. 11, 1848, WRHS IV A 5.
30. Letter of Ministry Canterbury to Ministry New Lebanon, April 23, 1851, WRHS IV A 6.
31. Letter of Church Family Elders New Lebanon to Ministry Canterbury, Oct. 10, 1852, WRHS IV A 6.
32. Wells, "Series of Remarks," pp. 31–32.
33. Wells, *Notebooks #5 and #6*, May 1855.
34. Damon, *Memoranda*, Feb. 16, 1854.
35. David Lamson, *Two Years' Experience Among the Shakers* (West Boylston, Mass., 1848).
36. Letter of Grove Wright to Grove Blanchard, Apr. 11, 1848, WRHS IV A 19.
37. Letter of Grove Wright to Grove Blanchard, May 22, 1848, WRHS IV A 19.
38. Damon, *Memoranda*, June 21, 1849.
39. Wells, *Journal Regarding Charges of Disorderly Conduct* (Watervliet, N.Y., 1849), WRHS V A 14.
40. Barber and Stewart, *Journal of Garden Accounts*, Aug. 25, 1847.
41. *Domestic Journal of Important Occurrences*, Aug. 25, 1847.
42. *Domestic Journal of Important*

Occurrences, Sept. 10, 1847—Apr. 14, 1851, passim.

43. Damon, *Memoranda*, June 23, 1847.

44. Letter of Ministry Hancock to Ministry Harvard, Apr. 11, 1851, WRHS IV A 20.

45. Damon, *Memoranda*, Nov. 1852.

46. For additional cases, see Weisbrod, *Boundaries*, pp. 36–58.

47. *Farm Journal*, Oct. 25, 1865.

48. Letter of William Miller to "Brother Hendryx," July 21, 1836. Quoted by James White, *Sketches of the Christian Life and Public Labors of William Miller* (Battle Creek, Mich., 1875), pp. 108–9.

49. White, *Sketches of the Christian Life*, pp. 360–61.

50. Gerald Carson, *Cornflake Crusade* (New York, 1957), p. 78 ff.

51. In Hammond, comp., *Sayings of Mother Ann*, pp. 98–99.

52. Letter of Ministry Canterbury to Ministry New Lebanon, Mar. 13, 1843, WRHS IV A 5.

53. Quoted in J.F.C. Harrison, *The Second Coming* (New Brunswick, N.J., 1979), p. 197.

54. Quoted in Harrison, *The Second Coming*, p. 197.

55. *Church Order Journal*, May 20, 1846.

56. Stewart and Crosman, *Confidential Journal*, Feb. 27, 1847.

57. Barber and Stewart, *Journal of Garden Accounts*, Mar. 11–12, 1847.

58. Wright, *Diary*, May 3, 1847.

59. Barber and Stewart, *Journal of Garden Accounts*, Mar. 5, 1848.

60. Andrews, *People Called Shakers*, p. 223.

61. Damon, *Travel Journal* (Hancock, Mass., 1849), Andrews Collection, SA 800, Oct. 5, 1849.

62. Youngs, *Concise View*, p. 179.

63. Letter of Jefferson White to unidentified member, Apr. 12, 1851, WRHS IV A 6.

64. *Domestic Journal of Important Occurrences*, Dec. 27, 1849. Cf. *Journal* (New Lebanon, N.Y., Center Family, 1848–1857), Shaker Museum, #8831, Dec. 31, 1849 for a lengthy account of the Rochester rappings.

65. Hammond, comp., *Sayings of Mother Ann*, pp. 160–61.

66. Jane D. Knight, "Journal in Verse" (New Lebanon, N.Y., 1850), WRHS V B 149.

67. Damon, *Memoranda*, May 17–18, 1851.

68. Blakeman, *Boys' Journal of Work*, Nov. 22, 1851.

69. Letter of Ministry Hancock to Ministry New Lebanon, Aug. 11, 1852, WRHS IV A 20.

70. William H. Dixon, *New America* (Philadelphia, 1867), p. 346.

71. Letter of Cassandana Brewster to Sally Loomis, Mar. 18, 1852, WRHS IV A 20.

72. For more information on Mother Rebecca Jackson and the Philadelphia Shakers see Jean M. Humez, ed., *Gifts of Power: The Writings of Rebecca Jackson, Black Visionary, Shaker Eldress* (Amherst, Mass., 1981); Richard E. Williams, *Called and Chosen: The Story of Mother Rebecca Jackson and the Philadelphia Shakers* (Metuchen, N.J., 1981); and Diane Sasson, *The Shaker Spiritual Narrative* (Knoxville, Tenn., 1983), pp. 158–88.

73. McLoughlin, *Revivals*, pp. 140–41.

74. Timothy L. Smith, *Revivalism and Social Reform* (New York, 1957), pp. 48–49.

75. Wells, "Series of Remarks," p. 34.

76. Letter of Joseph Gilman to Joseph Tillinghast, Apr. 17, 1853, WRHS IV A 2.

77. Examples of this incorrect interpretation can be found in Andrews, *People Called Shakers*, p. 224 and Whitworth, *God's Blueprints*, p. 78. Other recent scholarship supports my contention. See William Sims Bainbridge, "Shaker Demographics 1840–1900: An Example of the Use of U.S. Census Enumeration Schedules," *Journal for the Scientific Study of Religion* 21 (1982), p. 355.

78. Letter of Cassandana Brewster to Ministry Harvard, July 15, 1854, WRHS IV A 20.

79. Youngs, *Concise View*, pp. 176–77.

Chapter 9. A New Dress to Mother Ann's Gospel

1. Letter of Grove Wright to Ministry Harvard, Sept. 18, 1853, WRHS IV A 20.

2. *Ohio Ministry Travel Journal* (1854), WRHS V B 250, Sept. 11, 1854.

3. Letter of Thomas Damon to Ministry Harvard, Aug. 31, 1855, WRHS IV A 20.

4. Giles B. Avery, "An Address to the Believers Generally" (New Lebanon, N.Y., 1861), Andrews Collection, SA 823, pp. 24–25.

5. Quoted in Bathrick, comp., *Second Book*, p. 79.

6. Avery, "Address," pp. 7–8.

7. Youngs, *Concise View*, p. 509.

8. Wells, "Testimonies, Predictions and Remarks" (Watervliet, N.Y., 1865), WRHS VI B 51, p. 22.

9. Avery, *Journal* (New Lebanon, N.Y., 1864), Shaker Manuscript Collection, New York Public Library. Cited by Kern, *Ordered Love*, p. 103. For more discussion on this issue, see Kern, pp. 103–4.

10. *Travel Journal* (New Lebanon, N.Y., 1846), WRHS V B 140, Aug. 14, 1846.

11. Damon, *Memoranda*, June 9, 1847.

12. Amelia Lyman, *Travel Journal* (Enfield, Conn., 1858), WRHS V B 19, Aug. 20–26, 1858.

13. Dixon, *New America*, pp. 304–5.

14. Wells, "Series of Remarks," pp. 36–37.

15. Letter of Ministry Canterbury to Ministry New Lebanon, Nov. 18, 1841, WRHS IV A 5.

16. Dixon, *New America*, p. 313.

17. Youngs, *Concise View*, pp. 212–14.

18. *Farm Journal*, July 22, 1862.

19. *Farm Journal*, May 21, 1859.

20. Damon, *Travel Journal*, Sept. 25, 1849.

21. Damon, *Memoranda*, Sept. 20, 1856.

22. Sally Bushnell, *A few items written by Sally Bushnell for her own amusement* (Canaan and New Lebanon, N. Y., 1855–1865), Andrews Collection, SA 810, May 16, 1857.

23. Barber and Stewart, *Journal of Garden Accounts*, Dec. 14, 1847.

24. "A Choice Collection of Miscellaneous Matter &c. Calculated to Entertain, Amuse, and Instruct the Reader" (Watervliet, N.Y., 1858), WRHS VII B 274, p. 6.

25. Youngs, *Concise View*, pp. 505–6.

26. Bainbridge, "Shaker Demographics," p. 358.

27. Storer, *Journal*, June 16, 1849.

28. Bushnell, *A few items*, May 9, 1857.

29. Hancock Ministry Eldress, *Diary* (Hancock, Mass., 1867), Andrews Collection, SA 797.

30. Dixon, *New America*, p. 311.

31. Avery, *Journal*, Oct. 21, 1874.

32. *Brethren's Journal of Domestic Occurrences*, June 14, 1866.

33. *Brethren's Journal of Domestic Occurrences*, May 1, 1861.

34. Patterson, *Shaker Spiritual*, p. 443.

35. Luther Wells, "On Conversation Concerning Food, &c." (Watervliet, N.Y, 1858), WRHS VII B 271, p. 7.

36. Dixon, *New America*, p. 320.

37. Dixon, *New America*, pp. 336–37.

38. See, for example, Fanny Appleton Longfellow's description of the Sisters she saw in a public meeting of 1839. Quoted in Morse, *Shakers and World's People*, pp. 155–57.

39. David Macrae, *The Americans At Home* (Edinburgh, 1871; reprint, New York, 1952), p. 578.

40. Calvin Fairchild, *Sketchbook* (Hancock, Mass., 1868–1869), WRHS VII B 133, Dec. 24, 1868.

41. Blakeman, "The Propriety of Wearing a Beard" (New Lebanon, N.Y., 1858), WRHS VII B 113, passim.

42. Blakeman, "Propriety," passim.

43. Blakeman, "Propriety," p. 1.

44. Richmond, *Bibliography*, Vol. I, #84.

45. Letter of John M. Brown to Ministry New Lebanon, Jan. 30, 1873, WRHS VII A 6.

46. "Troubles in Shakerdom," *New York Times*, Dec. 31, 1875, p. 4. It is quite possible that Blakeman himself was the author of this article.

47. Patterson, *Shaker Spiritual*, p. 454.

48. "A New Years Covenant for the Sisters Under 50 Yrs. of Age"

(Canterbury, N.H., 1868), Andrews Collection, SA 763. Also in "Collection of Canterbury Letters Regarding Music," c. 1868, WRHS IV A 7.

49. "Collection of Canterbury Letters," c. 1868.

50. Calver et al., *School Journal*, Mar. 1870.

51. Stewart, *A Brief Weekly Journal* (New Lebanon, N.Y., 1870–1874), Andrews Collection, SA 776, May 1870.

52. Avery, *Journal*, Feb. 21, 1874.

53. Stewart, *Brief Weekly Journal*, Oct. 30, 1870.

54. Stewart, *Brief Weekly Journal*, Feb. 19, 1871.

55. Quoted in "New Years Covenant."

56. Calvin Green, "Biographic Memoir of the Life and Experience of Calvin Green" (New Lebanon, N.Y., 1861–1869), WRHS VI B 28. Quoted by

Sasson, *Shaker Spiritual Narrative*, p. 207.

57. Lists of Brethren of draft age, 1863, Andrews Collection, SA 977, 979, 980, and 981.

58. Kern, *Ordered Love*, pp. 104–5.

59. Bushnell, *A few items*, Oct. 6, 1858.

60. *Farm Journal*, Aug. 26, 1863.

61. *A Journal Kept by the Deaconesses of the Church Family at Watervliet* (Watervliet, N.Y., 1866–1870), Andrews Collection, SA 834, July 17, 1869.

62. Youngs, *Personal Journal*, Aug. 16, 1864.

63. *Farm Journal*, Aug. 9, 1865.

64. Stewart, *Brief Weekly Journal*, May 15, 1870.

65. *Book of Spirit Messages* (New Lebanon, N.Y., 1867), Andrews Collection, SA 1262.

Chapter 10. Plenty to Make the Brick—Few to Build the Temple

1. Elizabeth Sidle, *Tailoresses' Journal* (New Lebanon, N.Y., 1871), WRHS V B 139.

2. Stewart, *Brief Weekly Journal*, July 15, 1871.

3. Stewart, *Brief Weekly Journal*, Mar. 17, 1872.

4. *Record of Names, South and East Families of Young Believers* (Harvard, Mass., 1835–1882), Andrews Collection, SA 802.

5. Letter of Harriet Goodwin to Lydia Dole, Dec. 5, 1881, WRHS IV A 2.

6. Stewart, *Brief Weekly Journal*, Dec. 7, 1873.

7. Letter of John T. Cumings to Rosetta Cumings, Apr. 25, 1873. Manuscript at New Hampshire Historical Society, Concord, N.H. Quoted by Robert P. Emlen, "The Hard Choices of Brother John Cumings," *Historical New Hampshire* 34 (1979), p. 56.

8. Letter of Enoch Cumings to John Cumings, Jan. 25, 1871. Quoted by Emlen, "Hard Choices of Brother John Cumings," p. 60.

9. Letter of John T. Cumings to Rosetta Cumings, Apr. 25, 1873. Quoted by Emlen, "Hard Choices of Brother John Cumings," pp. 55–56.

10. Membership and occupation

records, Watervliet, N.Y., 1850 and 1880,WRHS III A 14.

11. Stewart, *Brief Weekly Journal*, Apr. 30, 1871.

12. Letter of Ministry New Lebanon to Elders Watervliet, Dec. 12, 1872, WRHS IV A 44.

13. Frederick W. Evans, "Shaker Land Limitation Laws" (New Lebanon, N.Y., c. 1870), copy in Andrews Collection, SA 1340.

14. Stewart, *Brief Weekly Journal*, Sept. 6, 1873.

15. William Dean Howells, "A Shaker Village," *Atlantic Monthly* (1876). Quoted by Morse, *Shakers and World's People*, p. 229.

16. Quoted in Bathrick, comp., *Second Book*, pp. 26–27.

17. Stewart, *Brief Weekly Journal*, May 1870.

18. Stewart, *Brief Weekly Journal*, Oct. 1, 1871.

19. Letter of Grove Wright to Ministry Harvard, Jan. 16, 1860, WRHS IV A 5.

20. Stewart, *Brief Weekly Journal*, June 5, 1871.

21. Letter of John T. Cumings to Rosetta Cumings, Apr. 5, 1873. Quoted by Emlen, "Hard Choices of Brother John Cumings," p. 56.

22. Avery, *Journal*, Jan. 30, 1874.

23. Robert F.W. Meader, "Gold and the Shakers," *Shaker Quarterly* 7 (1967), p. 5.

24. Biographical data on Lawson was drawn from *Biographical Review Containing Life Sketches of Leading Citizens of Berkshire County, Massachusetts* (Boston, 1899), Vol. XXXI, pp. 210–14. The story of Lawson's elopement with Van Valen was detailed in the *Springfield Republican*, Apr. 22, 1934, a clipping from which is included in *Scrapbook #99*, Vol. 2, Williams College Shaker Collection, Williamstown, Mass.

25. Stewart, *Brief Weekly Journal*, Aug. 5, 1871.

26. Stewart, *Brief Weekly Journal*, Aug. 20, 1871.

27. Letter of Emma J. Neale to Henry T. Clough, n.d., HSV.

28. Stewart, *Brief Weekly Journal*, Sept. 17, 1871.

29. Stewart, *Brief Weekly Journal*, Nov. 12 and 26, 1871.

30. [Thomas Damon], "Considerations Illustrating the necessity of some Revisions in the Direction and Management of Temporal Concerns" (Hancock, Mass., c. 1870), Andrews Collection, SA 766.

31. Recent research on the Canterbury, N.H., Church Family reveals that men outnumbered women for the first fourteen years of the Family's existence and that the male/female ratio remained near 50:50 until 1844. See Naomi Rosenblum, "The Church Family at Canterbury: An Age-Based Demographic Study of a Shaker Community" in *Historical Survey of Canterbury Shaker Village*, eds. David R. Starbuck and Margaret Supplee Smith (Boston, 1979), p. 191.

32. Damon, "Considerations." Underlined words are in Damon's personal shorthand.

33. White and Taylor, *Shakerism*, pp. 214–15.

34. Letter of Frederick W. Evans to Hervey Eads, Feb. 21, 1875, WRHS IV A 44.

35. Letter of Antoinette Doolittle to Ministry New Lebanon, Apr. 1, 1875, WRHS IV A 44.

36. Damon, *Memoranda*, Jan. 11, 1854.

37. Avery, *Journal*, Mar. 27, 1874.

38. Frederick W. Evans, *Tests of Divine Inspiration* (New Lebanon, N.Y., 1853), p. 115. Quoted by Whitworth, *God's Blueprints*, pp. 56–57.

39. Frederick W. Evans, *Autobiography of a Shaker* (1888, reprint; Philadelphia, 1971), p. x.

40. Angeline Brown, *Notebook* (Canaan, N.Y., 1869–1877), Andrews Collection, SA 1257, p. 22.

41. Dixon, *New America*, p. 336.

42. Willfrid Wylleys, "Prayer is Good, But Work is Better," *Banner of Light* (1865). Copied in Bathrick, *Visions*, p. 5.

43. Letter of Ministry New Lebanon to Ministry Canterbury, Nov. 16, 1863. In Bathrick, comp., *Second Book*, p. 22.

44. Quoted in Bathrick, comp., *Second Book*, p. 23.

45. See Andrews, *People Called Shakers*, p. 223.

46. New Lebanon Ministry, "Circulars Regarding Missionary Work," Dec. 1872 and Oct. 1873, WRHS IV A 44.

47. Letter of New Lebanon Ministry to Elders Watervliet, Feb. 15, 1871, WRHS IV A 44.

48. Quoted by Morse, *Shakers and World's People*, p. 217.

49. New Lebanon Ministry, "Circulars," Dec. 1872.

50. *Brethren's Journal of Domestic Occurrences*, Feb. 2, 1872.

51. Stewart, *Brief Weekly Journal*, Feb. 11, 1872.

52. Stewart, *Brief Weekly Journal*, May 11, 1872.

53. Stewart, *Brief Weekly Journal*, Feb. 25, 1872.

54. Frederick W. Evans in *Shaker and Shakeress* (New Lebanon, N.Y., 1875), p. 25. Quoted by Whitworth, *God's Blueprints*, p. 61.

55. Amelia J. Calver, *A Journal of the Various Literary Attempts of the Church Family* (New Lebanon, N.Y., 1880–1898), Andrews Collection, SA 827, Feb. 19, 1884.

56. Letter of Agnes E. Newton and Mabel E. Liscomb to John ———, Apr. 19, 1885, WRHS IV A 7.

57. Calver, *Journal*, 1884, passim.

58. Letter of Julia Briggs to Polly Reed, Jan. 1, 1878, WRHS IV A 7.

59. Letter of Sarah F. Wilson to Alonzo G. Hollister, Mar. 29, 1891, WRHS IV A 8.

60. *Union Village Ministry Journal* (1878–1896), vol. 3, p. 582. Quoted in Russell H. Anderson, "The Shaker Communities in Southeast Georgia," *Georgia Historical Quarterly* 50 (1966), p. 163.

61. Burnette Vanstory, "Shakerism and the Shakers in Georgia," *Georgia Historical Quarterly* 43 (1959), pp. 353–64, passim.

62. Anderson, "The Shaker Community in Florida," *Florida Historical Quarterly* 38 (1959), pp. 29–44, passim.

63. Letter of Abraham Perkins to Corinna Bishop, Mar. 20, 1896, WRHS IV A 8.

64. Letter of Andrew Barrett to Joseph Holden, Jan. 20, 1896, WRHS IV A 29.

65. White and Taylor, *Shakerism,* pp. 213–14.

66. Anderson, "Shaker Community in Florida," pp. 37–44.

67. Letter of Andrew Barrett to Joseph Holden, Jan. 20, 1896.

68. William A. Hinds, *American Communities* (1902). Quoted by Morse, *Shakers and World's People,* pp. 247–48.

69. White and Taylor, *Shakerism,* p. 42.

70. White and Taylor, *Shakerism,* pp. 385–87.

71. White and Taylor, *Shakerism.* Quoted by Morse, *Shakers and World's People,* p. 246.

72. White and Taylor, *Shakerism,* p. 81.

73. Stewart, *Brief Weekly Journal,* Sept. 6, 1873.

Conclusion

1. Dixon, *New America,* p. 321.

Bibliography

Abbreviations and Conventions

WRHS: Western Reserve Historical Society, Cleveland, Ohio.

HSV: Hancock Shaker Village, Inc., Pittsfield, Massachusetts.

SA: Manuscript numbering system used in Edward Deming Andrews Memorial Shaker Collection, Henry Francis du Pont Winterthur Museum, Winterthur, Delaware.

Shaker Museum: The Shaker Museum, Old Chatham, New York.

Brackets around an author's name signify that an author was not indicated on the title page, but the text reveals his or her identity.

I. Primary Sources

A. Shaker Manuscripts

Anonymous. *Account Book.* New Lebanon, N.Y., Church Family, 1817–1829. Hancock Shaker Village, Inc., Library, Pittsfield, Mass. (hereafter HSV).

———. *Book of Measurements of Brethren.* New Lebanon, N.Y., 1868–1880. Western Reserve Historical Society Shaker Collection, Cleveland, Ohio., III A 8 (hereafter WRHS).

———. *A Book of Orders given by Mother Lucy for all that Belong to the Children's Order.* New Lebanon, N.Y., 1840–1842. Edward Deming Andrews Memorial Shaker Collection, Henry Francis du Pont Winterthur Museum, Winterthur, Del., SA 756 (hereafter Andrews Collection).

———. *Book of Spirit Messages.* New Lebanon, N.Y., Church Family, 1867. Andrews Collection, SA 1262.

———. *Brethren's Journal of Domestic Occurrences.* New Lebanon, N.Y., 1790–1860. WRHS V B 63–71.

———. "A Choice Collection of Miscellaneous Matter &c. Calculated to Entertain, Amuse, and Instruct the Reader." Watervliet, N.Y., Nov. 15, 1858. WRHS VII B 274.

———. *Church Order Journal.* New Lebanon, N.Y., 1841–1846. WRHS V B 135.

———. *Daybook.* Hancock, Mass., Church Family, 1837–1913. HSV.

———. *Domestic Journal of Important Occurrences.* New Lebanon, N.Y., 1780–1860. WRHS V B 60–61.

———. *Farm Journal.* New Lebanon, N.Y., Second Order, 1858–1867. HSV.

———. *History of Lower Family.* Canaan, New York, n.d. WRHS V B 84.

———. "Instructions Concerning Church Order." New Lebanon, N.Y., n.d. WRHS I A 10.

———. "Inventory or Catalogue of Articles of Clothing &c. Delivered to those who have left our Society." Watervliet, N.Y., 1816–1884. WRHS II B 98.

———. *Journal*. Hancock, Mass., Second Family, 1829–1845. Andrews Collection, SA 783.

———. *Journal*. New Lebanon, N.Y., Center Family, 1848–1857. The Shaker Museum, Old Chatham, N.Y., no. 8831 (hereafter Shaker Museum).

———. *A Journal Kept by the Deaconesses of the Church Family*. Watervliet, N.Y., 1866–1870. Andrews Collection, SA 834.

———. *A Journal Kept by the Deaconesses at the Office*. New Lebanon, N.Y., 1830–1836. Andrews Collection, SA 894.

———. *A Journal of Domestic Events and Transactions*. New Lebanon, N.Y., 1851. HSV.

———. *Journal of Remarkable Events*. New Lebanon, N.Y., 1841–1846. WRHS III B 13.

———. *Kentucky Ministry Travel Journal*. Pleasant Hill, Ky., 1869. WRHS V B 228.

———. List of Contributions from Various Communities, c. 1805–1820. WRHS II A 17.

———. Lists of Brethren of Draft Age, 1863. Andrews Collection, SA 977, 979, 980, and 981.

———. *Ministry Daybook*. New Lebanon, N.Y., 1815–1829. WRHS V B 85.

———. *Mother's Pure Teaching*. Hancock, Mass., 1841–1845. WRHS I B 82.

———. "A New Years Covenant for the Sisters Under 50 Yrs. of Age." Canterbury, N.H., 1868. Andrews Collection, SA 763.

———. *Ohio Ministry Travel Journal*. Union Village, Ohio, 1854. WRHS V B 250.

———. *Orders Given by Mother Lucy*. Hancock, Mass., 1839–1842. Andrews Collection, SA 748.

———. *Record Book*. Hancock, Mass., Church Family, 1788–1815. Shaker Museum, no. 10,804.

———. *A Record of Messages and Communications given by Divine Inspiration*. Hancock, Mass., Church Family, 1840–1845. Andrews Collection, SA 1066.

———. *Record of Names, South and East Families of Young Believers*. Harvard, Mass., 1835–1882. Andrews Collection, SA 802.

———. *Record of Travels of Harvard Ministry*. Harvard, Mass., 1791–1880. WRHS V B 59.

———. "Report to Overseers of the Poor." Watervliet, N.Y., 1825. Typescript in New York State Library, Albany, N.Y., A2903.

———. *Travel Journal*. New Lebanon, N.Y., 1846. WRHS V B 140.

———. "Treatise on Simple Diet." n.p., n.d. WRHS VII B 289.

Avery, Giles B. "An Address to the Believers Generally." New Lebanon, N.Y., Dec. 1, 1861. Andrews Collection, SA 823.

———. *Book of Records*. New Lebanon, N.Y., n.d. HSV.

———. *Journal*. New Lebanon, N.Y., 1832–1881. WRHS V B 104–126.

Barber, Franklin and Philemon Stewart. *A Journal of Garden Accounts Commencing July 27th, 1840*. New Lebanon, N.Y., Church Family. HSV.

Bates, Betsy. *A Journal of Events*. New Lebanon, N.Y., 1833–1835. WRHS V B 128.

————. *Words of Mother Lucy.* New Lebanon, N.Y., n.d. WRHS VII B 61.

Bates, Issachar. *Sketch of the Life and Experience of Issachar Bates, Sr.* New Lebanon, N.Y., 1832–1836. Andrews Collection, SA 779.

Bathrick, Eunice, comp. *A Second Book Copied from Br. Alonzo Hollister's Manuscripts. Copied for Elder John Cloutman.* Harvard, Mass., 1874. Andrews Collection, SA 805.

————, comp. *Testimonies and Wise Sayings, Counsel and Instruction of Mother Ann and the Elders.* Harvard, Mass., 1869. WRHS VI B 10–13.

————, comp. *Visions, Spirit Communications, Religious Experience, Narrative Pieces, Poems and Sketches from different Authors.* Harvard, Mass., 1850–1865. Andrews Collection, SA 1077.

Bill, Aaron. *A Journal or Day Book.* New Lebanon, N.Y., 1834–1840. WRHS V B 132.

Bishop, Rufus, comp. *A Collection of the Writings of Father Joseph Meacham Respecting Church Order and Government.* New Lebanon, N.Y., 1850. WRHS VII B 59.

Blake, Rhoda. "A Sketch of the Life and Experience of Rhoda Blake." New Lebanon, N.Y., 1864. Andrews Collection, SA 780.

Blakeman, Elisha D. *The Boys' Journal of Work.* New Lebanon, N.Y., 1844–1865. WRHS V B 137.

————. *Daily Journal.* New Lebanon, N.Y., 1834–1840. WRHS V B 131.

————. "The Propriety of Wearing a Beard." New Lebanon, N.Y., 1858. WRHS VII B 113.

Blanchard, Grove B. *Diary.* Harvard, Mass., 1866. HSV.

————. *Names and Ages of those gathered into the Church.* Harvard, Mass., 1791–1860. Andrews Collection, SA 803.

Blanchard, Jemima. "Testimony." Harvard, Mass., n.d. WRHS VII B 107.

Blinn, Henry C. *Journal of a Trip to Kentucky, 1873.* Excerpted in *Shaker Quarterly* 5, no. 2 (Summer 1965).

Boynton, Mary. Letter to Mary Rust. Hancock, Mass., c. 1810. Andrews Collection, SA 1220.

[Brewster, Cassandana]. *Diary.* Hancock, Mass., 1865. Andrews Collection, SA 795.

Brewster, Cassandana. "Testimony." Hancock, Mass., n.d. Andrews Collection, SA 1548.

Brown, Angeline. *Notebook.* Canaan, N.Y., 1869–1877. Andrews Collection, SA 1257.

Bushnell, Sally. *A few items written by Sally Bushnell for her own Amusement.* Canaan, N.Y., 1855–1865. Andrews Collection, SA 810.

Buttrick, Amos. "Testimony." Harvard, Mass., c. 1792. WRHS I A 7.

Calver, Amelia J. *A Journal of the Various Literary Attempts of the Church Family.* New Lebanon, N.Y., 1880–1898. Andrews Collection, SA 827.

Calver, William et al. *School Journal.* New Lebanon, N.Y., 1852–1887. HSV.

Canterbury, N.H., Church Family Membership List, Oct. 26, 1819. WRHS III A 2.

Clark, Asenath. *Ministerial Journal.* New Lebanon and Watervliet, N.Y., 1831–1836. Copy at HSV.

Correspondence from various communities. WRHS IV A 1–36.

[Damon, Thomas]. "Considerations Illustrating the necessity of some Revisions in the Direction and Management of Temporal Concerns." Hancock, Mass., c.1870. Andrews Collection, SA 766.

Damon, Thomas. *Journal.* Enfield, Conn., 1834–1845. Andrews Collection, SA 774.

———. *Memoranda.* Hancock, Mass., 1846–1860. Shaker Museum, no. 13,357.

———. "Testimony." Enfield, Conn., 1843. WRHS VI A 2.

[Damon, Thomas]. *Travel Journal.* Hancock, Mass., c. 1849. Andrews Collection, SA 800.

Davis, Jennet. "Testimony." n.p., n.d. WRHS IV A 11.

DeWitt, Henry. *Journal.* New Lebanon, N.Y., 1827–1867. WRHS V B 97.

DeWitt, John. *Memo Book.* New Lebanon, N.Y. WRHS V B 92.

Evans, Frederick W. "Shaker Land Limitation Laws." New Lebanon, N.Y., c. 1870. Andrews Collection, SA 1340.

Fairchild, Calvin. *Sketchbook.* Hancock, Mass., 1868–1869. WRHS VII B 133.

Fowle, Robert et al. "Plain Dealing With Square Work." Canterbury, N.H., Sept. 1847. WRHS X B 1.

Gates, Benjamin. *A Day Book or Journal of Work and Various Things.* New Lebanon, N.Y., 1827–1838. Andrews Collection, SA 1030.

Goodrich, Daniel and Calvin Green. Letter to Mary Rust. Hancock, Mass., c. 1810. Andrews Collection, SA 1220.

Green, Calvin. "Biographic Memoir of the Life, Character and Important Events in the Ministration of Mother Lucy Wright." New Lebanon, N.Y., 1861. WRHS VI B 27.

———, comp. "Biography of Elder Henry Clough." New Lebanon, N.Y., 1860. WRHS VI B 24.

———. *Journal.* New Lebanon, N.Y., 1811–1822. WRHS V B 80.

———. *Journal of a Trip to Philadelphia.* New Lebanon, N.Y., 1828. WRHS V B 98.

———. *Journal of a Trip to Savoy.* New Lebanon, N.Y., 1821. WRHS V B 90.

Hammond, Thomas. *Harvard Church Family Record.* Harvard, Mass., 1791–1853 in Harvard, Massachusetts, Shaker Church Records. American Antiquarian Society, Worcester, Mass.

———, comp. *Sayings of Mother Ann and the first Elders, taken from Abijah Worster.* Harvard, Mass., n.d. WRHS VII B 22.

Hancock Ministry Eldress. *Diary.* Hancock, Mass., 1867. Andrews Collection, SA 797.

Hollister, Alonzo G., comp. *Autobiography of the Saints,* 2 vols. New Lebanon, N.Y., 1872. WRHS VI B 36–37.

———, comp. *Book of the Busy Hours.* New Lebanon, N.Y., 1877. HSV.

———. *Book of Remembrance.* New Lebanon, N.Y., n.d. WRHS VII B 109.

———, comp. *Copies of Various Letters.* New Lebanon, N.Y., n.d. WRHS IV B 35.

———, comp. *Writings of Deacon Daniel Goodrich.* New Lebanon, N.Y., n.d. Andrews Collection, SA 799.1

Knight, Jane D. *Journal in Verse.* New Lebanon, N.Y., 1850. WRHS V B 149.

Lovegrove, Elizabeth. *Journal.* New Lebanon, N.Y., 1827. WRHS V B 93.

——— and Anna Dodgson. *Dye House Journal.* New Lebanon, N.Y., 1837–1855. Andrews Collection, SA 817.

Lyman, Amelia. *Travel Journal*. Enfield, Conn., 1858. WRHS V B 19.

Lyon, Benjamin. *A Journal of Domestic Events*. New Lebanon, N.Y., 1839–1840. Andrews Collection, SA 1031.

Mosely, Sarah. "Affidavit." New Lebanon, N.Y., 1800. WRHS I A 6.

New Lebanon Ministry. "Circular Epistle." New Lebanon, N.Y., Sept. 1, 1829. WRHS IV A 35.

———. "Circular on Intemperance." New Lebanon, N.Y., c. 1827. Andrews Collection, SA 772.

———. "Circulars Regarding Missionary Work." New Lebanon, N.Y., Dec. 1872 and Oct. 1873. WRHS IV A 44.

———. *The Holy Orders of the Church, Written by Father Joseph*. New Lebanon, N.Y., Feb. 18, 1841. Andrews Collection, SA 750.

———. *Milenial Laws, or Gospel statutes and ordinances adapted to the day of Christ's second Appearing*. New Lebanon, N.Y., Aug. 7, 1821. WRHS I B 37.

Newspaper Scrapbook, no. 99. Williams College Shaker Collection, Williamstown, Mass.

Parker, David. "Remarks at the Close of Evening School." Canterbury, N.H., Mar. 18, 1833. WRHS IV A 4.

Prentiss, Ephraim. "Report of Interesting Experience with the Boys of whom he was Caretaker." Watervliet, N.Y., 1835–1837. WRHS VII B 258.

Prescott, Hannah. "Testimony." n.p., n.d. WRHS IV A 11.

Reed, Calvin. "Autobiography." New Lebanon, N.Y., n.d. WRHS VI B 29.

Reed, Polly, comp. *Book of Miscellaneous Writings*. New Lebanon, N.Y., 1847–1864. Andrews Collection, SA 1261.

Sears, Florinda, comp. "List of Visitors." Harvard, Mass., 1791–1879. WRHS V B 58.

Sidle, Elizabeth. *Tailoresses' Journal*. New Lebanon, N.Y., 1871. WRHS V B 139.

Southwick, Jonathan. "Testimony." Hancock, Mass., 1827. WRHS VI A 4.

Stewart, Philemon. *A Brief Weekly Journal*. New Lebanon, N.Y., 1870–1874. Andrews Collection, SA 776.

———. *Daily Journal*. New Lebanon, N.Y., 1833–1836. WRHS V B 130.

——— and Daniel Crosman. *A Confidential Journal Kept in the Elders' Lot*. New Lebanon, N.Y., First Order, 1842–1881. WRHS V B 136.

[Storer, Wealthy]. *Journal*. Hancock, Mass., 1846–1854. Andrews Collection, SA 789.

Warner, John. "A Short Account of the birth, character, and ministration of Father Eleazer and Mother Hannah." Harvard, Mass., 1824. WRHS VI B 7.

Watervliet, N.Y., Membership and Occupation Records, 1850 and 1880. WRHS III A 14.

Wells, Freegift. *Journal Regarding Charges of Disorderly Conduct*. Watervliet, N.Y., 1849. WRHS V A 14.

———. *Notebook #4*. Watervliet, N.Y., c. 1855. WRHS VII B 270.

———. *Notebooks #5 and #6*. Watervliet, N.Y., 1855–1856. WRHS VII B 270a.

———. "A Series of Remarks Showing the power of the Adversary in leading honest souls astray through the influence of inspired Messages. Or a Lamentation because the beauty of Zion hath faded, and Her Light become dim." Watervliet, N.Y., Jan. 31, 1850. WRHS VII B 266.

———. "Testimonies, Predictions and Remarks." Watervliet, N.Y., 1865. WRHS VI B 51.

———. "Various Protests Regarding Rules." Watervliet, N.Y., n.d. WRHS VII B 270a.

Wells, Luther. "On Conversation Concerning Food &c." Watervliet, N.Y., 1858. WRHS VII B 271.

Wells, Seth Y. "Counsel and instructions relative to Order." New Lebanon, N.Y., Dec. 30, 1832. WRHS I B 46.

———. "Remarks on Learning and the use of Boks." New Lebanon, N.Y., Mar. 10, 1836. Andrews Collection, SA 770.

———. "Testimony." New Lebanon, N.Y., n.d. WRHS I A 8.

Wetherbee, William H. *A Book Containing the Records of the Church . . . Shirley, Massachusetts*. 1844. Shaker Museum, no. 10,803.

Wheaton, Deborah and Anna Davis. "Testimony Regarding Henry Baker." New Lebanon, N.Y., c. 1828. Andrews Collection, SA 829.

Whittaker, James. Letter to Daniel Goodrich, Jr. n.p., n.d. WRHS VI A 11.

Wright, Grove. *Diary*. Hancock, Mass., 1854. Andrews Collection, SA 792.

Youngs, Isaac N. "Autobiography in Verse." New Lebanon, N.Y., July 4, 1837. Andrews Collection, SA 818.

———. *A Concise View of the Church of God and of Christ on Earth Having its foundation In the faith of Christ's first and Second Appearing*. New Lebanon, N.Y., 1856–1860. Andrews Collection, SA 760.

———. *Names and Ages of those who have been gathered into the church*. New Lebanon, N.Y., 1787–1854. HSV.

———. *Names and Ages of Those who have been gathered into the Church since 1787 . . . , some additions by J. M. Brown, 1870*. New Lebanon, N.Y., 1787–1875. Andrews Collection, SA 822.

———. *Personal Journal*. New Lebanon, N.Y., 1837–1857. Shaker Museum, no. 10,509.

B. Published Sources

Anonymous. "The Shakers At Niskeyuna." *Boston Palladium* (Aug. 20, 1829).

———. "Troubles in Shakerdom." *New York Times* (Dec. 31, 1875), p. 4.

[Bates, Paulina]. *The Divine Book of Holy and Eternal Wisdom, Revealing the Word of God, out of Whose Mouth Goeth a Sharp Sword*. Canterbury, N.H.: United Society Called Shakers, 1849.

Biographical Review Containing Life Sketches of Leading Citizens of Berkshire County, Massachusetts, Vol. XXXI. Boston: Biographical Review Publishing Co., 1899.

Bishop, Rufus and Seth Y. Wells, eds. *Testimonies of the Life, Character, Revelations and Doctrines of Mother Ann Lee and the Elders With Her*, 2nd edition. Albany, N.Y.: Weed, Parsons and Co., 1888.

Brown, Thomas. *An Account of the People Called Shakers: Their Faith, Doctrines, and Practice, Exemplified in the Life, Conversations, and Experience of the Author during the Time he Belonged to the Society, to Which is Affixed a History of Their Rise and Progress to the Present Day*. Troy, N.Y.: Parker & Bliss, 1812.

Cooper, Mary. *The Diary of Mary Cooper: Life on a Long Island Farm, 1768–1773*, ed. Field Horne. Oyster Bay, N.Y.: Oyster Bay Historical Society, 1981.

Dixon, William Hepworth. *New America.* Philadelphia: J. B. Lippincott & Co., 1867.

Dyer, Mary. *A Portraiture of Shakerism.* Concord, N.H.: for the author, 1822.

————. *The Rise and Progress of the Serpent from the Garden of Eden to the Present Day: With a Discourse of Shakerism, Exhibiting a General View of Their Real Character and Conduct from the first Appearance of Ann Lee: Also the Life and Sufferings of the Author.* Concord, N.H.: for the author, 1847.

Elkins, Hervey. *Fifteen Years in the Senior Order of Shakers: A Narration of the Facts concerning That Singular People.* Hanover, N.H.: Dartmouth Press, 1853.

Evans, Frederick W. *Autobiography of a Shaker and Revelation of the Apocalypse,* 2nd edition, 1888. Philadelphia: Porcupine Press, 1972, reprint.

————. *Tests of Divine Inspiration; Or, The Rudimental Principles by which True and False Revelation, in All Eras of the World, Can Be Unerringly Discriminated.* New Lebanon, N.Y.: United Society Called Shakers, 1853.

Graham, Sylvester. *A Lecture to Young Men, On Chastity, intended also for the serious consideration of parents and guardians.* Providence, R.I., 1834.

[Green, Calvin and Seth Y. Wells]. *A Summary View of the Millennial Church or United Society of Believers, Commonly Called Shakers, Comprising the Rise, Progress and Practical Order of the Society Together with the General Principles of their Faith and Testimony.* Albany, N.Y.: Packard & Van Benthuysen, 1823.

Lamson, David. *Two Years' Experience Among the Shakers: Being a Description of the Manners and Customs of That People; the Nature and Policy of TheirGovernment; Their Marvellous Intercourse with the Spiritual World; the Object and Uses of Confession, Their Inquisition; in Short, a Condensed View of Shakerism As It Is.* West Boylston, Mass.: for the author, 1848.

Macrae, David. *The Americans At Home.* 1871. New York: Dutton, 1952, reprint.

[Meacham, Joseph]. *A Concise Statement of the Principles of the Only True Church, according to the Gospel of the Present Appearance of Christ. As Held to and Practiced upon by the True Followers of the Living Saviour, at New Lebanon, &c. Together with a Letter from James Whittaker, Minister of the Gospel in this Day of Christ's Second Appearing—to his Natural Relations in England.* Bennington, Vt.: Haswell & Russell, 1790.

Nordhoff, Charles. *The Communistic Societies of the United States.* New York: Harper and Bros., 1875. New York: Dover Publications, Inc., 1966, reprint.

Perkins, Nathan. *A Narrative of a Tour Through the State of Vermont from April 27 to June 12, 1789.* Rutland, Vt.: Charles E. Tuttle Co., Inc., 1964.

Rathbun, Reuben. *Reasons Offered for Leaving the Shakers.* Pittsfield, Mass.: Chester Smith, 1800.

Rathbun, Valentine. "About the Shakers." *The New Star,* no. 5 (May 9, 1797), pp. 45–46.

Sedgwick, Catherine M. "Magnetism Among the Shakers." *Berkshire Culturist and Weekly Family Gazette* 2 (May 16, 1849), pp. 157–58.

Stewart, I. D. *The History of the Free Will Baptists.* Dover, N.H.: Free Will Baptist Printing Establishment, 1862.

Stiles, Ezra. *The Literary Diary of Ezra Stiles*, 3 vols., ed. F.B. Dexter. New York: Charles Scribner's Sons, 1901.

Wells, Seth Y. and Calvin Green. *Testimonies Concerning the Character and Ministry of Mother Ann Lee and the First Witnesses of the Gospel of Christ's Second Appearing; Given by Some of the Aged Brethren and Sisters of the United Society.* Albany, N.Y.: Packard & Van Benthuysen, 1827.

White, Anna and Leila S. Taylor. *Shakerism: Its Meaning and Message.* Columbus, Ohio: Fred J. Heer, 1904.

White, James. *Sketches of the Christian Life and Public Labors of William Miller.* Battle Creek, Mich.: Seventh Day Adventist Publishing Association, 1875.

Wright, Stephen, comp. *History of the Shaftesbury Baptist Association.* Troy, N.Y.: A.G. Johnson, 1853.

Yale, Cyrus. *The Godly Pastor. Life of the Rev. Jeremiah Hallock of Canton, Connecticut.* New York: American Tract Society, 1866.

Youngs, Benjamin S. and Calvin Green. *The Testimony of Christ's Second Appearing*, 2nd edition. Albany, N.Y.: E. & E. Hosford, 1810.

II. Secondary Sources

Anderson, Russell H. "The Shaker Communities in Southeast Georgia." *Georgia Historical Quarterly* 50 (1966), pp. 162–72.

————. "The Shaker Community in Florida." *Florida Historical Quarterly* 38 (1959), pp. 29–44.

Andrews, Edward Deming. *The Community Industries of the Shakers.* Albany, N.Y.: University of the State of New York, 1933.

————. *The People Called Shakers.* New York: Oxford University Press, 1953.

———— and Faith Andrews. *Work and Worship: The Economic Order of the Shakers.* Greenwich, Conn.: New York Graphic Society, 1974.

Bainbridge, William Sims. "Shaker Demographics 1840–1900: An Example of the Use of U.S. Census Enumeration Schedules." *Journal for the Scientific Study of Religion* 21 (1982), pp. 352–65.

Brewer, Priscilla J. "The Demographic Features of the Shaker Decline, 1787–1900." *Journal of Interdisciplinary History* 15 (1984), pp. 31–52.

————. "Emerson, Lane and the Shakers: A Case of Converging Ideologies." *New England Quarterly* 55 (1982), pp. 254–75.

Campbell, D'Ann. "Women's Life in Utopia: The Shaker Experiment in Sexual Equality Reappraised, 1810–1860." *New England Quarterly* 51 (1978), pp. 23–38.

Carson, Gerald. *Cornflake Crusade.* New York: Holt, Rinehart & Winston, 1957.

Desroche, Henri. *The American Shakers: From Neo-Christianity to Presocialism.* 1955. Amherst, Mass.: University of Massachusetts Press, 1971, trans. and ed., John K. Savacool.

Emlen, Robert P. "The Hard Choices of Brother John Cumings." *Historical New Hampshire* 34 (1979), pp. 54–65.

Filley, Dorothy M. *Recapturing Wisdom's Valley: The Watervliet Shaker Heritage, 1775–1975.* Albany, N.Y.: Albany Institute of History and Art, 1975.

Foster, Lawrence. *Religion and Sexuality: Three American Communal Experi-*

ments of the Nineteenth Century. New York: Oxford University Press, 1981.

Gordon, Beverly. *Shaker Textile Arts.* Hanover, N.H.: University Press of New England, 1980.

Greven, Philip. *The Protestant Temperament.* New York: Alfred A. Knopf, 1977.

Harrison, J.F.C. *The Second Coming: Popular Millenarianism, 1780–1850.* New Brunswick, N.J.: Rutgers University Press, 1979.

Hayden, Dolores. *Seven American Utopias: The Architecture of Communitarian Socialism, 1790–1975.* Cambridge, Mass.: MIT Press, 1976.

Horgan, Edward R. *The Shaker Holy Land: A Community Portrait.* Harvard, Mass.: Harvard Common Press, 1982.

Humez, Jean, ed. *Gifts of Power: The Writings of Rebecca Jackson, Black Visionary, Shaker Eldress.* Amherst, Mass.: University of Massachusetts Press, 1981.

Kern, Louis J. *An Ordered Love: Sex Roles and Sexuality in Victorian American Communes—the Shakers, the Mormons and the Oneida Community.* Chapel Hill, N.C.: University of North Carolina Press, 1981.

Lassiter, William L. *Shaker Architecture.* New York: Bonanza Books, 1966.

McLoughlin, William G. *Isaac Backus and the American Pietistic Tradition.* Boston: Little, Brown & Co., 1967.

———. *New England Dissent, 1630–1833*, 2 vols. Cambridge, Mass.: Harvard University Press, 1971.

———. *Revivals, Awakenings, and Reform.* Chicago: University of Chicago Press, 1978.

Marini, Stephen A. *Radical Sects of Revolutionary New England.* Cambridge, Mass.: Harvard University Press, 1982.

Meader, Robert F.W. "Gold and the Shakers." *Shaker Quarterly* 7 (1967).

———. *An Illustrated Guide to Shaker Furniture.* New York: Dover Publications, Inc., 1972.

Melcher, Marguerite. *The Shaker Adventure.* Princeton, N.J.: Princeton University Press, 1941.

Miller, Amy Bess and Persis Fuller. *The Best of Shaker Cooking.* New York: Macmillan, 1970.

Morse, Flo. *The Shakers and the World's People.* New York: Dodd, Mead & Co., 1980.

Neal, Julia. *By Their Fruits: The Story of Shakerism in South Union, Kentucky.* Chapel Hill, N.C.: University of North Carolina Press, 1947.

Nissenbaum, Stephen. *Sex, Diet, and Debility in Jacksonian America: Sylvester Graham and Health Reform.* Westport, Conn.: Greenwood Press, 1980.

Patterson, Daniel W. *Gift Drawing and Gift Song.* Sabbathday Lake, Maine: United Society of Shakers, 1983.

———. *The Shaker Spiritual.* Princeton, N.J.: Princeton University Press, 1979.

Piercy, Caroline B. *The Valley of God's Pleasure: A Saga of the North Union Shaker Community.* New York: Stratford House, 1951.

Richmond, Mary L. *Shaker Literature: A Bibliography*, 2 vols. Hanover, N.H.: University Press of New England, 1977.

Rosenblum, Naomi. "The Church Family at Canterbury: An Age-Based Demographic Study of a Shaker Family." *Historical Survey of Canterbury Shaker Village*, eds. David R. Starbuck and Margaret Supplee Smith. Boston: Boston University, 1979, pp. 190–214.

Rourke, Constance. "The Shakers." *Roots of American Culture and Other Essays*, ed. Van Wyck Brooks. New York: Harcourt, Brace & Co., 1942, pp. 195–237.

Sasson, Diane. *The Shaker Spiritual Narrative*. Knoxville, Tenn.: University of Tennessee Press, 1983.

Smith, Timothy L. *Revivalism and Social Reform*. New York: Abingdon Press, 1957.

Sprigg, June. *By Shaker Hands*. New York: Alfred A. Knopf, 1975.

Vanstory, Burnette. "Shakerism and the Shakers in Georgia." *Georgia Historical Quarterly* 43 (1959), pp. 353–64.

Weisbrod, Carol. *Boundaries of Utopia*. New York: Pantheon Books, 1980.

Whitworth, John M. *God's Blueprints: A Sociological Study of Three Utopian Sects*. London: Routledge & Kegan Paul, 1975.

Williams, Richard E. *Called and Chosen: The Story of Mother Rebecca Jackson and the Philadelphia Shakers*. Metuchen, N.J.: Scarecrow Press, Inc., 1981.

Index

Adventists, 150–53
Age distribution, 47, 69–70, 143, 166, 211, 212, 223–38; and children, 23–24, 30, 39, 69, 93, 115, 141, 147–48, 213–14; and elderly, 187, 196–97
Alcohol, 6, 39, 41. *See also* Diet
Allen, John, 139–40, 141–42
Andrews, Edward Deming, and Faith, xii
Ann (Mother). *See* Lee, Ann
Apostasy, 113–14, 139–50, 156–57; and economics, 113–14, 145; of females, 113, 210; of instruments and leaders, 126, 139–40, 184–88; of males, 47, 113, 178–81, 210; members' response to, 140–42, 156–57, 158–59, 180–84; rate of, 28, 47, 87, 141–45, 156, 160–61, 178, 210; for sexual reasons, 93–96, 139–40, 186–87, 248n27, 252n18; of young, 28, 30–31, 138–39, 141, 178–79, 210
Apostates, 89–92; exposés by, 8–9, 54, 91–92, 156; property given to, 24, 91, 113; return of, 89, 90–91, 95, 186, 252n18
Avery, Giles, 108–9, 115, 124, 126, 131, 159–60, 185, 187

Backus, Isaac, 2, 8
Baker, Henry, 97
Baptists, 3–4, 6–8, 10; Freewill, 155
Barns, John, 26, 57–58, 98
Bates, Issachar, 32, 34, 71, 86
Bates, Paulina: *The Divine Book of Holy and Eternal Wisdom*, 122, 134
Bathrick, Eunice, 193
Beards, 169–71
Behavior, 36–37, 70–72, 82–83; rules of, 38–42, 93, 119–21, 128, 145–46
Bennet, Nicholas, 141
Berkshire county, Massachusetts, 106, 249n66
Bishop, Ebenezer, 50, 96, 119, 144
Bishop, Job, 26–27, 242n43
Bishop, Rufus, 46, 50, 96, 112, 119, 120–40, 144, 176–77
Blake, Rhoda, 46, 81

Blakeman, Elisha, 75, 77–78, 82, 83, 113, 154, 169–71
Blanchard, Grove, 60, 61
Blinn, Henry, 190
Brewster, Cassandana, 61–62, 155, 156–57
Brewster, Justus, 32
Briggs, Nicholas, 164
Brown, Thomas, 52, 53, 54, 56
Businessman's Revival, 155

Calver, William, 76
Campbell, D'Ann, xiii
Celibacy, 5, 13–15, 160. *See also* Sexes, relations between
Chandler, Hewitt, 164
Chase, Edward, 187
Children, 11–14, 74–79; indentured, 147–50; percentage of, 23–24, 30, 39, 93, 115, 141, 147–48, 213–14
Civil War, 174
Clark, Asenath, 96, 103, 119, 144
Clough, Henry, 20, 26–27, 28, 30, 55, 56–57, 67
Communalism, 5, 13, 20, 21–24
Confession, 5, 13, 20, 50–51, 71
Congregationalists, 3–4
Converts: and children, 147–50; early, 6–10, 22–24; economically motivated, 39, 85–90, 99, 105, 113–14, 155; lack of, 176, 196–201; non-Christian, 66–67; outside of communities, 33; revivalists, 66–68, 118, 150–56; under Wright, 31–36, 38. *See also* Members; Missionary activities; Revivals, Shaker
Cooley, Ebenezer, 31
Copley, Luther, 75
Cumings, John, 180–81, 185

Damon, Thomas, 55–56, 62–63, 140, 142, 154, 159, 188–89
Dance, 6, 8–9, 21, 124, 195
Darrow, David, 20, 34
Davis, Benjamin B., 173
Deacons and Deaconesses, 22, 49–50, 85, 185–89